Ghost Diary
カイダンにっき
3

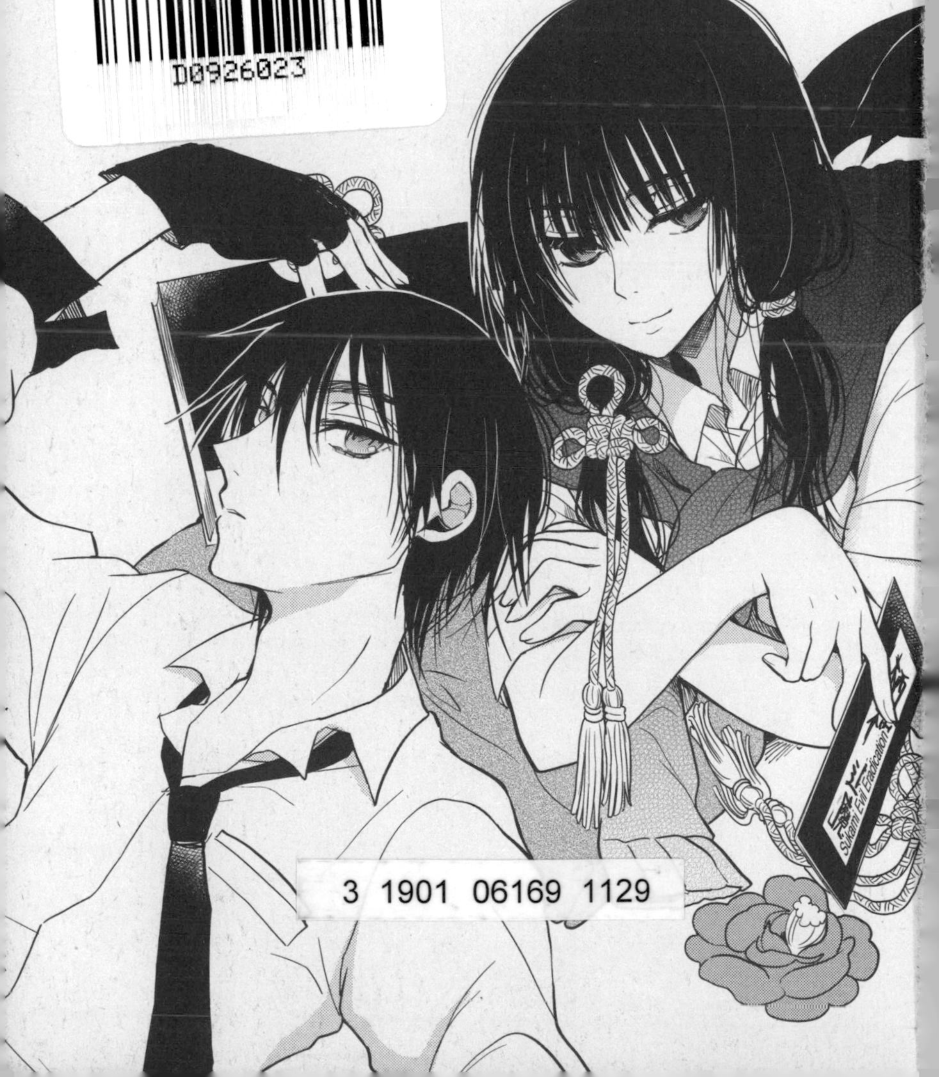

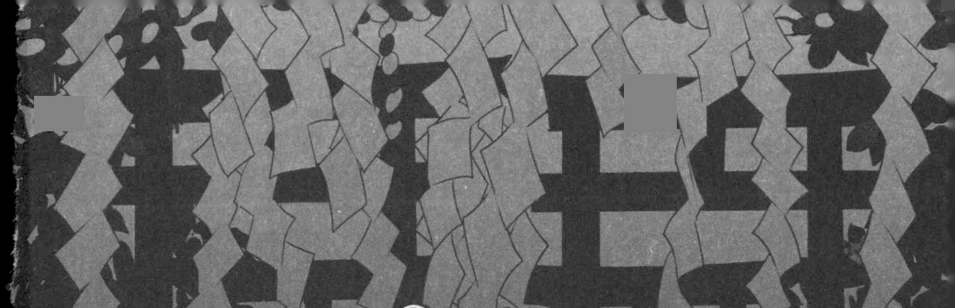

Greetings

Hello again--or nice to meet you.
I am Seiju Natsumegu.

Thank you for picking up volume three of my strange, occultic young-adult manga *Ghost Diary.* The series has reached the final volume, at long last!

After coming to the last chapter, I noticed several things I definitely want to fix. I'm going to redraw them when time permits. Those who followed the story in the magazine should try comparing the two. *Ha ha!*

Since this is the final volume, there are many bittersweet moments. Please watch over Kyouichi, Chloe, the Occult Club members, and Hanaichi as we go on one last journey with them.

As usual, I have written various things in these little author notes. (For a detailed explanation, see Volumes 1 and 2!) Feel free to come back and read them after you've finished the final chapter.

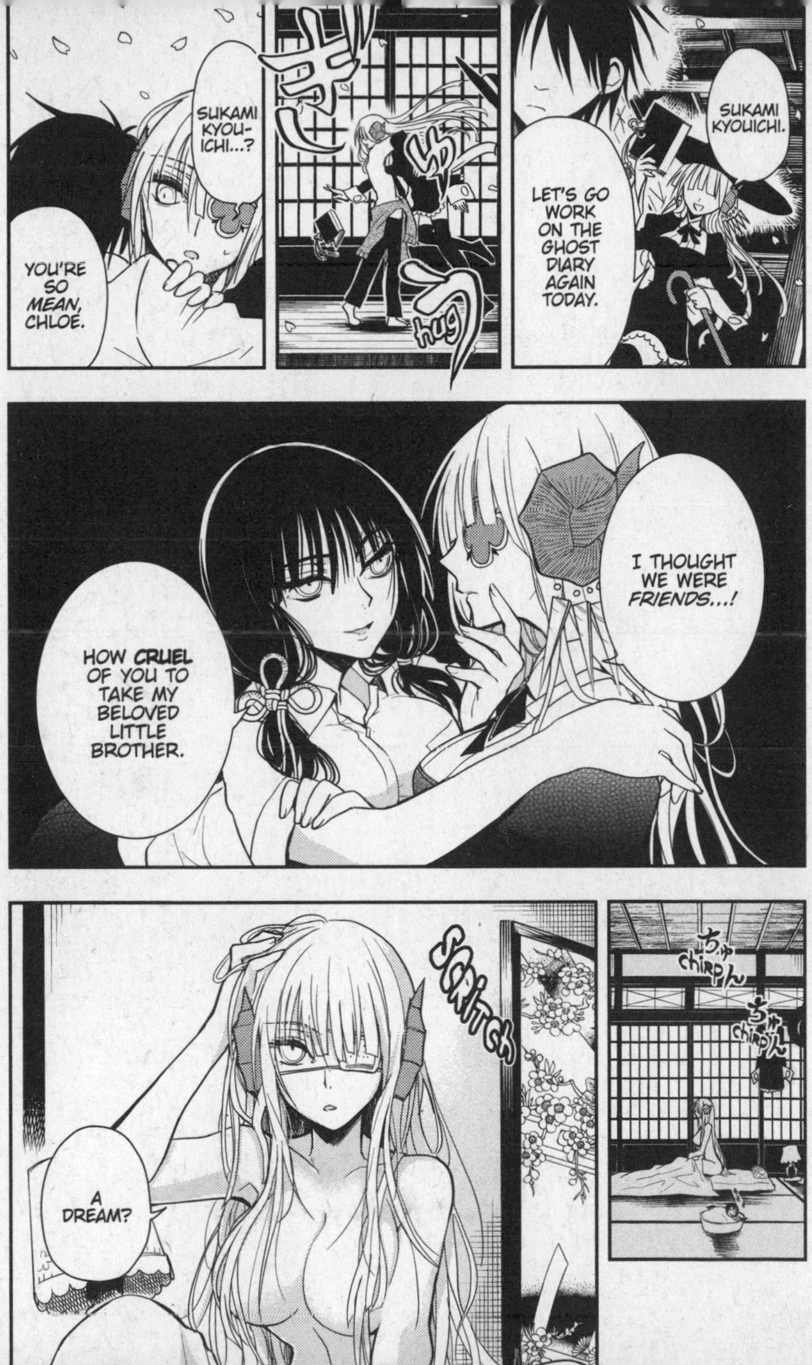

SUKAMI KYOUICHI.
LET'S GO WORK ON THE GHOST DIARY AGAIN TODAY.
hug
SUKAMI KYOUICHI...?
YOU'RE SO MEAN, CHLOE.
I THOUGHT WE WERE FRIENDS...!
HOW CRUEL OF YOU TO TAKE MY BELOVED LITTLE BROTHER.
chirp
chirp
SCRITCH
A DREAM?

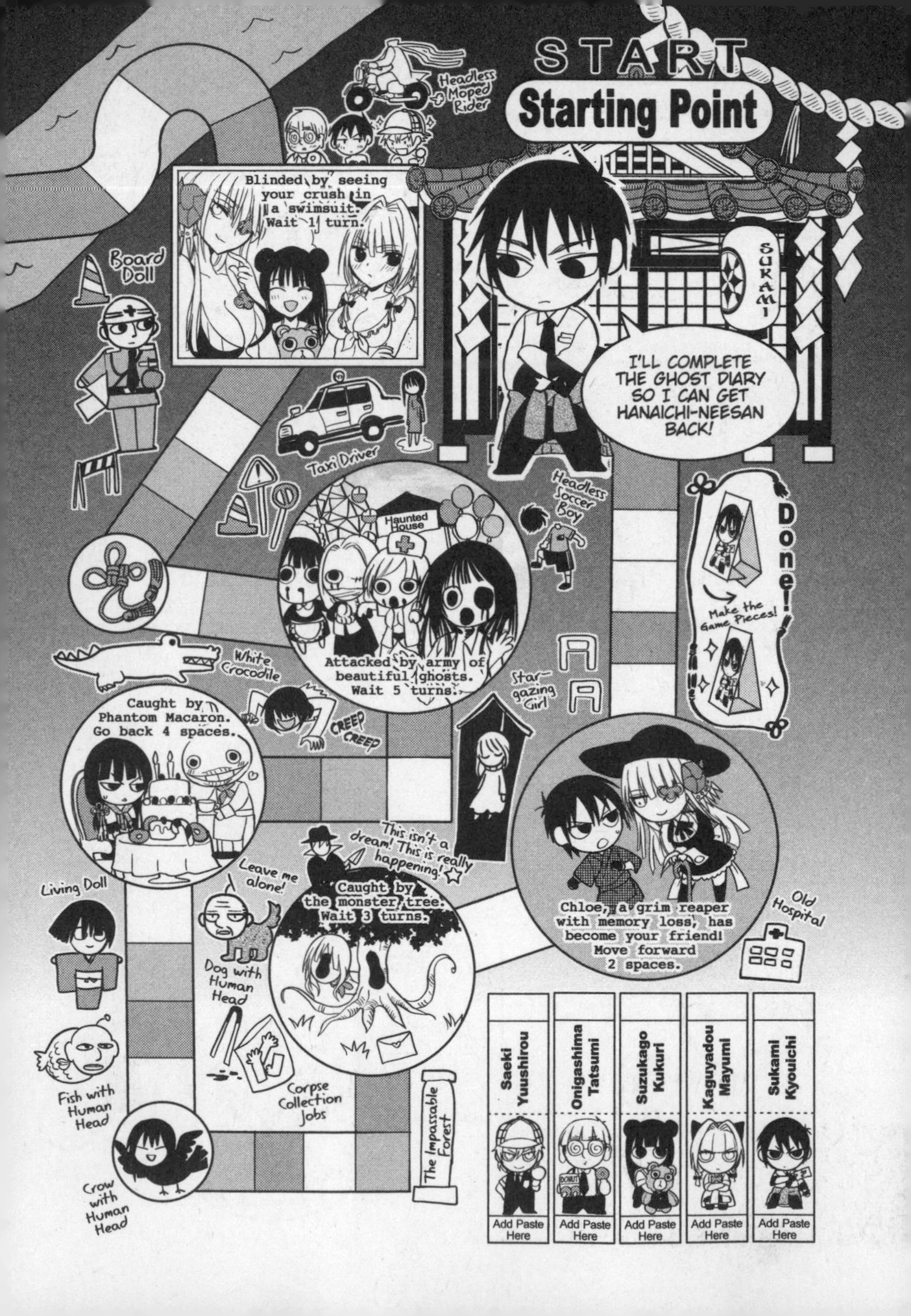
START
Starting Point
Headless Moped Rider
Blinded by seeing your crush in a swimsuit. Wait 1 turn.
Board Doll
SUKAMI
I'LL COMPLETE THE GHOST DIARY SO I CAN GET HANAICHI-NEESAN BACK!
Taxi Driver
Headless Soccer Boy
Haunted House
Done!
Make the Game Pieces!
White Crocodile
Attacked by army of beautiful ghosts. Wait 5 turns.
Star-gazing Girl
Caught by Phantom Macaron. Go back 4 spaces.
CREEP CREEP
This isn't a dream! This is really happening!
Leave me alone!
Living Doll
Caught by the monster tree. Wait 3 turns.
Chloe, a grim reaper with memory loss, has become your friend! Move forward 2 spaces.
Old Hospital
Dog with Human Head
Fish with Human Head
Corpse Collection Jobs
The Impassable Forest
Crow with Human Head
Saeki Yuushirou
Onigashima Tatsumi
DONUT
Suzukago Kukuri
Kaguyadou Mayumi
Sukami Kyouichi
Add Paste Here
Add Paste Here
Add Paste Here
Add Paste Here
Add Paste Here

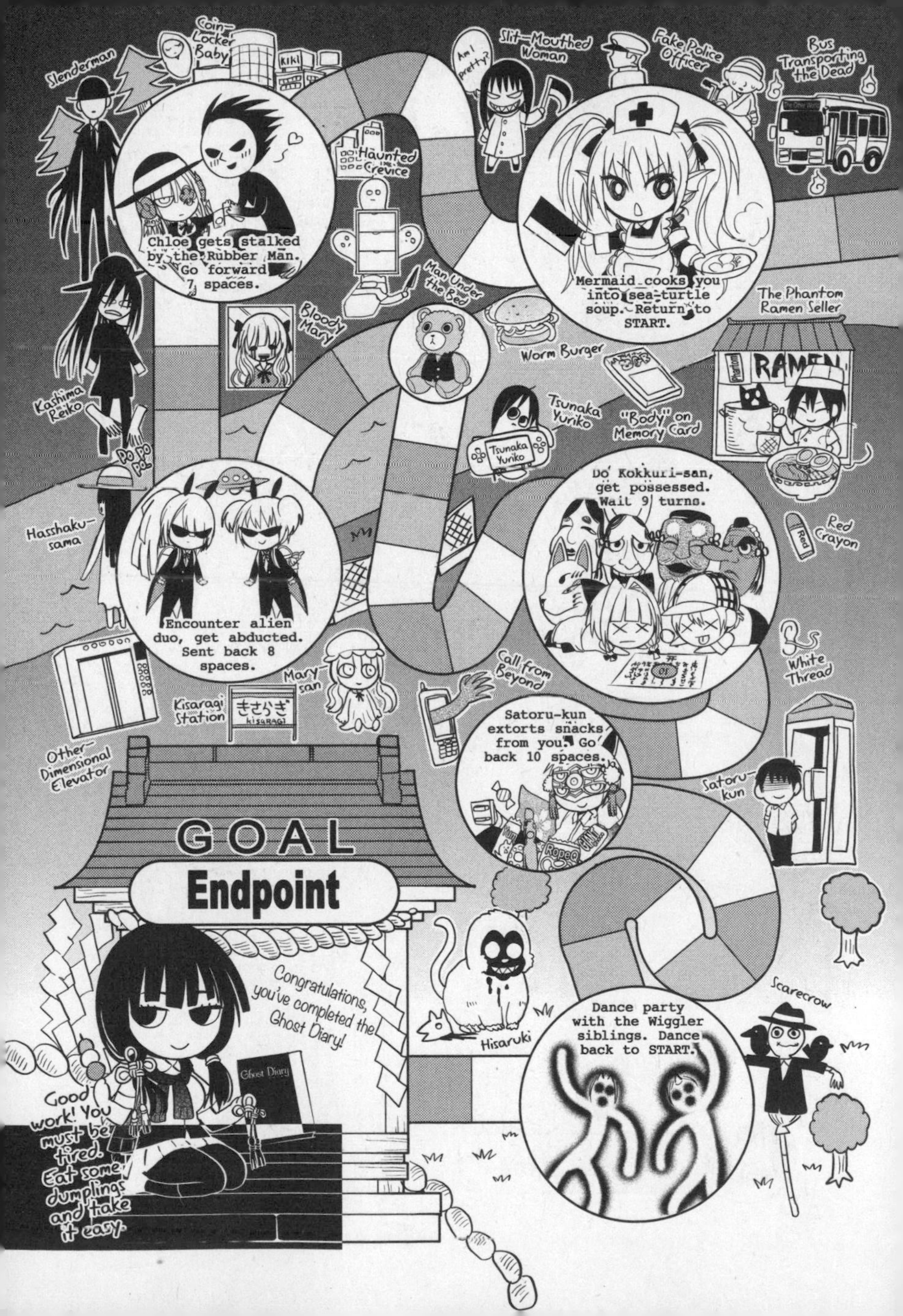

Slenderman
Coin-Locker Baby
Am I pretty?
Slit-Mouthed Woman
Fake Police Officer
Bus Transporting the Dead
Haunted Crevice
Chloe gets stalked by the Rubber Man. Go forward 7 spaces.
Mermaid cooks you into sea-turtle soup. Return to START.
Man Under the Bed
Bloody Mary
The Phantom Ramen Seller
RAMEN
Phantom
Worm Burger
Kashima Reiko
Tsunaka Yuriko
Tsunaka Yuriko
"Body" on Memory Card
Po po po.
Do Kokkuri-san, get possessed. Wait 9 turns.
Hasshaku-sama
Red Crayon
Red
Encounter alien duo, get abducted. Sent back 8 spaces.
White Thread
Mary-san
Call from Beyond
Kisaragi Station
きさらぎ
kisaragi
Satoru-kun extorts snacks from you. Go back 10 spaces.
Other-Dimensional Elevator
Satoru-kun
GOAL
Endpoint
Congratulations, you've completed the Ghost Diary!
Scarecrow
Hisaruki
Dance party with the Wiggler siblings. Dance back to START.
Ghost Diary
Good work! You must be tired. Eat some dumplings and take it easy.

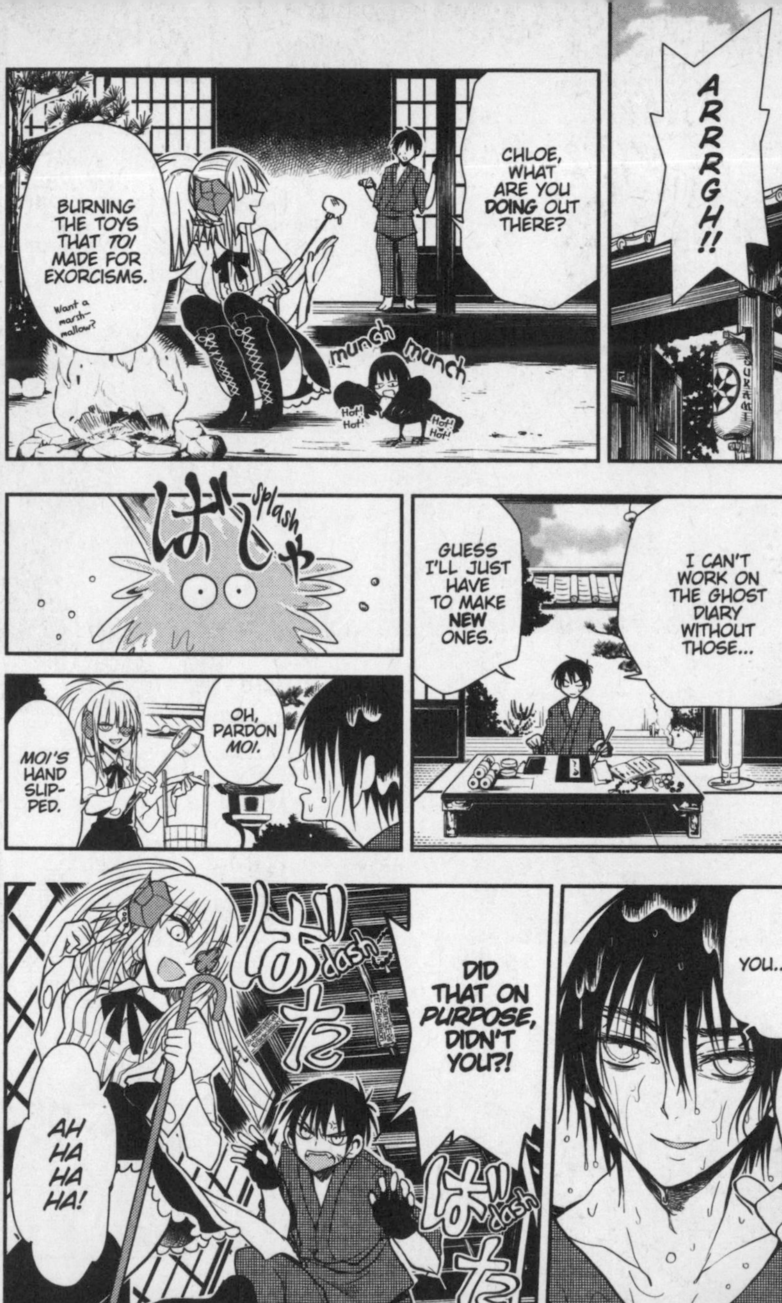

ARRRGH!!
CHLOE, WHAT ARE YOU DOING OUT THERE?
BURNING THE TOYS THAT TOI MADE FOR EXORCISMS.
Want a marsh-mallow?
munch munch
Hot! Hot!
Hot! Hot!
I CAN'T WORK ON THE GHOST DIARY WITHOUT THOSE...
GUESS I'LL JUST HAVE TO MAKE NEW ONES.
ばしゃ splash
OH, PARDON MOI.
MOI'S HAND SLIP-PED.
YOU...
DID THAT ON PURPOSE, DIDN'T YOU?!
ばた dash
ばた dash
AH HA HA HA!

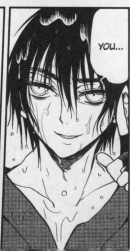

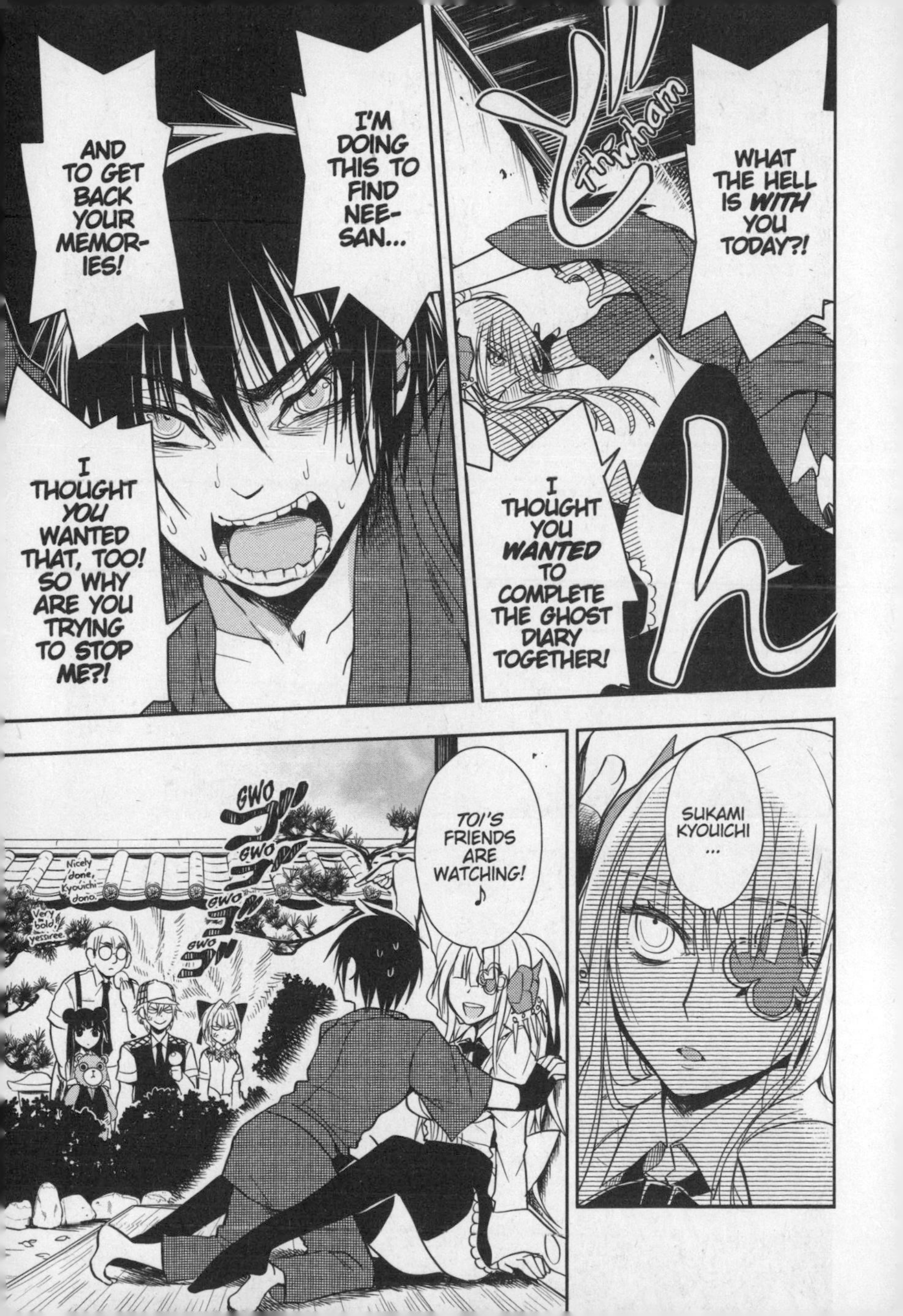

Thwham
WHAT THE HELL IS WITH YOU TODAY?!
I THOUGHT YOU WANTED TO COMPLETE THE GHOST DIARY TOGETHER!
I'M DOING THIS TO FIND NEE-SAN...
AND TO GET BACK YOUR MEMORIES!
I THOUGHT YOU WANTED THAT, TOO! SO WHY ARE YOU TRYING TO STOP ME?!
SUKAMI KYOUICHI ...
TOI'S FRIENDS ARE WATCHING! ♪
GWO GWO GWO GWO
Nicely done, Kyouichi-dono.
Very bold, yessiree.

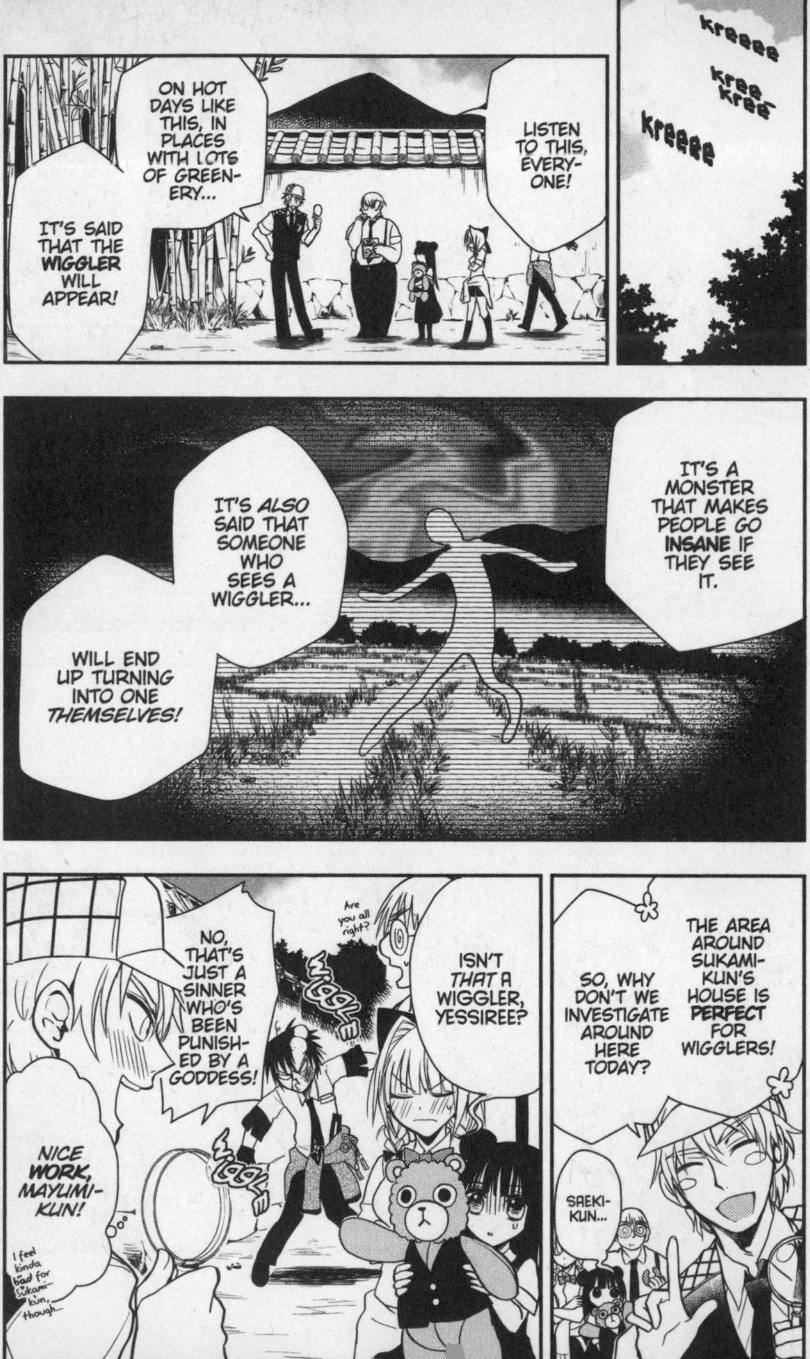
kreeee
kree kree
kreeee
LISTEN TO THIS, EVERYONE!
ON HOT DAYS LIKE THIS, IN PLACES WITH LOTS OF GREENERY...
IT'S SAID THAT THE WIGGLER WILL APPEAR!
IT'S A MONSTER THAT MAKES PEOPLE GO INSANE IF THEY SEE IT.
IT'S ALSO SAID THAT SOMEONE WHO SEES A WIGGLER...
WILL END UP TURNING INTO ONE THEMSELVES!
THE AREA AROUND SUKAMI-KUN'S HOUSE IS PERFECT FOR WIGGLERS!
SO, WHY DON'T WE INVESTIGATE AROUND HERE TODAY?
SAEKI-KUN...
ISN'T THAT A WIGGLER, YESSIREE?
Are you all right?
WIGGLE
WIGGLE
NO, THAT'S JUST A SINNER WHO'S BEEN PUNISHED BY A GODDESS!
NICE WORK, MAYUMI-KUN!
I feel kinda bad for Sukami-kun, though...

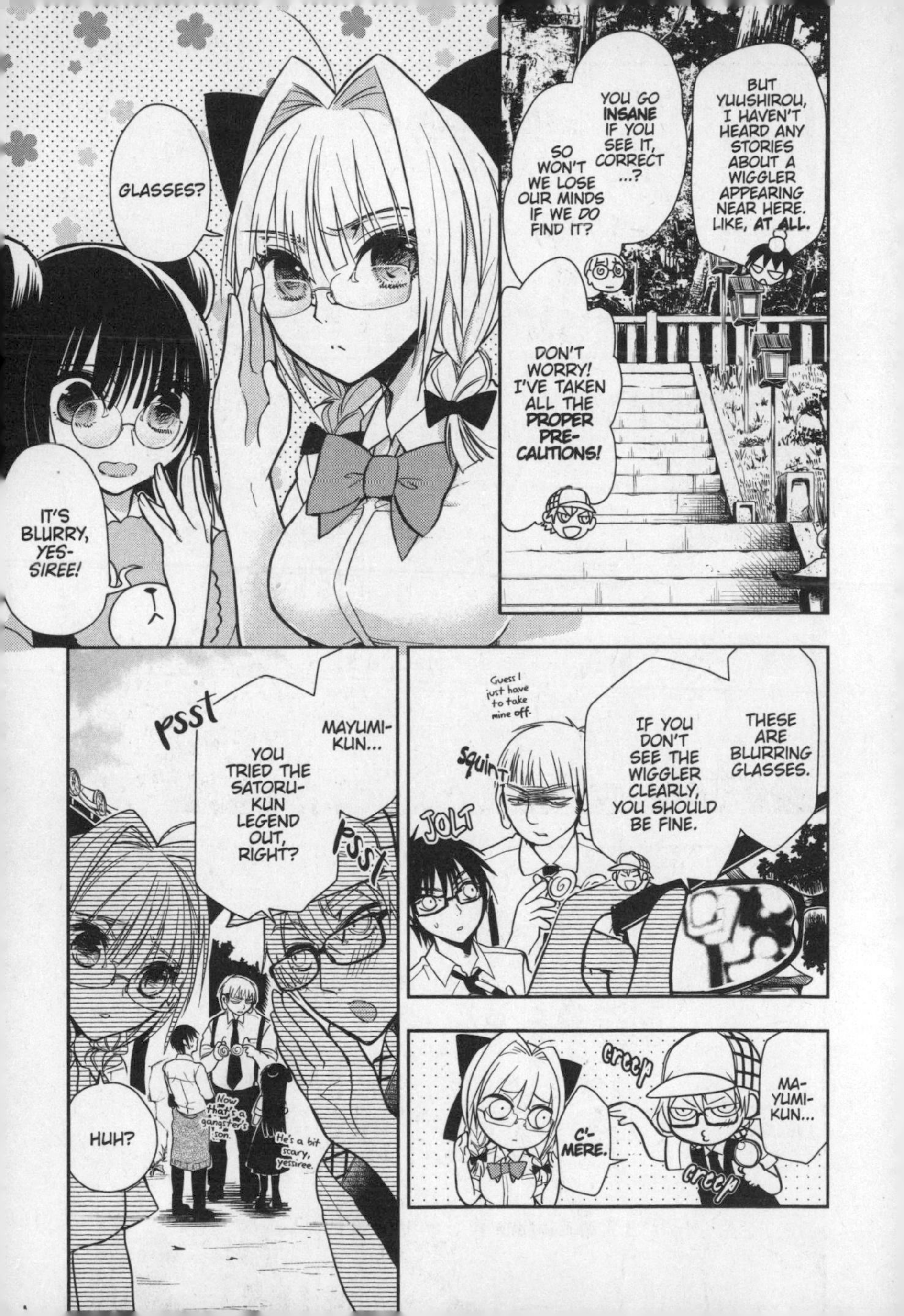

BUT YUUSHIROU, I HAVEN'T HEARD ANY STORIES ABOUT A WIGGLER APPEARING NEAR HERE. LIKE, AT ALL.
YOU GO INSANE IF YOU SEE IT, CORRECT ...?
SO WON'T WE LOSE OUR MINDS IF WE DO FIND IT?
DON'T WORRY! I'VE TAKEN ALL THE PROPER PRE-CAUTIONS!
GLASSES?
IT'S BLURRY, YES-SIREE!
THESE ARE BLURRING GLASSES.
IF YOU DON'T SEE THE WIGGLER CLEARLY, YOU SHOULD BE FINE.
Guess I just have to take mine off.
Squint
JOLT
MAYUMI-KUN...
psst
YOU TRIED THE SATORU-KUN LEGEND OUT, RIGHT?
psst
HUH?
Now that's a gangster's son.
He's a bit scary, yessiree.
MA-YUMI-KUN...
creep
C'-MERE.
creep

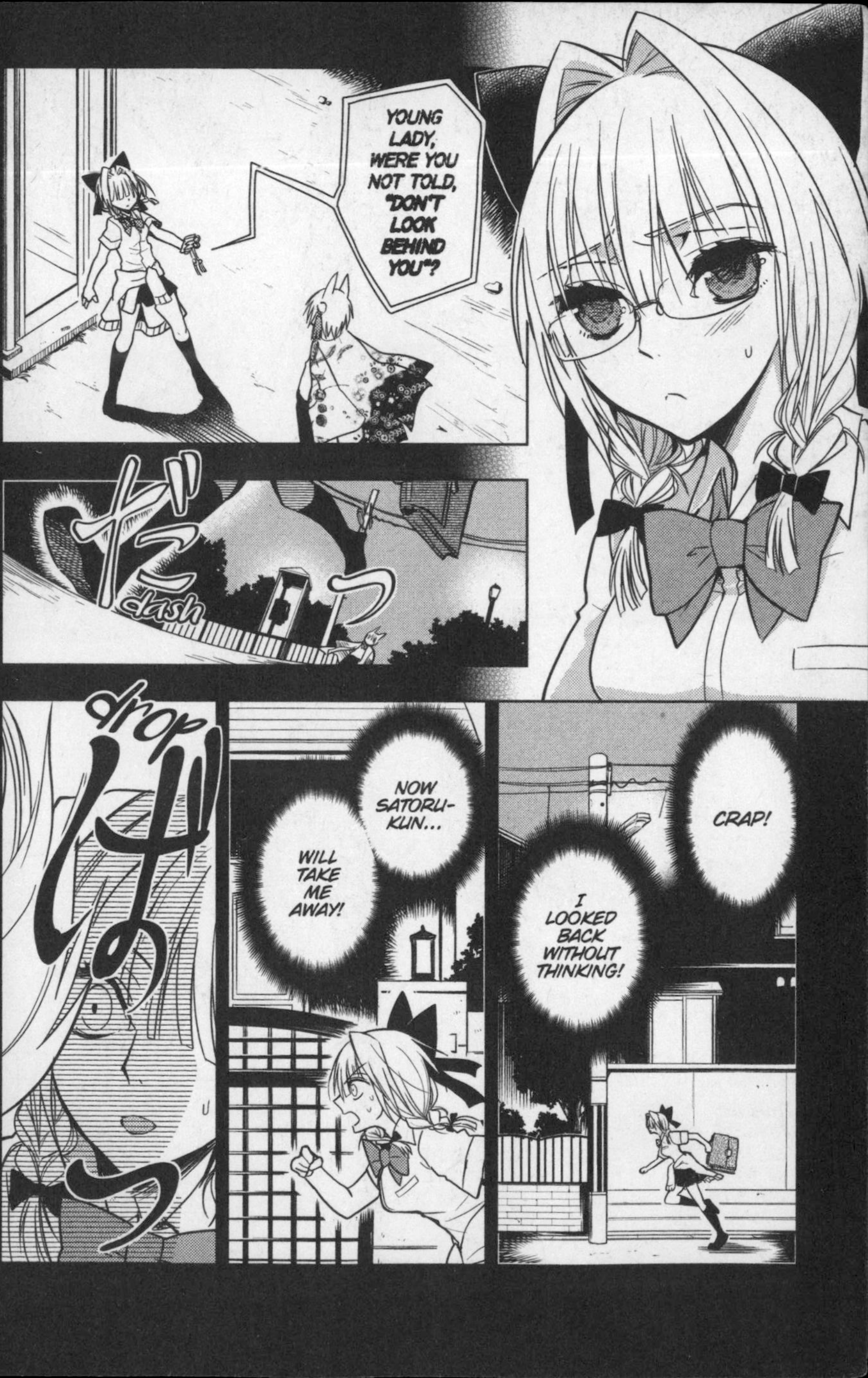

YOUNG LADY, WERE YOU NOT TOLD, "DON'T LOOK BEHIND YOU"?
dash
CRAP!
I LOOKED BACK WITHOUT THINKING!
NOW SATORU-KUN...
WILL TAKE ME AWAY!
drop

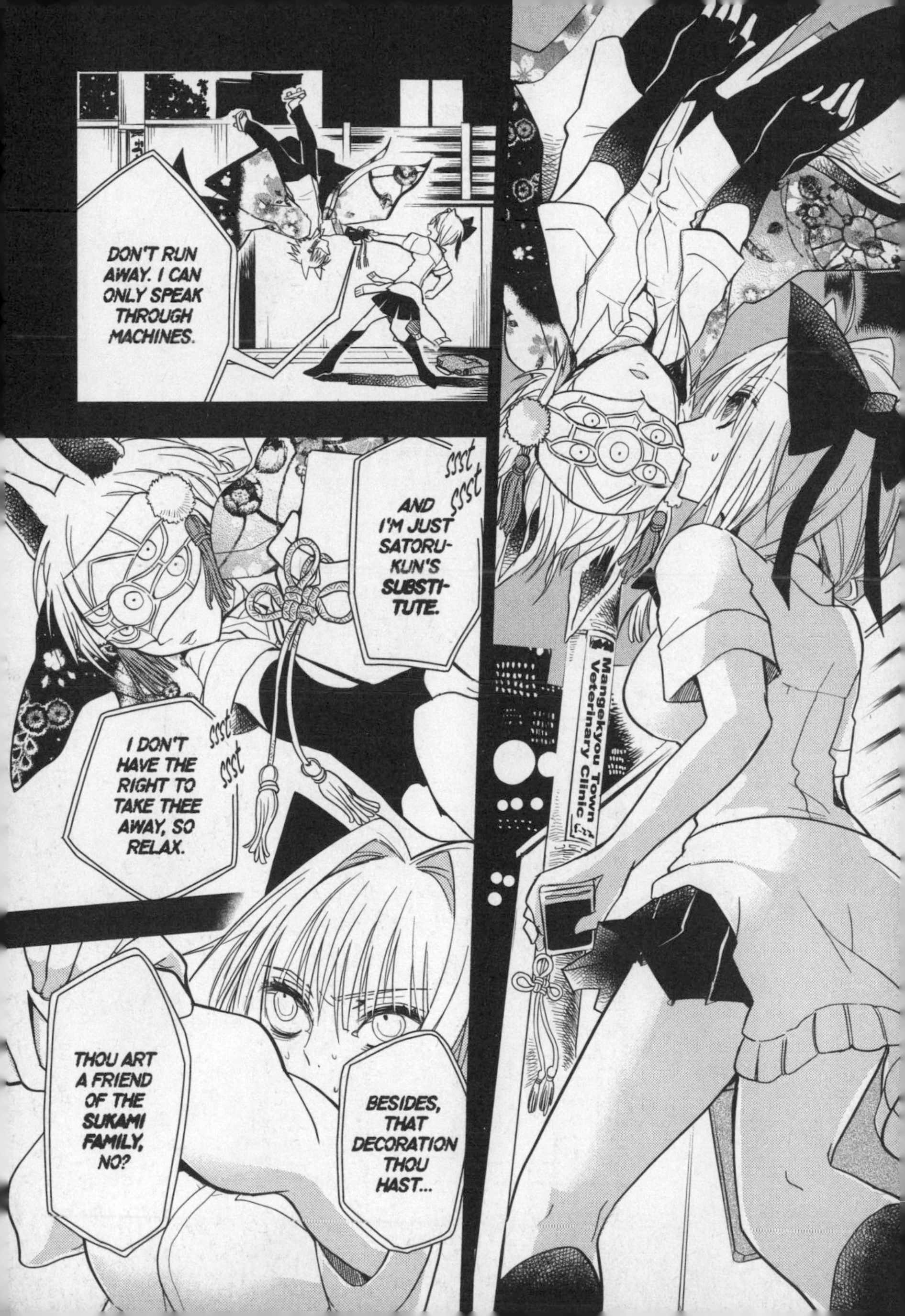
Mangekyou Town Veterinary Clinic
DON'T RUN AWAY. I CAN ONLY SPEAK THROUGH MACHINES.
AND I'M JUST SATORU-KUN'S SUBSTITUTE.
SSST SSST
I DON'T HAVE THE RIGHT TO TAKE THEE AWAY, SO RELAX.
SSST SSST
BESIDES, THAT DECORATION THOU HAST...
THOU ART A FRIEND OF THE SUKAMI FAMILY, NO?

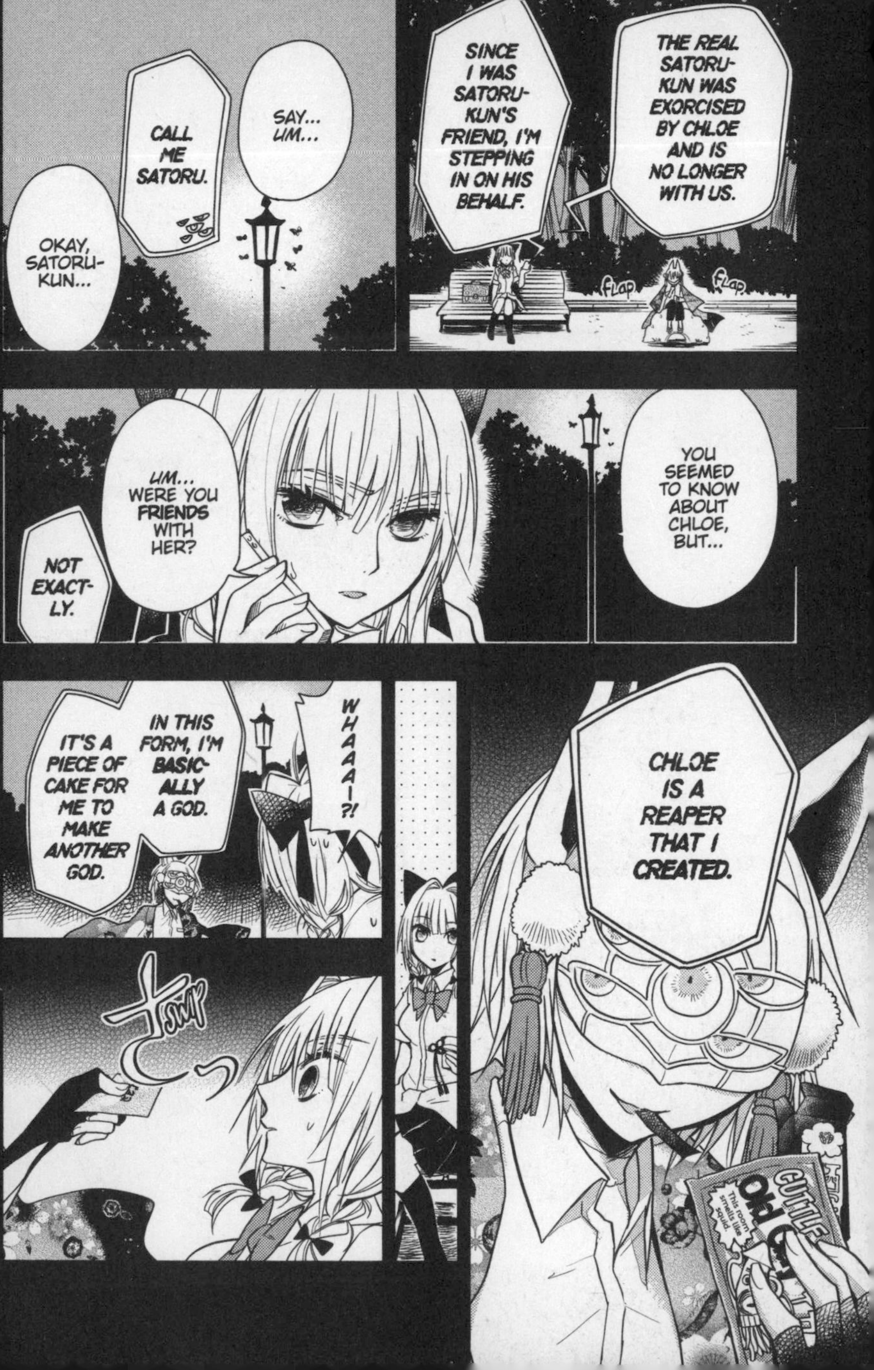
THE REAL SATORU-KUN WAS EXORCISED BY CHLOE AND IS NO LONGER WITH US.
SINCE I WAS SATORU-KUN'S FRIEND, I'M STEPPING IN ON HIS BEHALF.
FLAP
FLAP
SAY... UM...
CALL ME SATORU.
OKAY, SATORU-KUN...
YOU SEEMED TO KNOW ABOUT CHLOE, BUT...
UM... WERE YOU FRIENDS WITH HER?
NOT EXACTLY.
CHLOE IS A REAPER THAT I CREATED.
WHAAAAI?!
IN THIS FORM, I'M BASICALLY A GOD.
IT'S A PIECE OF CAKE FOR ME TO MAKE ANOTHER GOD.
SWIP
CUTTLE
Old
This room smells like squid.

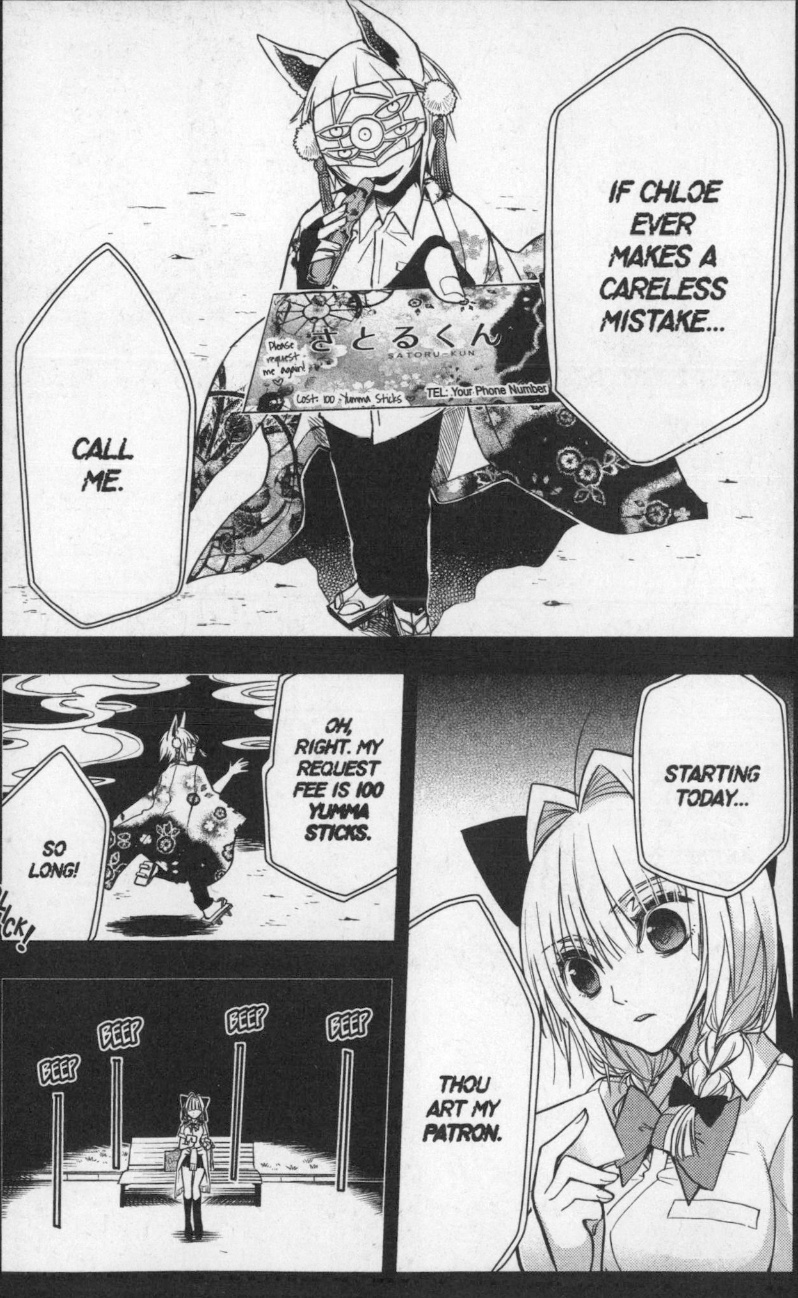
IF CHLOE EVER MAKES A CARELESS MISTAKE...
さとるくん
SATORU-KUN
Please request me again! ♡
Cost: 100 Yumma Sticks ♡
TEL: Your Phone Number
CALL ME.
STARTING TODAY...
THOU ART MY PATRON.
OH, RIGHT. MY REQUEST FEE IS 100 YUMMA STICKS.
SO LONG!
CLICK!
BEEP
BEEP
BEEP
BEEP

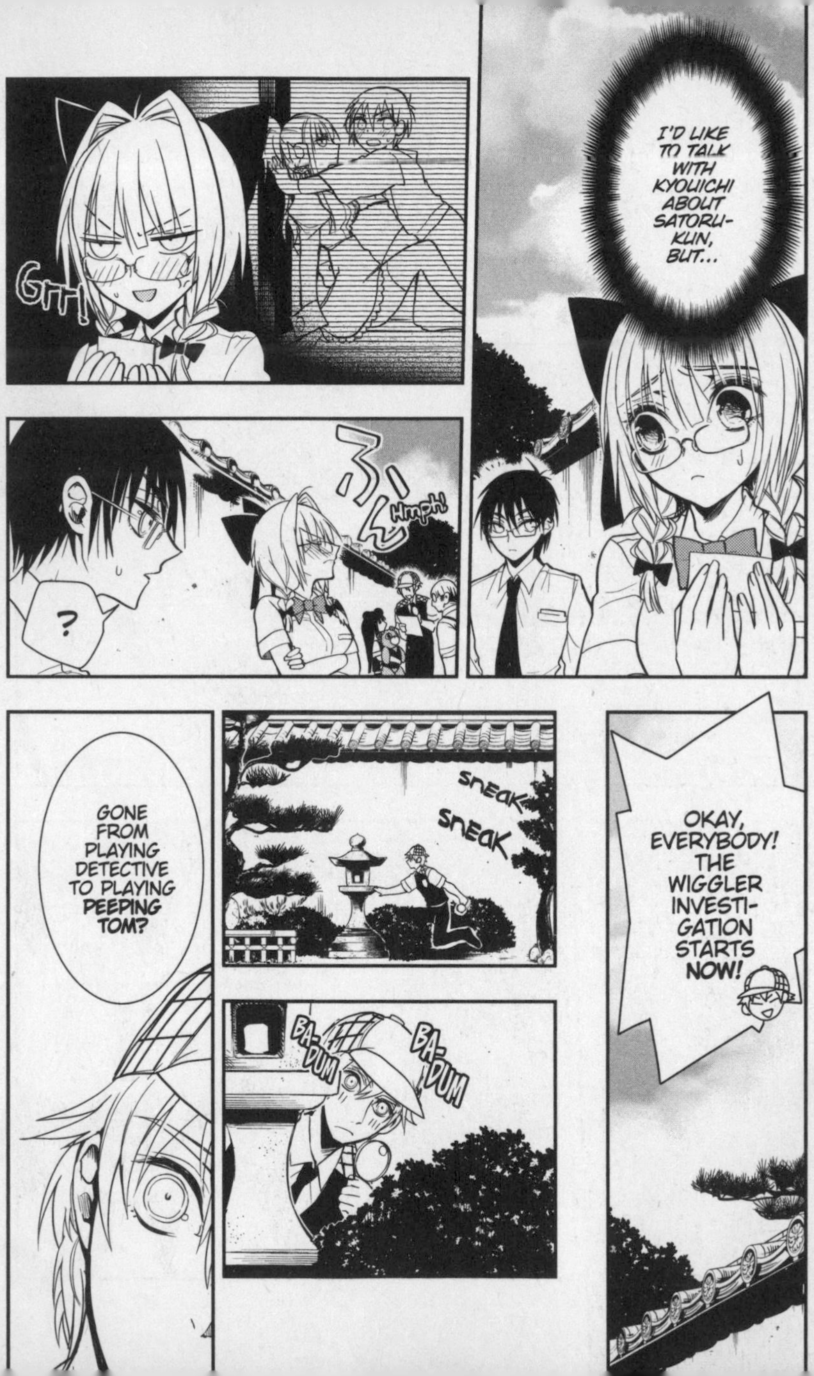
I'D LIKE TO TALK WITH KYOUICHI ABOUT SATORU-KUN, BUT...
Grrr!
ふん
Hmph!
?
OKAY, EVERYBODY! THE WIGGLER INVESTIGATION STARTS NOW!
sneak
sneak
BA-DUM
BA-DUM
GONE FROM PLAYING DETECTIVE TO PLAYING PEEPING TOM?

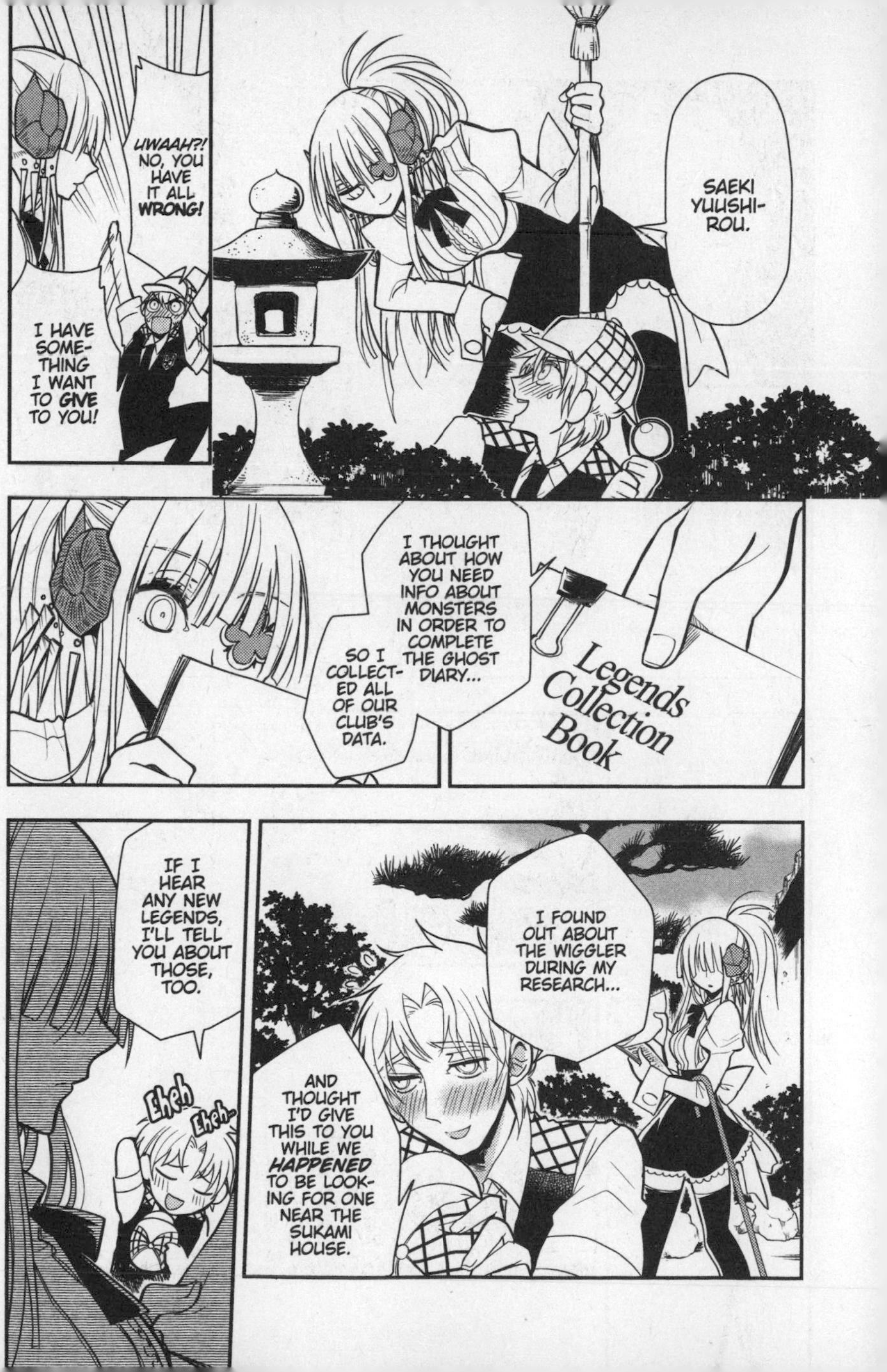

SAEKI YUUSHIROU.
UWAAH?! NO, YOU HAVE IT ALL WRONG!
I HAVE SOMETHING I WANT TO GIVE TO YOU!
Legends Collection Book
I THOUGHT ABOUT HOW YOU NEED INFO ABOUT MONSTERS IN ORDER TO COMPLETE THE GHOST DIARY...
SO I COLLECTED ALL OF OUR CLUB'S DATA.
I FOUND OUT ABOUT THE WIGGLER DURING MY RESEARCH...
AND THOUGHT I'D GIVE THIS TO YOU WHILE WE HAPPENED TO BE LOOKING FOR ONE NEAR THE SUKAMI HOUSE.
IF I HEAR ANY NEW LEGENDS, I'LL TELL YOU ABOUT THOSE, TOO.
Eheh
Eheh...

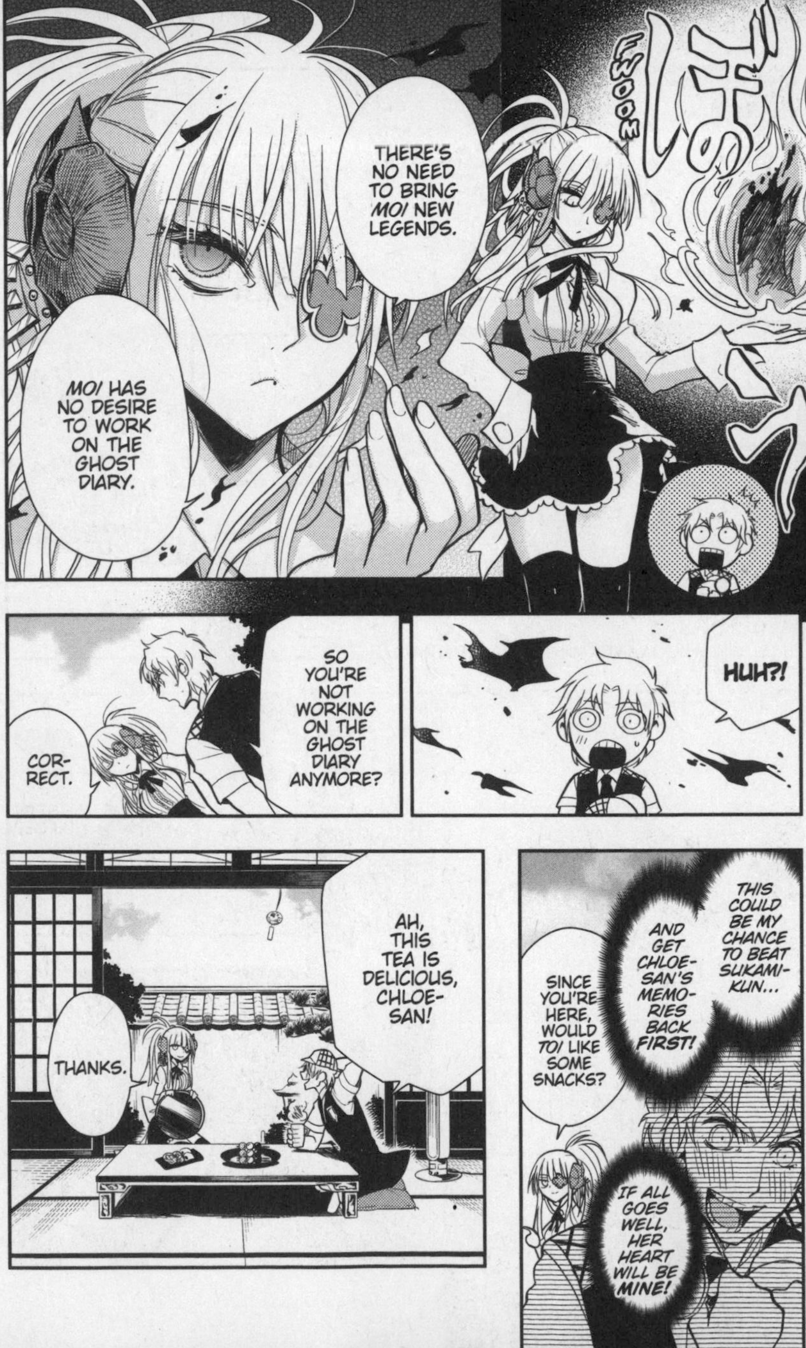
FWOOM
THERE'S NO NEED TO BRING *MOI* NEW LEGENDS.
MOI HAS NO DESIRE TO WORK ON THE GHOST DIARY.
HUH?!
SO YOU'RE NOT WORKING ON THE GHOST DIARY ANYMORE?
COR-RECT.
THIS COULD BE MY CHANCE TO BEAT SUKAMI-KUN...
AND GET CHLOE-SAN'S MEMORIES BACK FIRST!
SINCE YOU'RE HERE, WOULD *TOI* LIKE SOME SNACKS?
IF ALL GOES WELL, HER HEART WILL BE MINE!
AH, THIS TEA IS DELICIOUS, CHLOE-SAN!
THANKS.

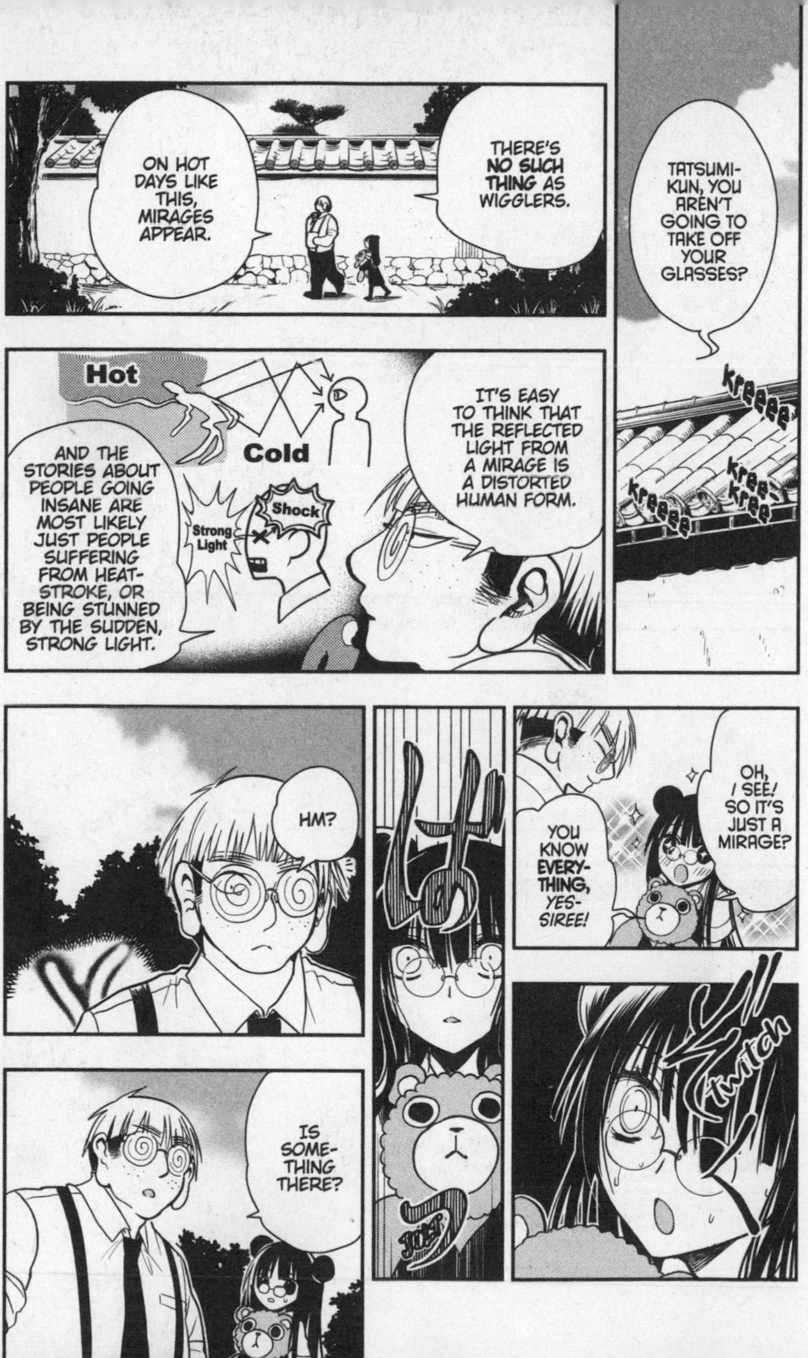

TATSUMI-KUN, YOU AREN'T GOING TO TAKE OFF YOUR GLASSES?
kreeee
kree-kree
kreeee
THERE'S **NO SUCH THING** AS WIGGLERS.
ON HOT DAYS LIKE THIS, MIRAGES APPEAR.
IT'S EASY TO THINK THAT THE REFLECTED LIGHT FROM A MIRAGE IS A DISTORTED HUMAN FORM.
Hot
Cold
Shock
Strong Light
AND THE STORIES ABOUT PEOPLE GOING INSANE ARE MOST LIKELY JUST PEOPLE SUFFERING FROM HEAT-STROKE, OR BEING STUNNED BY THE SUDDEN, STRONG LIGHT.
OH, I SEE! SO IT'S JUST A MIRAGE?
YOU KNOW **EVERYTHING**, YES-SIREE!
twitch
HM?
IS SOMETHING THERE?

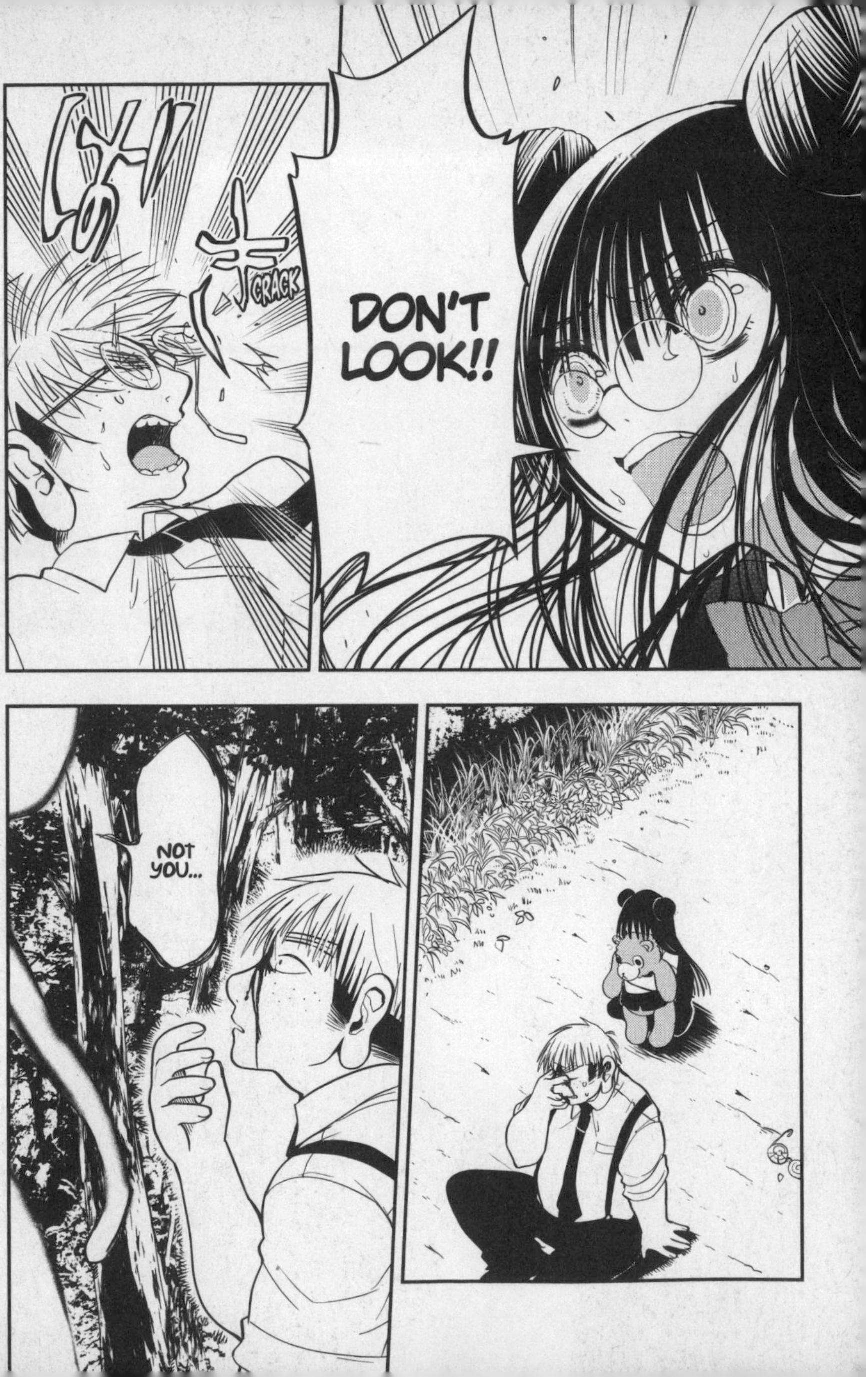
CRACK
DON'T LOOK!!
NOT YOU...

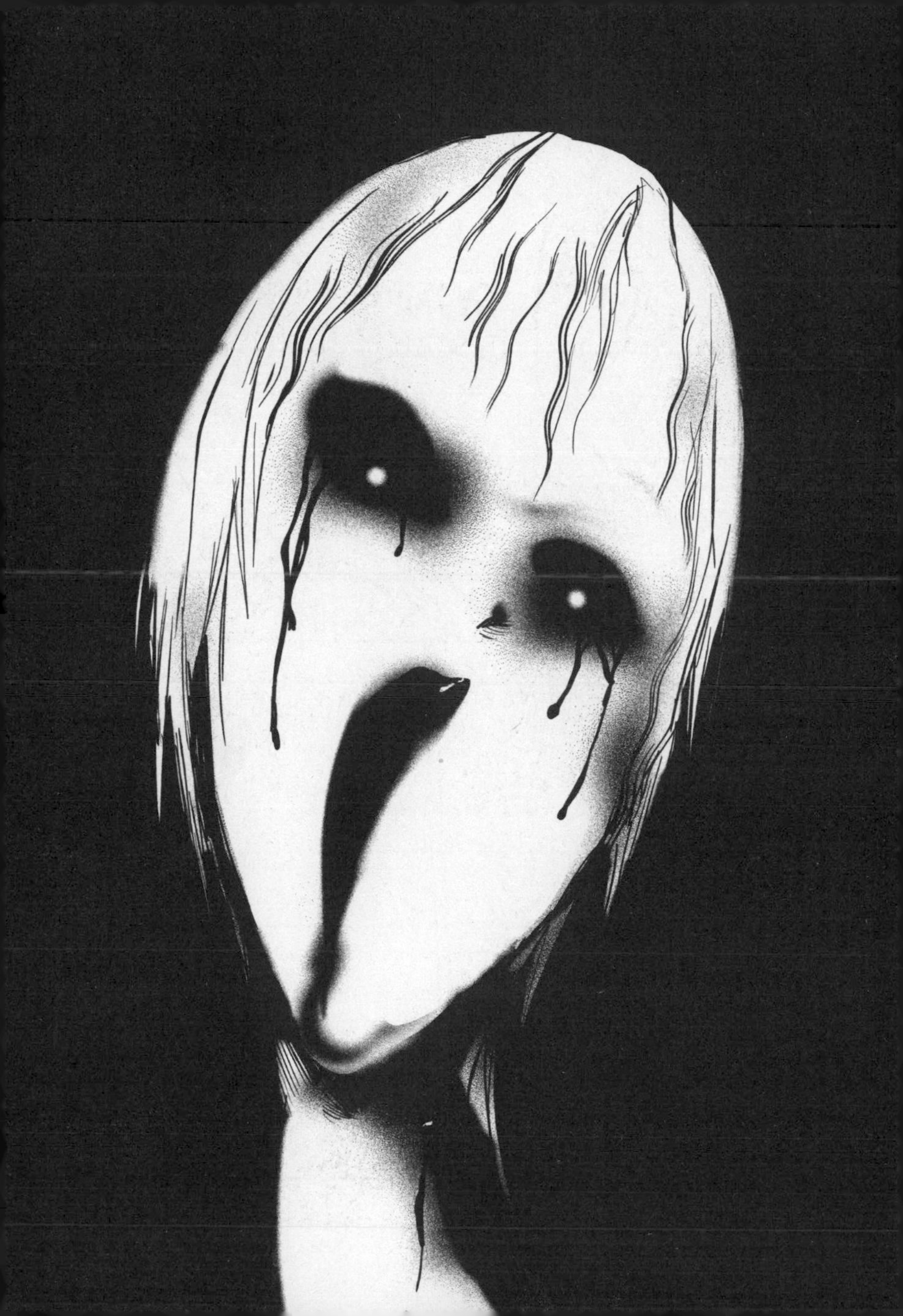

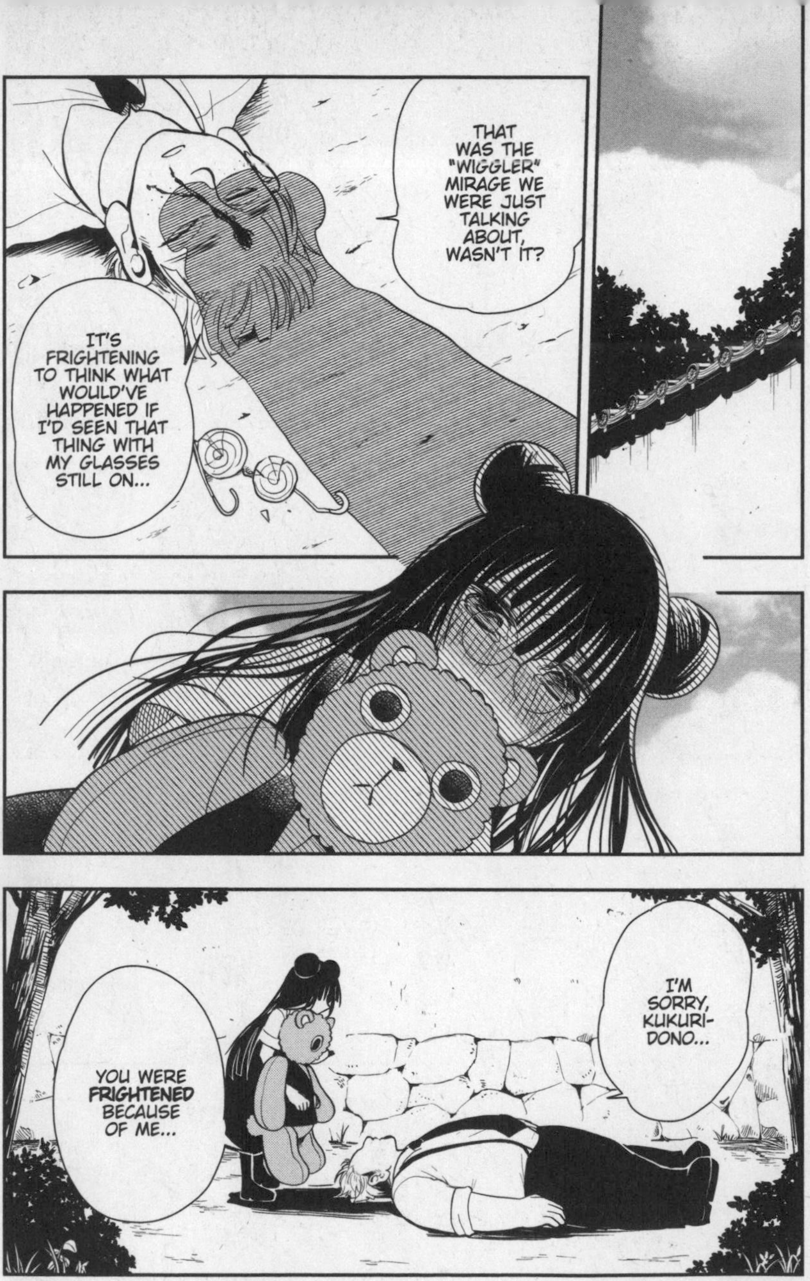
THAT WAS THE "WIGGLER" MIRAGE WE WERE JUST TALKING ABOUT, WASN'T IT?
IT'S FRIGHTENING TO THINK WHAT WOULD'VE HAPPENED IF I'D SEEN THAT THING WITH MY GLASSES STILL ON...
I'M SORRY, KUKURI-DONO...
YOU WERE **FRIGHTENED** BECAUSE OF ME...

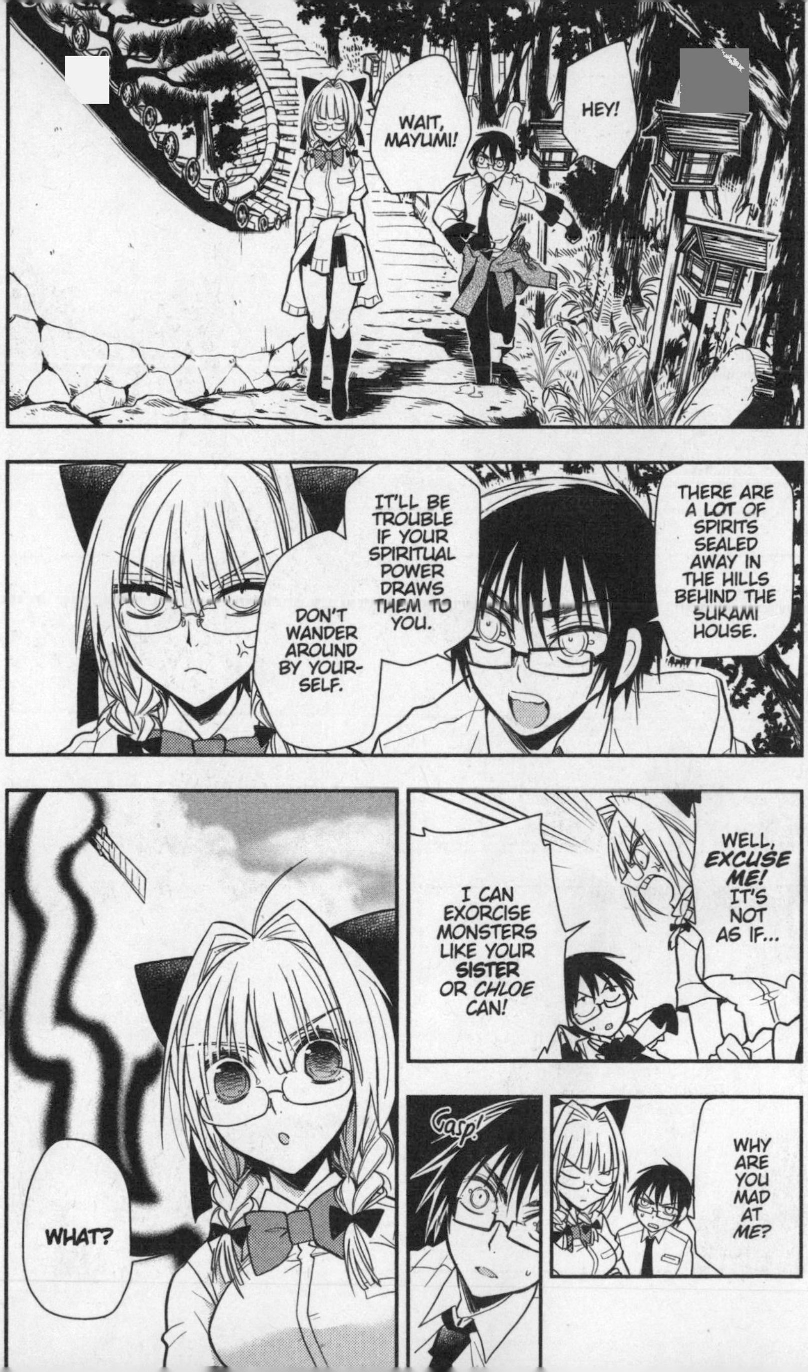
HEY!
WAIT, MAYUMI!
THERE ARE A LOT OF SPIRITS SEALED AWAY IN THE HILLS BEHIND THE SUKAMI HOUSE.
IT'LL BE TROUBLE IF YOUR SPIRITUAL POWER DRAWS THEM TO YOU.
DON'T WANDER AROUND BY YOUR-SELF.
WELL, EXCUSE ME! IT'S NOT AS IF...
I CAN EXORCISE MONSTERS LIKE YOUR SISTER OR CHLOE CAN!
WHY ARE YOU MAD AT ME?
Gasp!
WHAT?

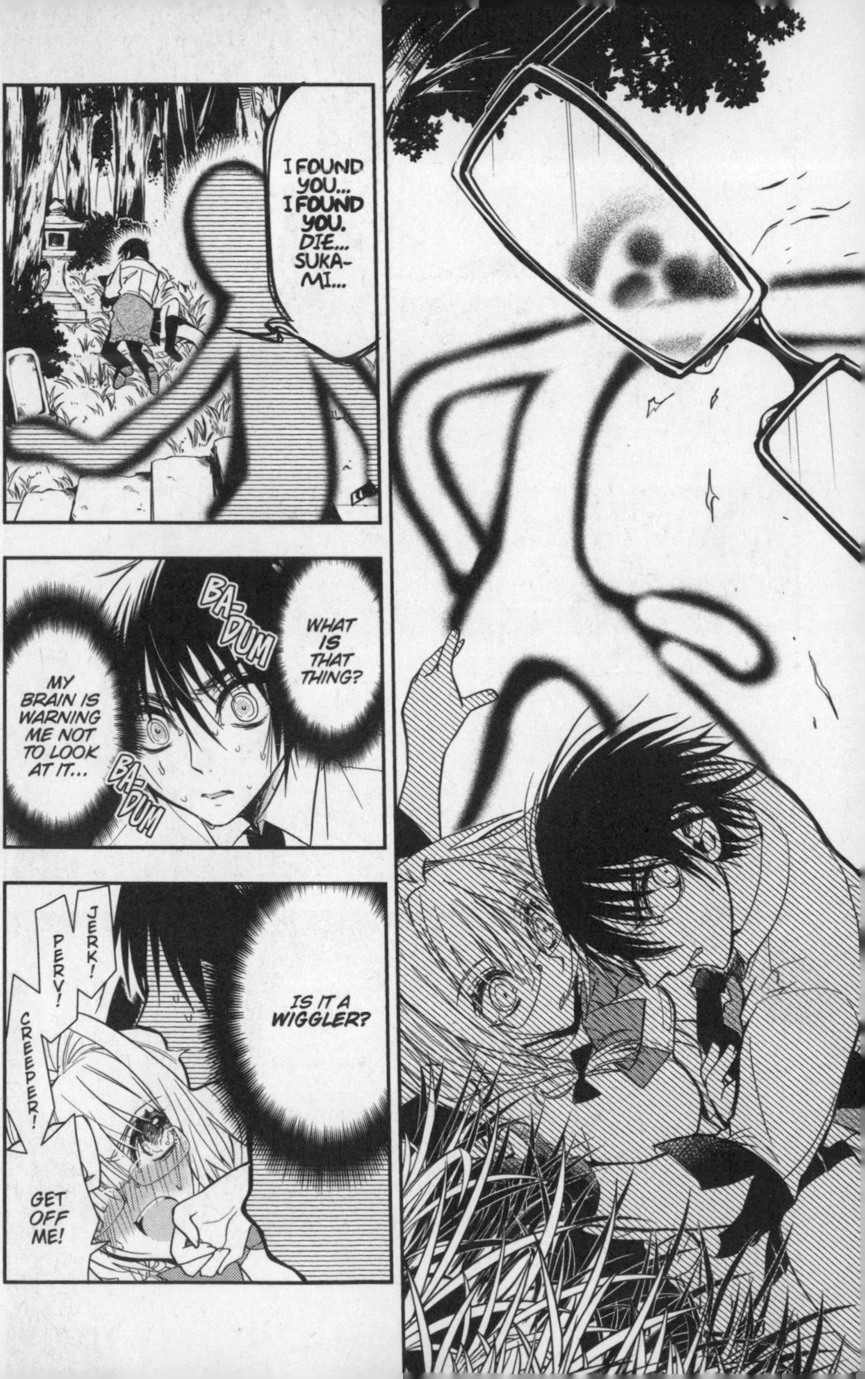
I FOUND YOU... I FOUND YOU. DIE... SUKA-MI...
WHAT IS THAT THING?
BA-DUM
MY BRAIN IS WARNING ME NOT TO LOOK AT IT...
BA-DUM
IS IT A WIGGLER?
JERK!
PERV!
CREEPER!
GET OFF ME!

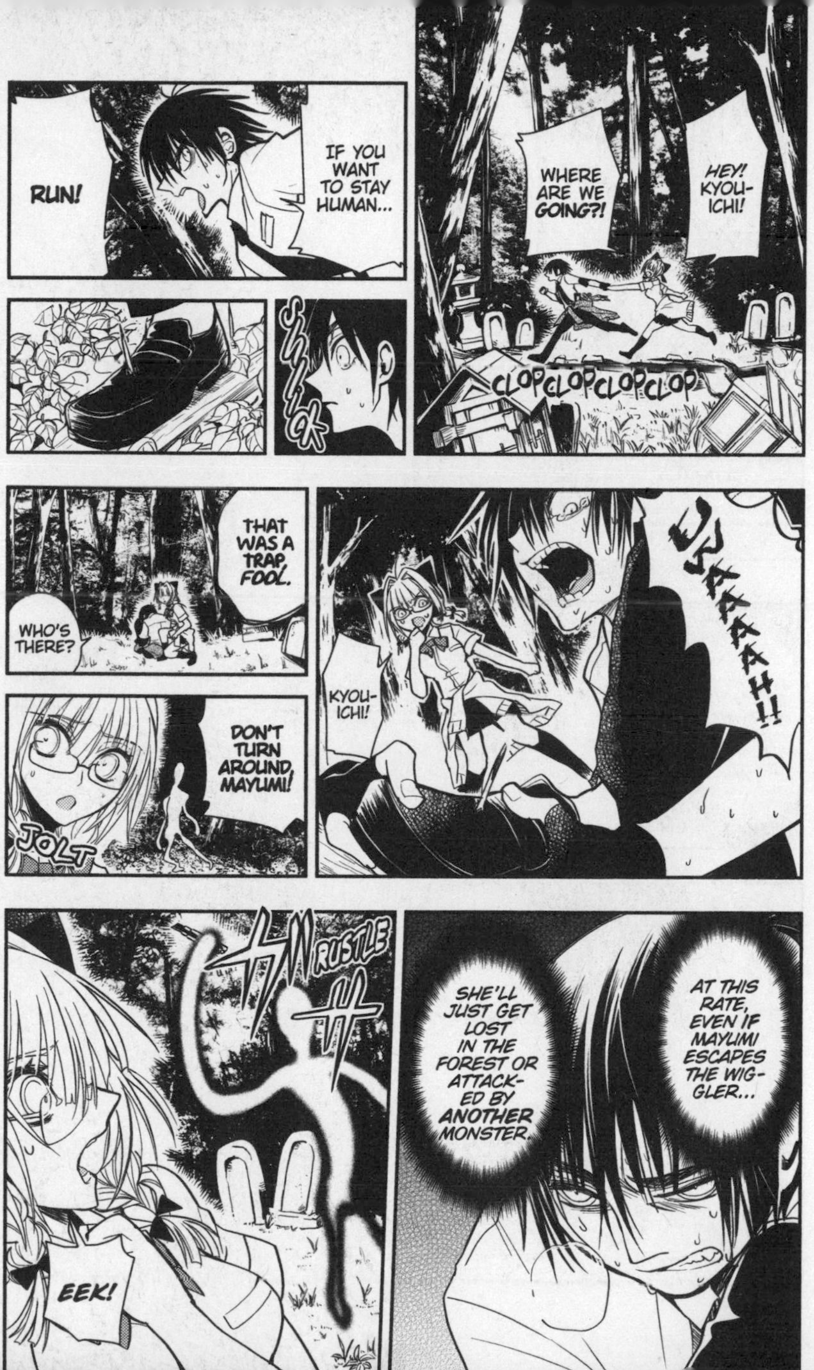
HEY! KYOU-ICHI!
WHERE ARE WE GOING?!
CLOP CLOP CLOP CLOP
IF YOU WANT TO STAY HUMAN...
RUN!
GYAAAAH!!
KYOU-ICHI!
THAT WAS A TRAP, FOOL.
WHO'S THERE?
DON'T TURN AROUND, MAYUMI!
JOLT
AT THIS RATE, EVEN IF MAYUMI ESCAPES THE WIGGLER...
SHE'LL JUST GET LOST IN THE FOREST OR ATTACKED BY ANOTHER MONSTER.
RUSTLE
EEK!

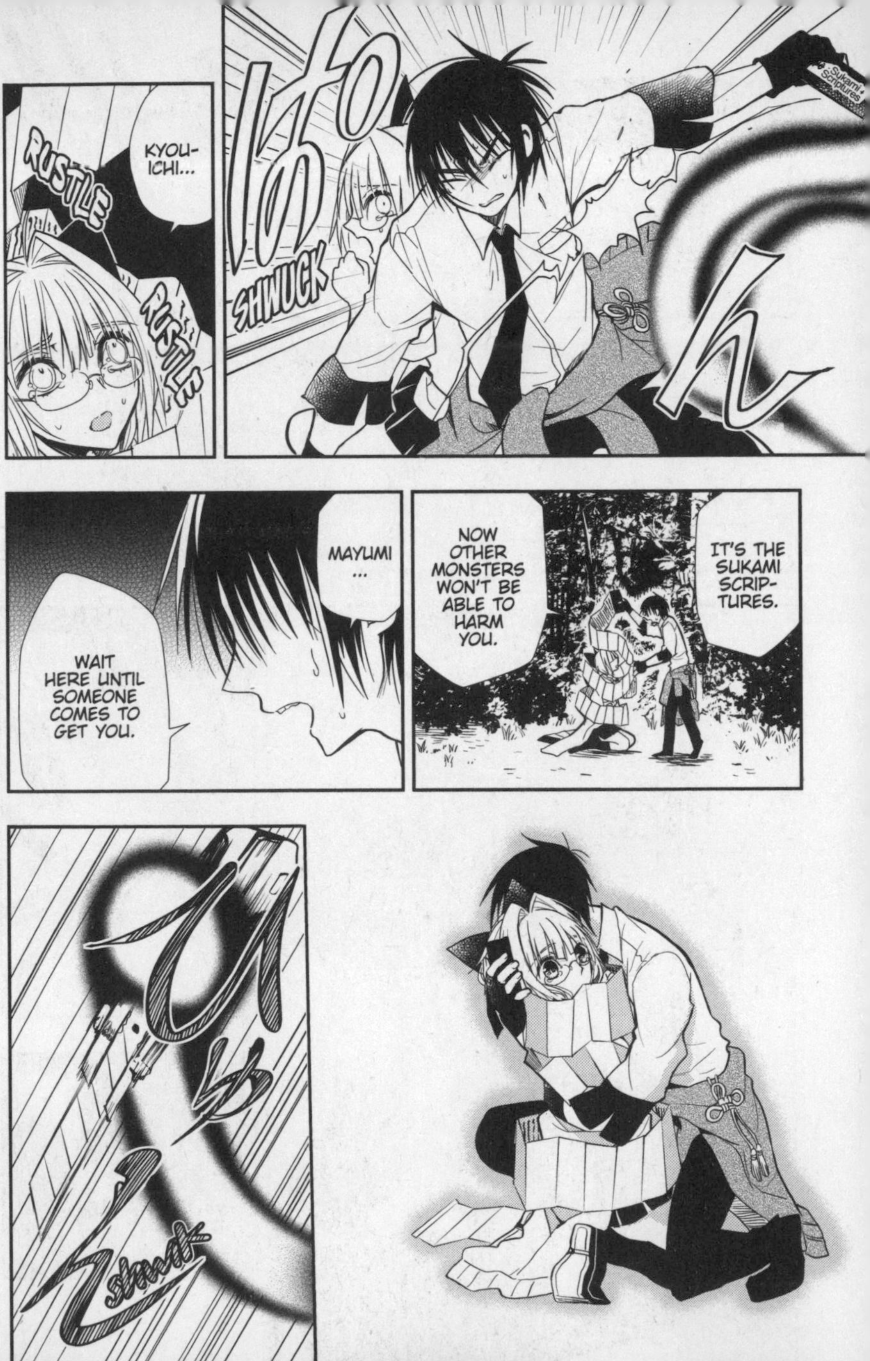
Sukami Scriptures
SHWUCK
RUSTLE
KYOU-ICHI...
RUSTLE
IT'S THE SUKAMI SCRIP-TURES.
NOW OTHER MONSTERS WON'T BE ABLE TO HARM YOU.
MAYUMI ...
WAIT HERE UNTIL SOMEONE COMES TO GET YOU.

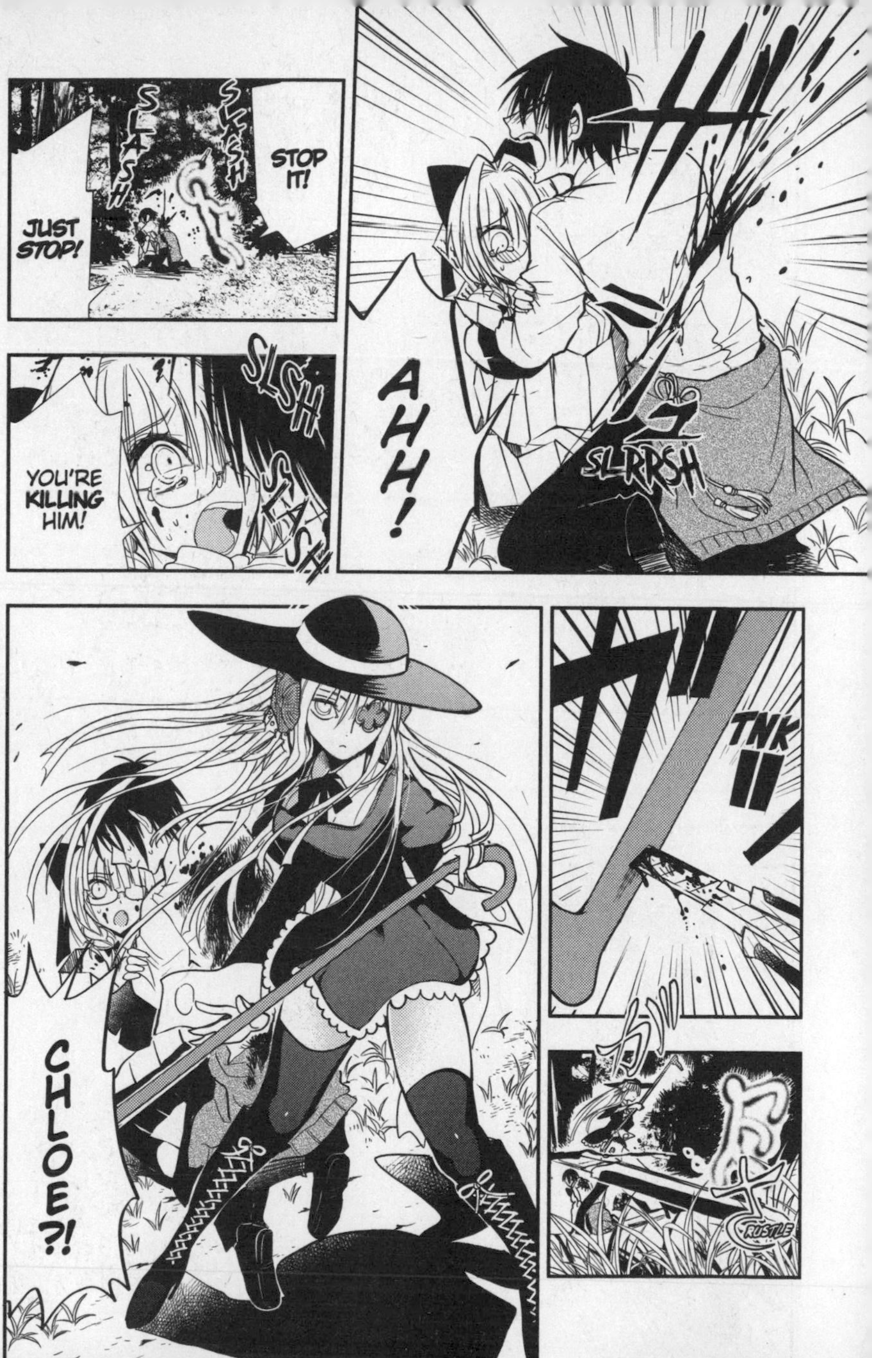
AHH!
SLRRSH
STOP IT!
JUST STOP!
SLASH
SLASH
SLSH
SLASH
YOU'RE KILLING HIM!
TNK
RUSTLE
CHLOE?!

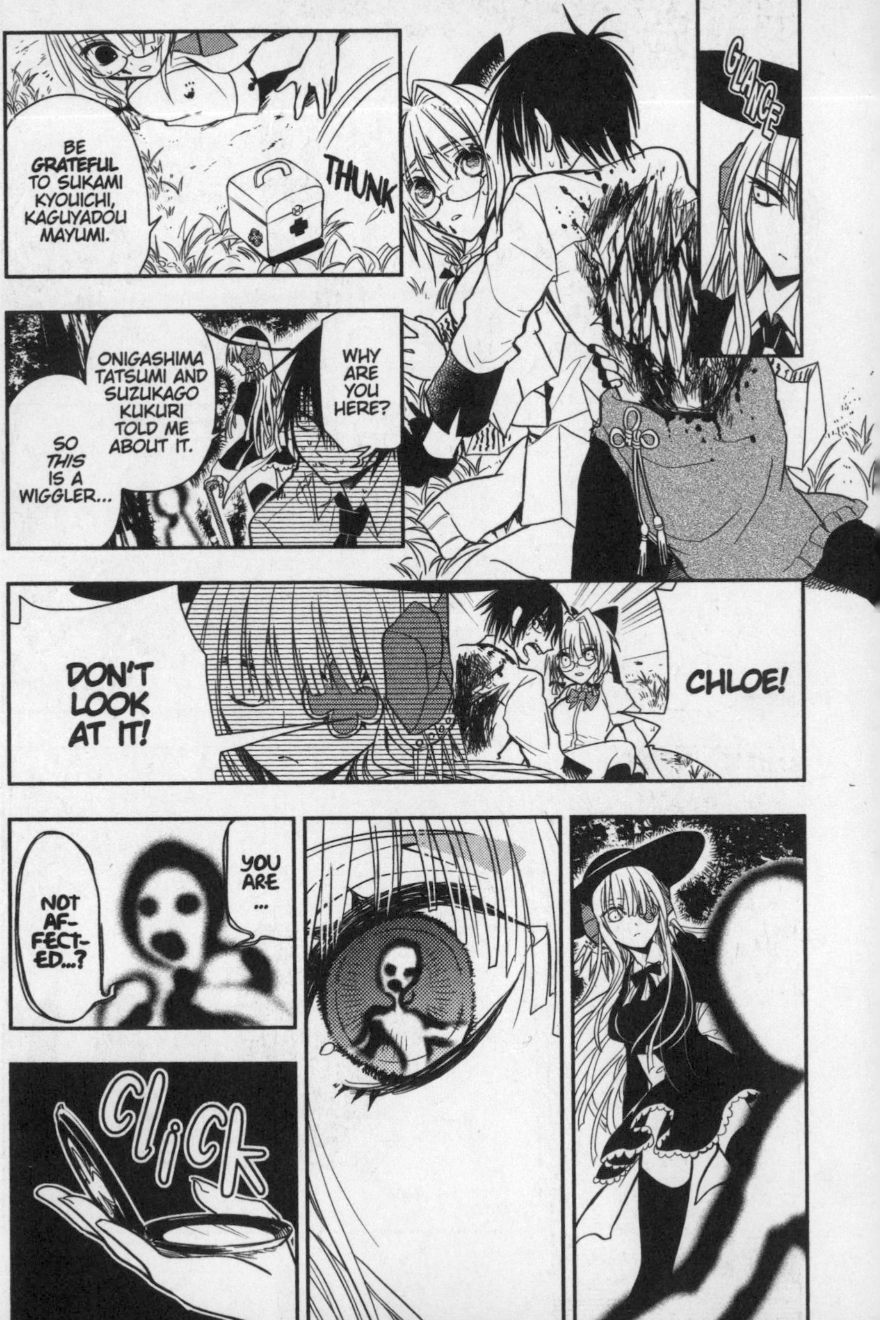
GLANCE
THUNK
BE GRATEFUL TO SUKAMI KYOUICHI, KAGUYADOU MAYUMI.
WHY ARE YOU HERE?
ONIGASHIMA TATSUMI AND SUZUKAGO KUKURI TOLD ME ABOUT IT.
SO THIS IS A WIGGLER...
CHLOE!
DON'T LOOK AT IT!
YOU ARE ...
NOT AF-FECT-ED...?
Click

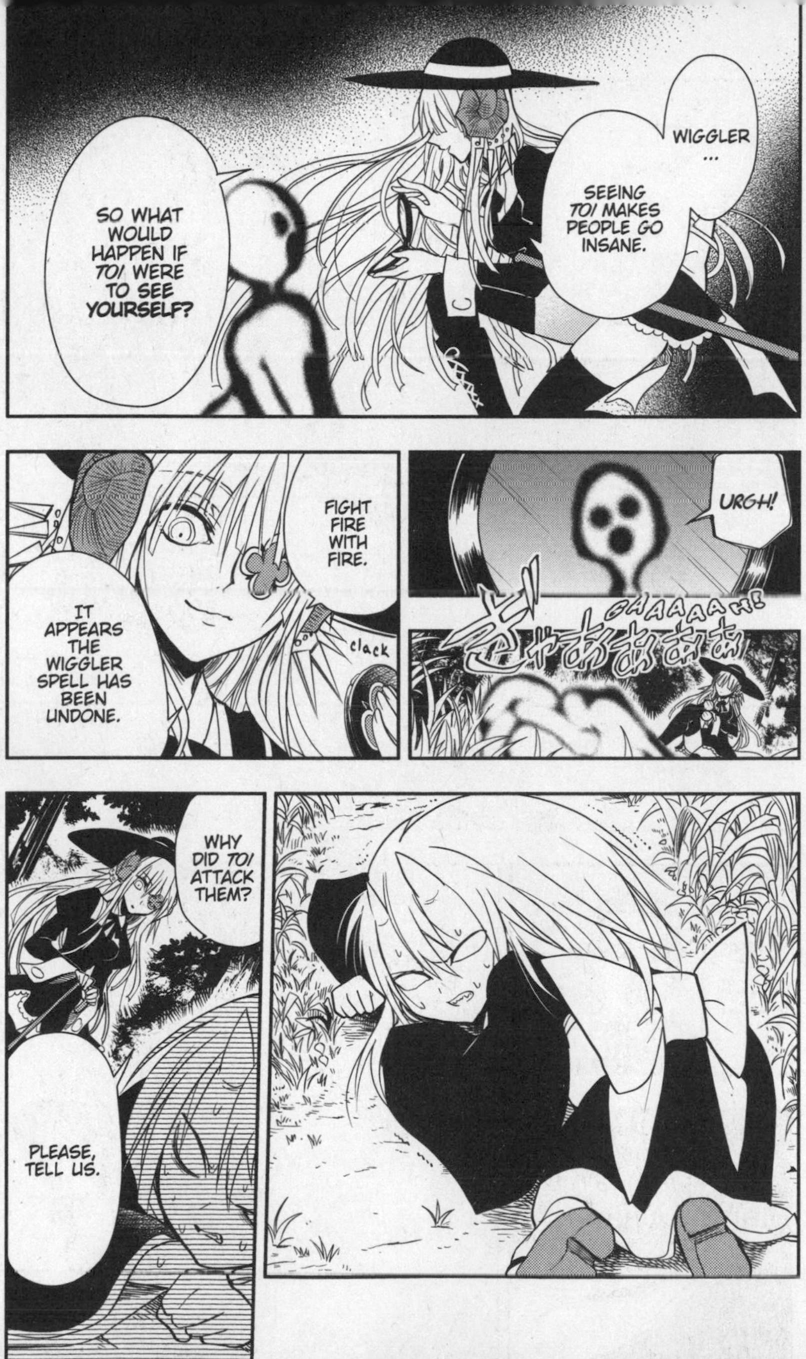
WIGGLER ...
SEEING TOI MAKES PEOPLE GO INSANE.
SO WHAT WOULD HAPPEN IF TOI WERE TO SEE YOURSELF?
URGH!
GAAAAAH!
FIGHT FIRE WITH FIRE.
clack
IT APPEARS THE WIGGLER SPELL HAS BEEN UNDONE.
WHY DID TOI ATTACK THEM?
PLEASE, TELL US.

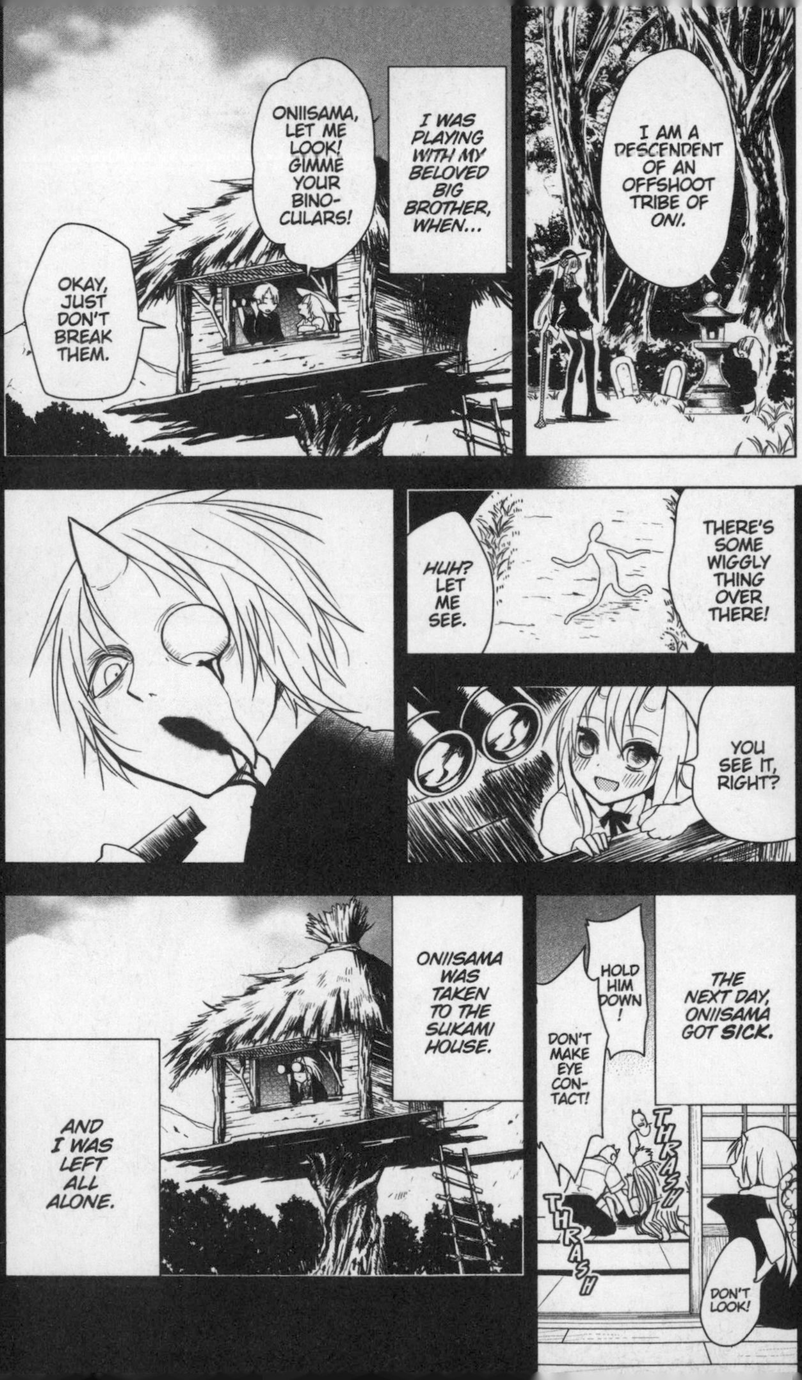
I AM A DESCENDENT OF AN OFFSHOOT TRIBE OF ONI.
I WAS PLAYING WITH MY BELOVED BIG BROTHER, WHEN...
ONIISAMA, LET ME LOOK! GIMME YOUR BINOCULARS!
OKAY, JUST DON'T BREAK THEM.
THERE'S SOME WIGGLY THING OVER THERE!
HUH? LET ME SEE.
YOU SEE IT, RIGHT?
THE NEXT DAY, ONIISAMA GOT SICK.
HOLD HIM DOWN!
DON'T MAKE EYE CONTACT!
THRASH
THRASH
DON'T LOOK!
ONIISAMA WAS TAKEN TO THE SUKAMI HOUSE.
AND I WAS LEFT ALL ALONE.

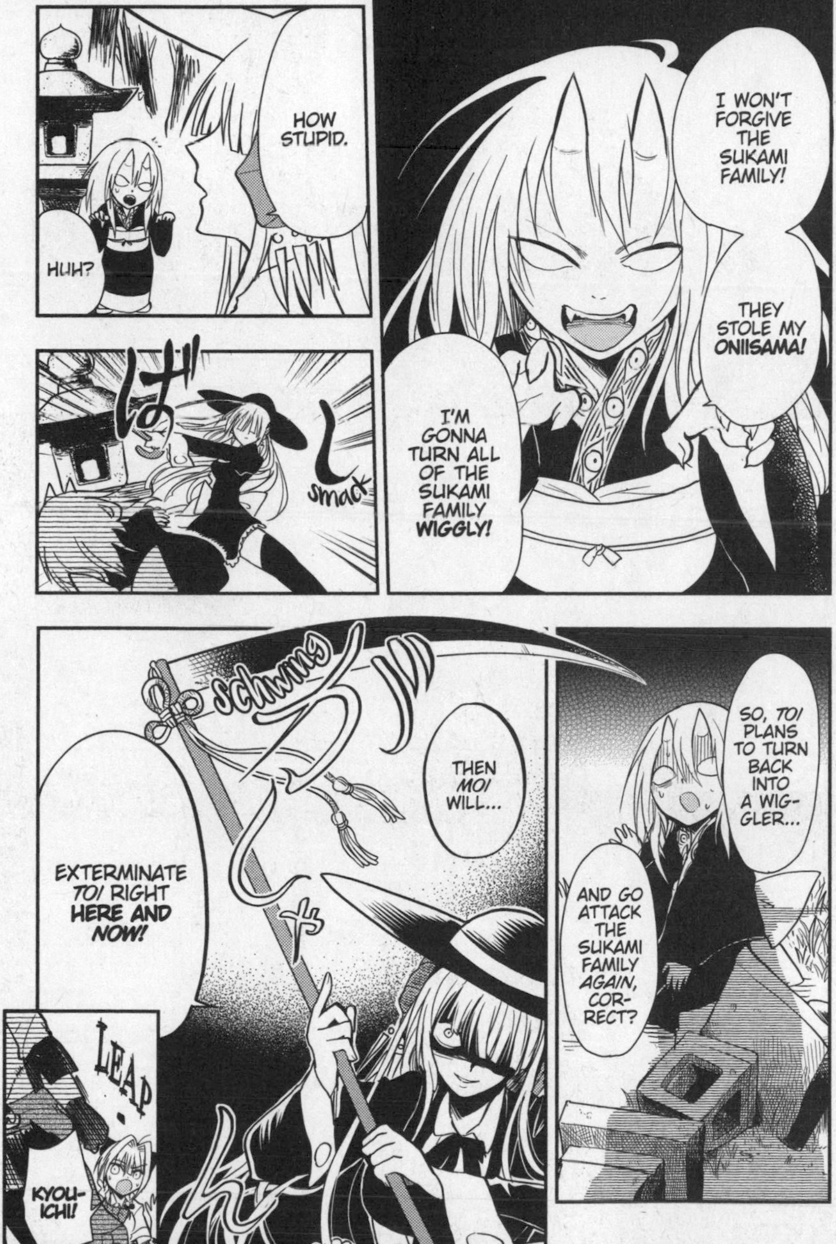
I WON'T FORGIVE THE SUKAMI FAMILY!
THEY STOLE MY ONIISAMA!
I'M GONNA TURN ALL OF THE SUKAMI FAMILY WIGGLY!
HOW STUPID.
HUH?
ばし
smack
SO, TOI PLANS TO TURN BACK INTO A WIG-GLER...
AND GO ATTACK THE SUKAMI FAMILY AGAIN, COR-RECT?
schwing
THEN MOI WILL...
EXTERMINATE TOI RIGHT HERE AND NOW!
LEAP
KYOU-ICHI!

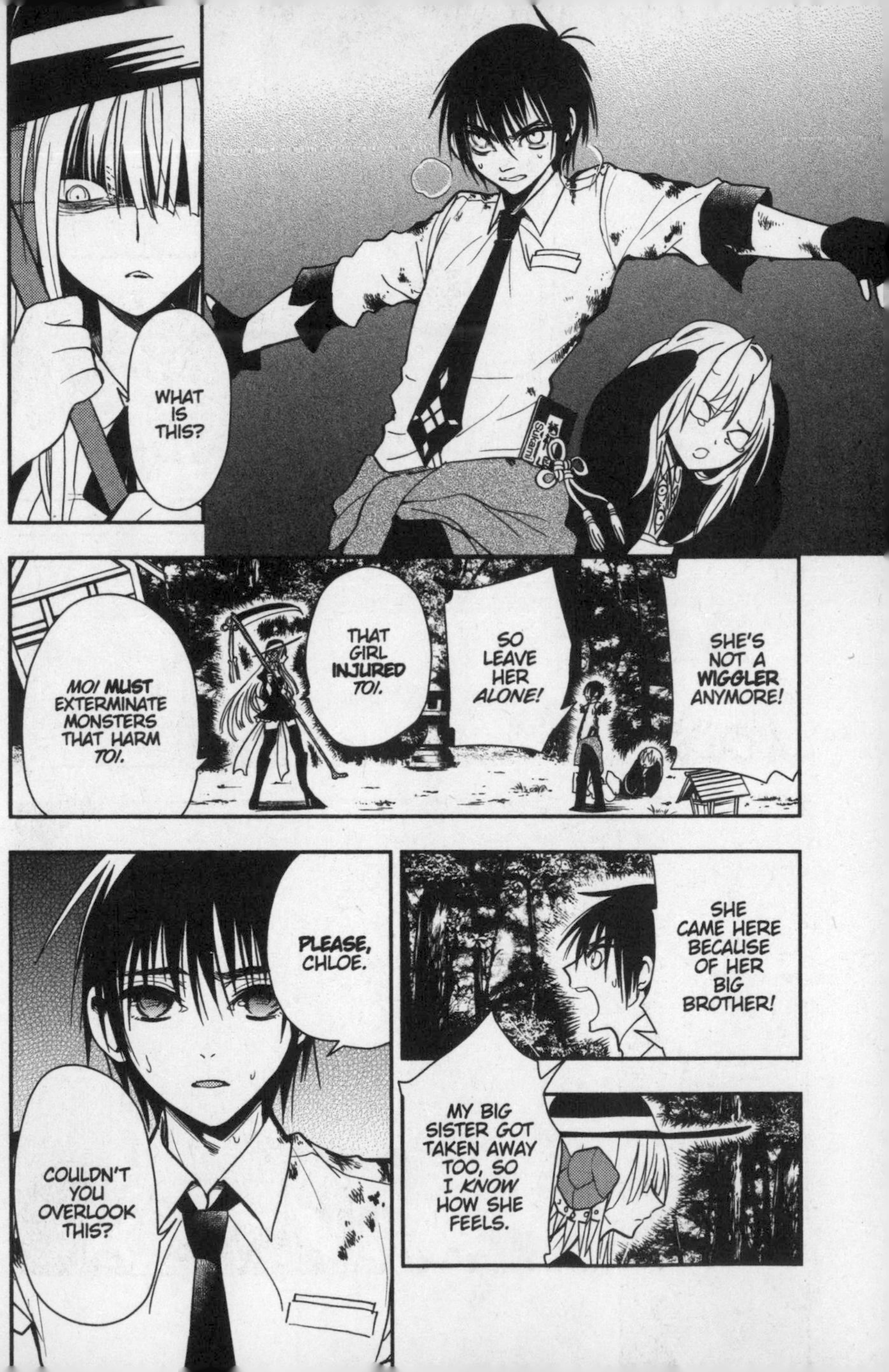
WHAT IS THIS?
SHE'S NOT A WIGGLER ANYMORE!
SO LEAVE HER ALONE!
THAT GIRL INJURED TOI.
MOI MUST EXTERMINATE MONSTERS THAT HARM TOI.
SHE CAME HERE BECAUSE OF HER BIG BROTHER!
MY BIG SISTER GOT TAKEN AWAY TOO, SO I KNOW HOW SHE FEELS.
PLEASE, CHLOE.
COULDN'T YOU OVERLOOK THIS?

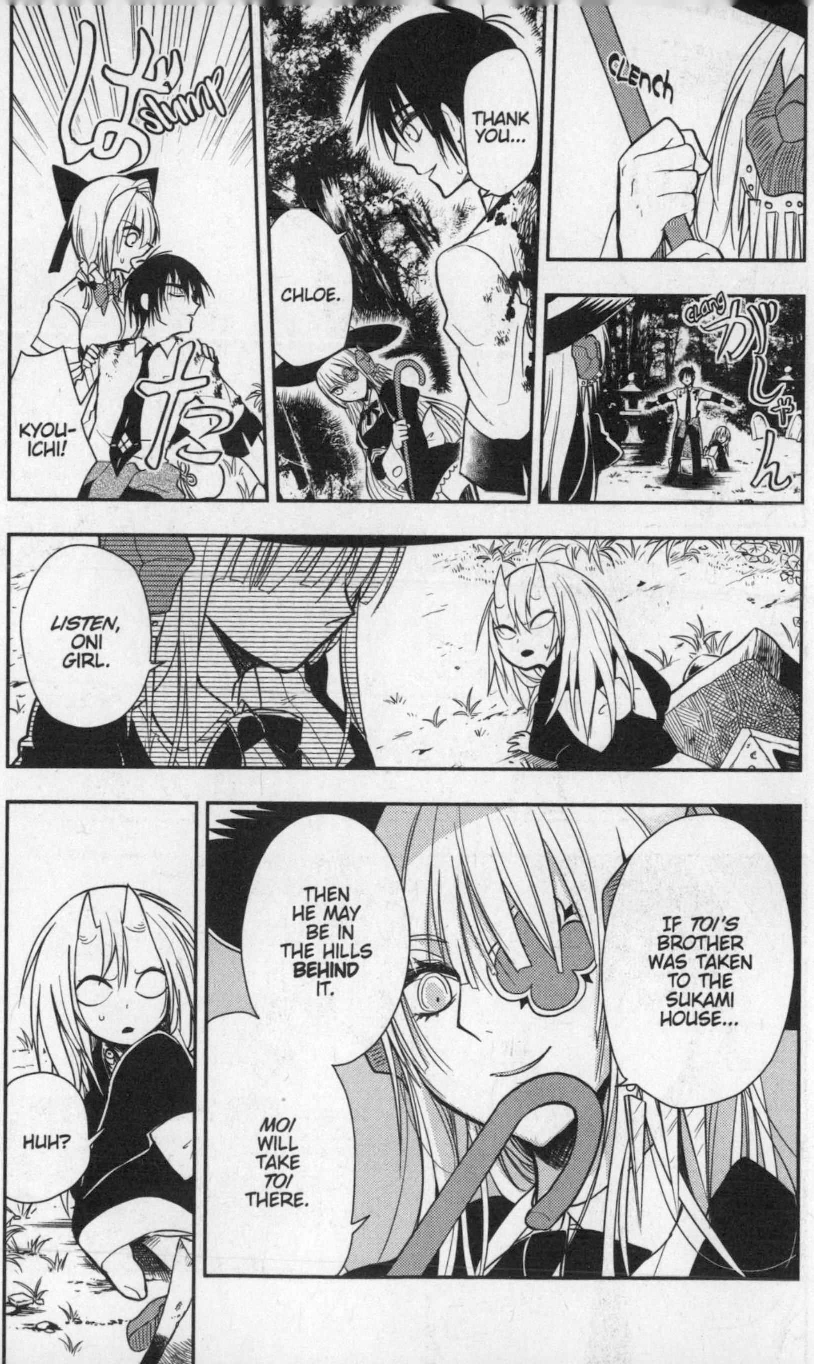

CLENCH
CLANG
がしゃん
THANK YOU...
CHLOE.
KYOU-ICHI!
LISTEN, ONI GIRL.
IF *TOI's* BROTHER WAS TAKEN TO THE SUKAMI HOUSE...
THEN HE MAY BE IN THE HILLS BEHIND IT.
MOI WILL TAKE *TOI* THERE.
HUH?

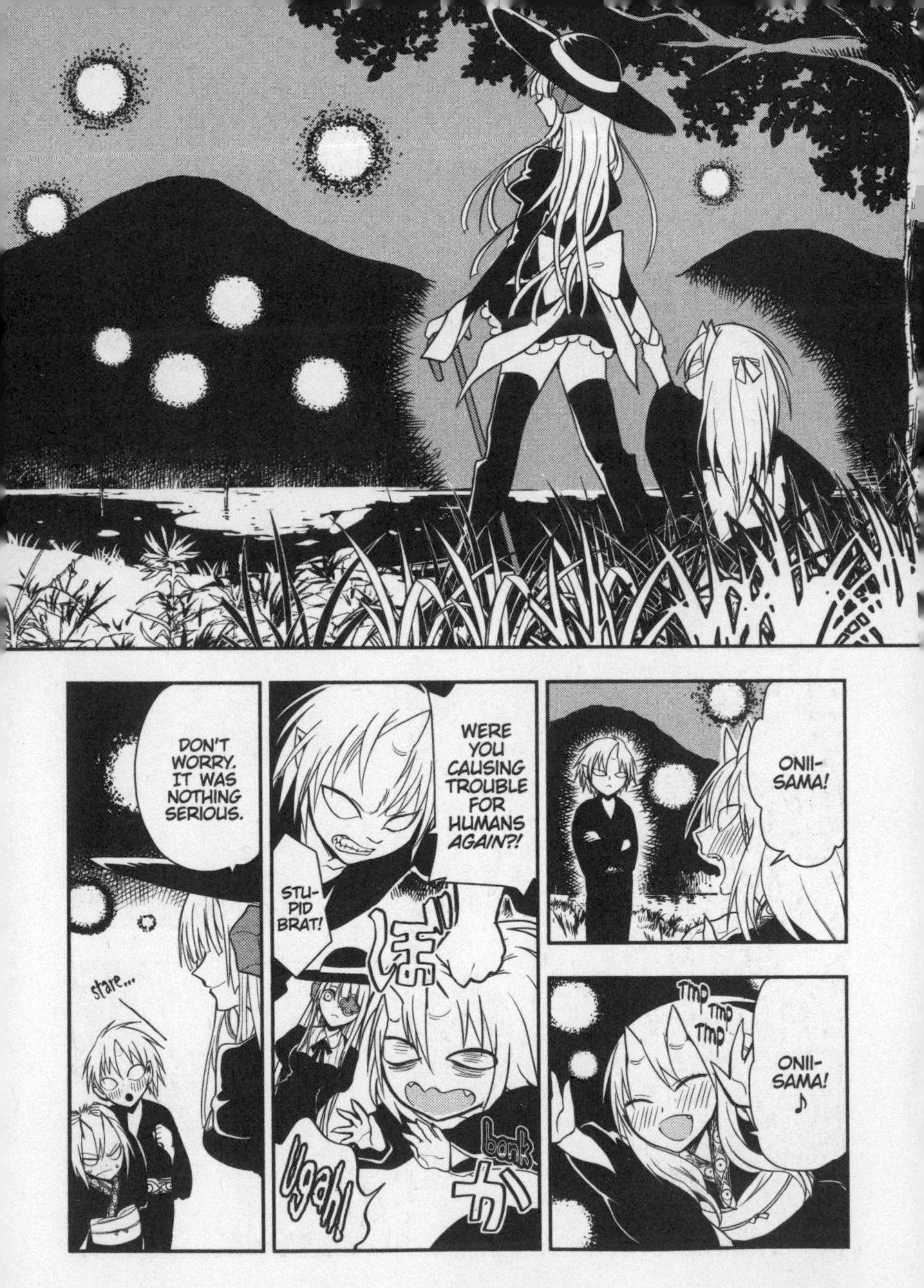
ONII-SAMA!
TMP TMP TMP
ONII-SAMA! ♪
WERE YOU CAUSING TROUBLE FOR HUMANS AGAIN?!
STU-PID BRAT!
bank
Ugah!
DON'T WORRY. IT WAS NOTHING SERIOUS.
stare...

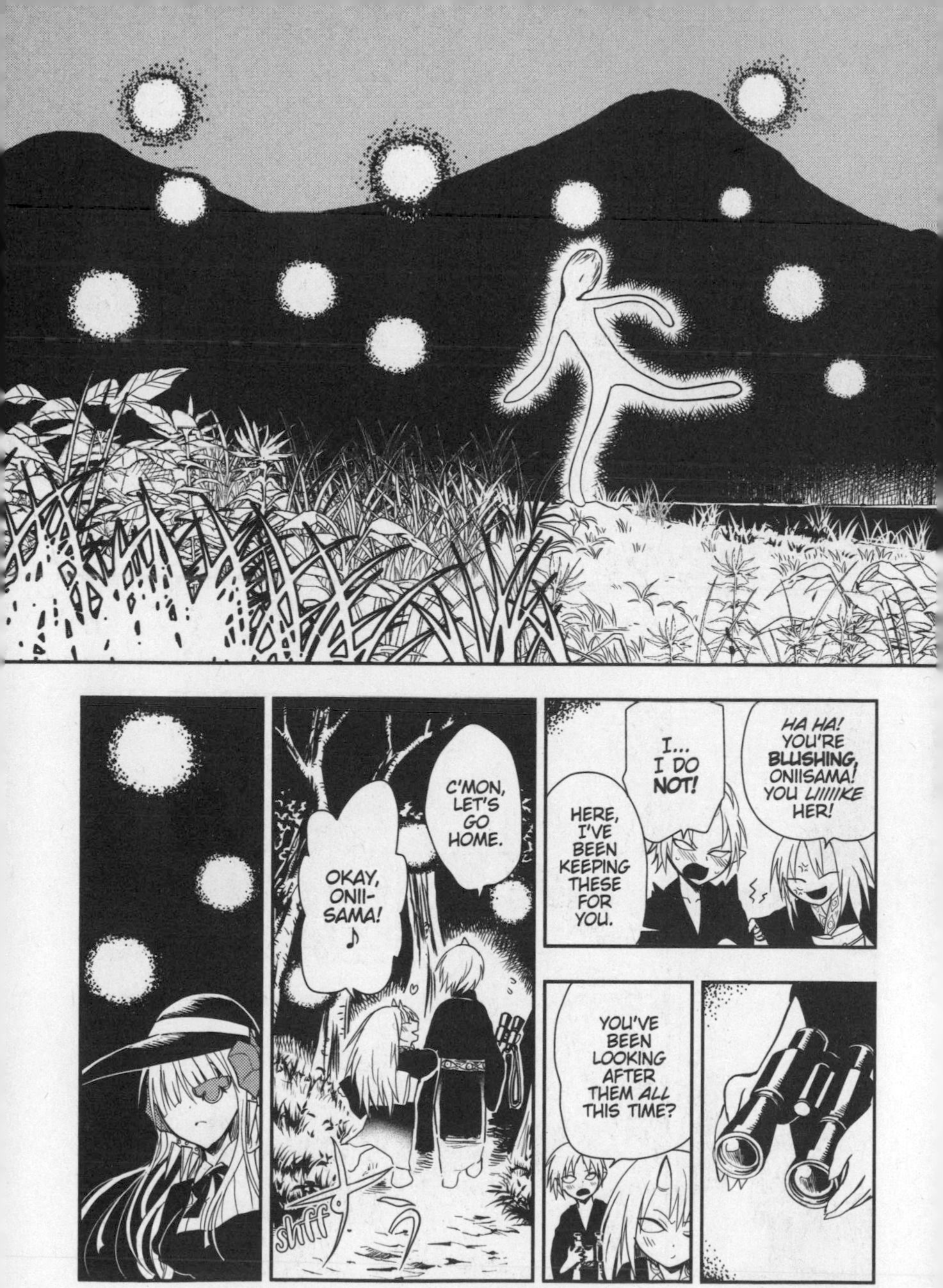
HA HA! YOU'RE BLUSHING, ONIISAMA! YOU LIIIIIKE HER!
I... I DO NOT!
HERE, I'VE BEEN KEEPING THESE FOR YOU.
YOU'VE BEEN LOOKING AFTER THEM ALL THIS TIME?
C'MON, LET'S GO HOME.
OKAY, ONII-SAMA! ♪
shff

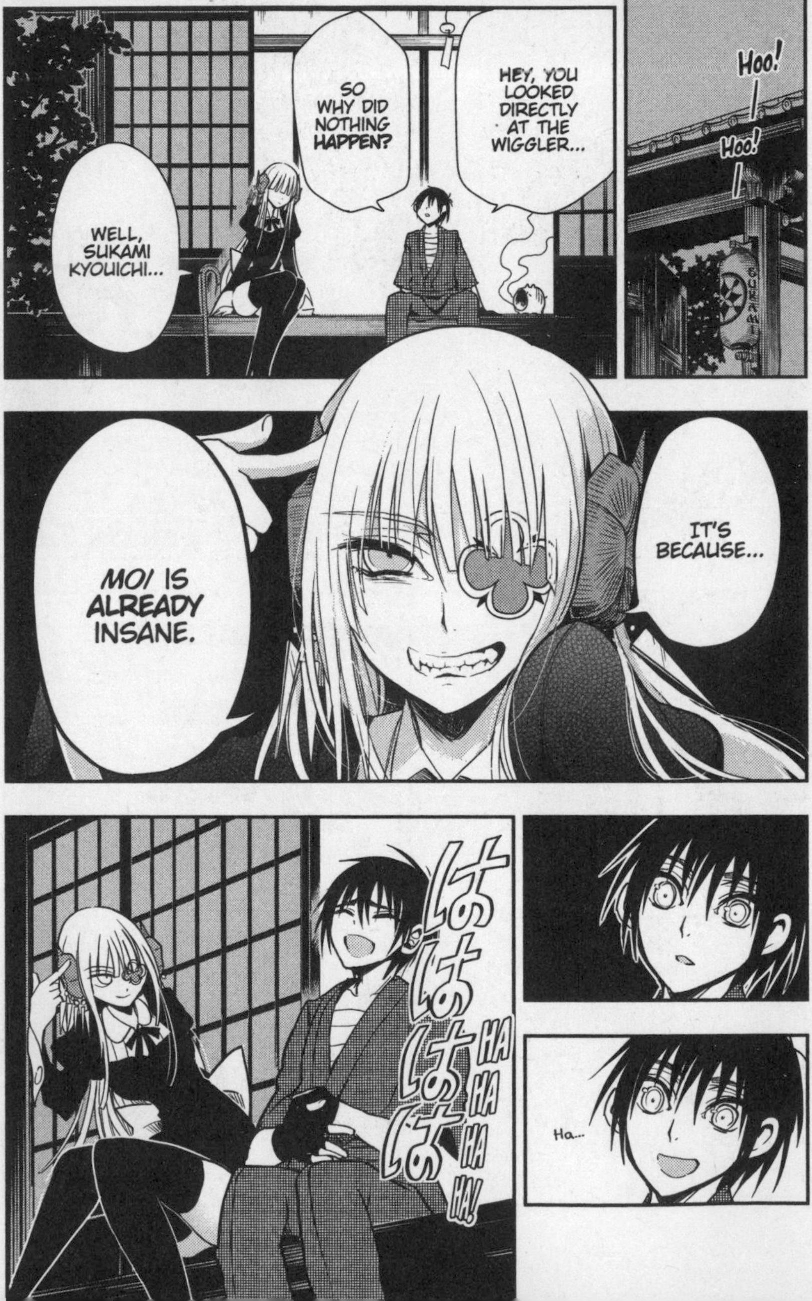

Hoo! Hoo!
HEY, YOU LOOKED DIRECTLY AT THE WIGGLER...
SO WHY DID NOTHING HAPPEN?
WELL, SUKAMI KYOUICHI...
IT'S BECAUSE...
MOI IS ALREADY INSANE.
Ha...
HA HA HA HA HA!

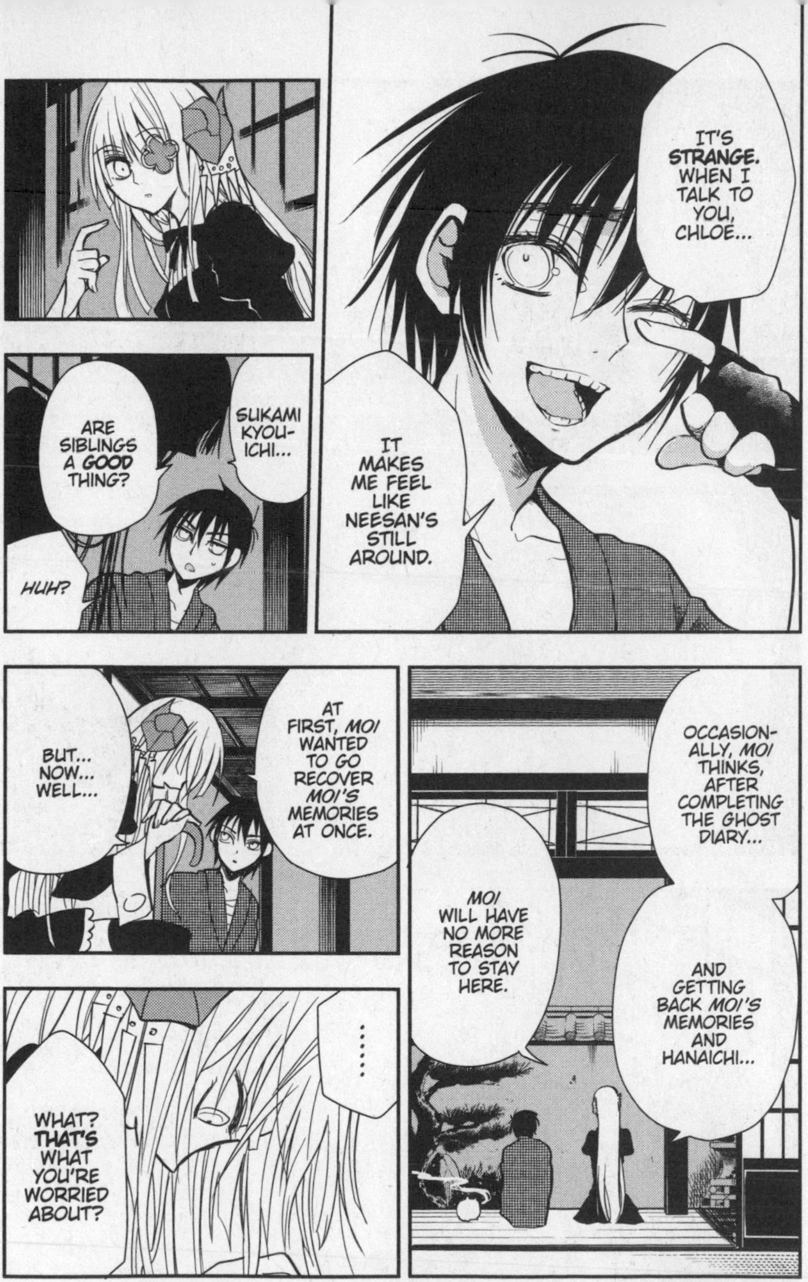
IT'S STRANGE. WHEN I TALK TO YOU, CHLOE...
IT MAKES ME FEEL LIKE NEESAN'S STILL AROUND.
SUKAMI KYOUICHI...
ARE SIBLINGS A GOOD THING?
HUH?
OCCASIONALLY, MOI THINKS, AFTER COMPLETING THE GHOST DIARY...
AND GETTING BACK MOI'S MEMORIES AND HANAICHI...
MOI WILL HAVE NO MORE REASON TO STAY HERE.
AT FIRST, MOI WANTED TO GO RECOVER MOI'S MEMORIES AT ONCE.
BUT... NOW... WELL...
......
WHAT? THAT'S WHAT YOU'RE WORRIED ABOUT?

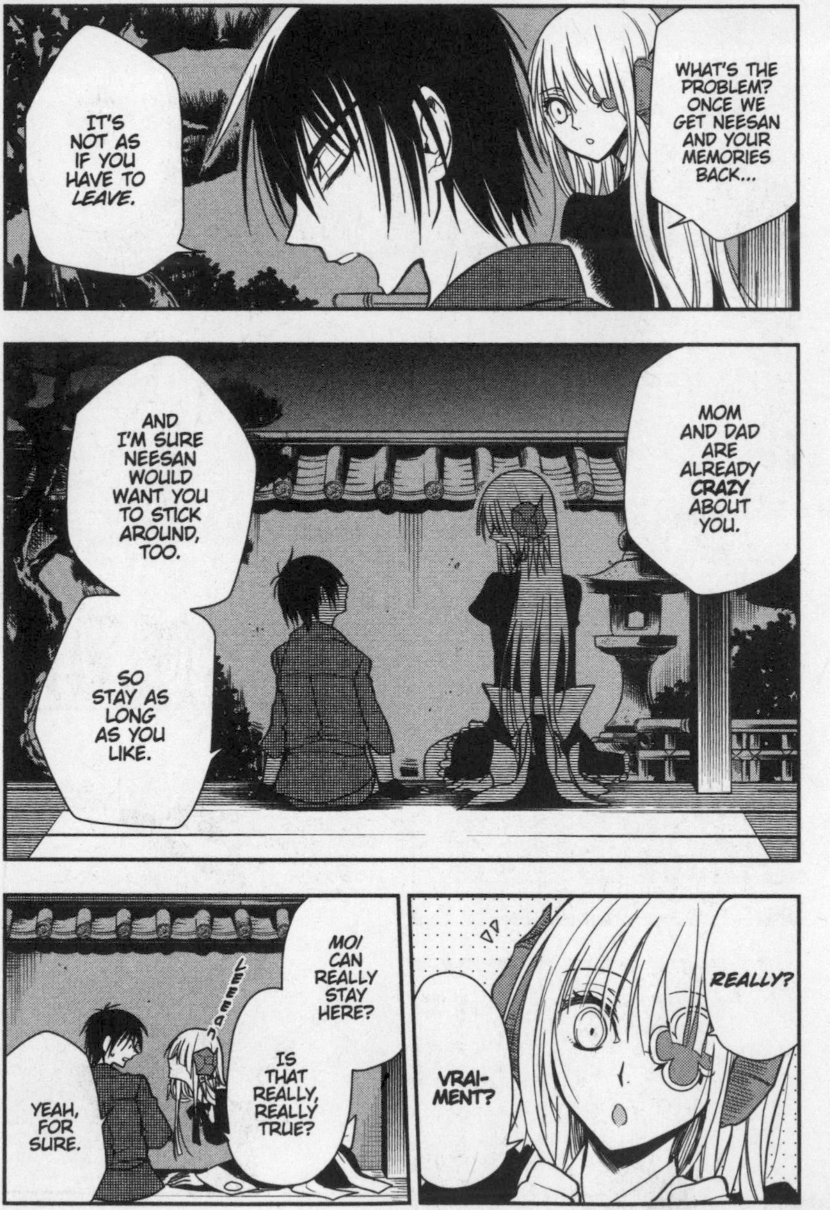
WHAT'S THE PROBLEM? ONCE WE GET NEESAN AND YOUR MEMORIES BACK...
IT'S NOT AS IF YOU HAVE TO *LEAVE*.
MOM AND DAD ARE ALREADY **CRAZY** ABOUT YOU.
AND I'M SURE NEESAN WOULD WANT YOU TO STICK AROUND, TOO.
SO STAY AS LONG AS YOU LIKE.
REALLY?
VRAI-MENT?
MOI CAN REALLY STAY HERE?
IS THAT REALLY, REALLY TRUE?
YEAH, FOR SURE.

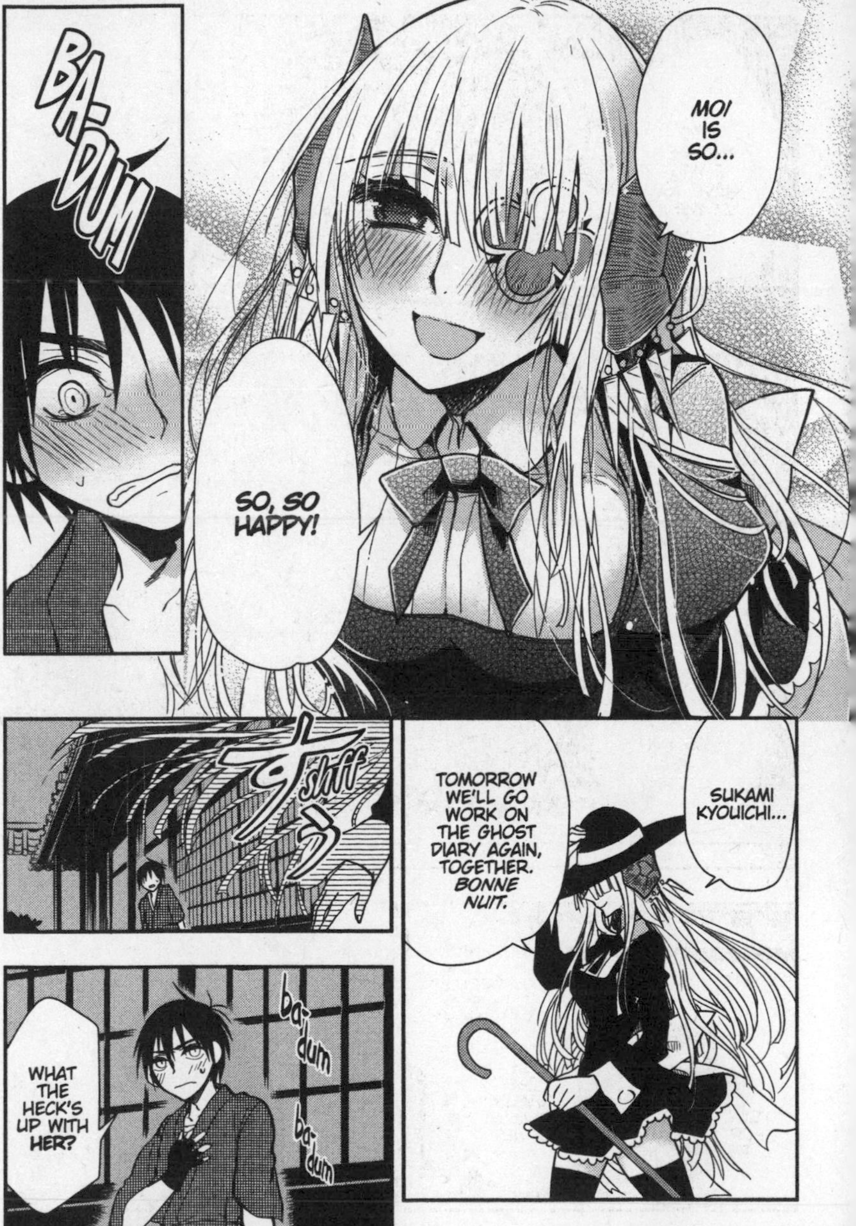
MOI IS SO...
SO, SO HAPPY!
BA-DUM
SUKAMI KYOUICHI...
TOMORROW WE'LL GO WORK ON THE GHOST DIARY AGAIN, TOGETHER. *BONNE NUIT.*
すう shff
ba-dum ba-dum
WHAT THE HECK'S UP WITH HER?

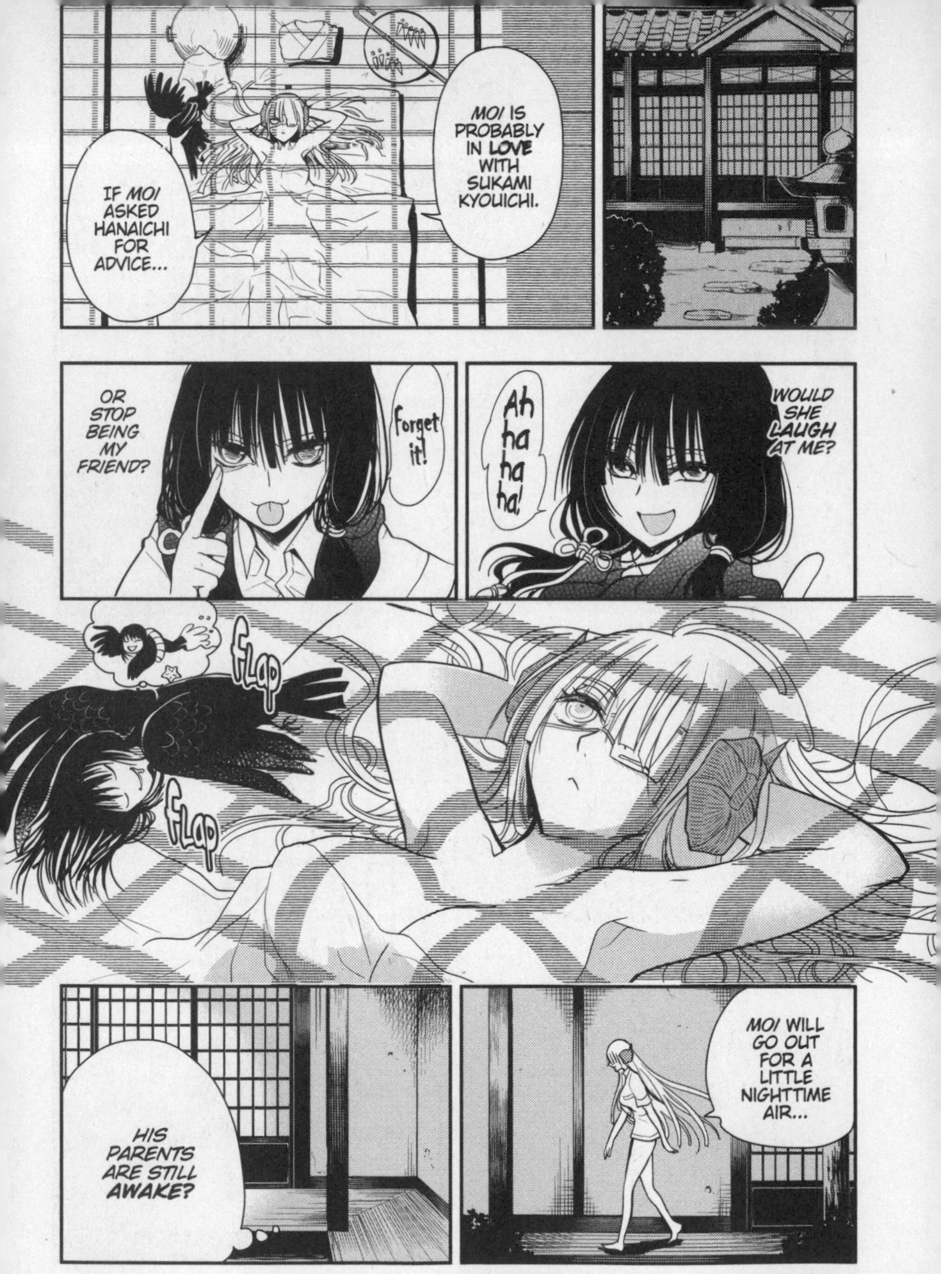
MOI IS PROBABLY IN LOVE WITH SUKAMI KYOUICHI.
IF MOI ASKED HANAICHI FOR ADVICE...
WOULD SHE LAUGH AT ME?
Ah ha ha ha!
Forget it!
OR STOP BEING MY FRIEND?
FLAP
FLAP
MOI WILL GO OUT FOR A LITTLE NIGHTTIME AIR...
HIS PARENTS ARE STILL AWAKE?

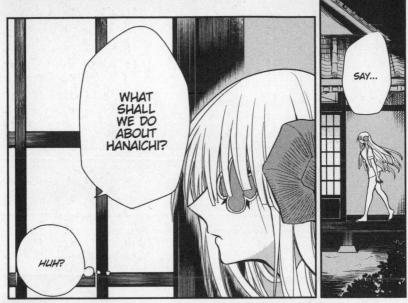

SAY...
WHAT SHALL WE DO ABOUT HANAICHI?
HUH?
I THOUGHT SHE WAS LOST FOREVER AFTER GETTING KIDNAPPED BY A GOD...
SO I'M TRULY GLAD, REALLY...
BUT SHE'S STILL NOT ALIVE.
HOW SHOULD WE TELL KYOUICHI?
DON'T WORRY. KYOUICHI'S A GOOD BOY.
WE'LL TELL HIM SOMEDAY SOON. HE'LL UNDER-STAND.

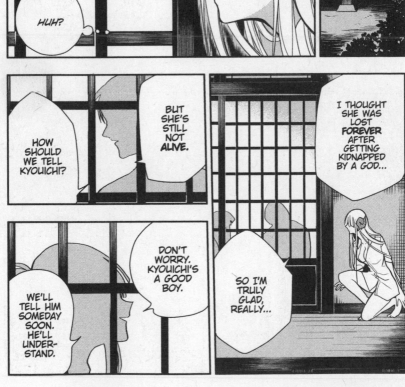

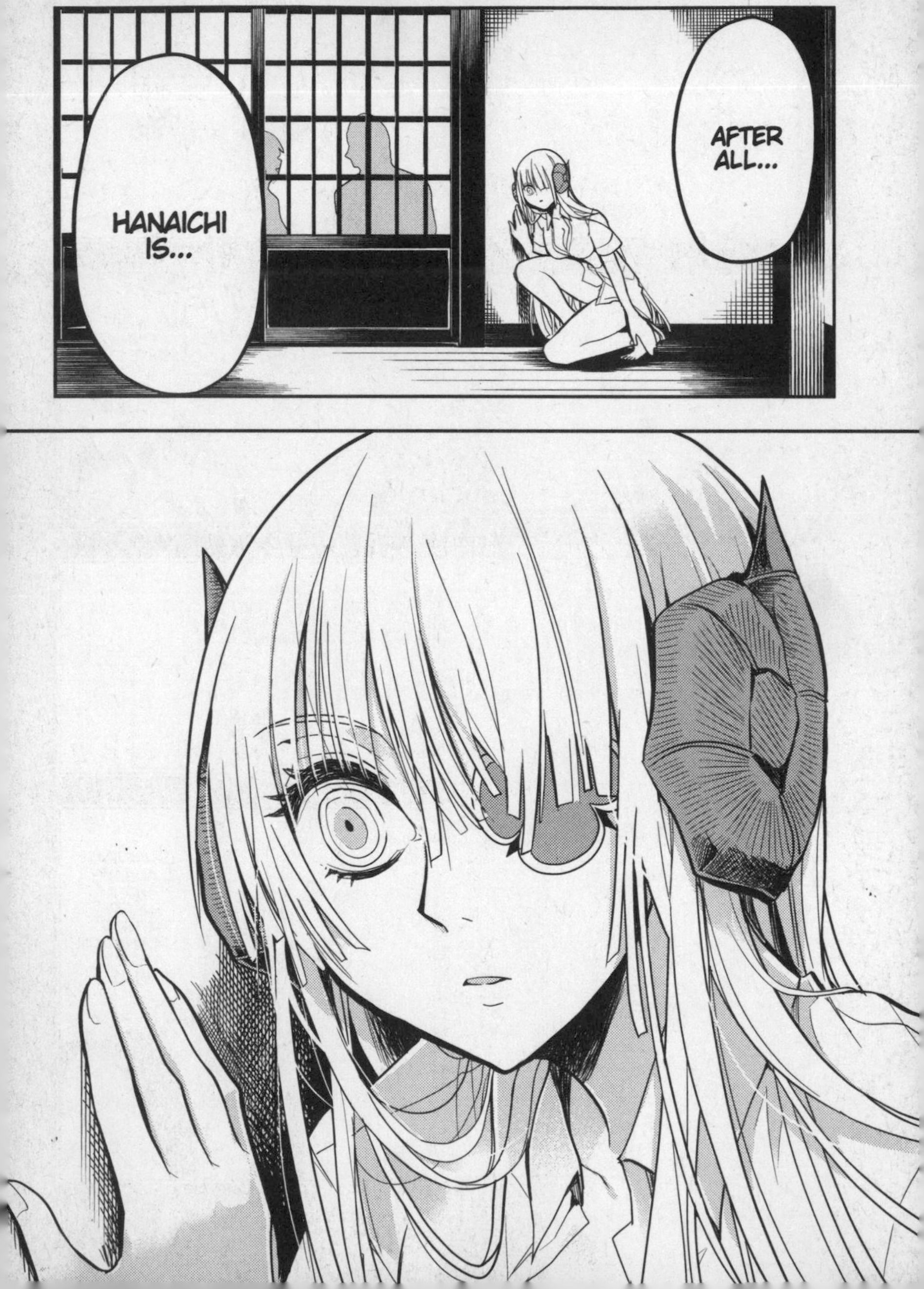
AFTER ALL...
HANAICHI IS...

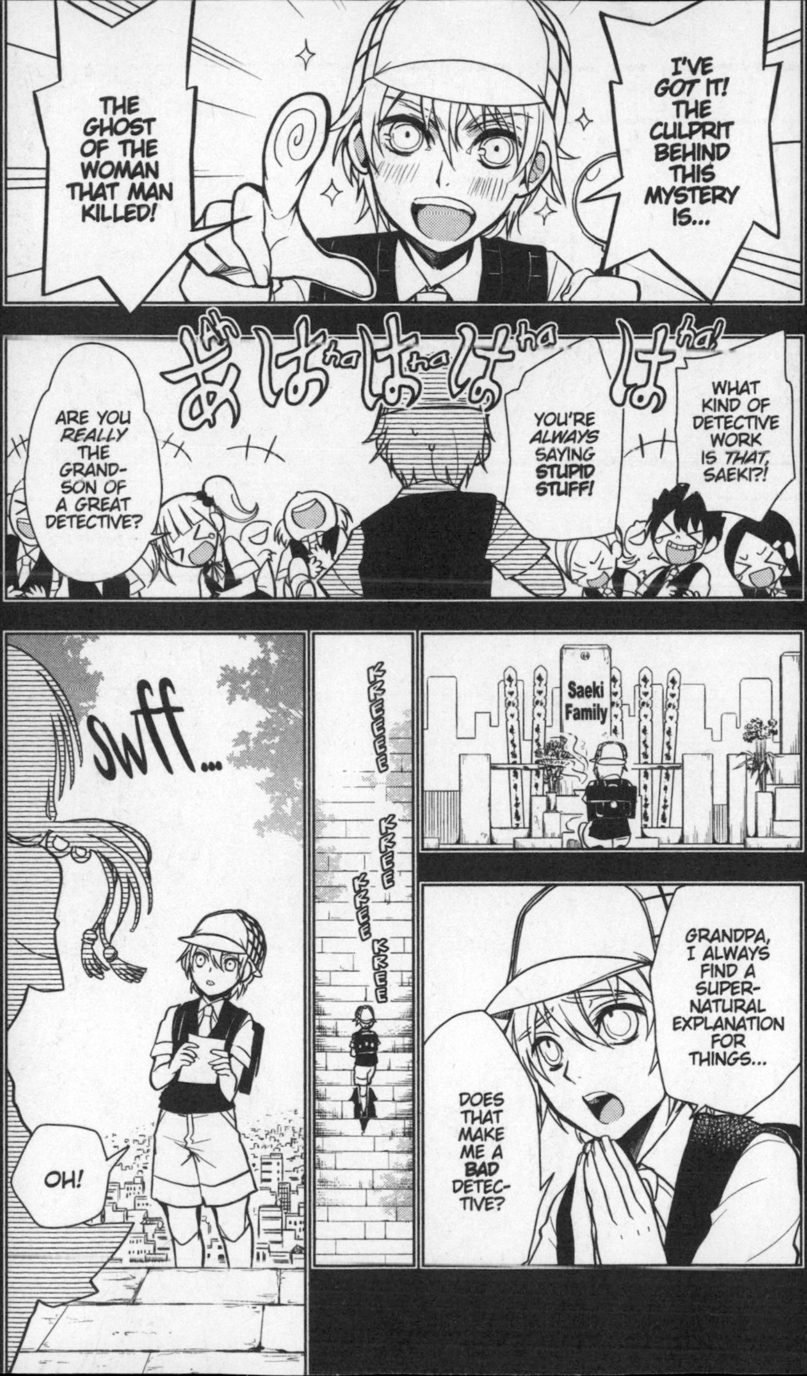
I'VE GOT IT! THE CULPRIT BEHIND THIS MYSTERY IS...
THE GHOST OF THE WOMAN THAT MAN KILLED!
あははは は
ah ha ha ha ha!
WHAT KIND OF DETECTIVE WORK IS *THAT*, SAEKI?!
YOU'RE *ALWAYS* SAYING STUPID STUFF!
ARE YOU *REALLY* THE GRANDSON OF A GREAT DETECTIVE?
Saeki Family
GRANDPA, I ALWAYS FIND A SUPERNATURAL EXPLANATION FOR THINGS...
DOES THAT MAKE ME A BAD DETECTIVE?
KREEEEE
KREE
KREE
KREE
swff...
OH!

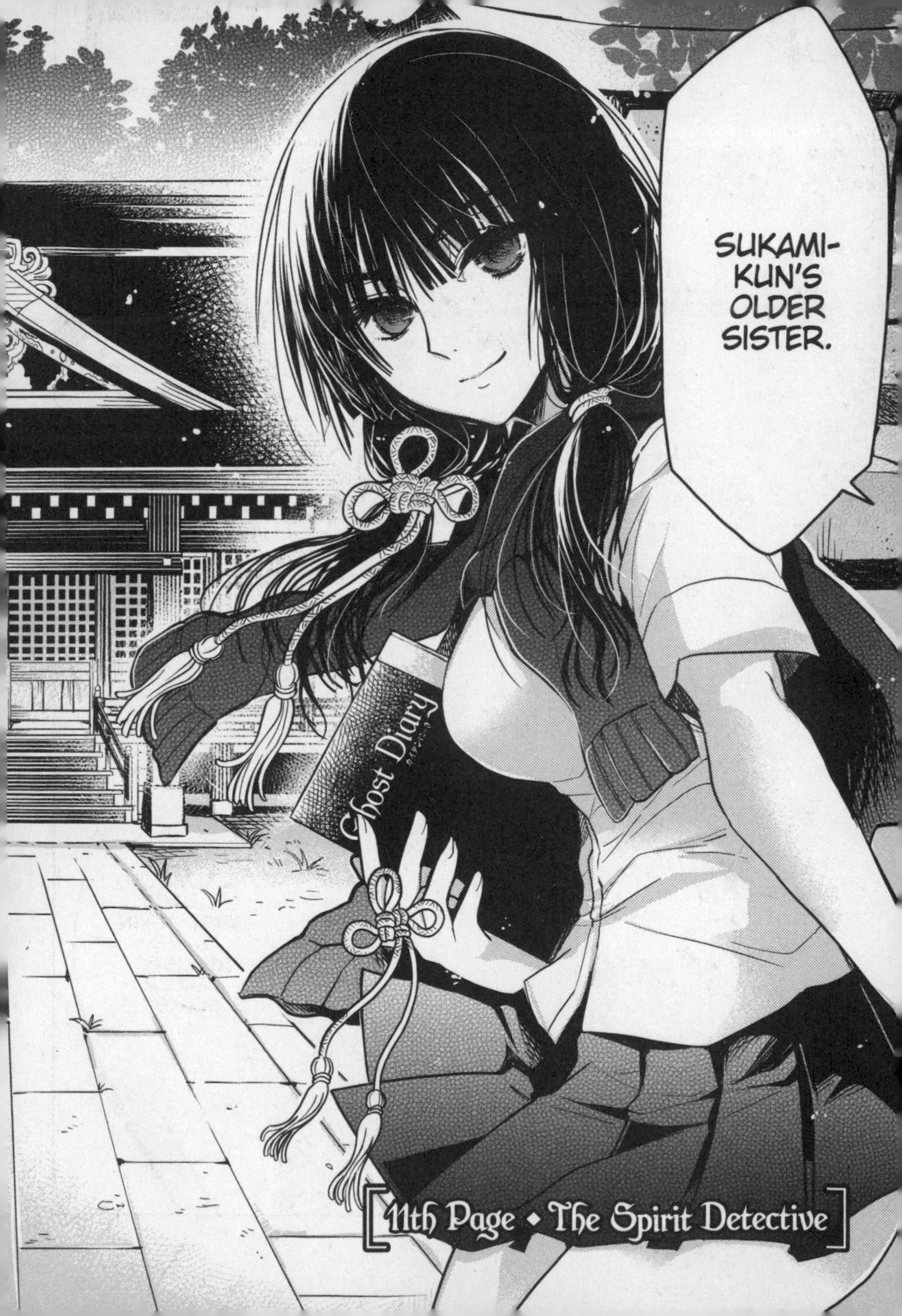
SUKAMI-KUN'S OLDER SISTER.
Ghost Diary
11th Page ◆ The Spirit Detective

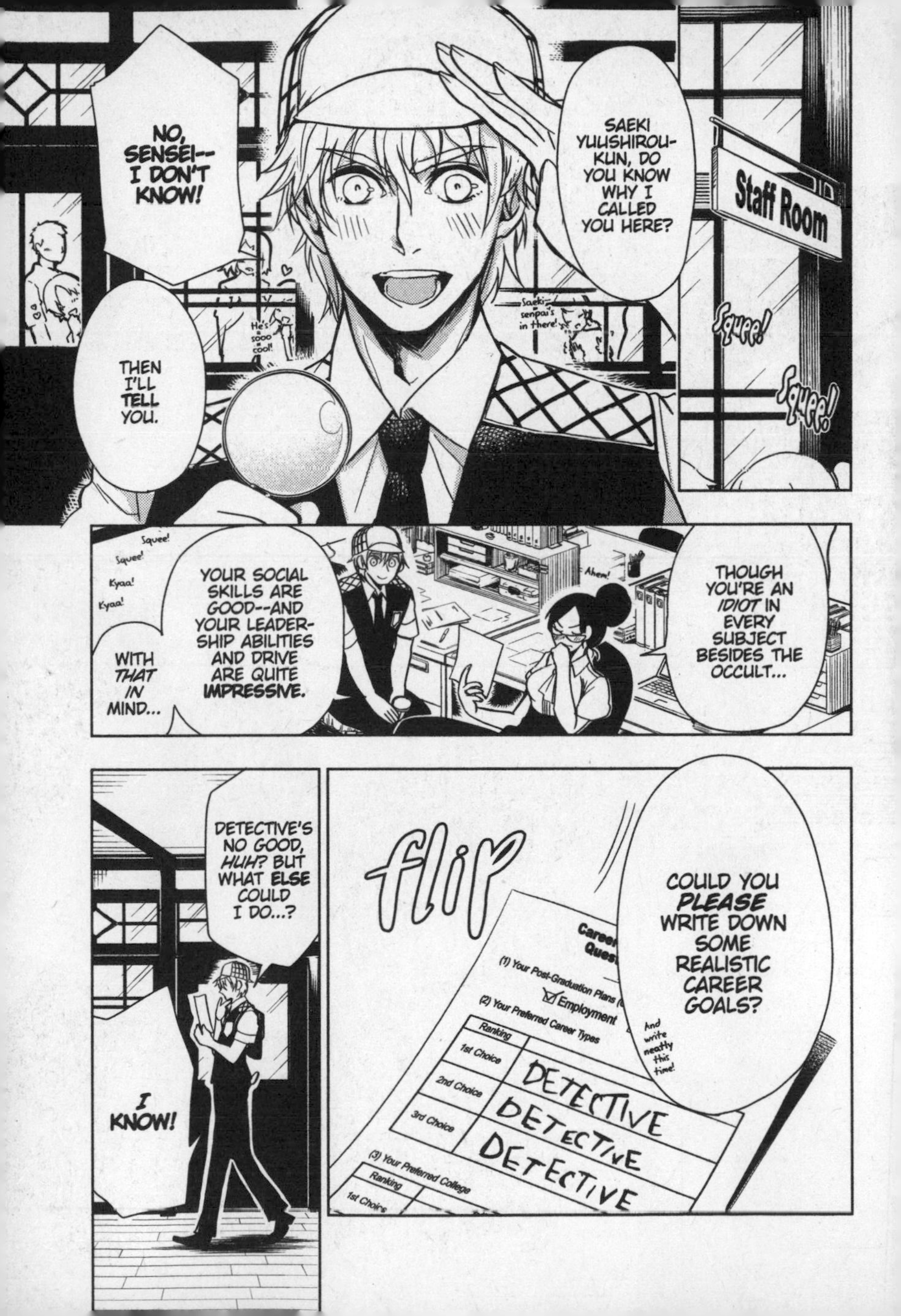
SAEKI YUUSHIROU-KUN, DO YOU KNOW WHY I CALLED YOU HERE?
Staff Room
Squee!
Squee!
Saeki-senpai's in there!
He's sooo cool!
NO, SENSEI-- I DON'T KNOW!
THEN I'LL TELL YOU.
THOUGH YOU'RE AN IDIOT IN EVERY SUBJECT BESIDES THE OCCULT...
Ahem!
YOUR SOCIAL SKILLS ARE GOOD--AND YOUR LEADERSHIP ABILITIES AND DRIVE ARE QUITE IMPRESSIVE.
WITH THAT IN MIND...
Squee!
Squee!
Kyaa!
Kyaa!
COULD YOU PLEASE WRITE DOWN SOME REALISTIC CAREER GOALS?
And write neatly this time!
flip
(1) Your Post-Graduation Plans
Employment
(2) Your Preferred Career Types
Ranking
1st Choice DETECTIVE
2nd Choice DETECTIVE
3rd Choice DETECTIVE
(3) Your Preferred College
Ranking
DETECTIVE'S NO GOOD, HUH? BUT WHAT ELSE COULD I DO...?
I KNOW!

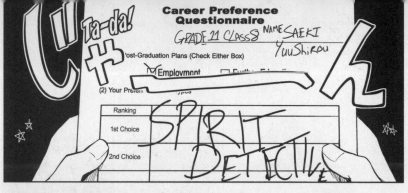

Career Preference Questionnaire

GRADE *11* CLASS *8* NAME *SAEKI Yuu Shirou*

Post-Graduation Plans (Check Either Box)

☑ Employment   ☐ Further Education

(2) Your Prefer...

Ranking	
1st Choice	SPIRIT DETECTIVE
2nd Choice	

Ta-da!

murmur

murmur

WHAT DO YOU MEAN CHLOE-SAN'S GONE MISSING?!

WHAT'S THE MATTER, EVERY-BODY?

shunk

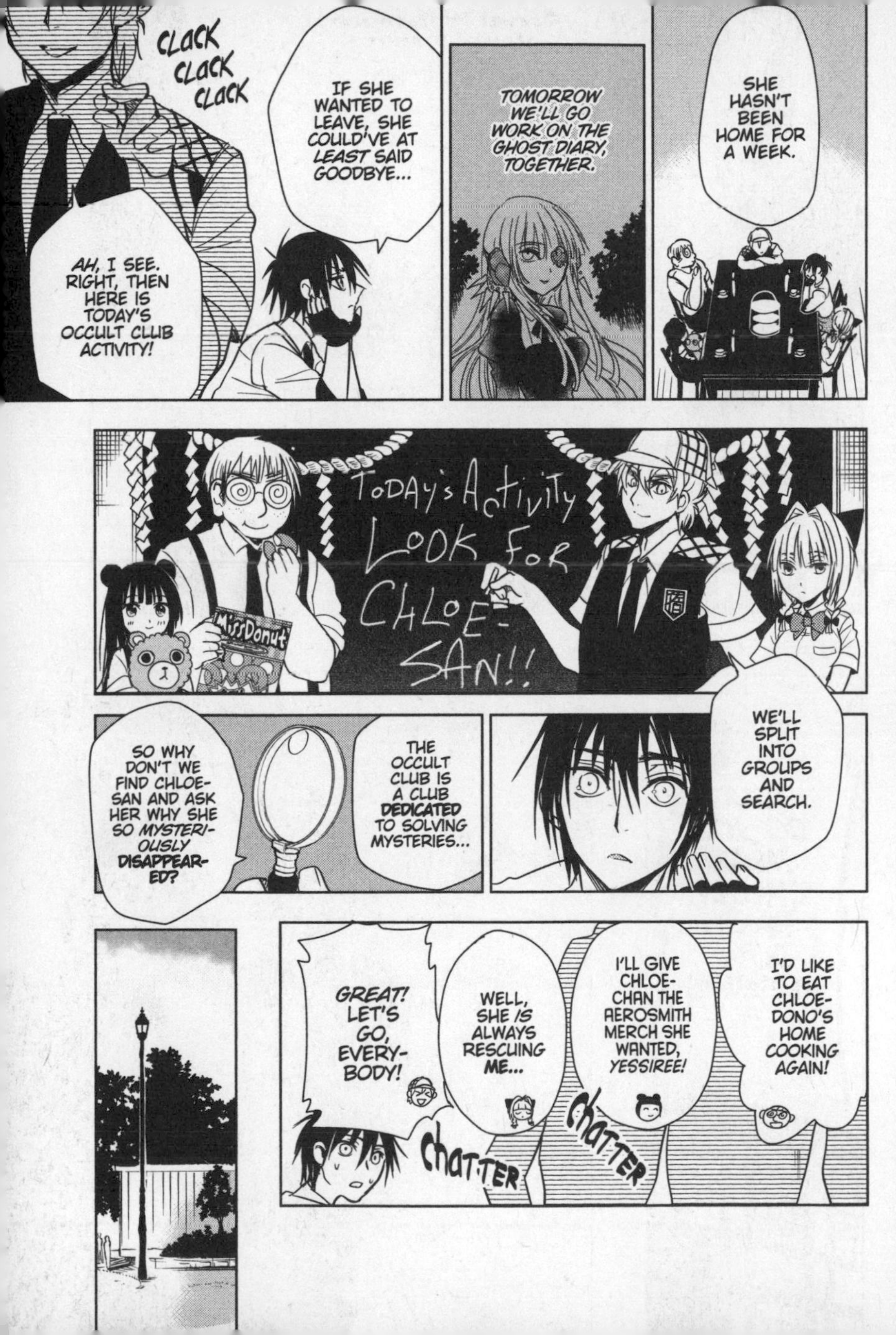
SHE HASN'T BEEN HOME FOR A WEEK.
TOMORROW WE'LL GO WORK ON THE GHOST DIARY, TOGETHER.
IF SHE WANTED TO LEAVE, SHE COULD'VE AT LEAST SAID GOODBYE...
CLACK CLACK CLACK
AH, I SEE. RIGHT, THEN HERE IS TODAY'S OCCULT CLUB ACTIVITY!
TODAY'S ACTIVITY LOOK FOR CHLOE-SAN!!
MissDonut
WE'LL SPLIT INTO GROUPS AND SEARCH.
THE OCCULT CLUB IS A CLUB DEDICATED TO SOLVING MYSTERIES...
SO WHY DON'T WE FIND CHLOE-SAN AND ASK HER WHY SHE SO MYSTERIOUSLY DISAPPEARED?
I'D LIKE TO EAT CHLOE-DONO'S HOME COOKING AGAIN!
I'LL GIVE CHLOE-CHAN THE AEROSMITH MERCH SHE WANTED, YESSIREE!
WELL, SHE IS ALWAYS RESCUING ME...
GREAT! LET'S GO, EVERYBODY!
CHATTER
CHATTER

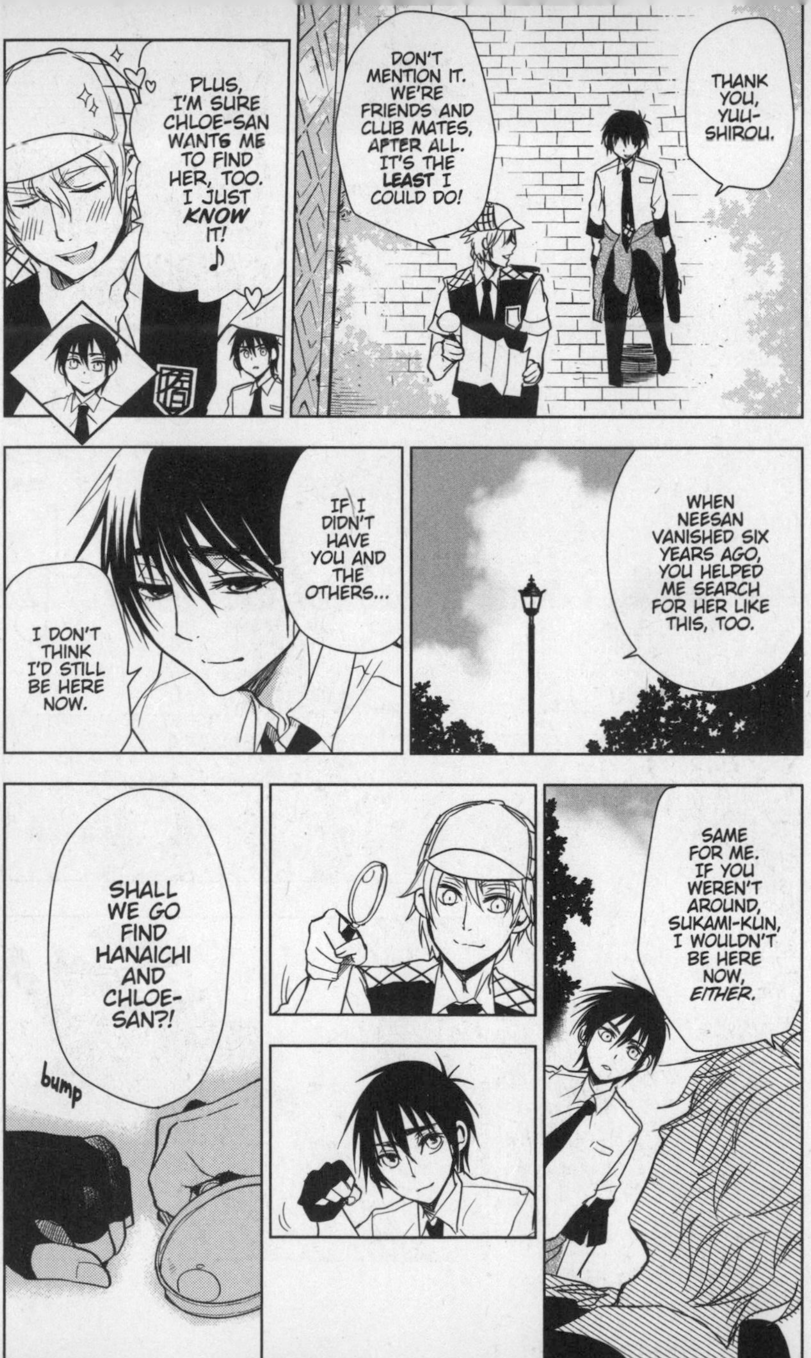
THANK YOU, YUU-SHIROU.
DON'T MENTION IT. WE'RE FRIENDS AND CLUB MATES, AFTER ALL. IT'S THE **LEAST** I COULD DO!
PLUS, I'M SURE CHLOE-SAN WANTS ME TO FIND HER, TOO. I JUST ***KNOW*** IT! ♪
WHEN NEESAN VANISHED SIX YEARS AGO, YOU HELPED ME SEARCH FOR HER LIKE THIS, TOO.
IF I DIDN'T HAVE YOU AND THE OTHERS...
I DON'T THINK I'D STILL BE HERE NOW.
SAME FOR ME. IF YOU WEREN'T AROUND, SUKAMI-KUN, I WOULDN'T BE HERE NOW, *EITHER*.
SHALL WE GO FIND HANAICHI AND CHLOE-SAN?!
bump

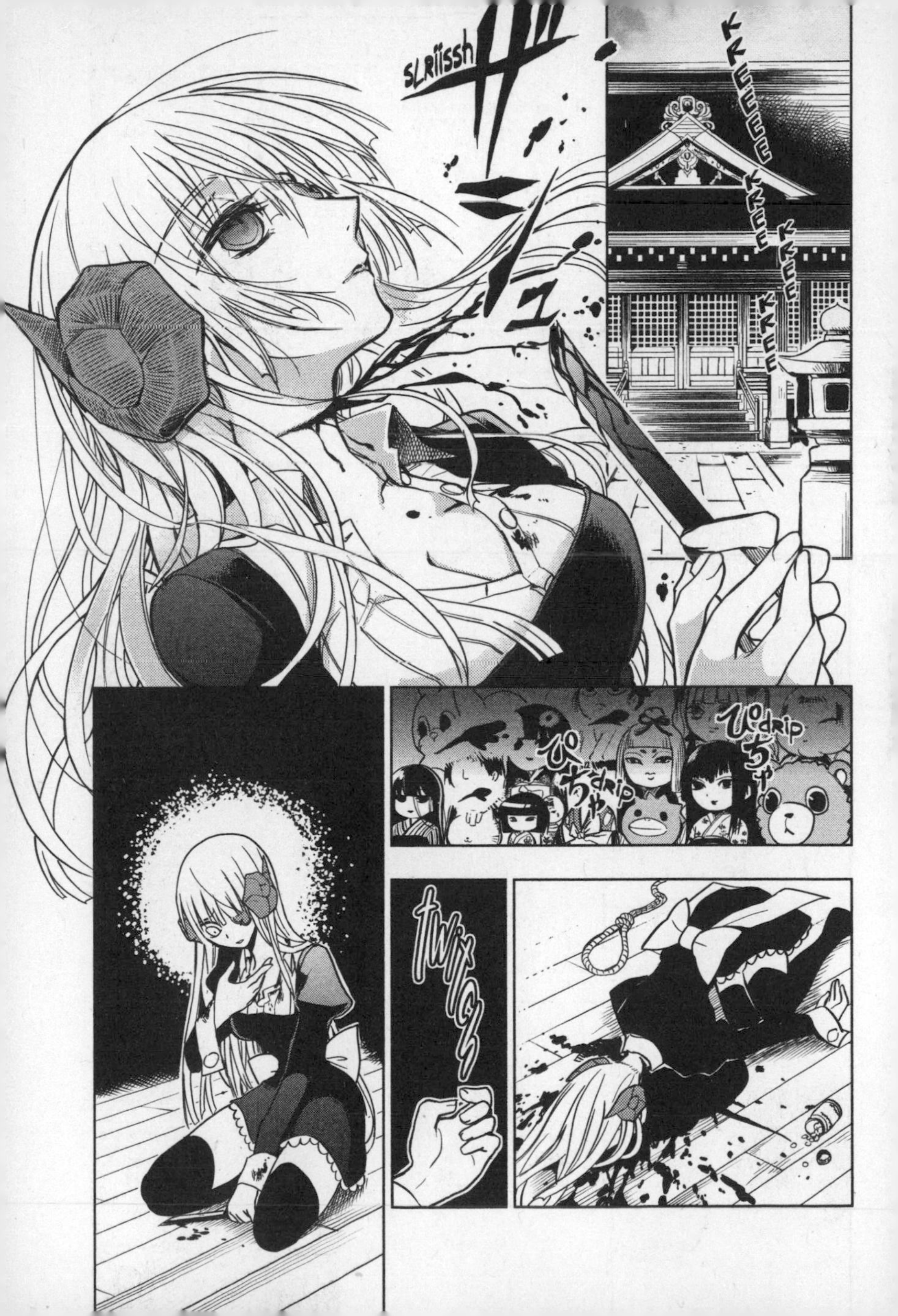
KREEEEE
KREE
KREE
KREE
SLRIISSH
ザシュ
ぴちゃ drip
ぴちゃ drip
twitch

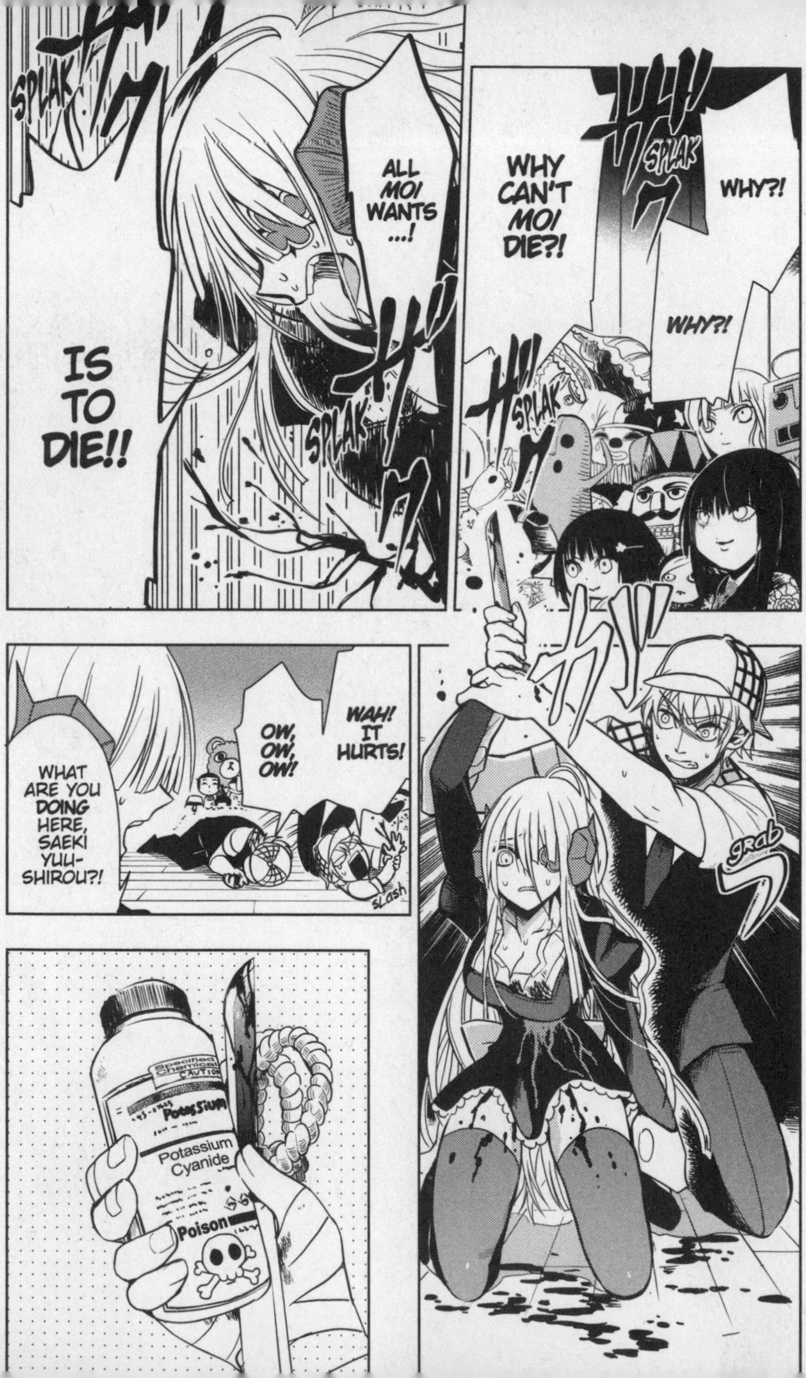

WHY?!
SPLAK
WHY CAN'T MOI DIE?!
WHY?!
SPLAK
SPLAK
ALL MOI WANTS ...!
SPLAK
IS TO DIE!!
grab
WAH! IT HURTS!
OW, OW, OW!
slash
WHAT ARE YOU DOING HERE, SAEKI YUU-SHIROU?!
Specified Chemical
CAUTION
Potassium
Potassium Cyanide
Poison

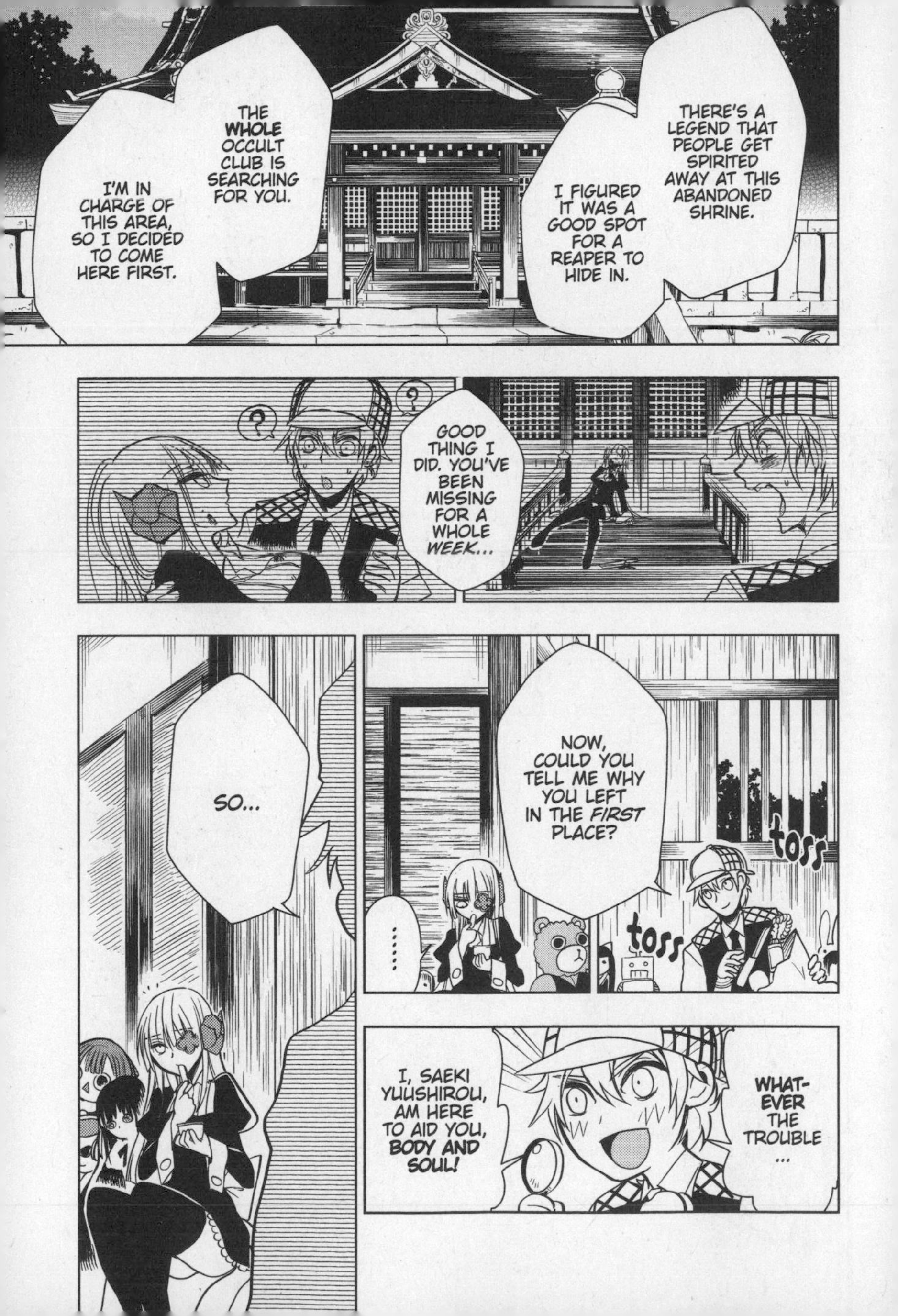
THERE'S A LEGEND THAT PEOPLE GET SPIRITED AWAY AT THIS ABANDONED SHRINE.
I FIGURED IT WAS A GOOD SPOT FOR A REAPER TO HIDE IN.
THE WHOLE OCCULT CLUB IS SEARCHING FOR YOU.
I'M IN CHARGE OF THIS AREA, SO I DECIDED TO COME HERE FIRST.
?
?
GOOD THING I DID. YOU'VE BEEN MISSING FOR A WHOLE WEEK...
toss
toss
NOW, COULD YOU TELL ME WHY YOU LEFT IN THE FIRST PLACE?
......
SO...
WHAT-EVER THE TROUBLE...
I, SAEKI YUUSHIROU, AM HERE TO AID YOU, BODY AND SOUL!

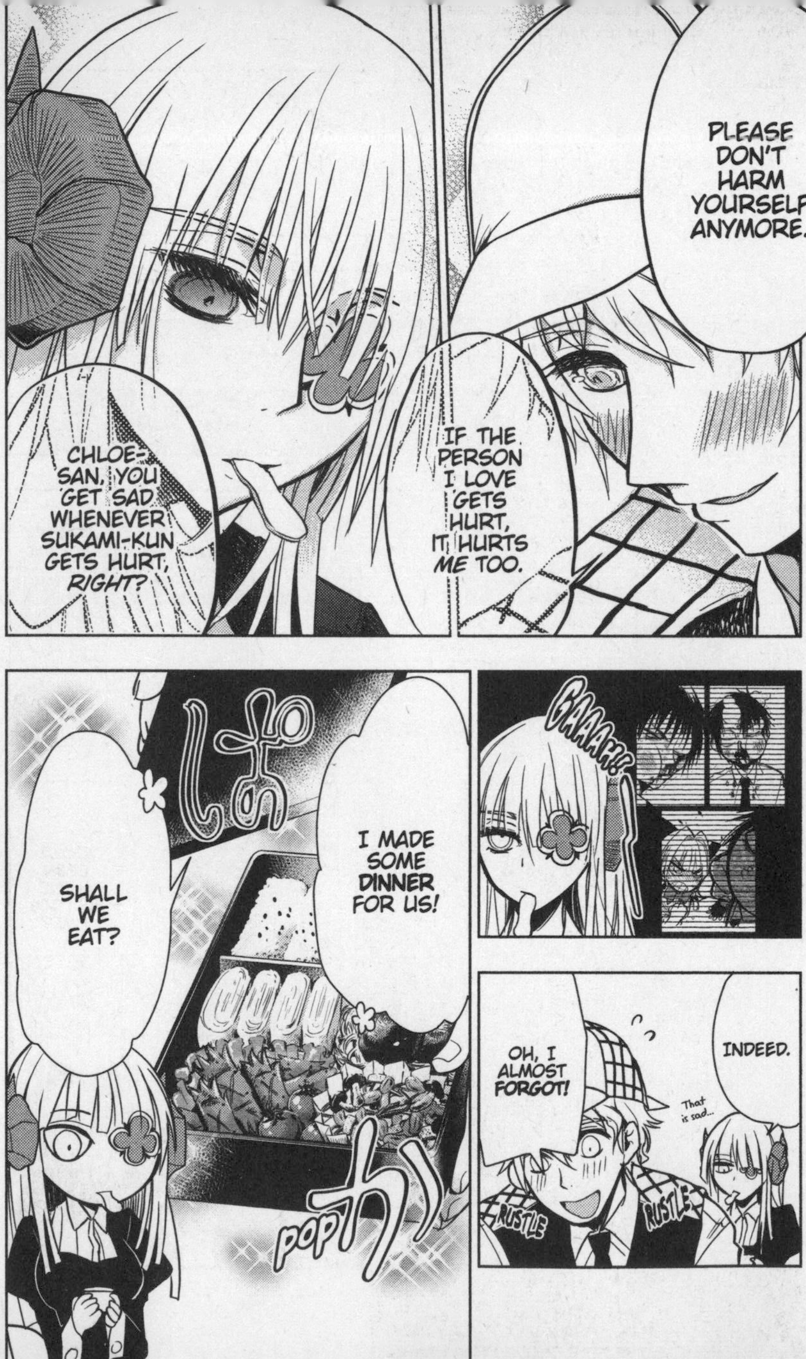
PLEASE DON'T HARM YOURSELF ANYMORE.
IF THE PERSON I LOVE GETS HURT, IT HURTS *ME* TOO.
CHLOE-SAN, YOU GET SAD WHENEVER SUKAMI-KUN GETS HURT, *RIGHT?*
INDEED.
That is sad...
OH, I ALMOST **FORGOT!**
RUSTLE
RUSTLE
I MADE SOME **DINNER** FOR US!
SHALL WE EAT?
pop

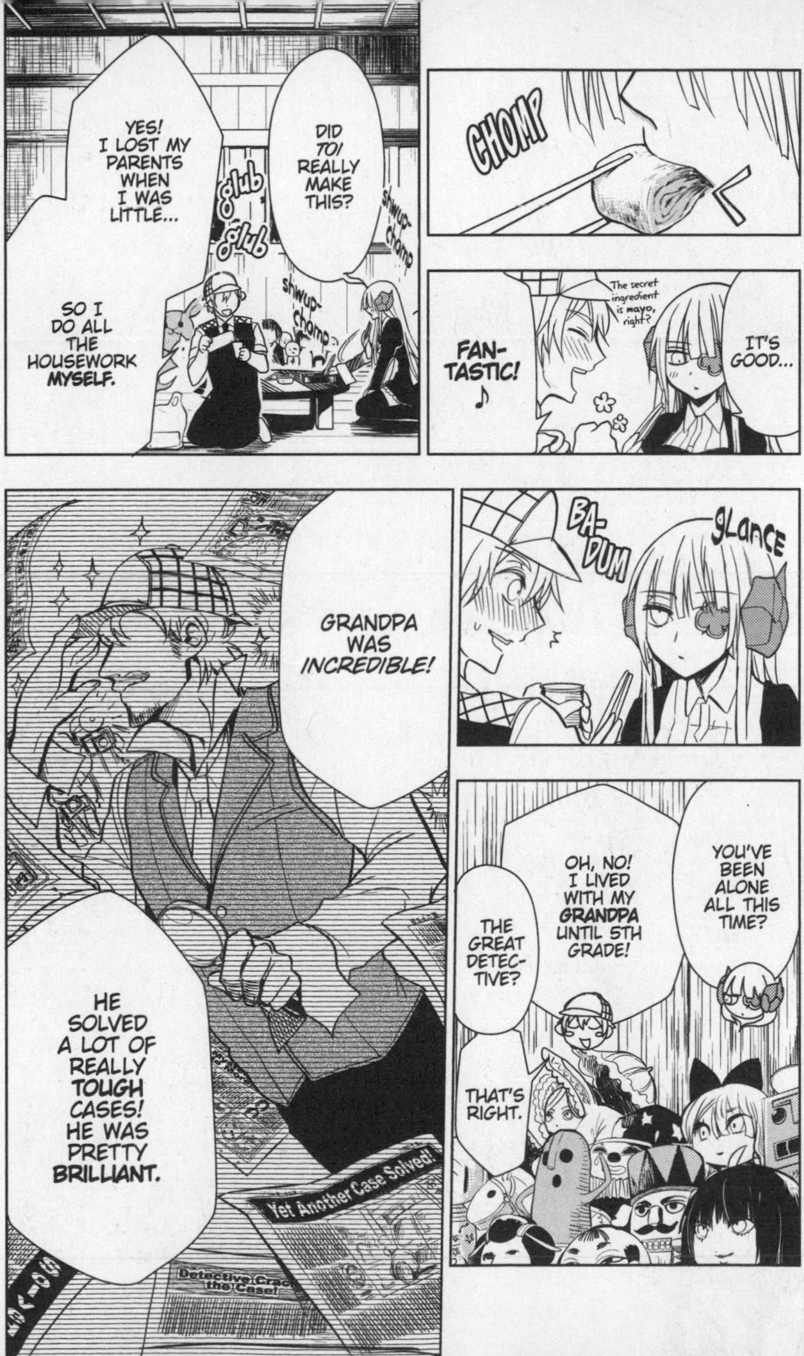
CHOMP
IT'S GOOD...
FAN-TASTIC! ♪
The secret ingredient is mayo, right?
DID TOI REALLY MAKE THIS?
shwup-chomp
shwup-chomp
glub glub
YES! I LOST MY PARENTS WHEN I WAS LITTLE...
SO I DO ALL THE HOUSEWORK MYSELF.
glance
BA-DUM
YOU'VE BEEN ALONE ALL THIS TIME?
OH, NO! I LIVED WITH MY GRANDPA UNTIL 5TH GRADE!
THE GREAT DETECTIVE?
THAT'S RIGHT.
GRANDPA WAS INCREDIBLE!
HE SOLVED A LOT OF REALLY TOUGH CASES! HE WAS PRETTY BRILLIANT.
Yet Another Case Solved!
Detective Crac the Case!

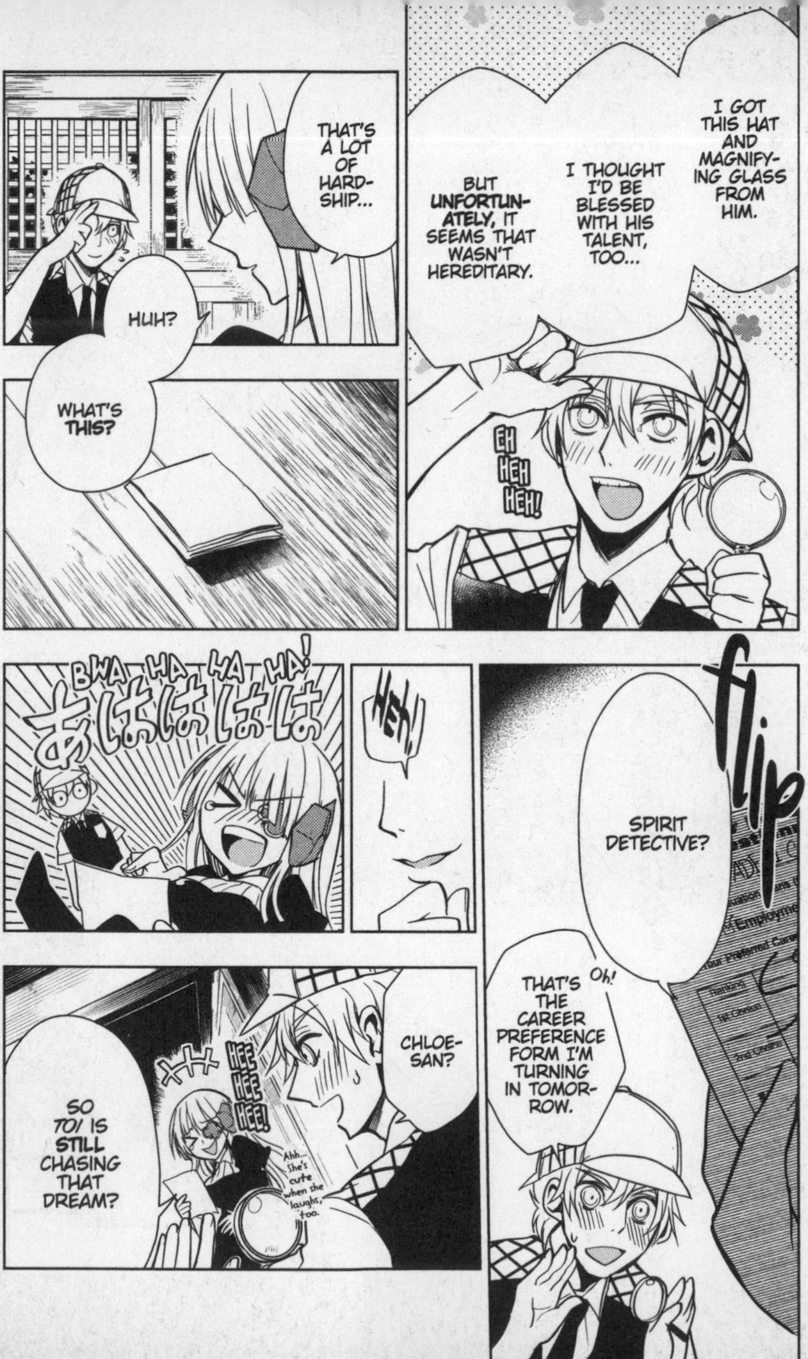
I GOT THIS HAT AND MAGNIFYING GLASS FROM HIM.
I THOUGHT I'D BE BLESSED WITH HIS TALENT, TOO...
BUT **UNFORTUNATELY,** IT SEEMS THAT WASN'T HEREDITARY.
EH HEH HEH!
THAT'S A LOT OF HARDSHIP...
HUH?
WHAT'S **THIS?**
flip
SPIRIT DETECTIVE?
Oh!
THAT'S THE CAREER PREFERENCE FORM I'M TURNING IN TOMORROW.
HEH!
BWA HA HA HA!
CHLOE-SAN?
HEE HEE HEE!
Ahh... She's cute when she laughs, too.
SO *TOI* IS **STILL** CHASING THAT DREAM?

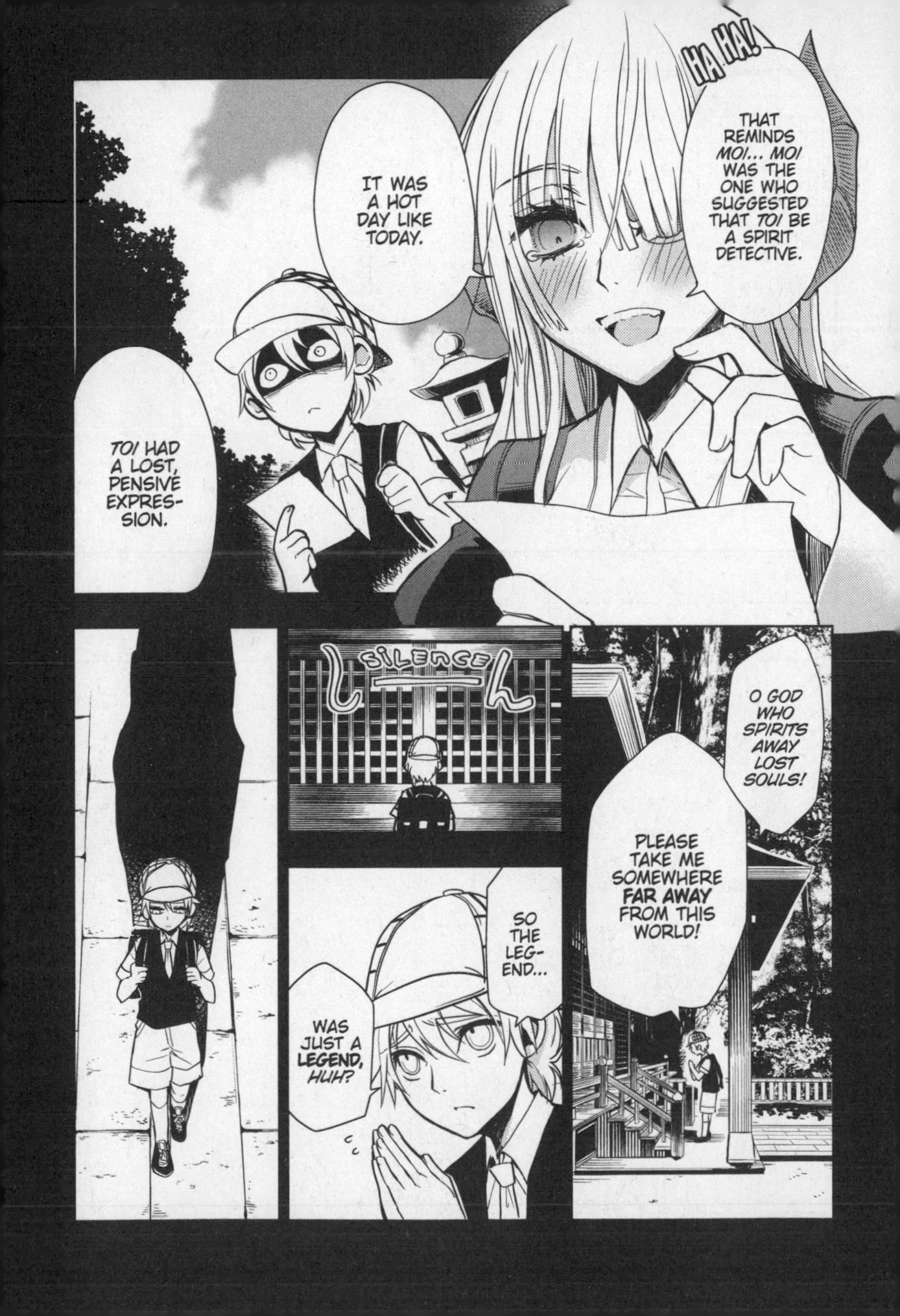
HA HA!
THAT REMINDS *MOI*... *MOI* WAS THE ONE WHO SUGGESTED THAT *TOI* BE A SPIRIT DETECTIVE.
IT WAS A HOT DAY LIKE TODAY.
TOI HAD A LOST, PENSIVE EXPRESSION.
O GOD WHO SPIRITS AWAY LOST SOULS!
PLEASE TAKE ME SOMEWHERE **FAR AWAY** FROM THIS WORLD!
SILENCE
SO THE LEGEND...
WAS JUST A **LEGEND**, *HUH?*

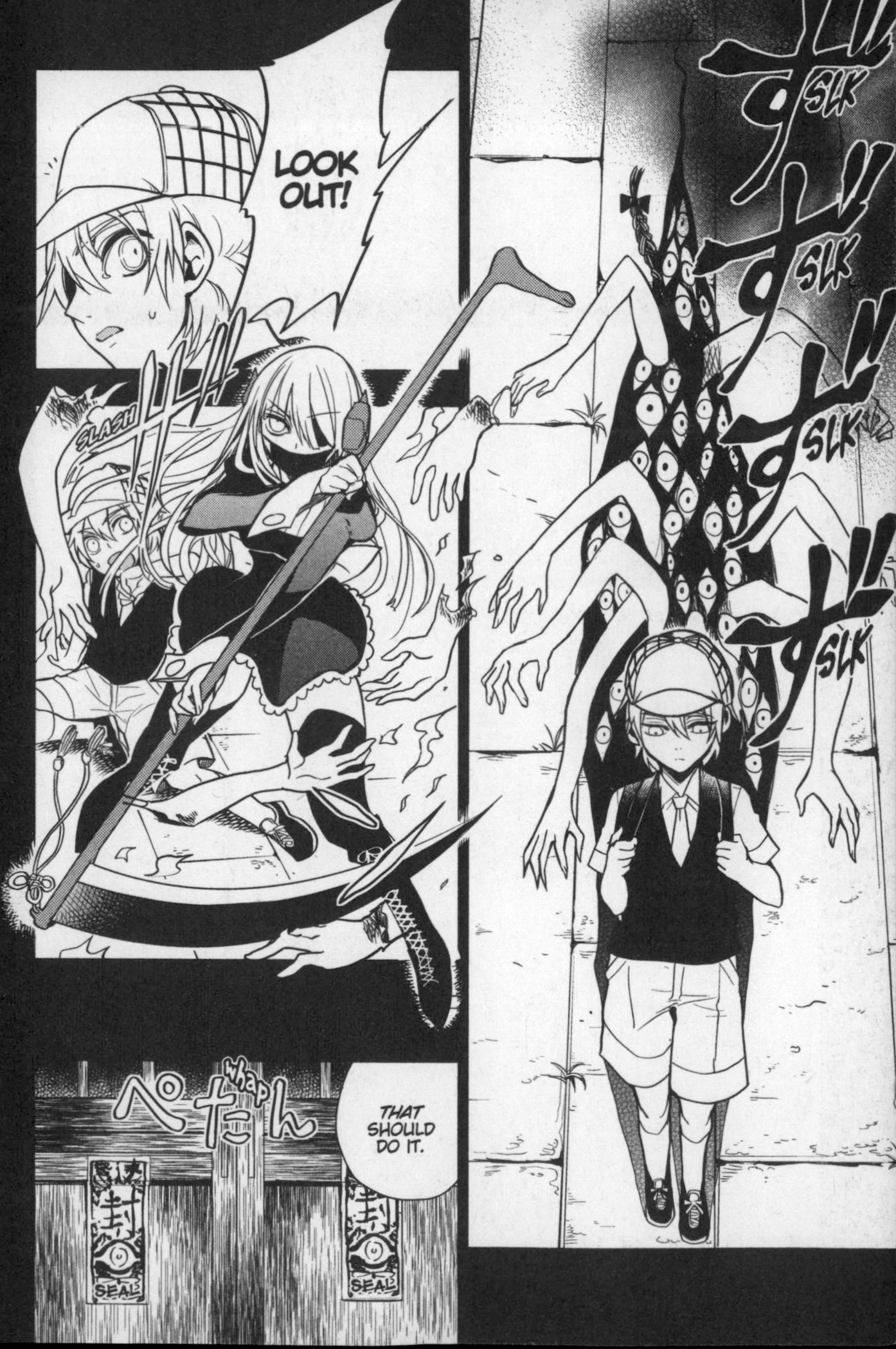
SLK
SLK
SLK
SLK
LOOK OUT!
SLASH
ぺたん
whap
THAT SHOULD DO IT.
SEAL
SEAL

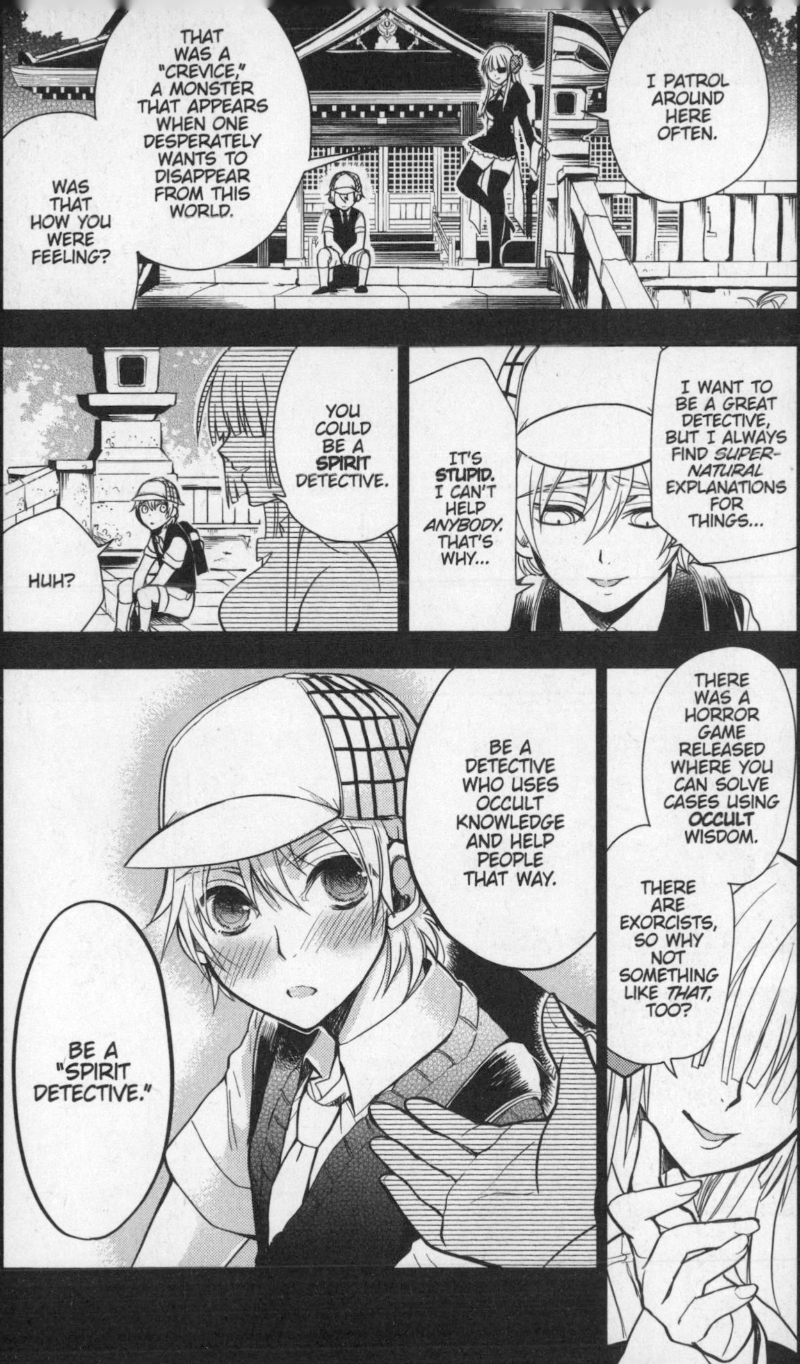
I PATROL AROUND HERE OFTEN.
THAT WAS A "CREVICE," A MONSTER THAT APPEARS WHEN ONE DESPERATELY WANTS TO DISAPPEAR FROM THIS WORLD.
WAS THAT HOW YOU WERE FEELING?
I WANT TO BE A GREAT DETECTIVE, BUT I ALWAYS FIND *SUPER-NATURAL* EXPLANATIONS FOR THINGS...
IT'S **STUPID.** I CAN'T HELP *ANYBODY.* THAT'S WHY...
YOU COULD BE A **SPIRIT** DETECTIVE.
HUH?
THERE WAS A HORROR GAME RELEASED WHERE YOU CAN SOLVE CASES USING **OCCULT** WISDOM.
THERE ARE EXORCISTS, SO WHY NOT SOMETHING LIKE *THAT,* TOO?
BE A DETECTIVE WHO USES OCCULT KNOWLEDGE AND HELP PEOPLE THAT WAY.
BE A "SPIRIT DETECTIVE."

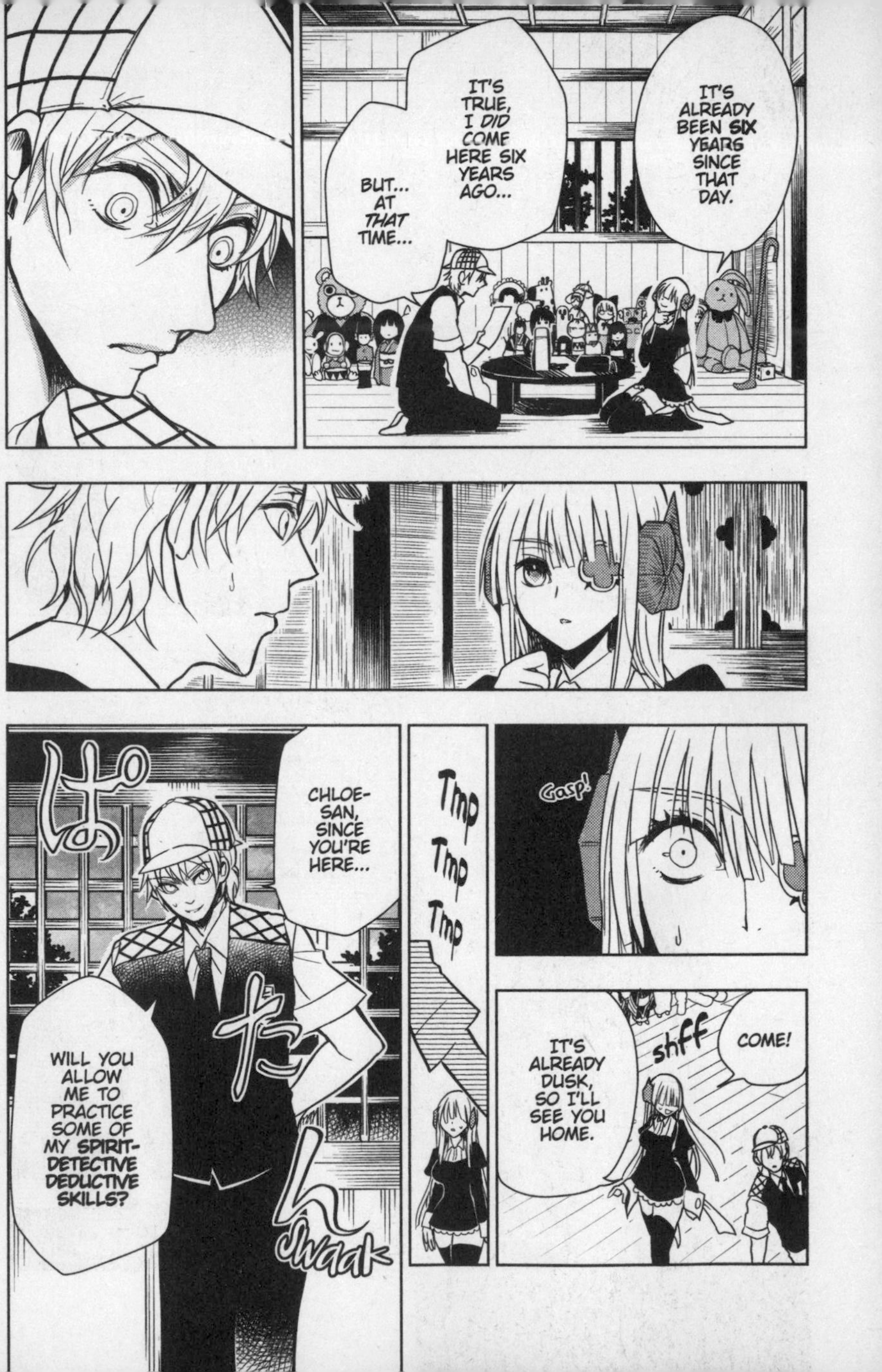
IT'S ALREADY BEEN SIX YEARS SINCE THAT DAY.
IT'S TRUE, I DID COME HERE SIX YEARS AGO...
BUT... AT THAT TIME...
Gasp!
Tmp Tmp Tmp
COME!
shff
IT'S ALREADY DUSK, SO I'LL SEE YOU HOME.
CHLOE-SAN, SINCE YOU'RE HERE...
WILL YOU ALLOW ME TO PRACTICE SOME OF MY SPIRIT-DETECTIVE DEDUCTIVE SKILLS?
shwaak

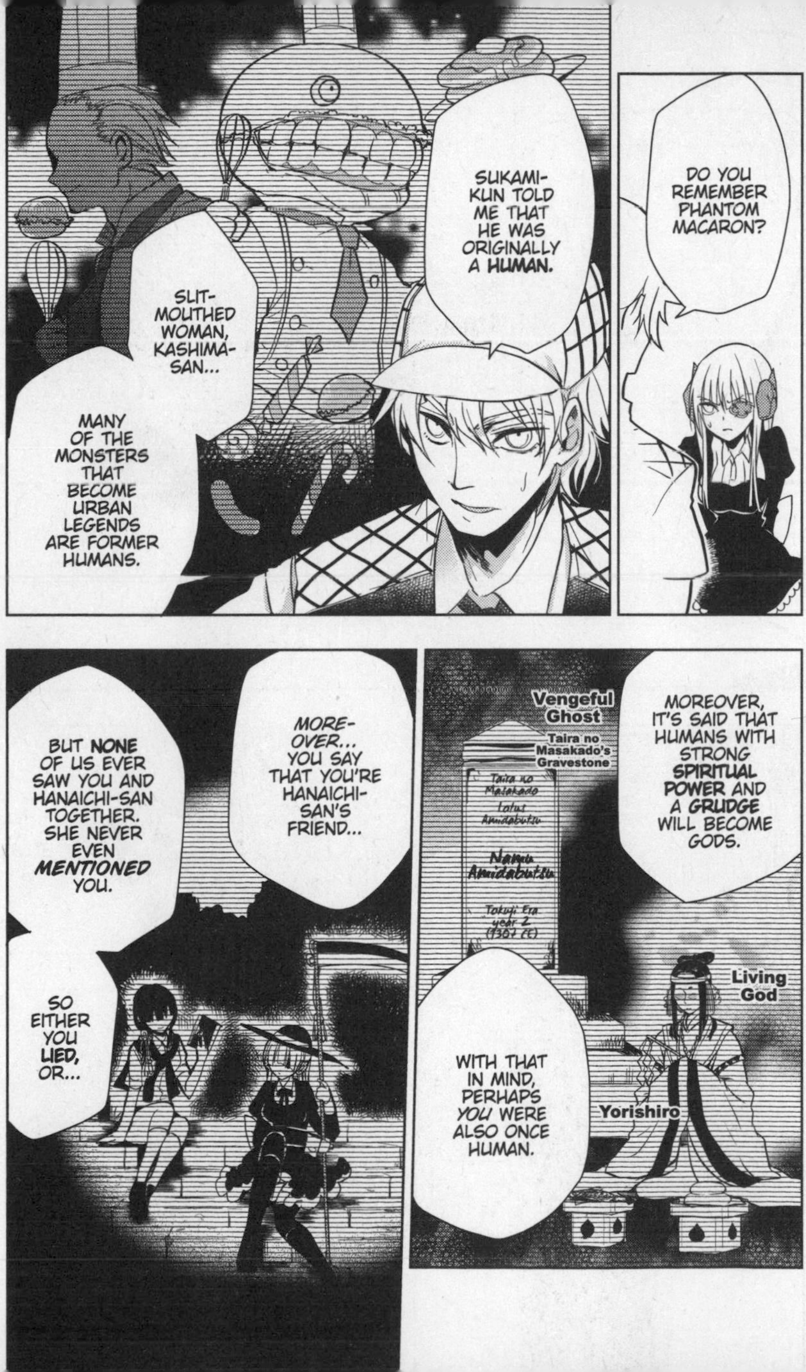
DO YOU REMEMBER PHANTOM MACARON?
SUKAMI-KUN TOLD ME THAT HE WAS ORIGINALLY A **HUMAN.**
SLIT-MOUTHED WOMAN, KASHIMA-SAN...
MANY OF THE MONSTERS THAT BECOME URBAN LEGENDS ARE FORMER HUMANS.
MOREOVER, IT'S SAID THAT HUMANS WITH STRONG **SPIRITUAL POWER** AND A **GRUDGE** WILL BECOME GODS.
Vengeful Ghost
Taira no Masakado's Gravestone
Namu Amidabutsu
Living God
Yorishiro
WITH THAT IN MIND, PERHAPS *YOU* WERE ALSO ONCE HUMAN.
MORE-OVER... YOU SAY THAT YOU'RE HANAICHI-SAN'S FRIEND...
BUT **NONE** OF US EVER SAW YOU AND HANAICHI-SAN TOGETHER. SHE NEVER EVEN ***MENTIONED*** YOU.
SO EITHER YOU **LIED,** OR...

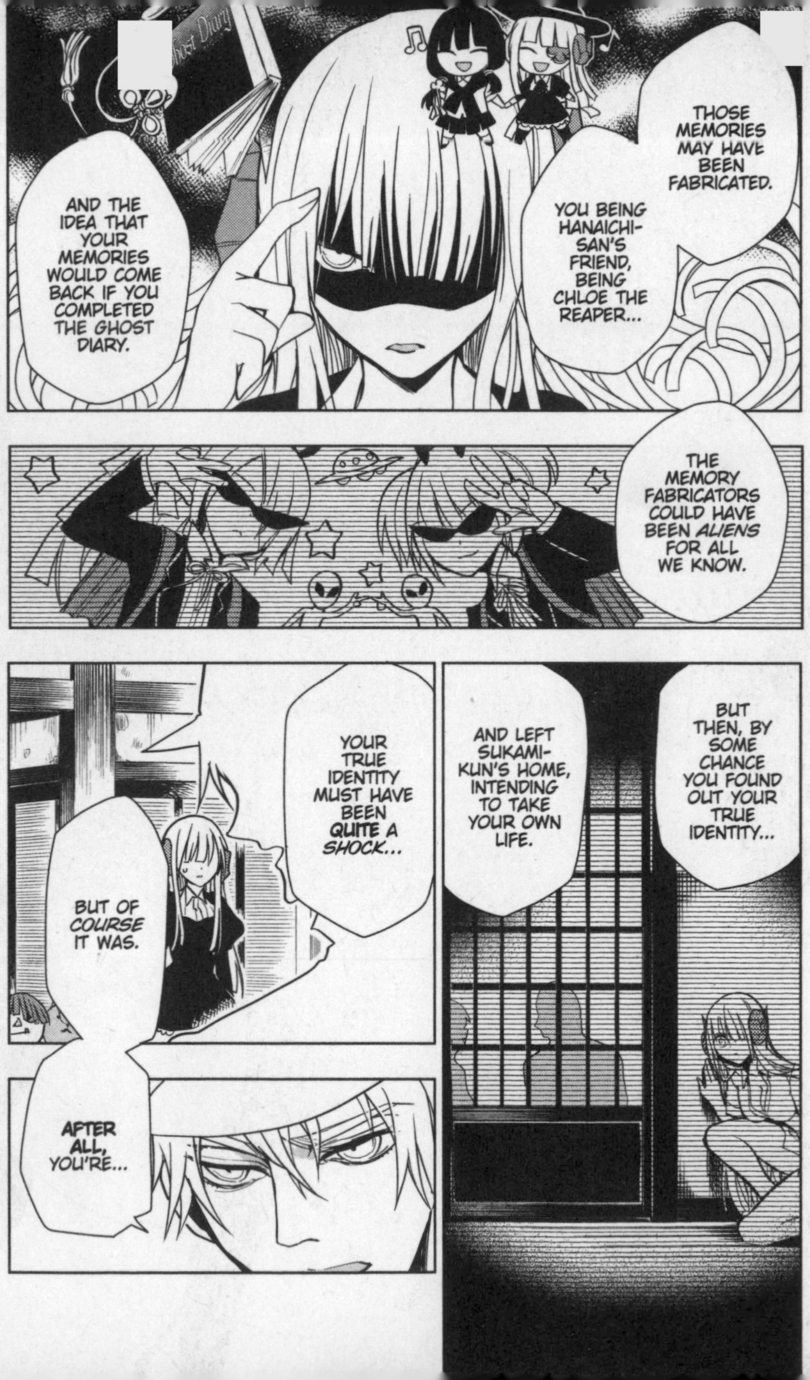
THOSE MEMORIES MAY HAVE BEEN FABRICATED.
YOU BEING HANAICHI-SAN'S FRIEND, BEING CHLOE THE REAPER...
AND THE IDEA THAT YOUR MEMORIES WOULD COME BACK IF YOU COMPLETED THE GHOST DIARY.
THE MEMORY FABRICATORS COULD HAVE BEEN *ALIENS* FOR ALL WE KNOW.
BUT THEN, BY SOME CHANCE YOU FOUND OUT YOUR TRUE IDENTITY...
AND LEFT SUKAMI-KUN'S HOME, INTENDING TO TAKE YOUR OWN LIFE.
YOUR TRUE IDENTITY MUST HAVE BEEN **QUITE** A *SHOCK*...
BUT OF *COURSE* IT WAS.
AFTER ALL, YOU'RE...

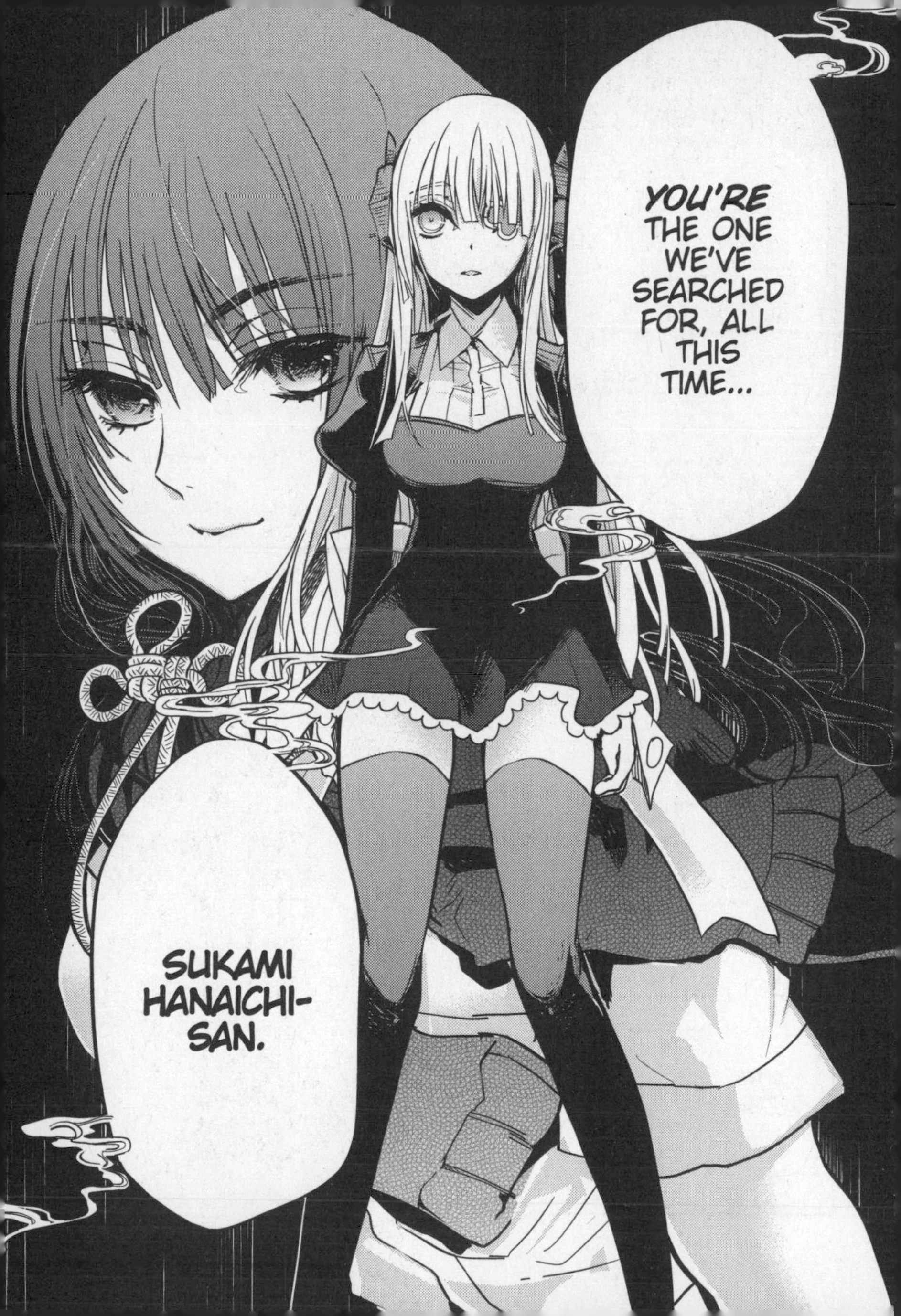
YOU'RE THE ONE WE'VE SEARCHED FOR, ALL THIS TIME...
SUKAMI HANAICHI-SAN.

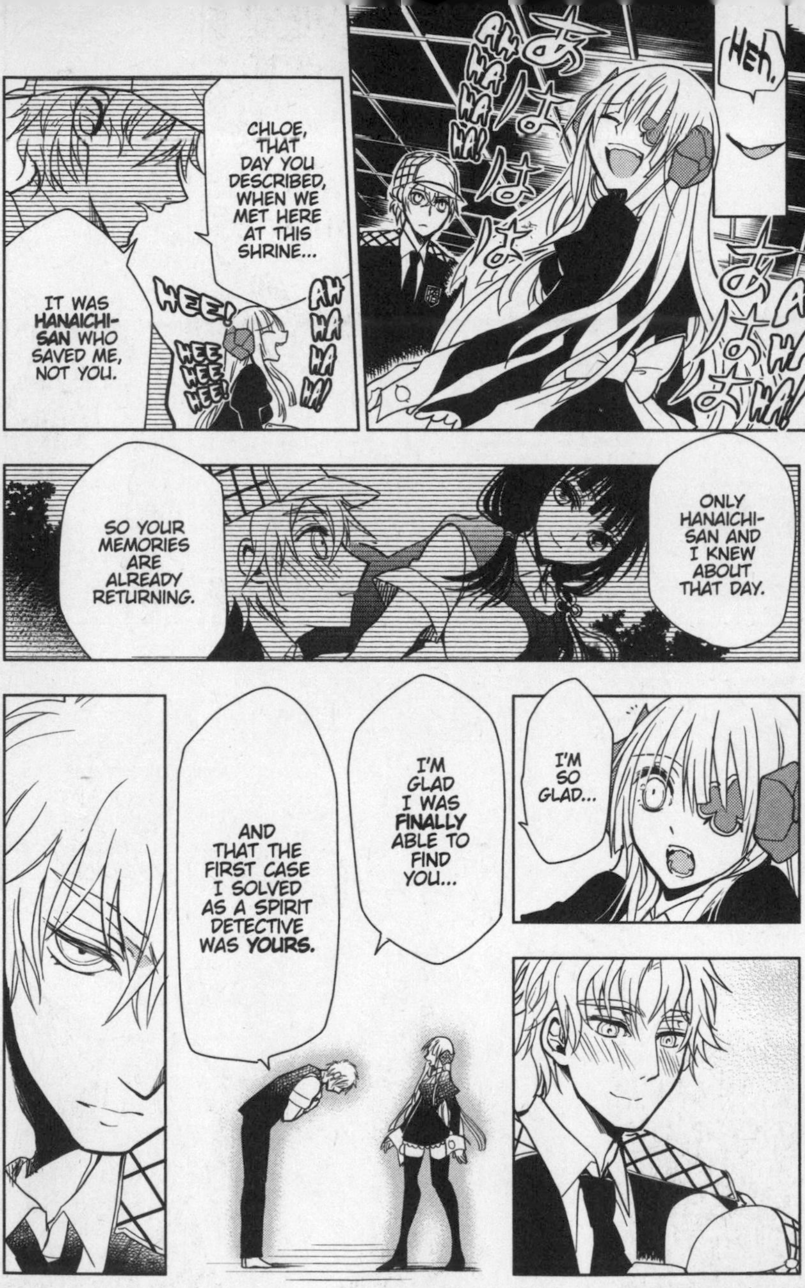
Heh.
AH HA HA HA!
あははは
AH HA HA HA!
あははは
CHLOE, THAT DAY YOU DESCRIBED, WHEN WE MET HERE AT THIS SHRINE...
AH HA HA HA HA!
HEE! HEE HEE HEE!
IT WAS HANAICHI-SAN WHO SAVED ME, NOT YOU.
ONLY HANAICHI-SAN AND I KNEW ABOUT THAT DAY.
SO YOUR MEMORIES ARE ALREADY RETURNING.
I'M SO GLAD...
I'M GLAD I WAS FINALLY ABLE TO FIND YOU...
AND THAT THE FIRST CASE I SOLVED AS A SPIRIT DETECTIVE WAS YOURS.

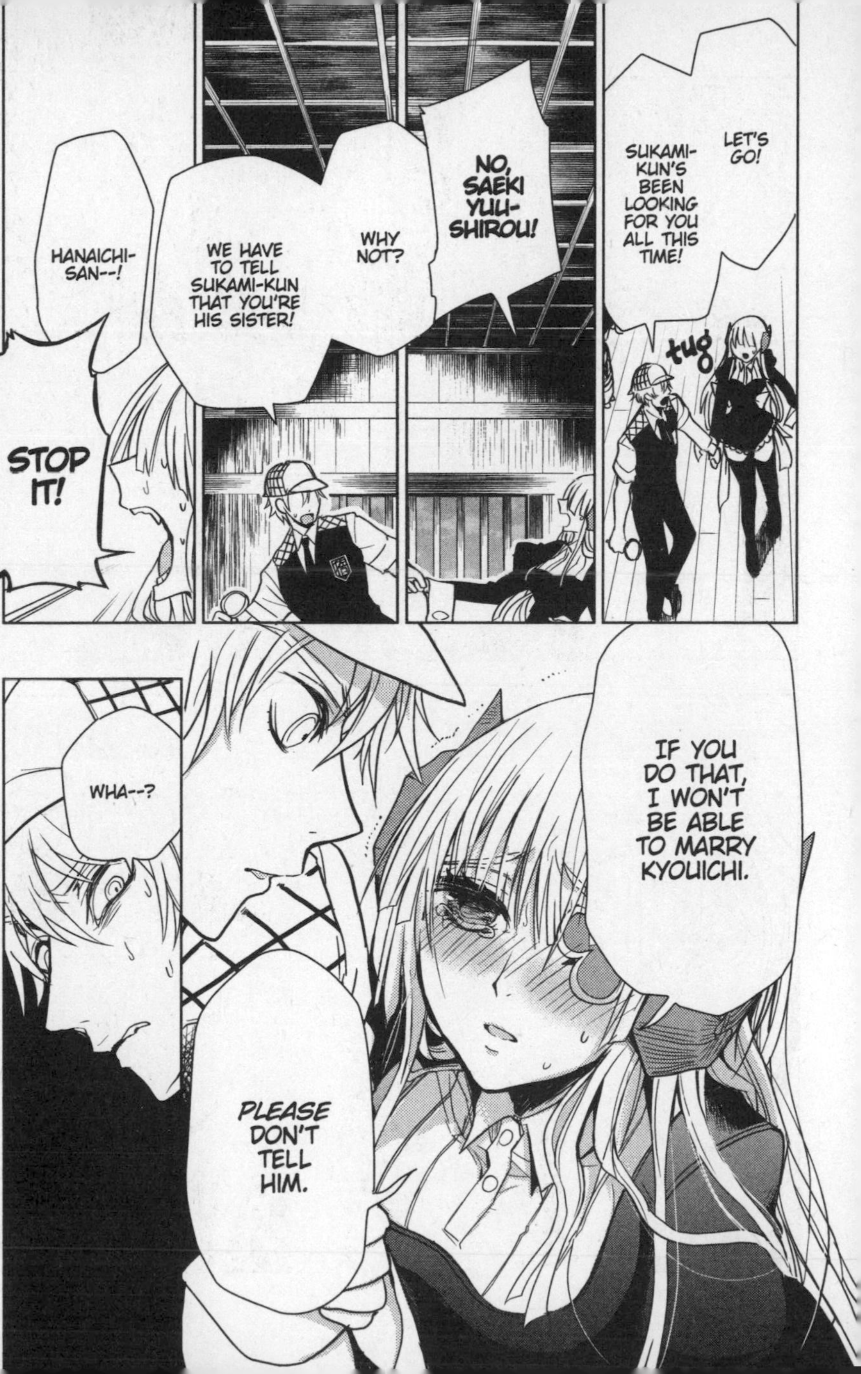
LET'S GO!
SUKAMI-KUN'S BEEN LOOKING FOR YOU ALL THIS TIME!
tug
NO, SAEKI YUU-SHIROU!
WHY NOT?
WE HAVE TO TELL SUKAMI-KUN THAT YOU'RE HIS SISTER!
HANAICHI-SAN--!
STOP IT!
IF YOU DO THAT, I WON'T BE ABLE TO MARRY KYOUICHI.
WHA--?
PLEASE DON'T TELL HIM.

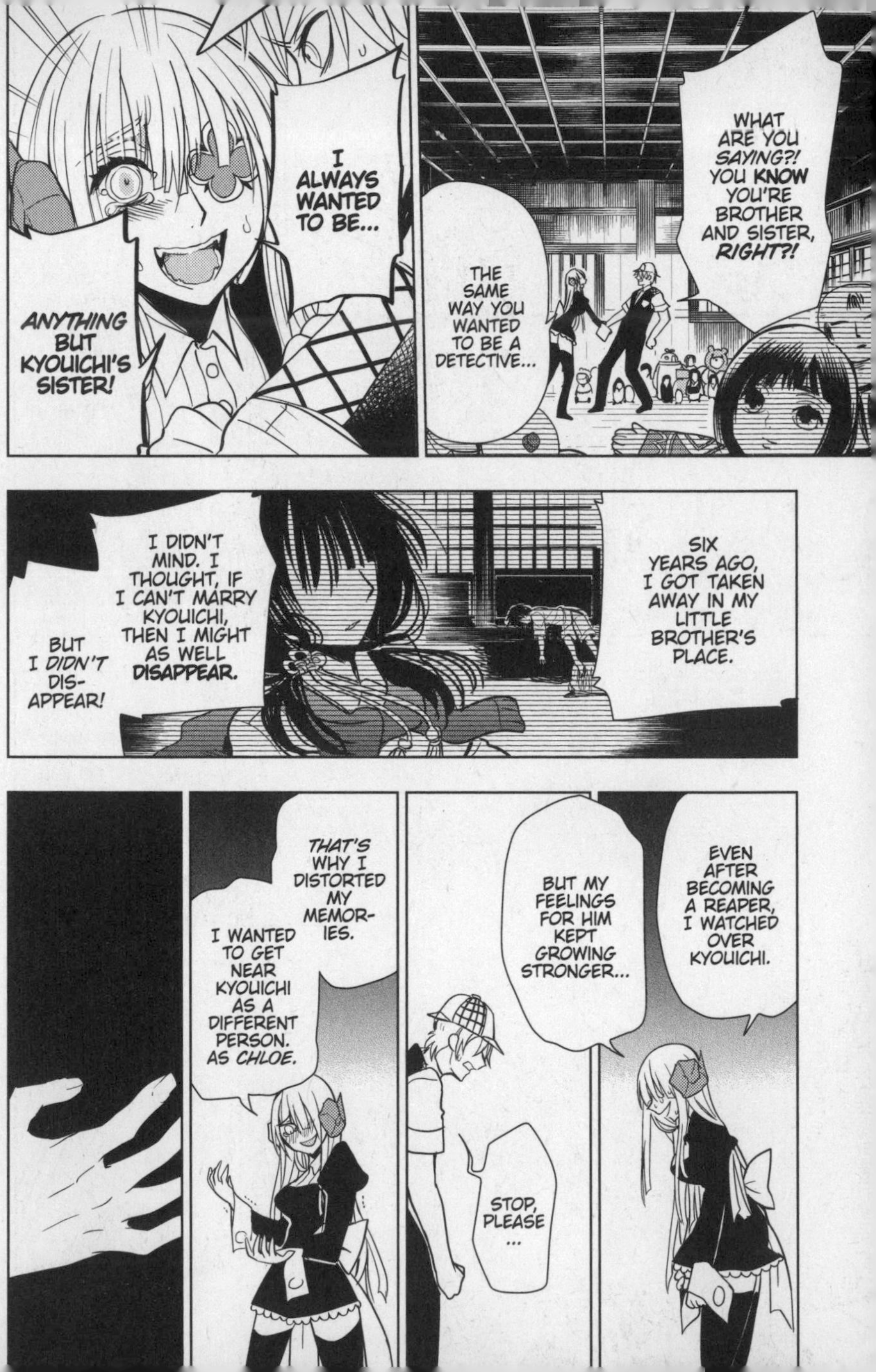
WHAT ARE YOU *SAYING?!* YOU **KNOW** YOU'RE BROTHER AND SISTER, ***RIGHT?!***
THE SAME WAY YOU WANTED TO BE A DETECTIVE...
I ALWAYS WANTED TO BE...
ANYTHING BUT KYOUICHI'S SISTER!
SIX YEARS AGO, I GOT TAKEN AWAY IN MY LITTLE BROTHER'S PLACE.
I DIDN'T MIND. I THOUGHT, IF I CAN'T MARRY KYOUICHI, THEN I MIGHT AS WELL **DISAPPEAR.**
BUT I *DIDN'T* DIS-APPEAR!
EVEN AFTER BECOMING A REAPER, I WATCHED OVER KYOUICHI.
BUT MY FEELINGS FOR HIM KEPT GROWING STRONGER...
STOP, PLEASE...
THAT'S WHY I DISTORTED MY MEMOR-IES.
I WANTED TO GET NEAR KYOUICHI AS A DIFFERENT PERSON. AS *CHLOE.*

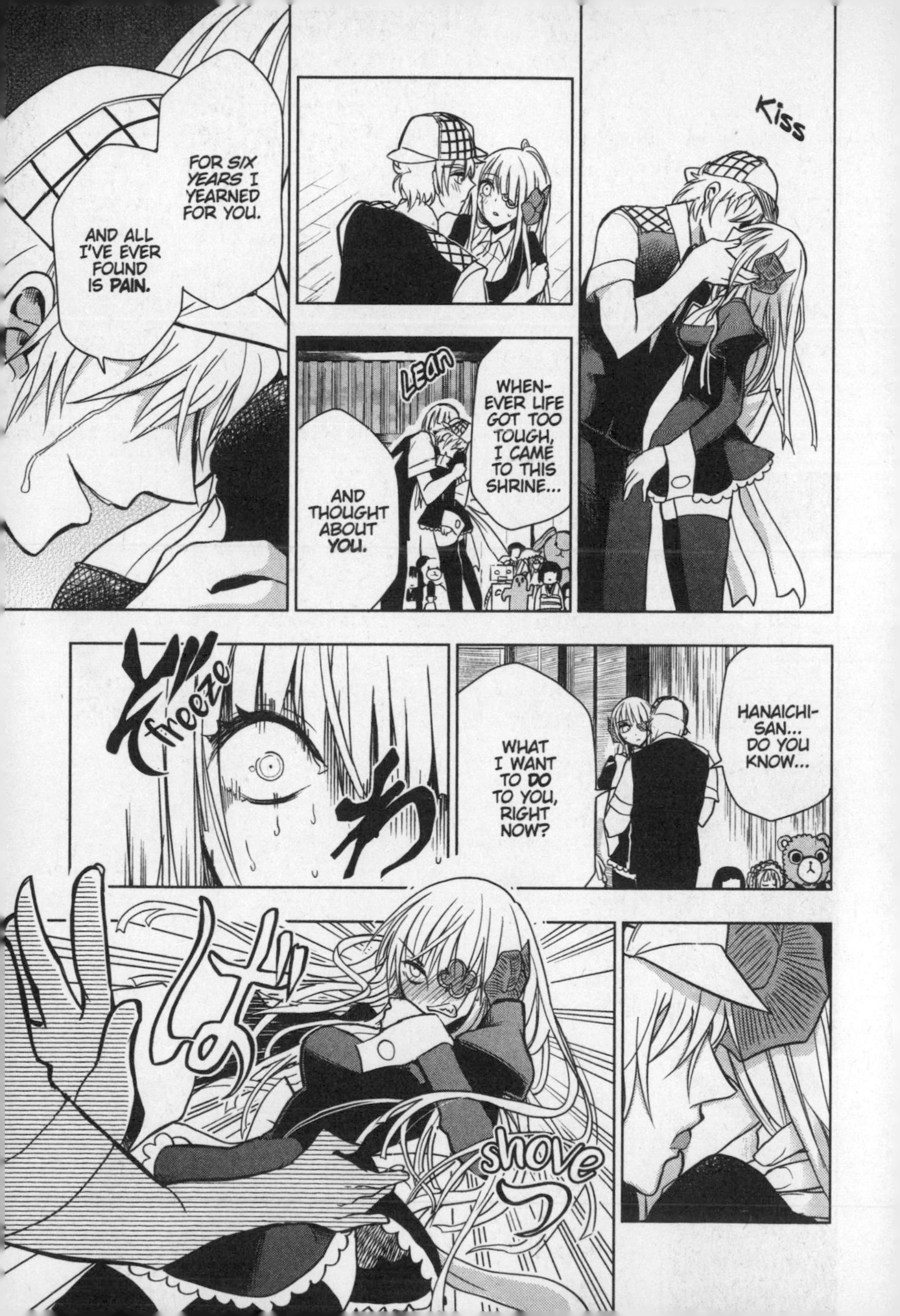

Kiss
LEan
WHEN-EVER LIFE GOT TOO TOUGH, I CAME TO THIS SHRINE...
AND THOUGHT ABOUT YOU.
FOR SIX YEARS I YEARNED FOR YOU.
AND ALL I'VE EVER FOUND IS PAIN.
HANAICHI-SAN... DO YOU KNOW...
WHAT I WANT TO DO TO YOU, RIGHT NOW?
freeze
shove

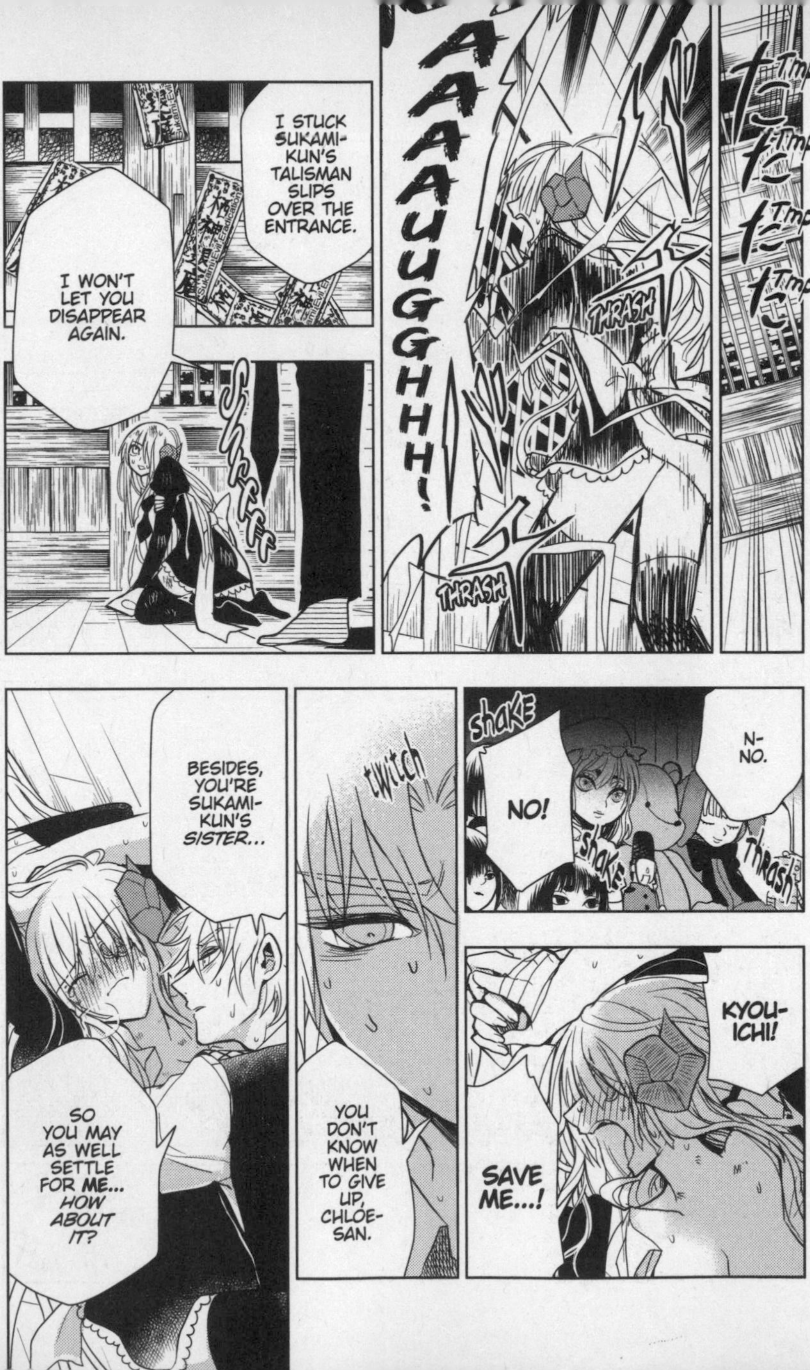

Tmp Tmp Tmp Tmp
AAAAUUGGHHH!
THRASH
THRASH
I STUCK SUKAMI-KUN'S TALISMAN SLIPS OVER THE ENTRANCE.
I WON'T LET YOU DISAPPEAR AGAIN.
Shffff
shake
N-NO.
NO!
shake
thrash
KYOU-ICHI!
SAVE ME...!
twitch
YOU DON'T KNOW WHEN TO GIVE UP, CHLOE-SAN.
BESIDES, YOU'RE SUKAMI-KUN'S *SISTER*...
SO YOU MAY AS WELL SETTLE FOR ME... *HOW ABOUT IT?*

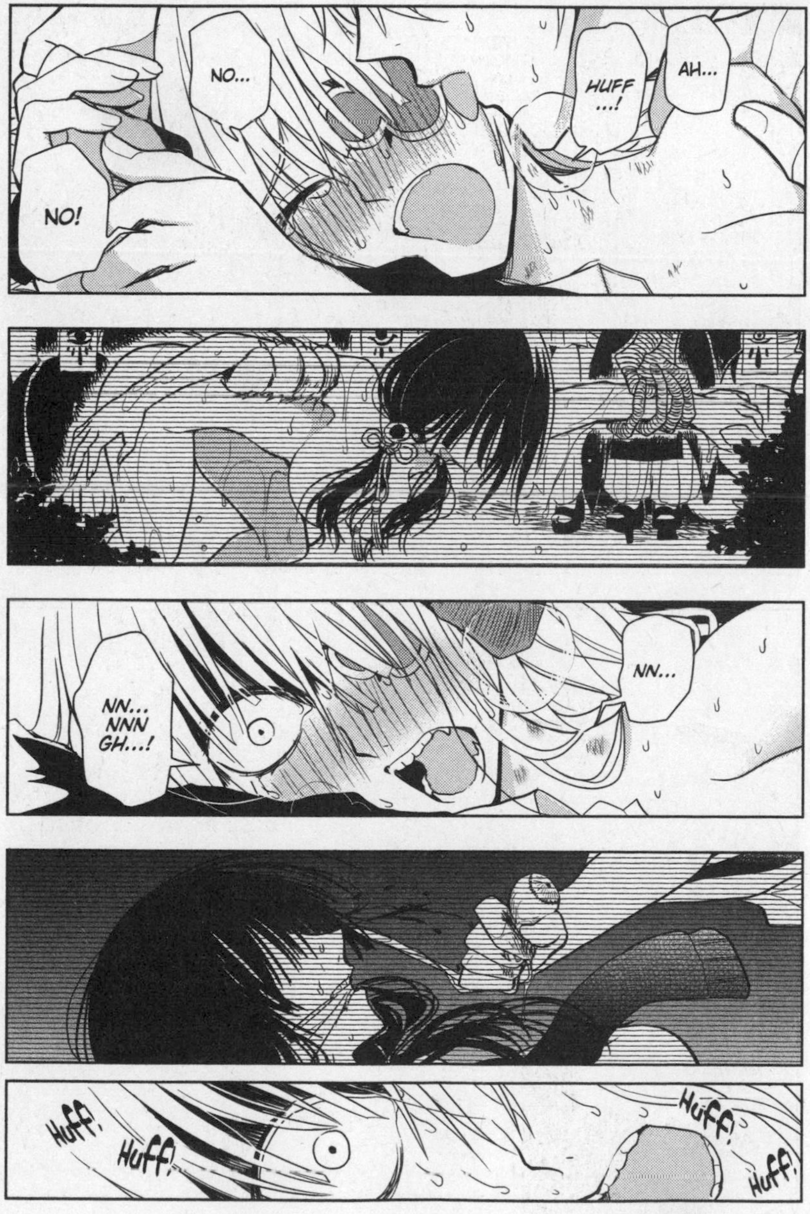
AH...
HUFF ...!
NO...
NO!
NN...
NN... NNNGH...!
Huff!
Huff!
Huff!
Huff!

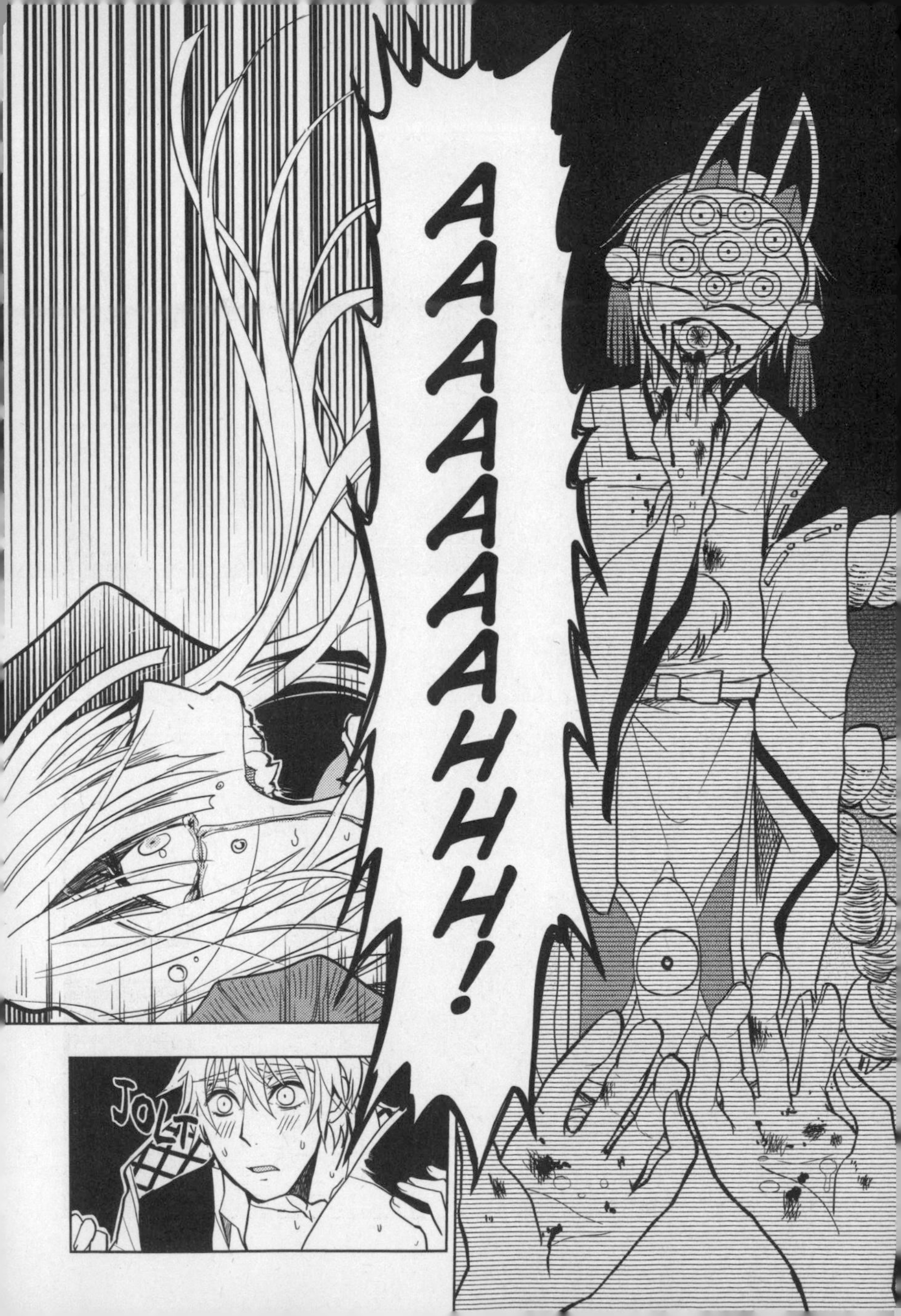
AAAAAAAHHH!
JOLT

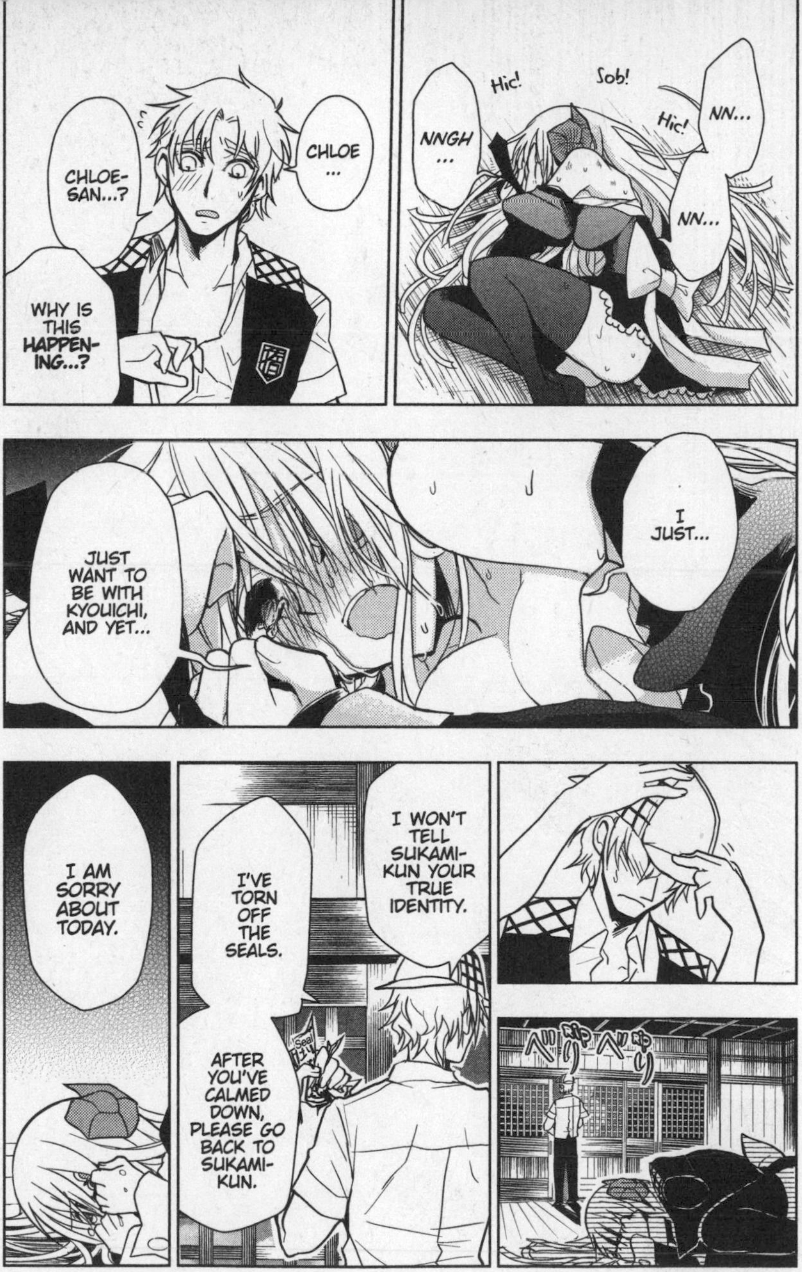

NN...
Hic!
Sob!
Hic!
NNGH ...
NN...
CHLOE ...
CHLOE-SAN...?
WHY IS THIS HAPPEN-ING...?
I JUST...
JUST WANT TO BE WITH KYOUICHI, AND YET...
I WON'T TELL SUKAMI-KUN YOUR TRUE IDENTITY.
RIP
RIP
I'VE TORN OFF THE SEALS.
Seal
AFTER YOU'VE CALMED DOWN, PLEASE GO BACK TO SUKAMI-KUN.
I AM SORRY ABOUT TODAY.

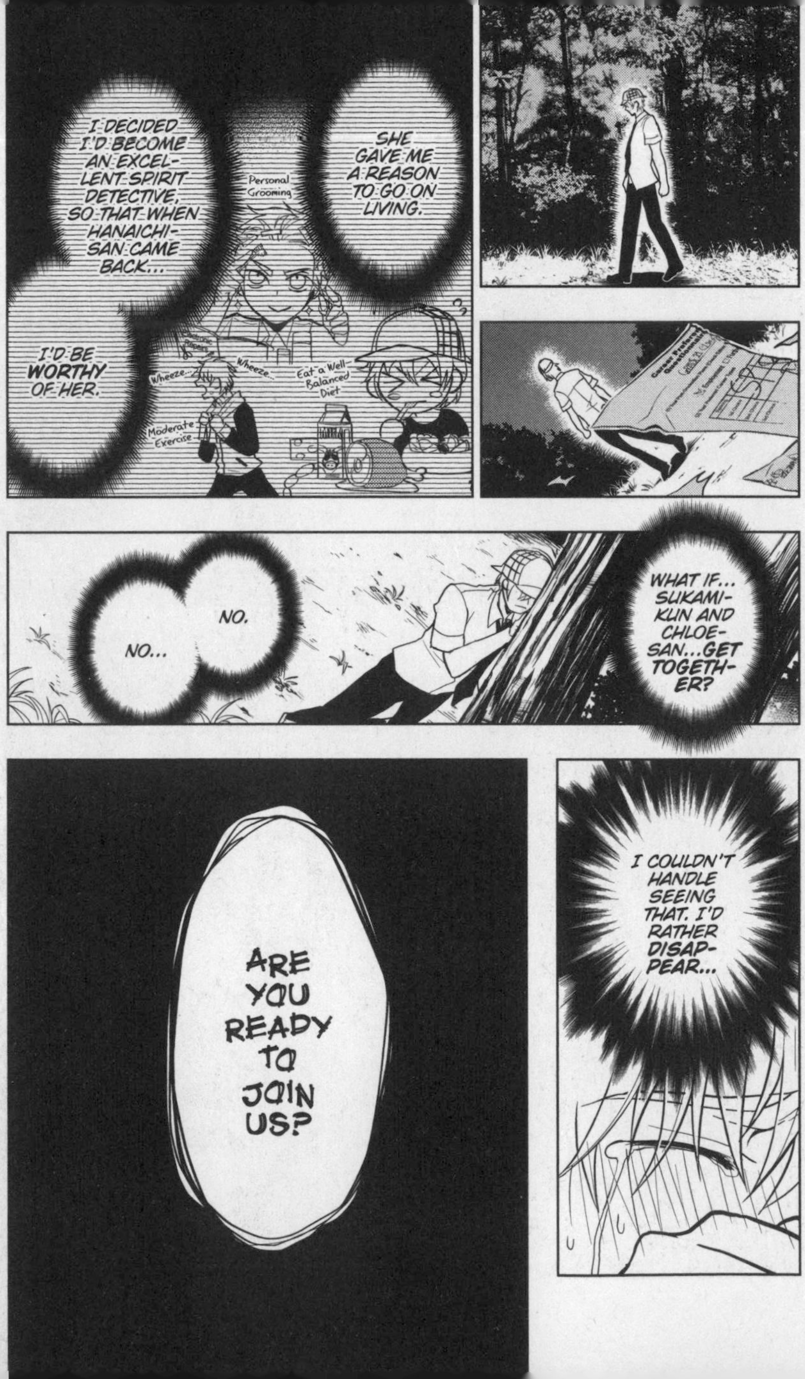
SHE GAVE ME A REASON TO GO ON LIVING.
I DECIDED I'D BECOME AN EXCEL-LENT SPIRIT DETECTIVE, SO THAT WHEN HANAICHI-SAN CAME BACK...
Personal Grooming
Wheeze...
Wheeze...
Eat a Well-Balanced Diet
Moderate Exercise
I'D BE **WORTHY** OF HER.
WHAT IF... SUKAMI-KUN AND CHLOE-SAN...GET TOGETH-ER?
NO.
NO...
I COULDN'T HANDLE SEEING THAT. I'D RATHER DISAP-PEAR...
ARE YOU READY TO JOIN US?

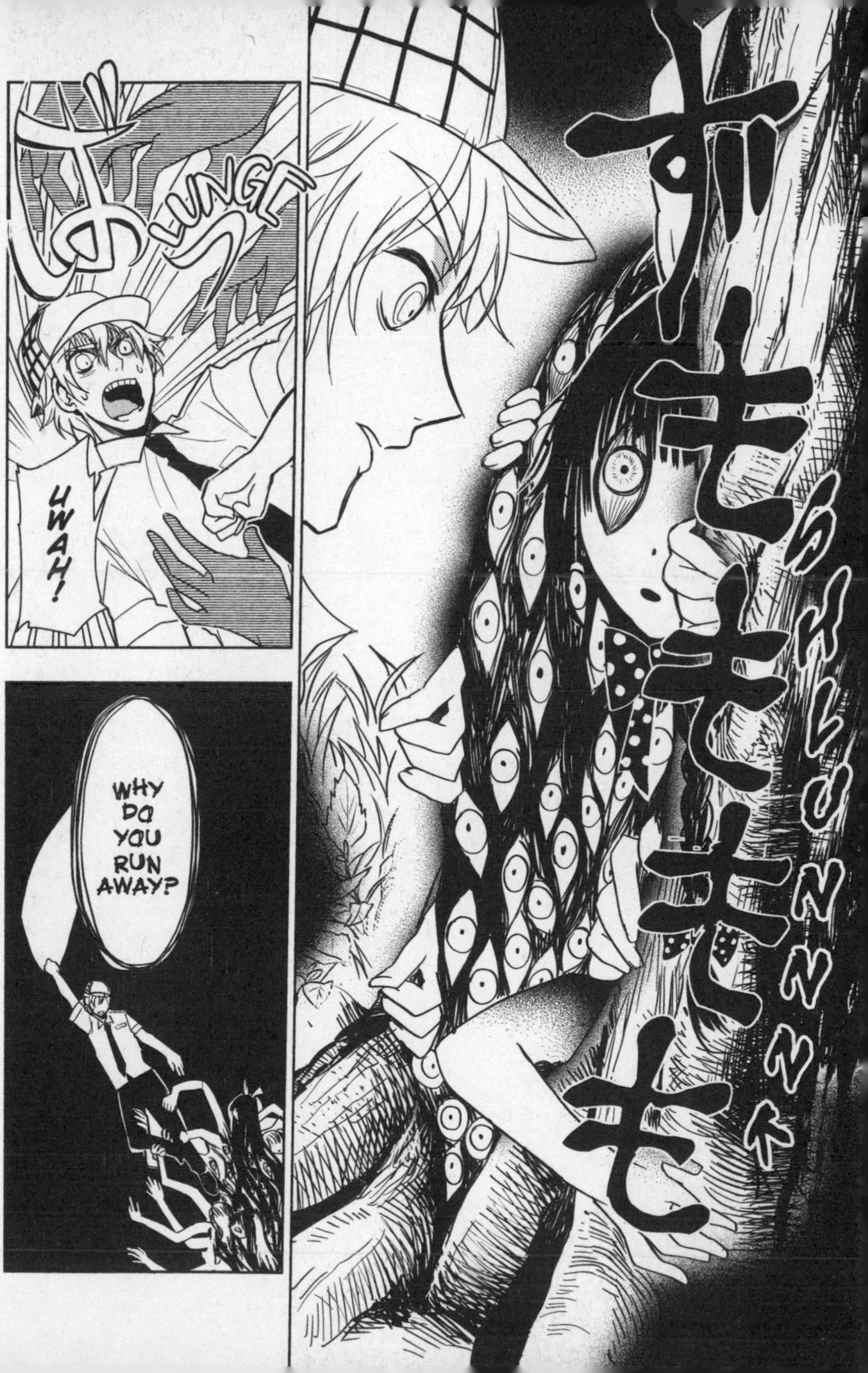

SHUNNN
PLUNGE
UWAH!
WHY DO YOU RUN AWAY?

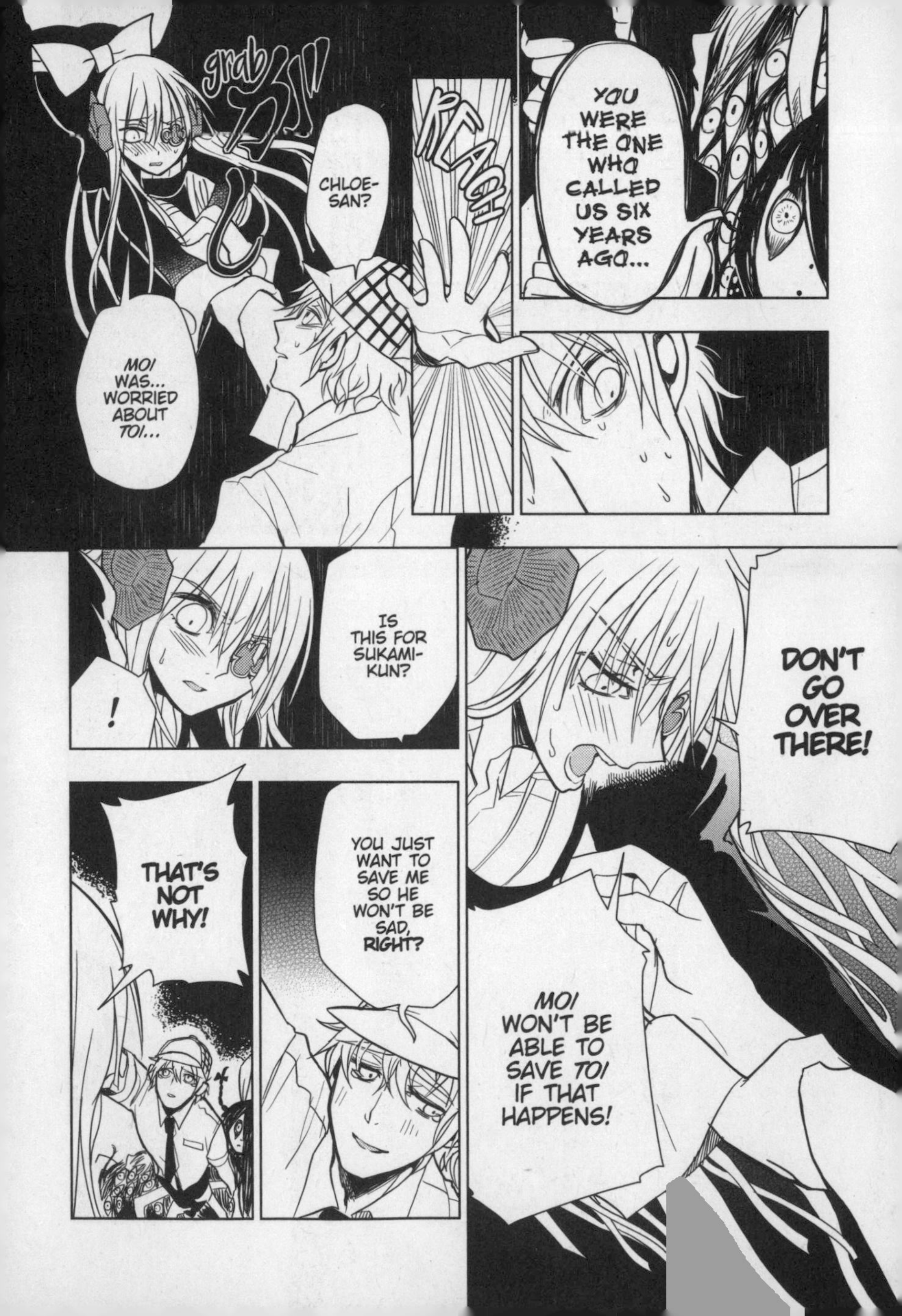
YOU WERE THE ONE WHO CALLED US SIX YEARS AGO...
REACH
CHLOE-SAN?
grab
MOI WAS... WORRIED ABOUT TOI...
DON'T GO OVER THERE!
IS THIS FOR SUKAMI-KUN?
!
MOI WON'T BE ABLE TO SAVE TOI IF THAT HAPPENS!
YOU JUST WANT TO SAVE ME SO HE WON'T BE SAD, RIGHT?
THAT'S NOT WHY!

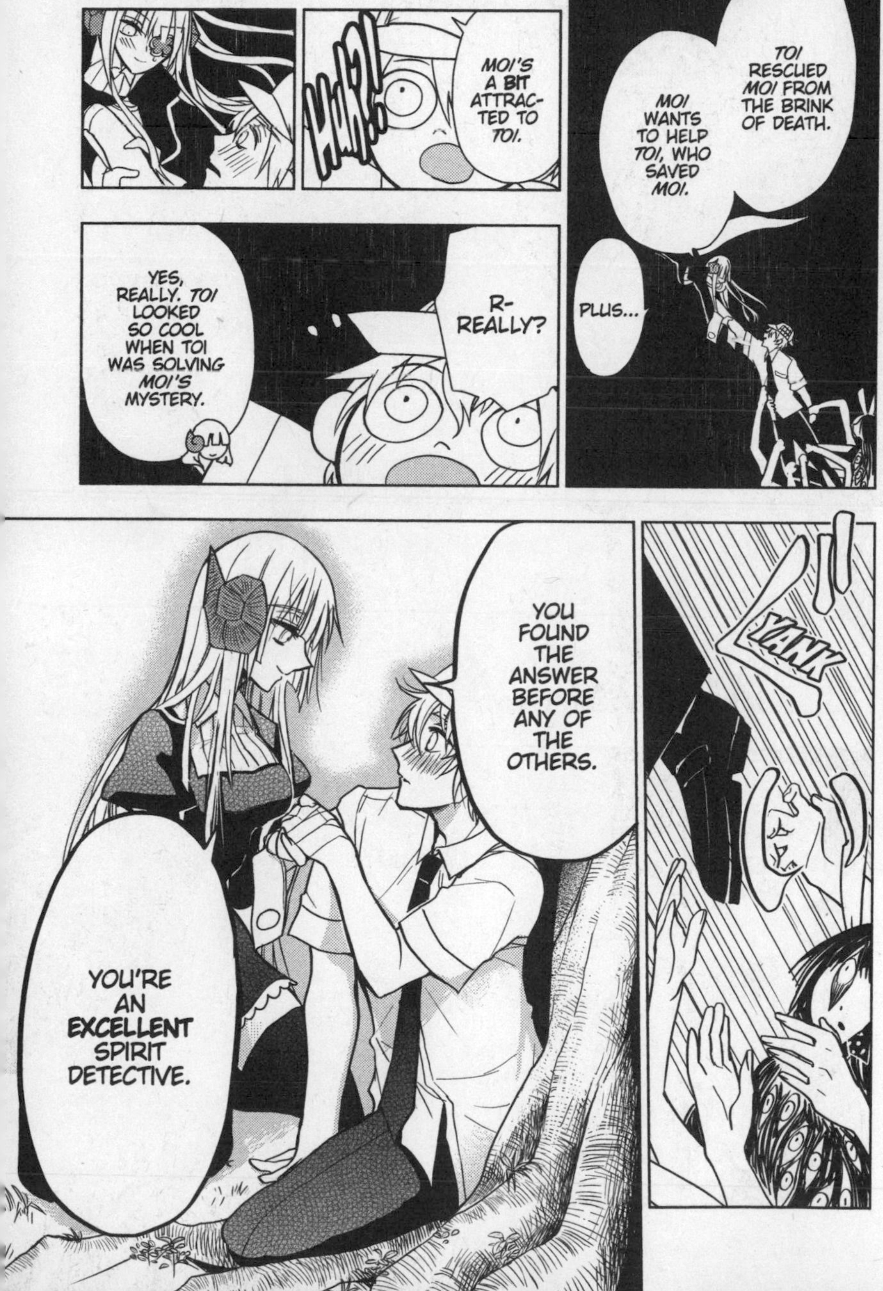
TOI RESCUED MOI FROM THE BRINK OF DEATH.
MOI WANTS TO HELP TOI, WHO SAVED MOI.
PLUS...
MOI'S A BIT ATTRACTED TO TOI.
R-REALLY?
YES, REALLY. TOI LOOKED SO COOL WHEN TOI WAS SOLVING MOI'S MYSTERY.
YANK
YOU FOUND THE ANSWER BEFORE ANY OF THE OTHERS.
YOU'RE AN EXCELLENT SPIRIT DETECTIVE.

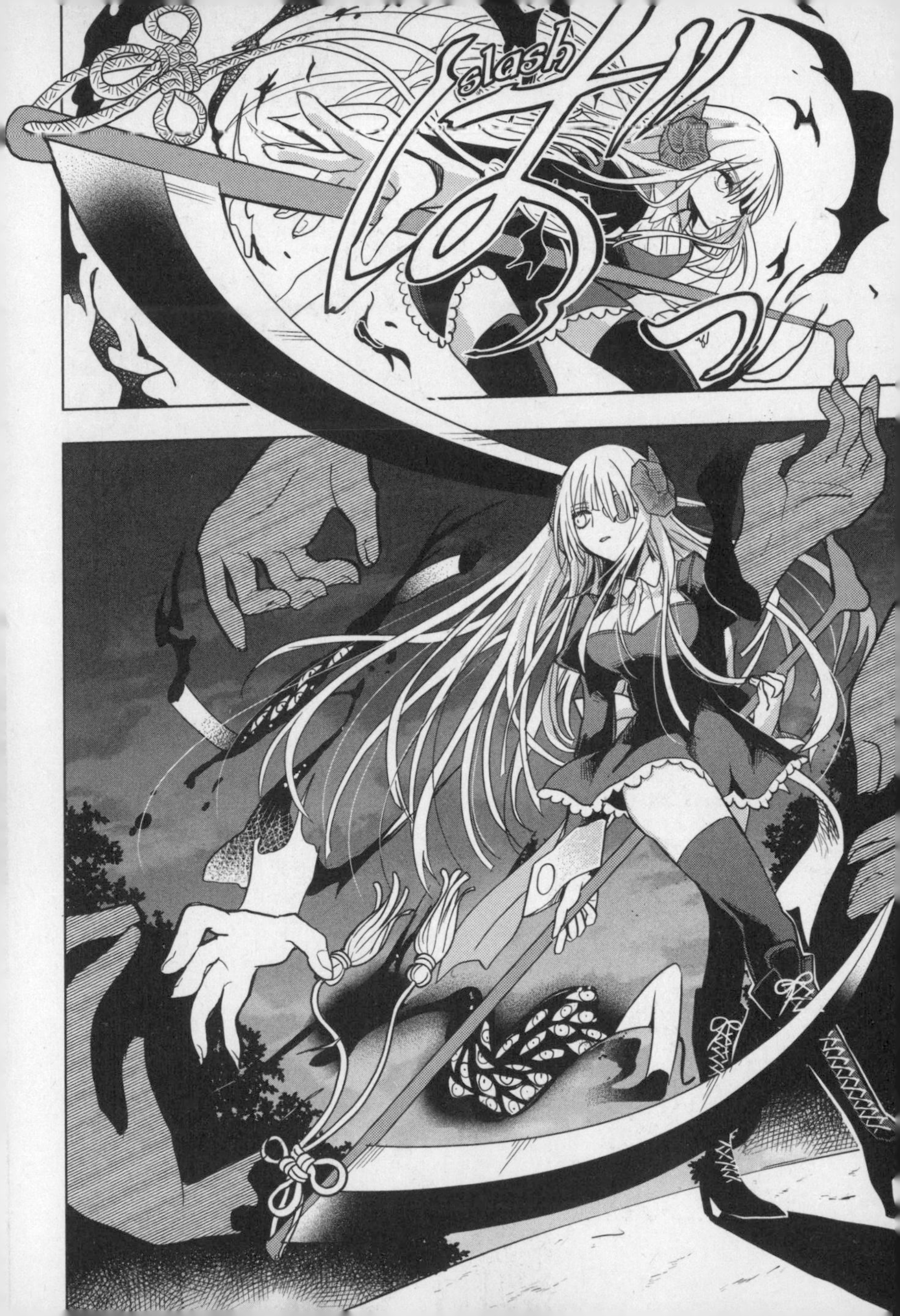
slash

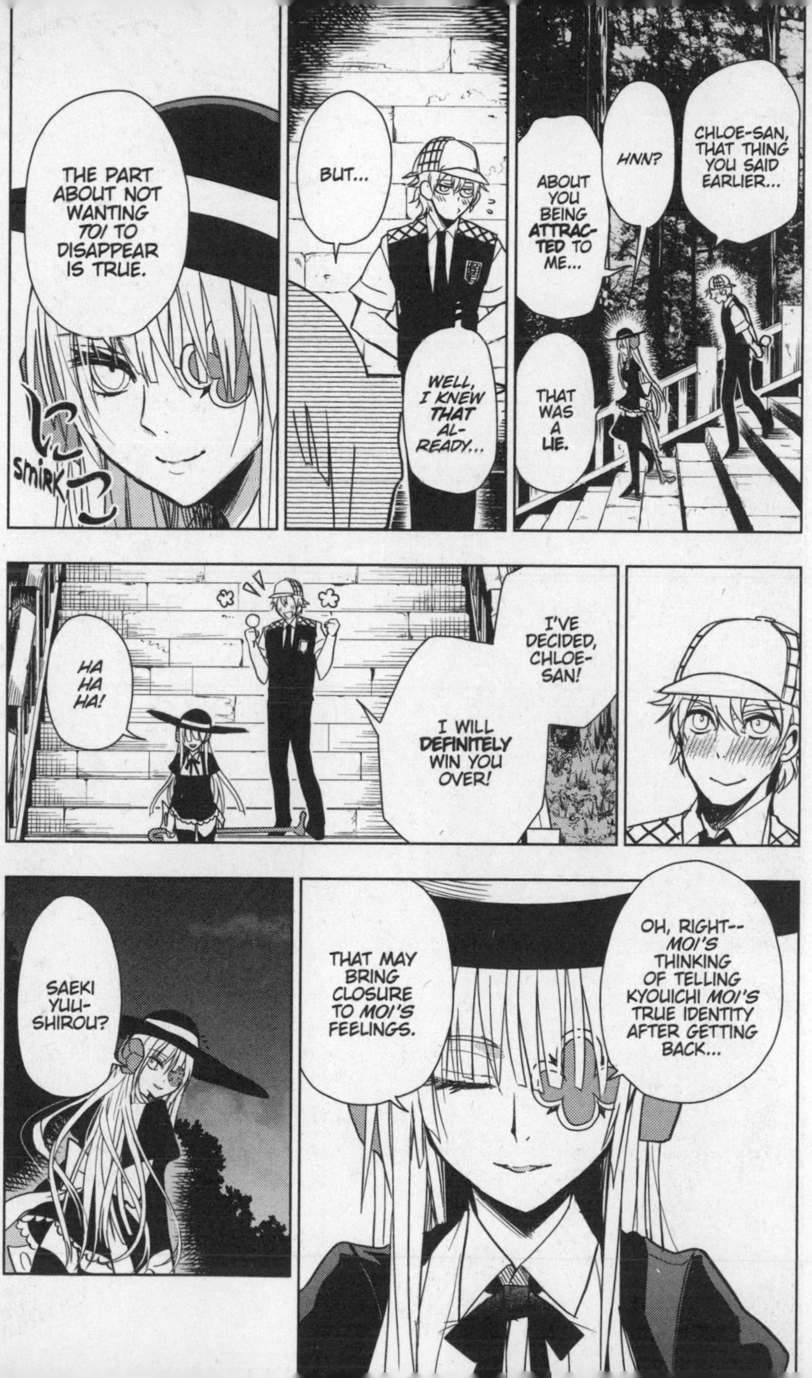
CHLOE-SAN, THAT THING YOU SAID EARLIER...
HNN?
ABOUT YOU BEING ATTRACTED TO ME...
THAT WAS A LIE.
BUT...
WELL, I KNEW THAT AL-READY...
THE PART ABOUT NOT WANTING TOI TO DISAPPEAR IS TRUE.
smirk
I'VE DECIDED, CHLOE-SAN!
I WILL DEFINITELY WIN YOU OVER!
HA HA HA!
OH, RIGHT-- MOI'S THINKING OF TELLING KYOUICHI MOI'S TRUE IDENTITY AFTER GETTING BACK...
THAT MAY BRING CLOSURE TO MOI'S FEELINGS.
SAEKI YUU-SHIROU?

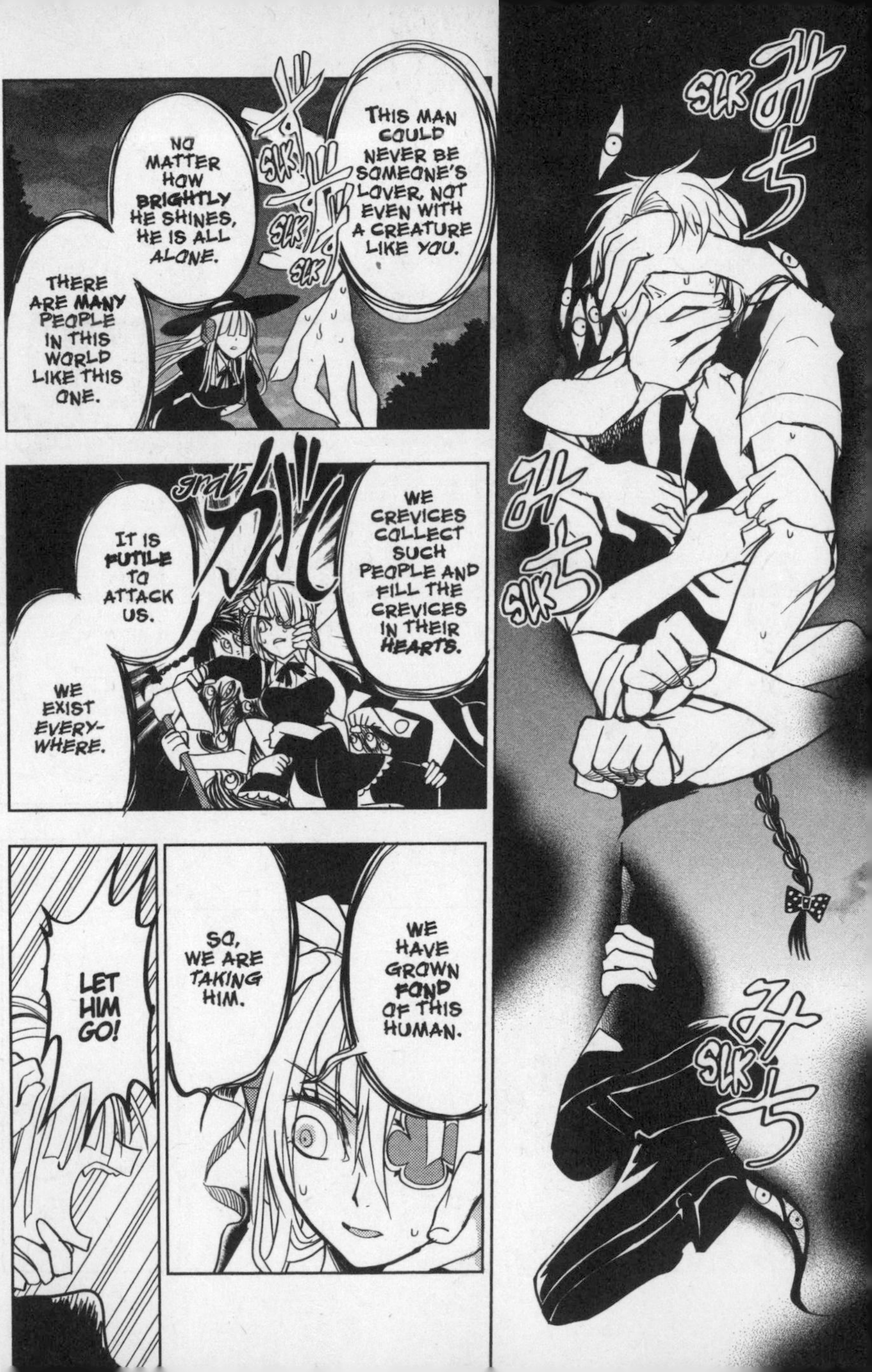
SLK
SLK
SLK
THIS MAN COULD NEVER BE SOMEONE'S LOVER, NOT EVEN WITH A CREATURE LIKE YOU.
SLK
SLK
SLK
NO MATTER HOW BRIGHTLY HE SHINES, HE IS ALL ALONE.
THERE ARE MANY PEOPLE IN THIS WORLD LIKE THIS ONE.
WE CREVICES COLLECT SUCH PEOPLE AND FILL THE CREVICES IN THEIR HEARTS.
grab
IT IS FUTILE TO ATTACK US.
WE EXIST EVERY-WHERE.
WE HAVE GROWN FOND OF THIS HUMAN.
SO, WE ARE TAKING HIM.
LET HIM GO!

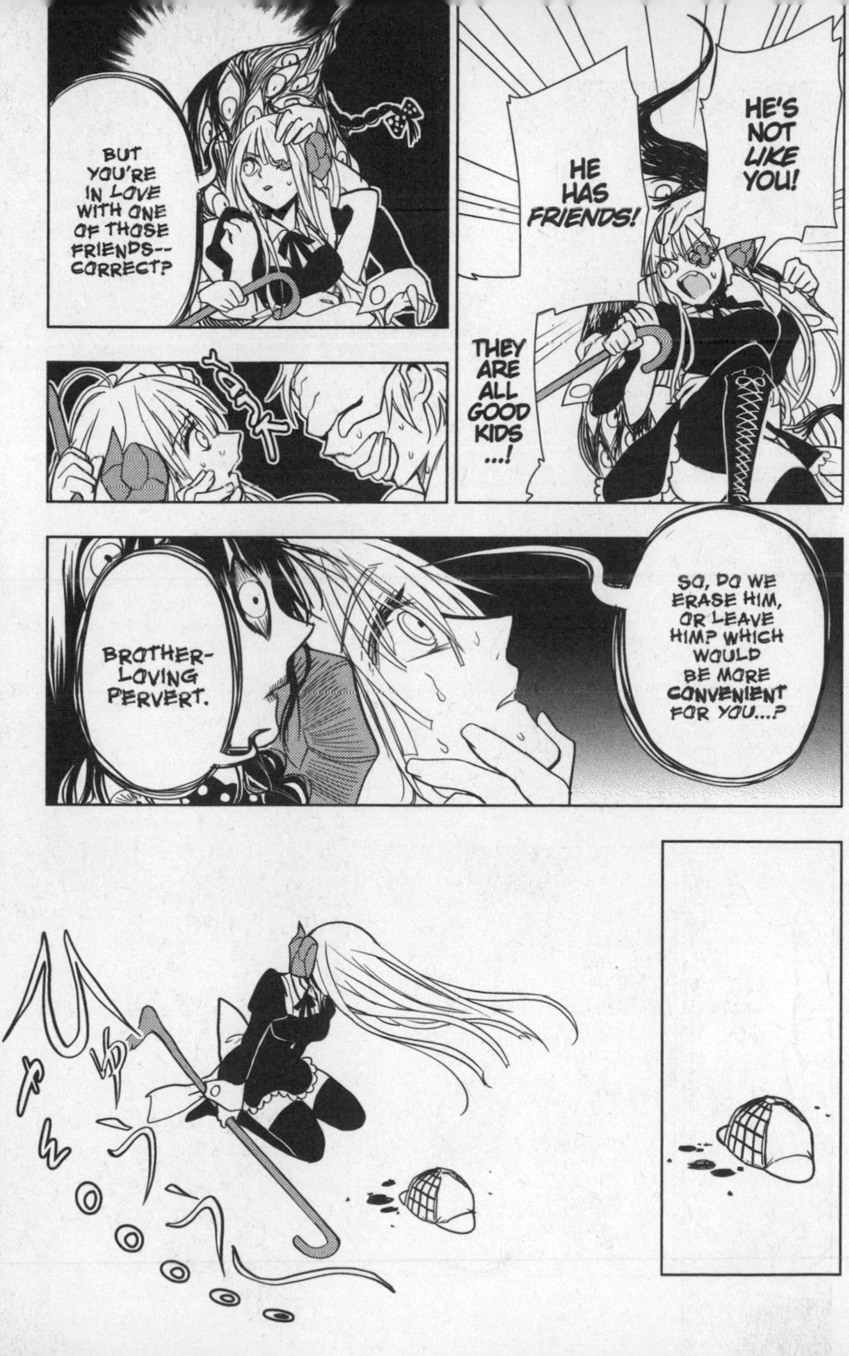
HE'S NOT LIKE YOU!
HE HAS FRIENDS!
THEY ARE ALL GOOD KIDS ...!
BUT YOU'RE IN LOVE WITH ONE OF THOSE FRIENDS-- CORRECT?
YANK
SO, DO WE ERASE HIM, OR LEAVE HIM? WHICH WOULD BE MORE CONVENIENT FOR YOU...?
BROTHER-LOVING PERVERT.

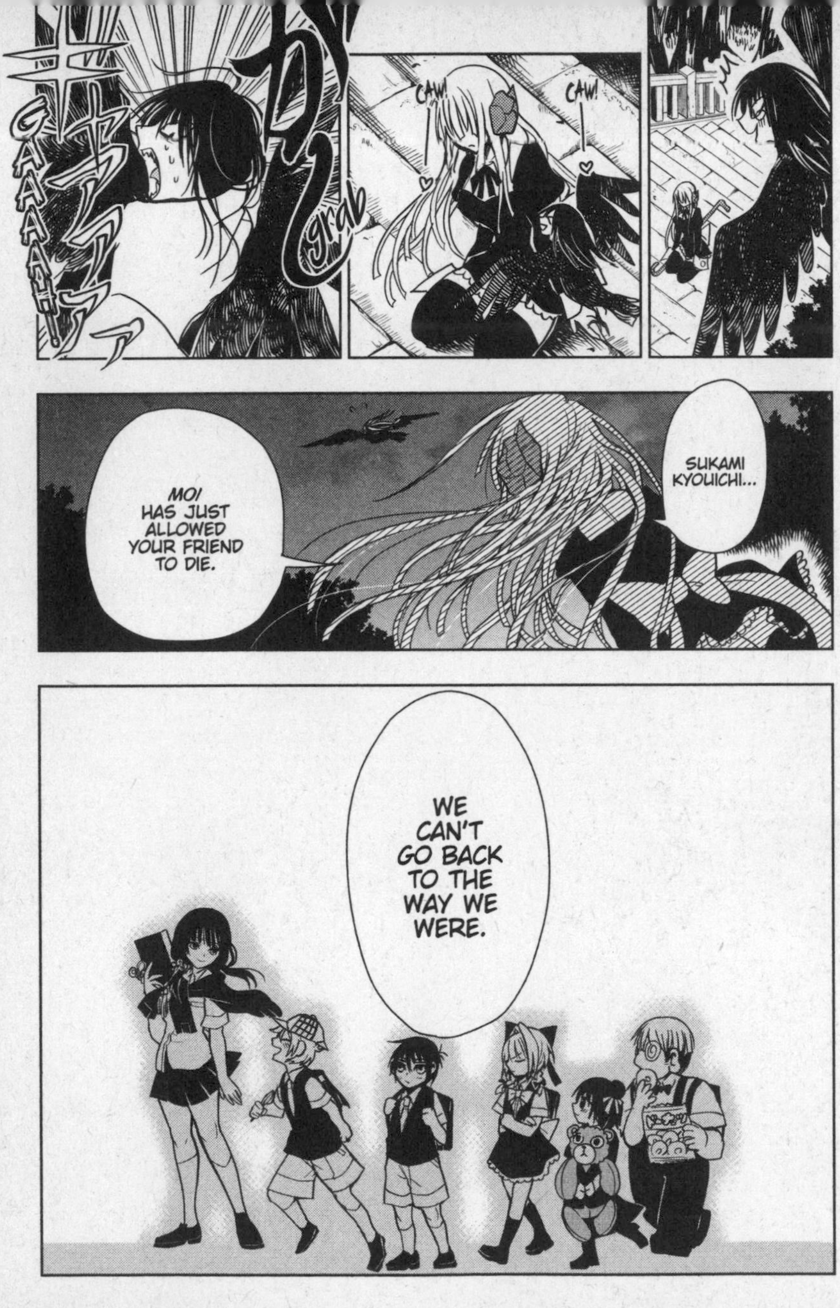
CAW!
CAW!
grab
GAAAAAAH!!
SUKAMI KYOUICHI...
MOI HAS JUST ALLOWED YOUR FRIEND TO DIE.
WE CAN'T GO BACK TO THE WAY WE WERE.

Ghost Diary
カイダンにっき

K a i d a n n i k k i

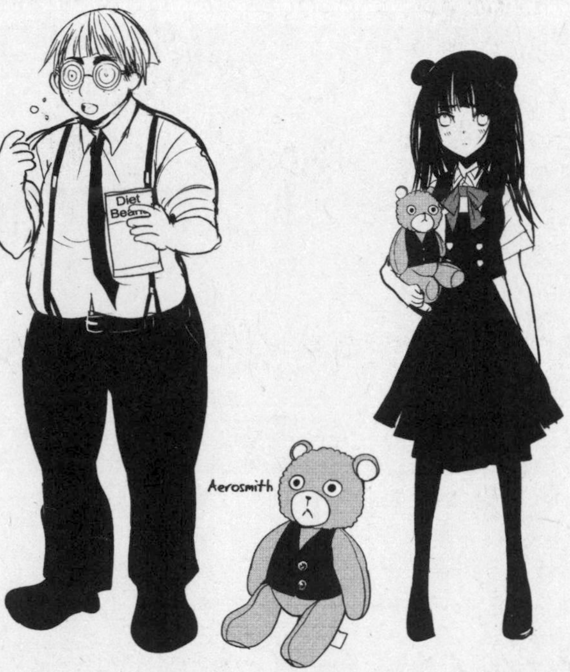
Diet Beans
Aerosmith

The Mascot-Type Occult Club Members Suzukago Kukuri and Onigashima Tatsumi

I wanted the Occult Club to be colorful, so I made their designs pretty strange--but I still think they're both cute. I like these two a lot!

After making Kukuri-chan, I chuckled and thought, "The boys are *sure* to like her"--so I was happy when people told me they thought she was cute.

Since this is an occultic column, I thought I'd bring in an occult topic. I hear that dolls or plush-toys that get played with for a long time will eventually house a human soul. Famous ghost stories with dolls would include Inagawa Junji-san's "Living Doll" and "Cursed Doll Annabelle," right? Being famous stories, they're deeply interesting, so please look into them.

Since Tatsumi is a gangster's son, here's a story from that world. It's said that people in organized crime or police work don't eat mantis shrimp sushi. The story goes that it's because crustaceans eat drowned corpses that have sunk into the sea. That's not necessarily true, so please eat them without worrying about that. I always pass on eating them, though (ha ha!).

Since many gangster or police insider stories have become urban legends, people interested in that kind of thing may find it worthwhile to check out.

Today's Theme: Suzukago Kukuri and Onigashima Tatsumi

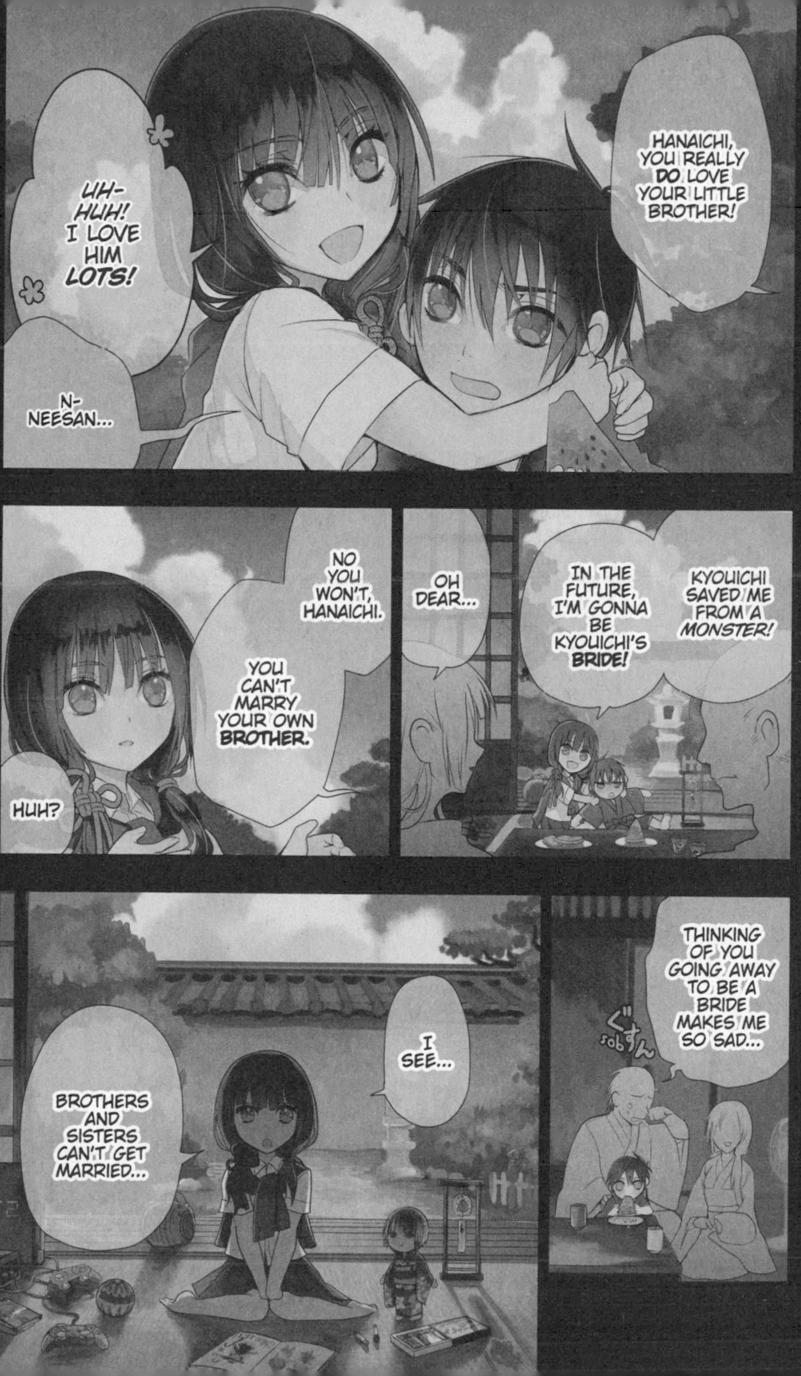
HANAICHI, YOU REALLY DO LOVE YOUR LITTLE BROTHER!
UH-HUH! I LOVE HIM LOTS!
N-NEESAN...
KYOUICHI SAVED ME FROM A MONSTER!
IN THE FUTURE, I'M GONNA BE KYOUICHI'S BRIDE!
OH DEAR...
NO YOU WON'T, HANAICHI.
YOU CAN'T MARRY YOUR OWN BROTHER.
HUH?
THINKING OF YOU GOING AWAY TO BE A BRIDE MAKES ME SO SAD...
ぐすん sob
I SEE...
BROTHERS AND SISTERS CAN'T GET MARRIED...

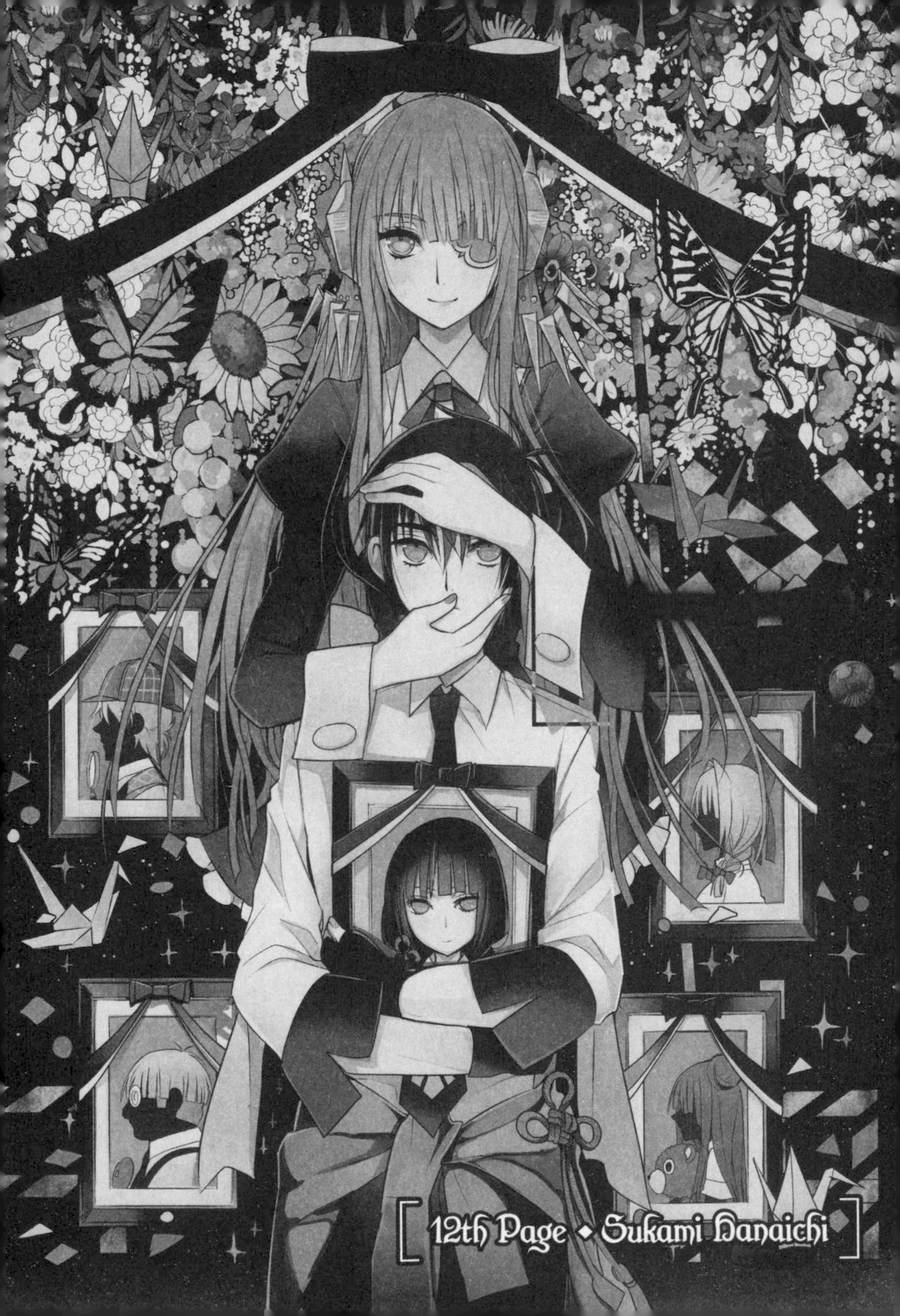
12th Page ◆ Sukami Hanaichi

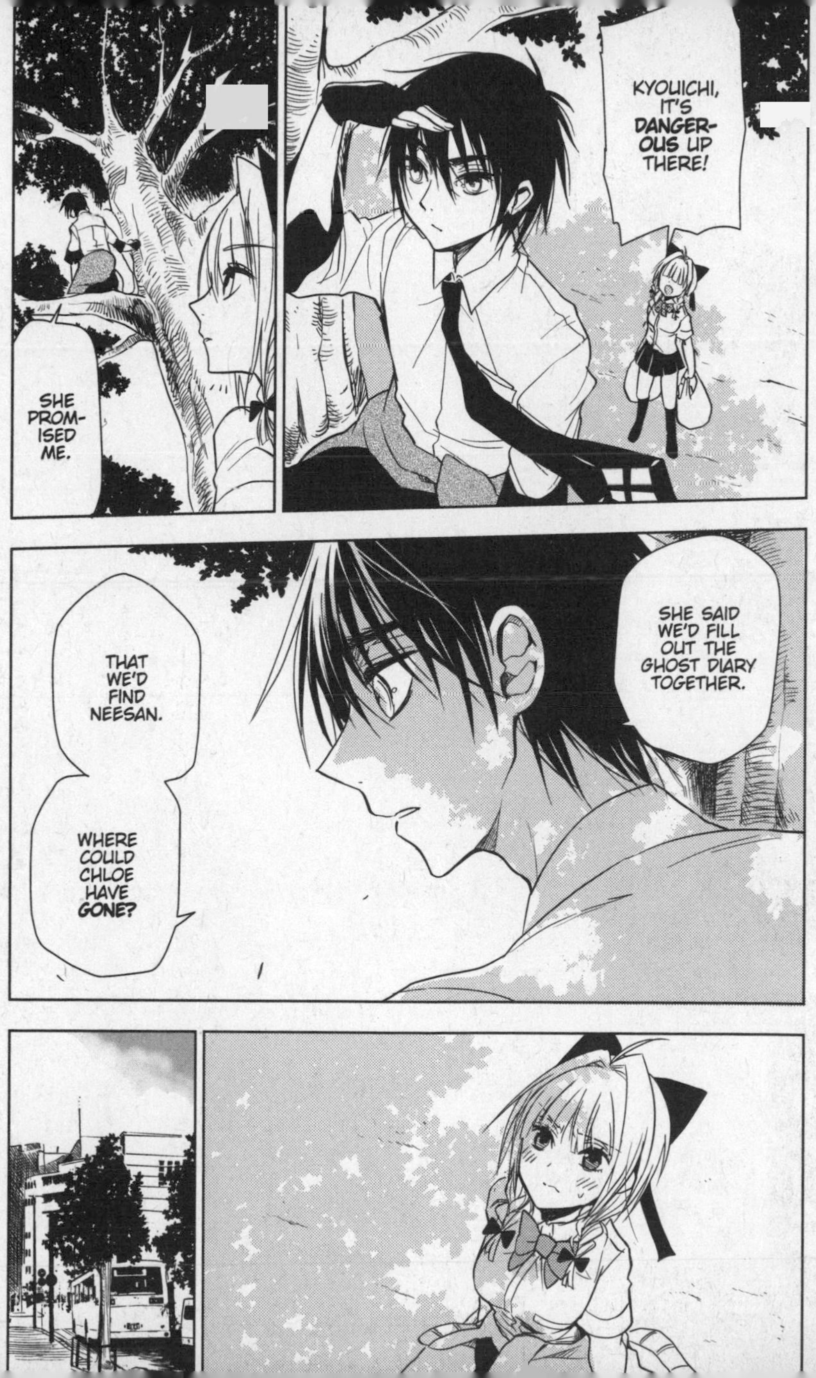
KYOUICHI, IT'S DANGER-OUS UP THERE!
SHE PROM-ISED ME.
SHE SAID WE'D FILL OUT THE GHOST DIARY TOGETHER.
THAT WE'D FIND NEESAN.
WHERE COULD CHLOE HAVE GONE?

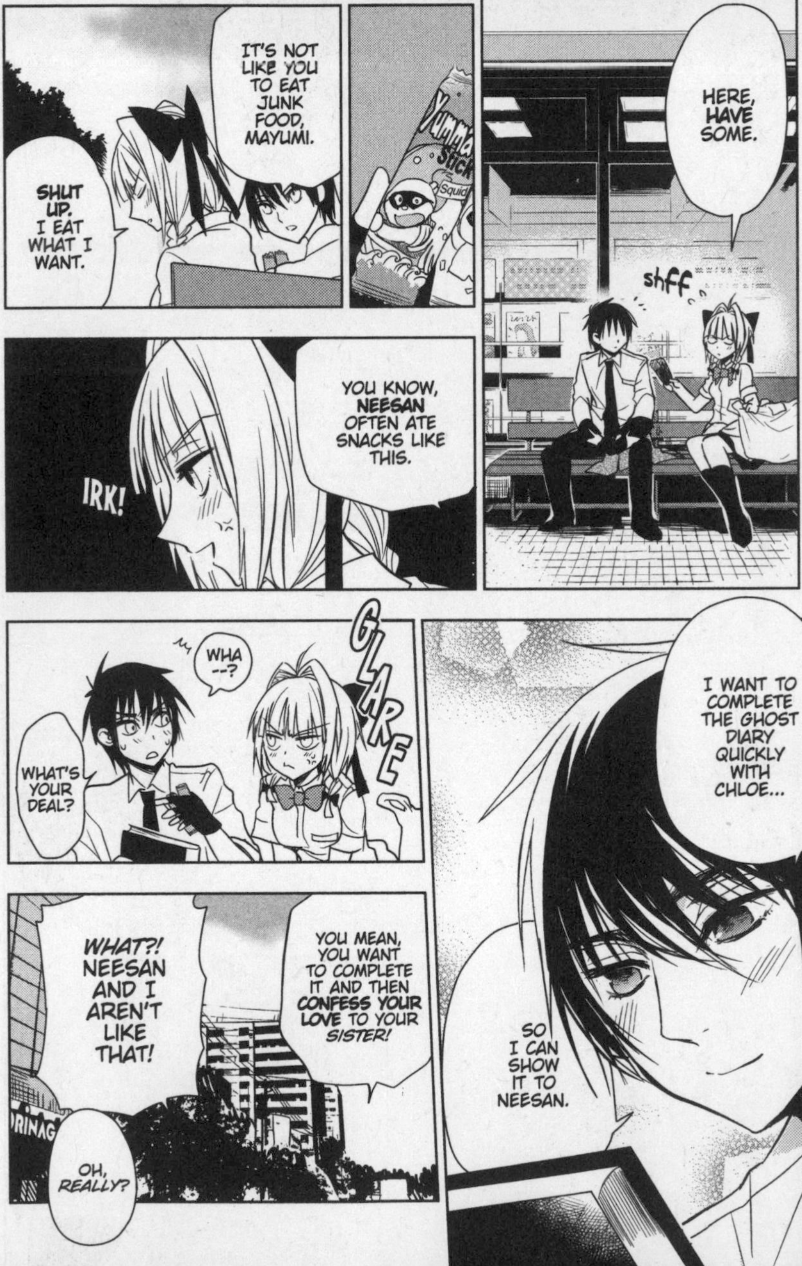
HERE, HAVE SOME.
shff
IT'S NOT LIKE YOU TO EAT JUNK FOOD, MAYUMI.
SHUT UP. I EAT WHAT I WANT.
YOU KNOW, NEESAN OFTEN ATE SNACKS LIKE THIS.
IRK!
I WANT TO COMPLETE THE GHOST DIARY QUICKLY WITH CHLOE...
SO I CAN SHOW IT TO NEESAN.
GLARE
WHA--?
WHAT'S YOUR DEAL?
YOU MEAN, YOU WANT TO COMPLETE IT AND THEN CONFESS YOUR LOVE TO YOUR SISTER!
WHAT?! NEESAN AND I AREN'T LIKE THAT!
OH, REALLY?

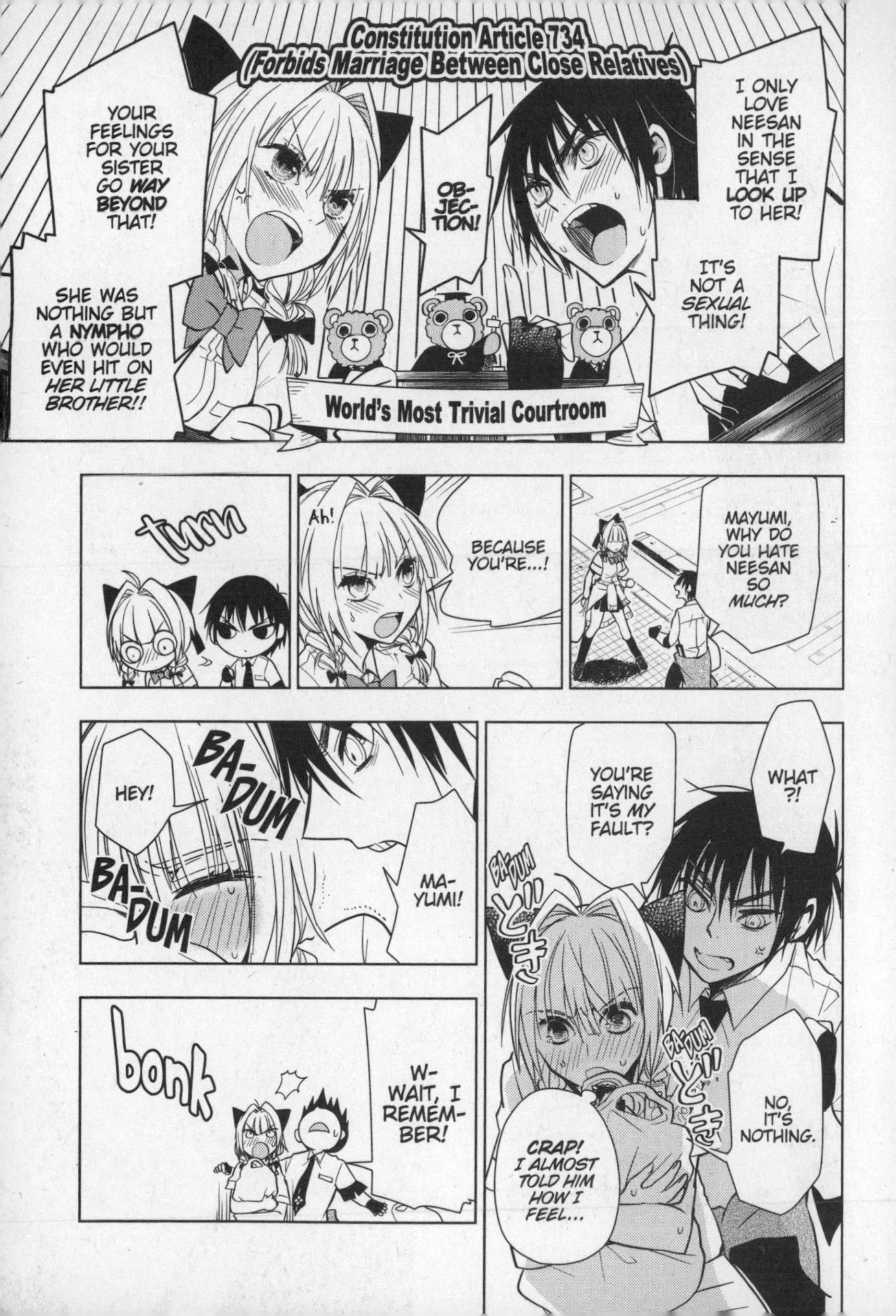
Constitution Article 734 (Forbids Marriage Between Close Relatives)
I ONLY LOVE NEESAN IN THE SENSE THAT I LOOK UP TO HER!
IT'S NOT A SEXUAL THING!
OBJECTION!
YOUR FEELINGS FOR YOUR SISTER GO WAY BEYOND THAT!
SHE WAS NOTHING BUT A NYMPHO WHO WOULD EVEN HIT ON HER LITTLE BROTHER!!
World's Most Trivial Courtroom
MAYUMI, WHY DO YOU HATE NEESAN SO MUCH?
Ah!
BECAUSE YOU'RE...!
turn
WHAT?!
YOU'RE SAYING IT'S MY FAULT?
BA-DUM どき
BA-DUM どき
NO, IT'S NOTHING.
CRAP! I ALMOST TOLD HIM HOW I FEEL...
HEY!
BA-DUM
BA-DUM
MA-YUMI!
W-WAIT, I REMEMBER!
bonk

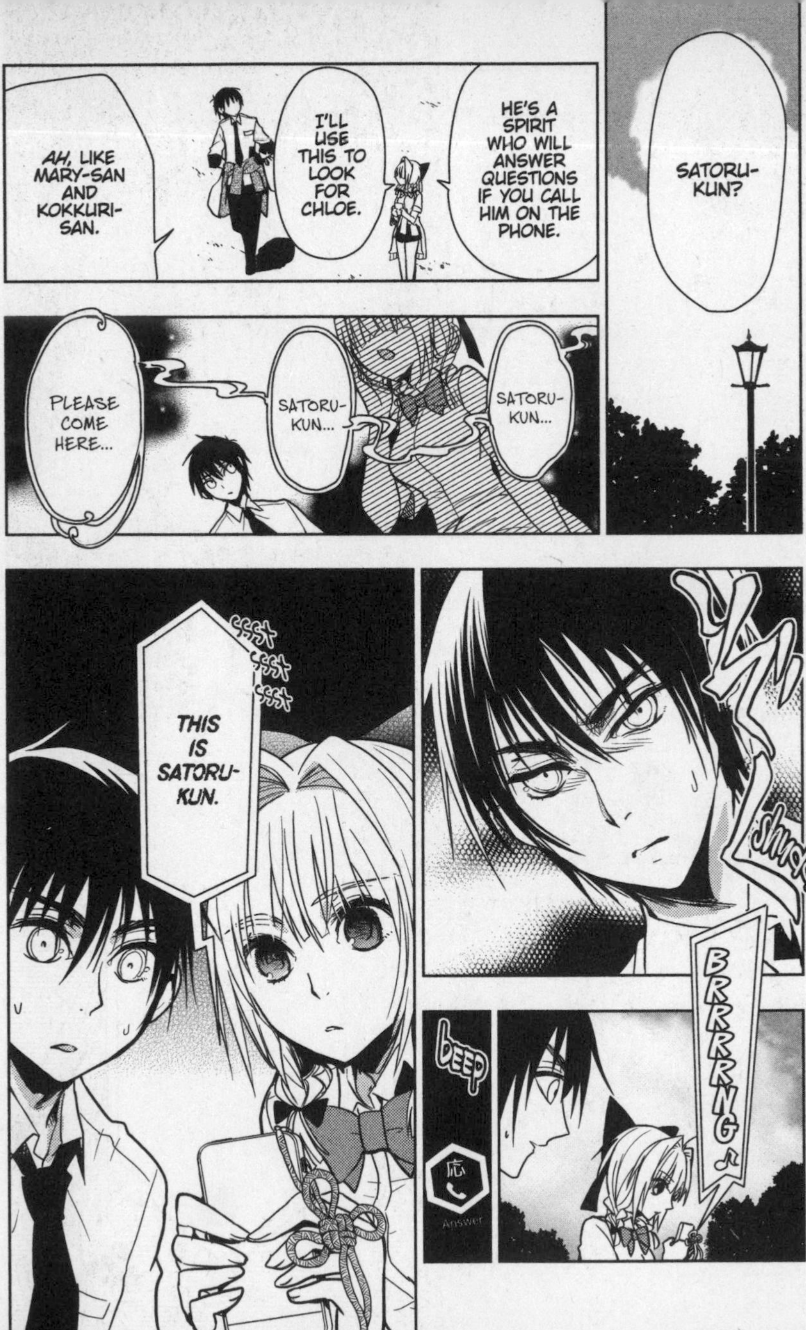
SATORU-KUN?
HE'S A SPIRIT WHO WILL ANSWER QUESTIONS IF YOU CALL HIM ON THE PHONE.
I'LL USE THIS TO LOOK FOR CHLOE.
AH, LIKE MARY-SAN AND KOKKURI-SAN.
SATORU-KUN...
SATORU-KUN...
PLEASE COME HERE...
shudder
BRRRRNG
beep
応
Answer
ssst
ssst
ssst
THIS IS SATORU-KUN.

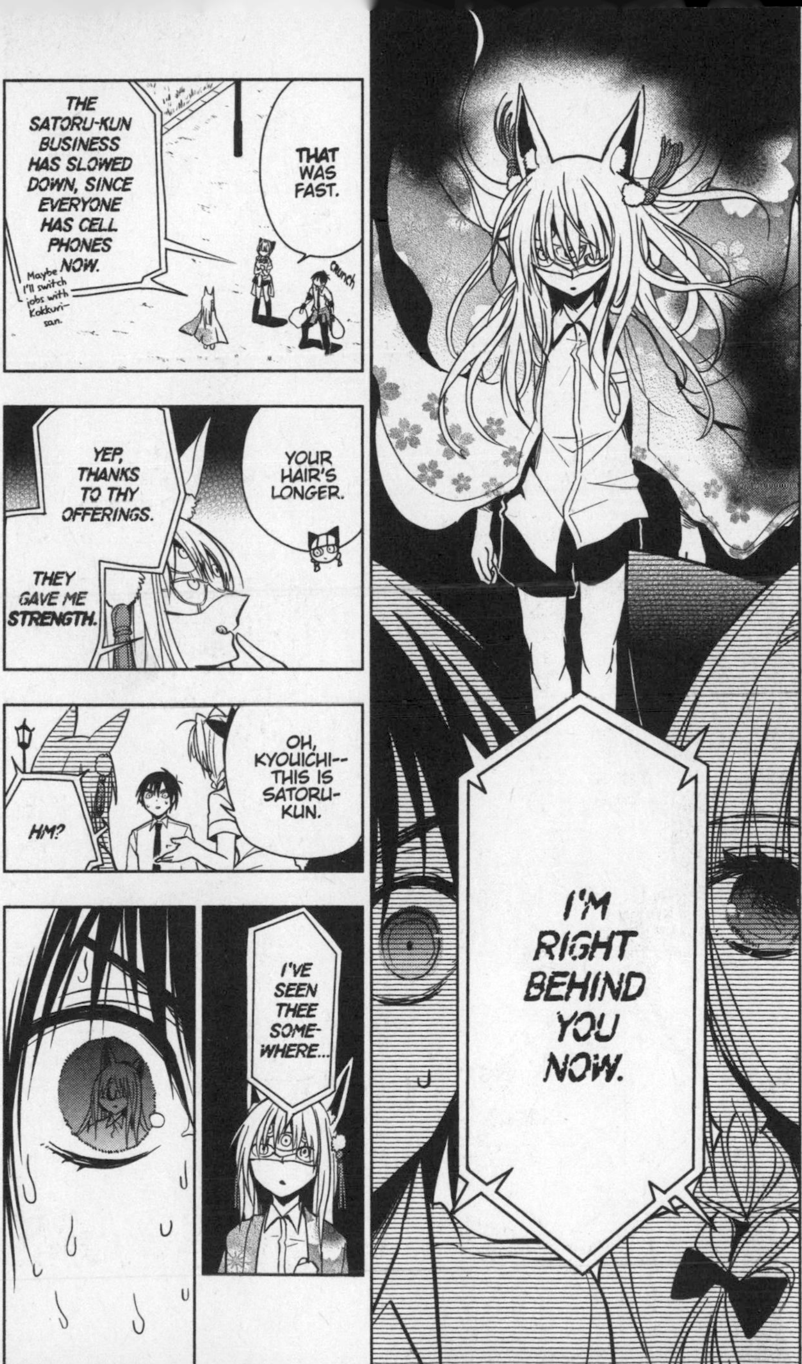
THAT WAS FAST.
THE SATORU-KUN BUSINESS HAS SLOWED DOWN, SINCE EVERYONE HAS CELL PHONES NOW.
Maybe I'll switch jobs with Kokkuri-san.
Crunch
YOUR HAIR'S LONGER.
YEP, THANKS TO THY OFFERINGS.
THEY GAVE ME STRENGTH.
OH, KYOUICHI-- THIS IS SATORU-KUN.
HM?
I'VE SEEN THEE SOMEWHERE...
I'M RIGHT BEHIND YOU NOW.

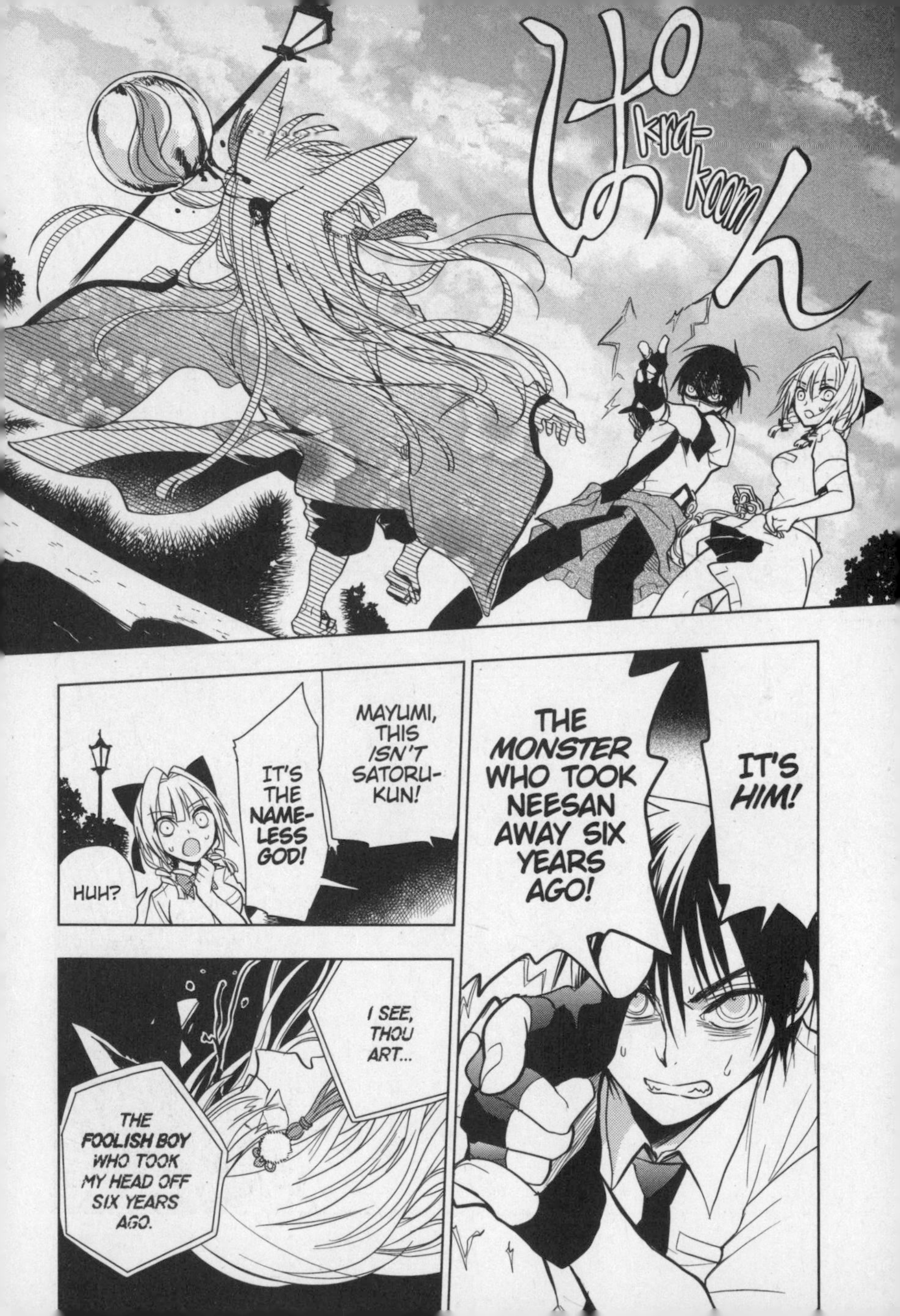

kra-koom
IT'S HIM!
THE MONSTER WHO TOOK NEESAN AWAY SIX YEARS AGO!
MAYUMI, THIS ISN'T SATORU-KUN!
IT'S THE NAMELESS GOD!
HUH?
I SEE, THOU ART...
THE FOOLISH BOY WHO TOOK MY HEAD OFF SIX YEARS AGO.

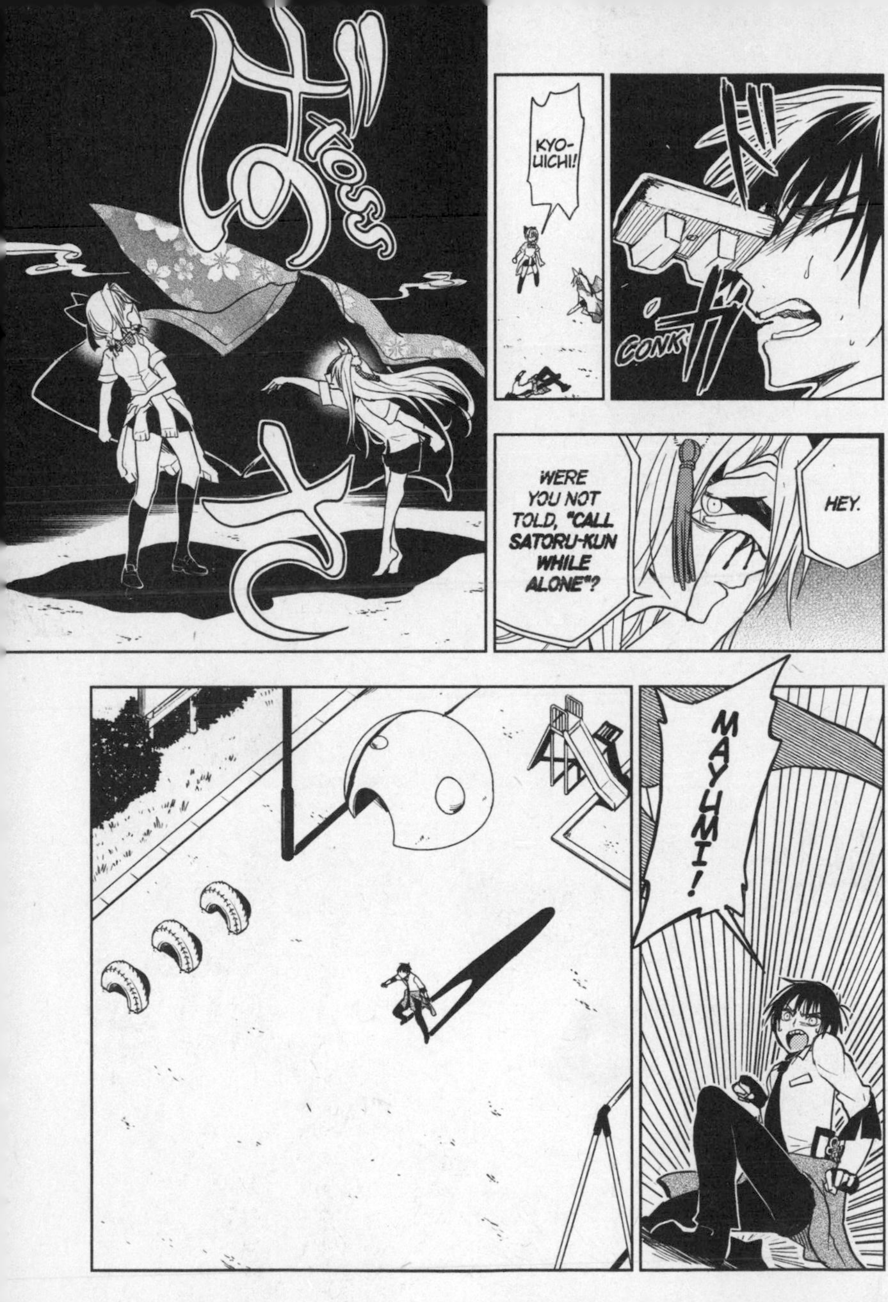
TOSS
CONK
KYO-UICHI!
HEY.
WERE YOU NOT TOLD, "CALL SATORU-KUN WHILE ALONE"?
MAYUMI!

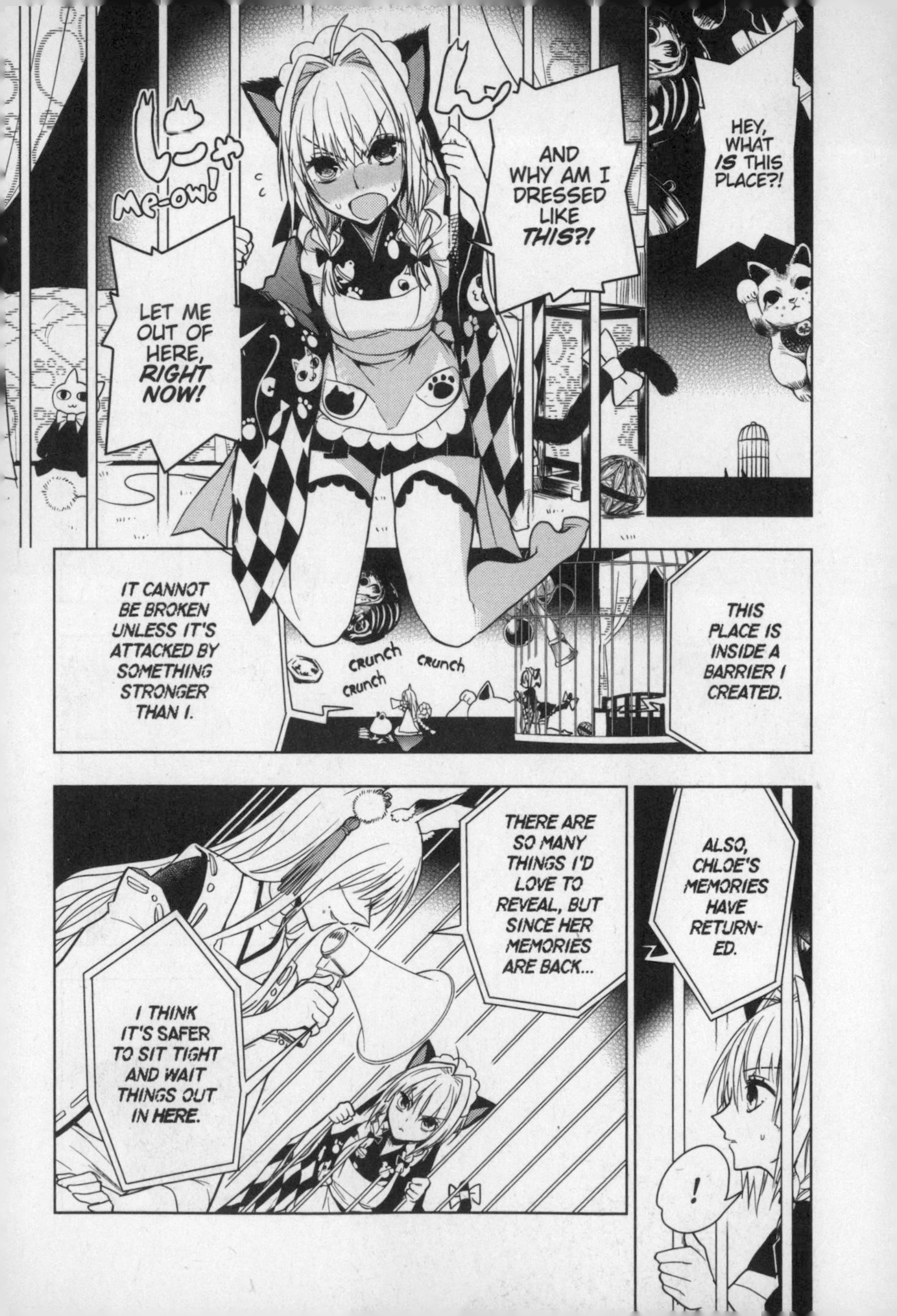
HEY, WHAT *IS* THIS PLACE?!
AND WHY AM I DRESSED LIKE *THIS?!*
Me-ow!
LET ME OUT OF HERE, *RIGHT NOW!*
THIS PLACE IS INSIDE A BARRIER I CREATED.
IT CANNOT BE BROKEN UNLESS IT'S ATTACKED BY SOMETHING STRONGER THAN I.
crunch crunch crunch
ALSO, CHLOE'S MEMORIES HAVE RETURN-ED.
!
THERE ARE SO MANY THINGS I'D LOVE TO REVEAL, BUT SINCE HER MEMORIES ARE BACK...
I THINK IT'S SAFER TO SIT TIGHT AND WAIT THINGS OUT IN HERE.

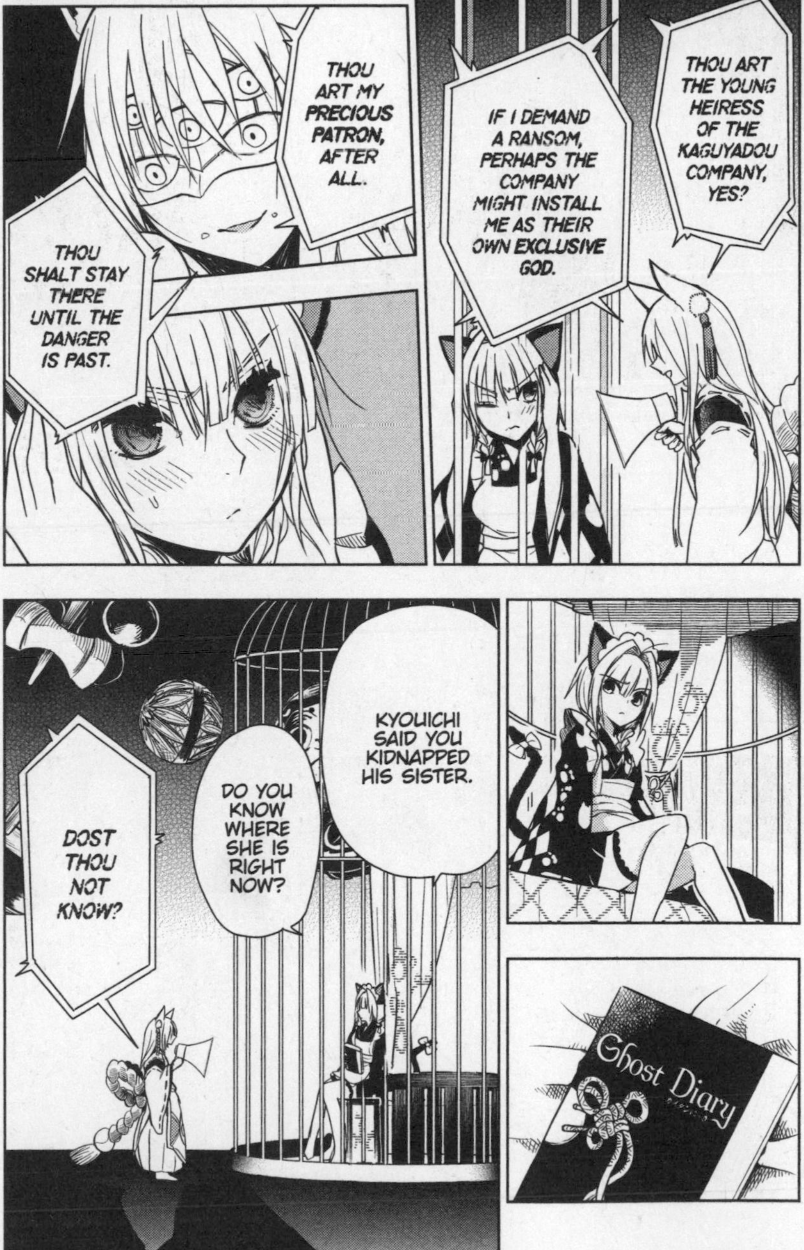

THOU ART THE YOUNG HEIRESS OF THE KAGUYADOU COMPANY, YES?
IF I DEMAND A RANSOM, PERHAPS THE COMPANY MIGHT INSTALL ME AS THEIR OWN EXCLUSIVE GOD.
THOU ART MY PRECIOUS PATRON, AFTER ALL.
THOU SHALT STAY THERE UNTIL THE DANGER IS PAST.
KYOUICHI SAID YOU KIDNAPPED HIS SISTER.
DO YOU KNOW WHERE SHE IS RIGHT NOW?
DOST THOU NOT KNOW?
Ghost Diary

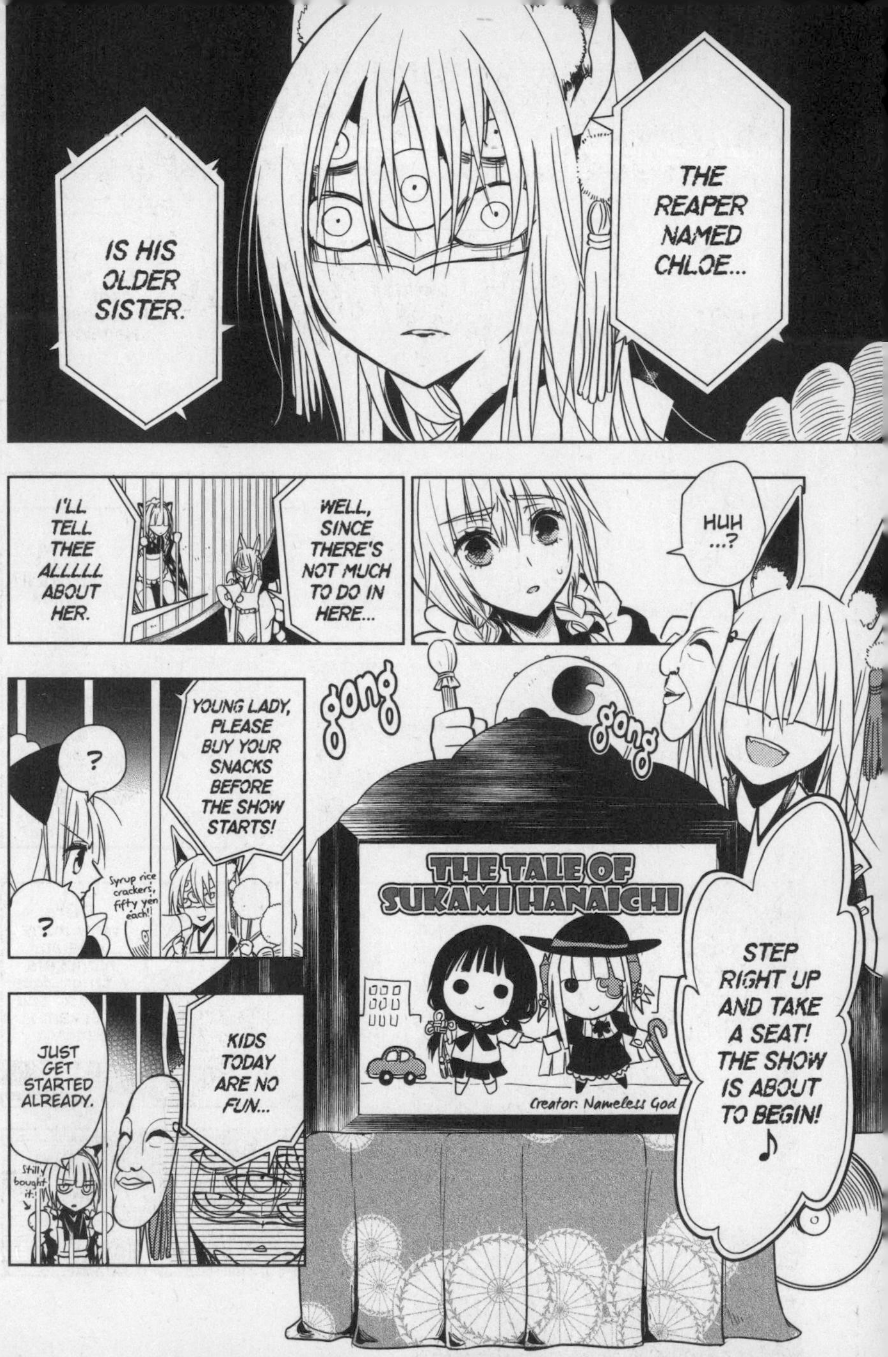
THE REAPER NAMED CHLOE...
IS HIS OLDER SISTER.
HUH ...?
WELL, SINCE THERE'S NOT MUCH TO DO IN HERE...
I'LL TELL THEE ALLLLL ABOUT HER.
gong
gong
THE TALE OF SUKAMI HANAICHI
Creator: Nameless God
STEP RIGHT UP AND TAKE A SEAT! THE SHOW IS ABOUT TO BEGIN! ♪
YOUNG LADY, PLEASE BUY YOUR SNACKS BEFORE THE SHOW STARTS!
?
Syrup rice crackers, fifty yen each!!
?
KIDS TODAY ARE NO FUN...
JUST GET STARTED ALREADY.
Still bought it.

THE TALE OF SUKAMI HANAICHI

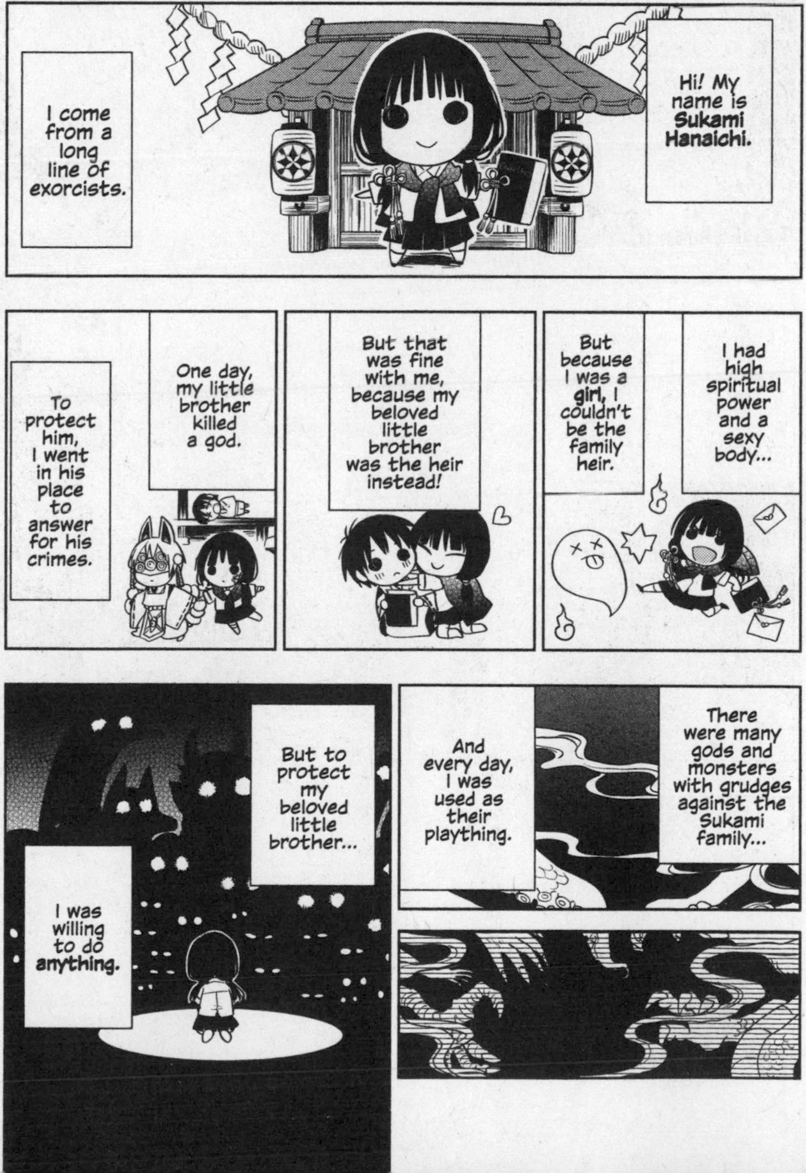
Hi! My name is Sukami Hanaichi.
I come from a long line of exorcists.
I had high spiritual power and a sexy body...
But because I was a girl, I couldn't be the family heir.
But that was fine with me, because my beloved little brother was the heir instead!
One day, my little brother killed a god.
To protect him, I went in his place to answer for his crimes.
There were many gods and monsters with grudges against the Sukami family...
And every day, I was used as their plaything.
But to protect my beloved little brother...
I was willing to do anything.

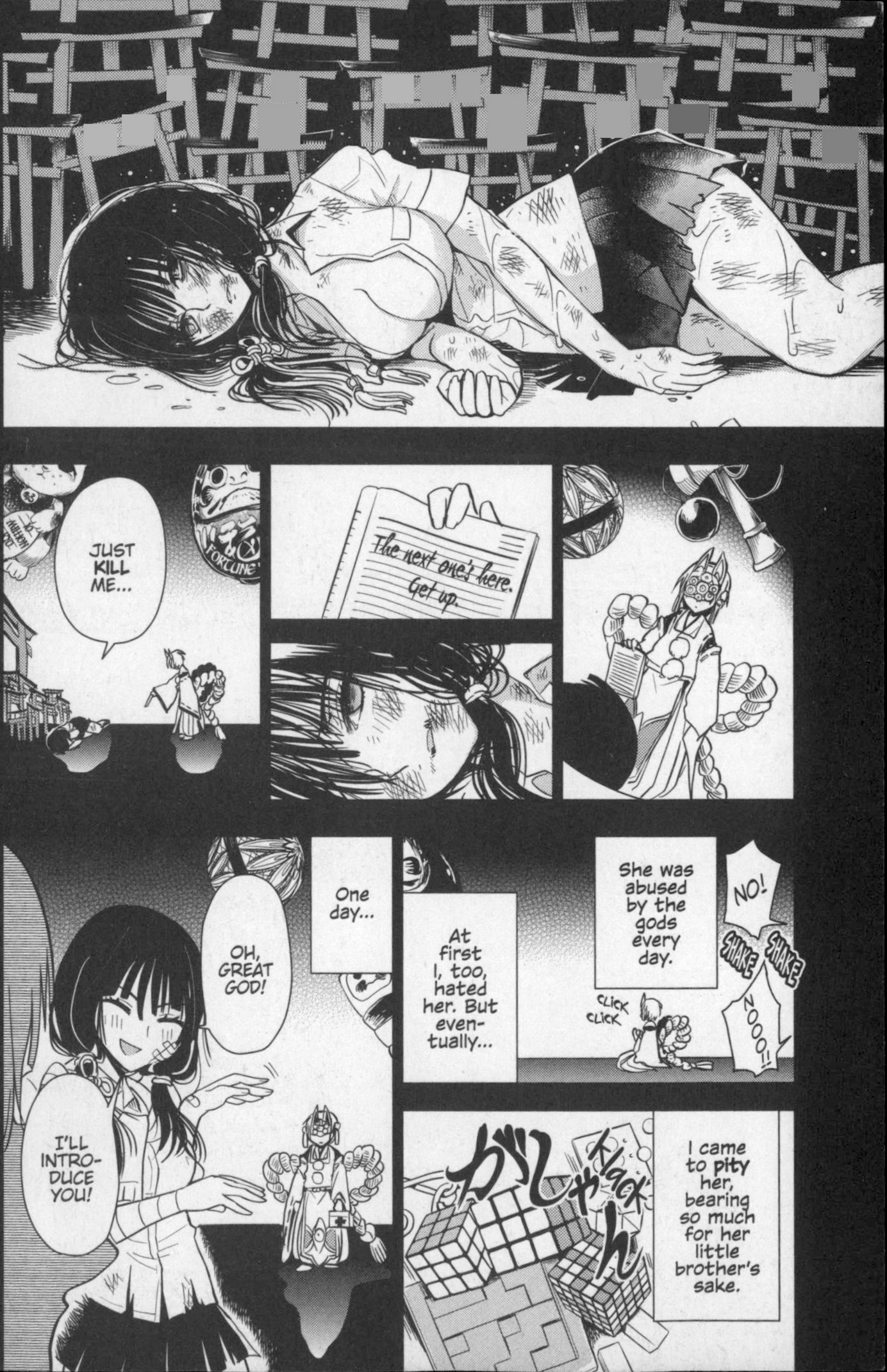
The next one's here. Get up.
JUST KILL ME...
FORTUNE
She was abused by the gods every day.
NO!
SHAKE
SHAKE
NOOOO!!
CLICK CLICK
At first I, too, hated her. But eventually...
I came to pity her, bearing so much for her little brother's sake.
Klack
One day...
OH, GREAT GOD!
I'LL INTRODUCE YOU!

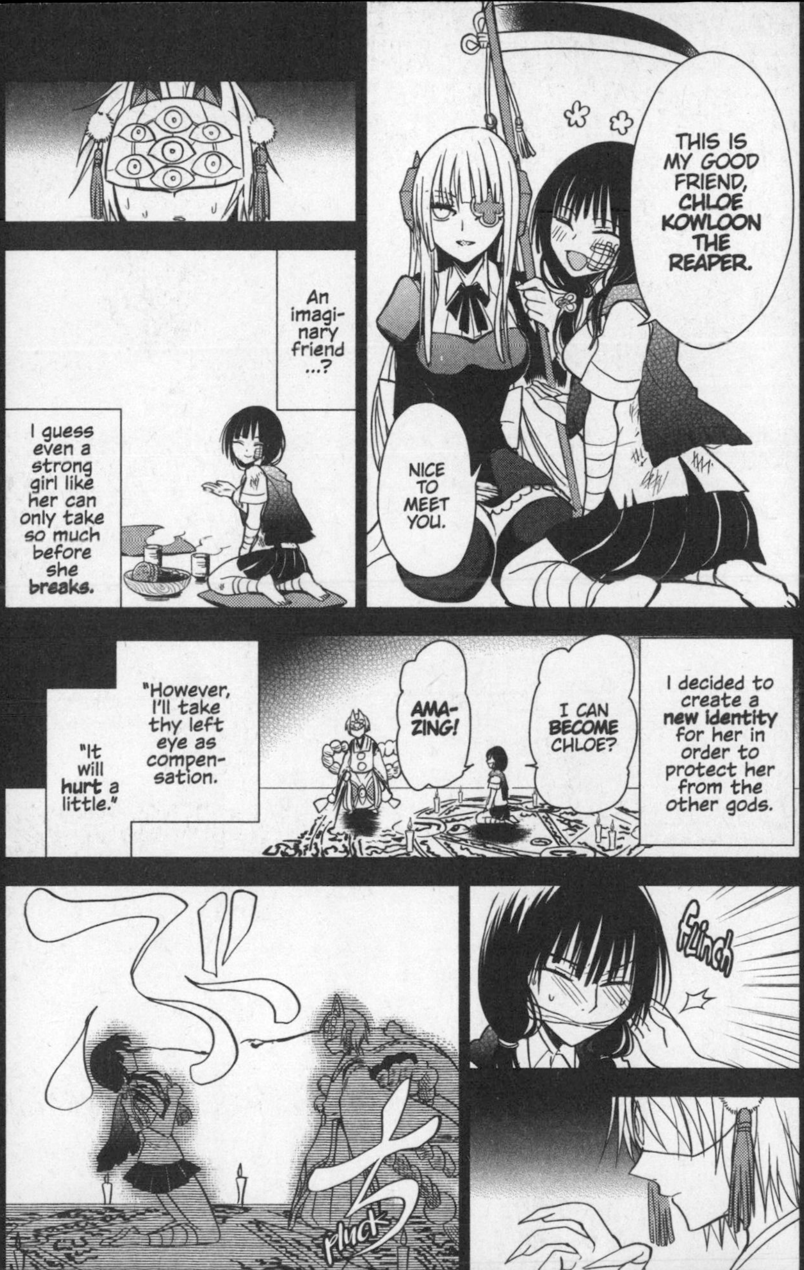
THIS IS MY GOOD FRIEND, CHLOE KOWLOON THE REAPER.
NICE TO MEET YOU.
An imaginary friend ...?
I guess even a strong girl like her can only take so much before she breaks.
I decided to create a new identity for her in order to protect her from the other gods.
I CAN BECOME CHLOE?
AMA-ZING!
"However, I'll take thy left eye as compensation.
"It will hurt a little."
flinch
pluck

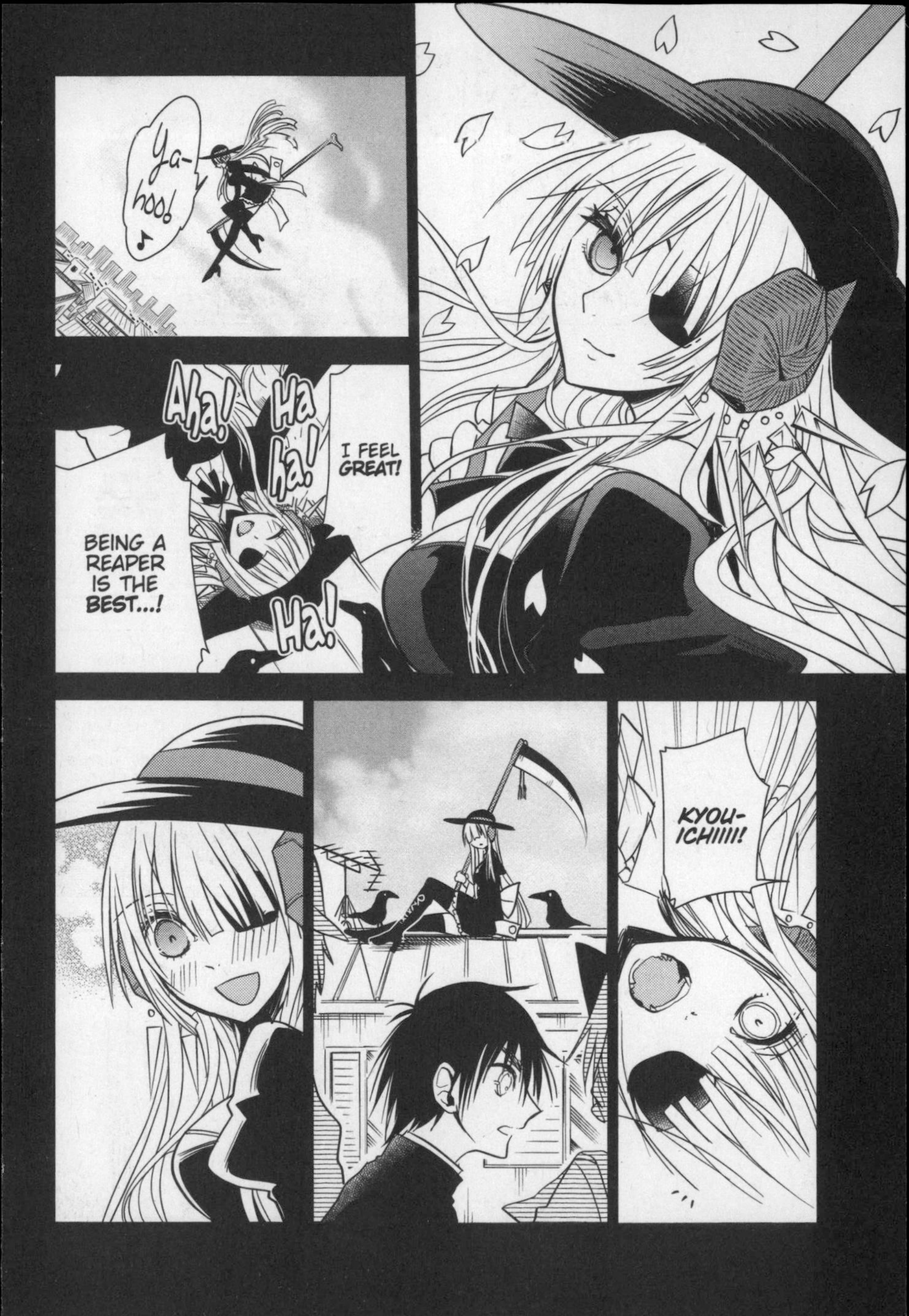
Ya-hoo! ♪
Aha! Ha ha! Ha!
I FEEL GREAT!
BEING A REAPER IS THE BEST...!
KYOU-ICHIIIII!

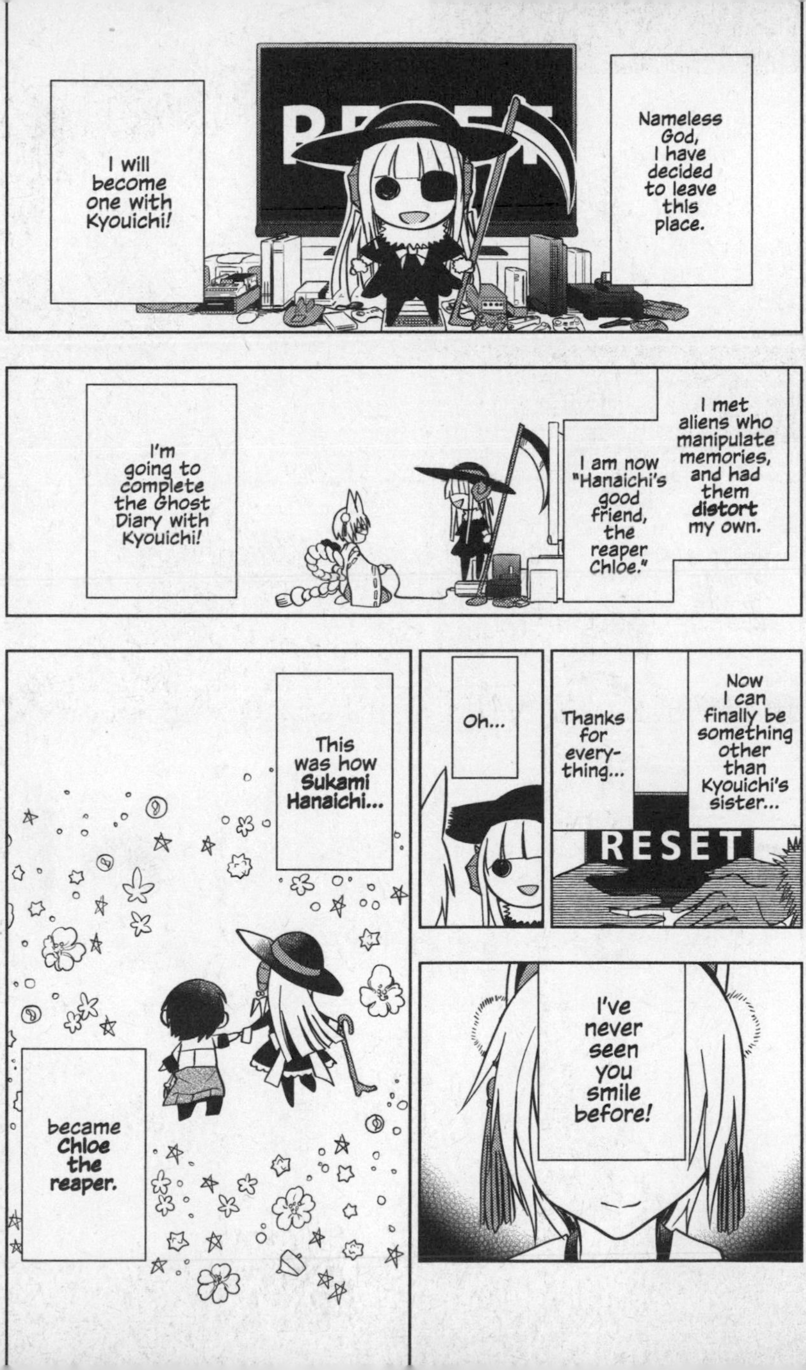
Nameless God, I have decided to leave this place.
I will become one with Kyouichi!
I met aliens who manipulate memories, and had them distort my own.
I am now "Hanaichi's good friend, the reaper Chloe."
I'm going to complete the Ghost Diary with Kyouichi!
Now I can finally be something other than Kyouichi's sister...
Thanks for every-thing...
RESET
Oh...
I've never seen you smile before!
This was how Sukami Hanaichi...
became Chloe the reaper.

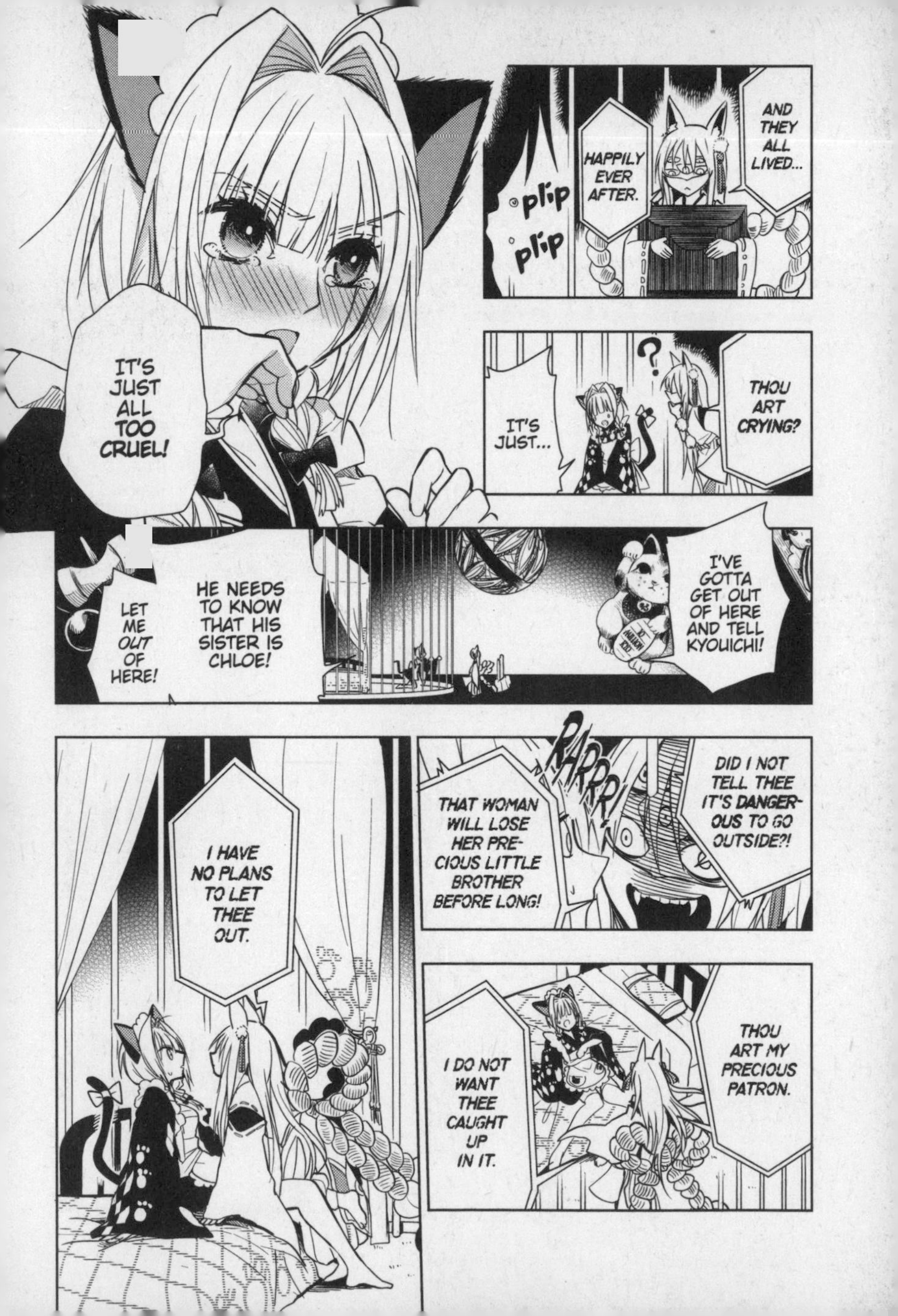
AND THEY ALL LIVED...
HAPPILY EVER AFTER.
plip
plip
THOU ART CRYING?
IT'S JUST...
IT'S JUST ALL TOO CRUEL!
I'VE GOTTA GET OUT OF HERE AND TELL KYOUICHI!
HE NEEDS TO KNOW THAT HIS SISTER IS CHLOE!
LET ME OUT OF HERE!
RARRR!
DID I NOT TELL THEE IT'S DANGER-OUS TO GO OUTSIDE?!
THAT WOMAN WILL LOSE HER PRE-CIOUS LITTLE BROTHER BEFORE LONG!
THOU ART MY PRECIOUS PATRON.
I DO NOT WANT THEE CAUGHT UP IN IT.
I HAVE NO PLANS TO LET THEE OUT.

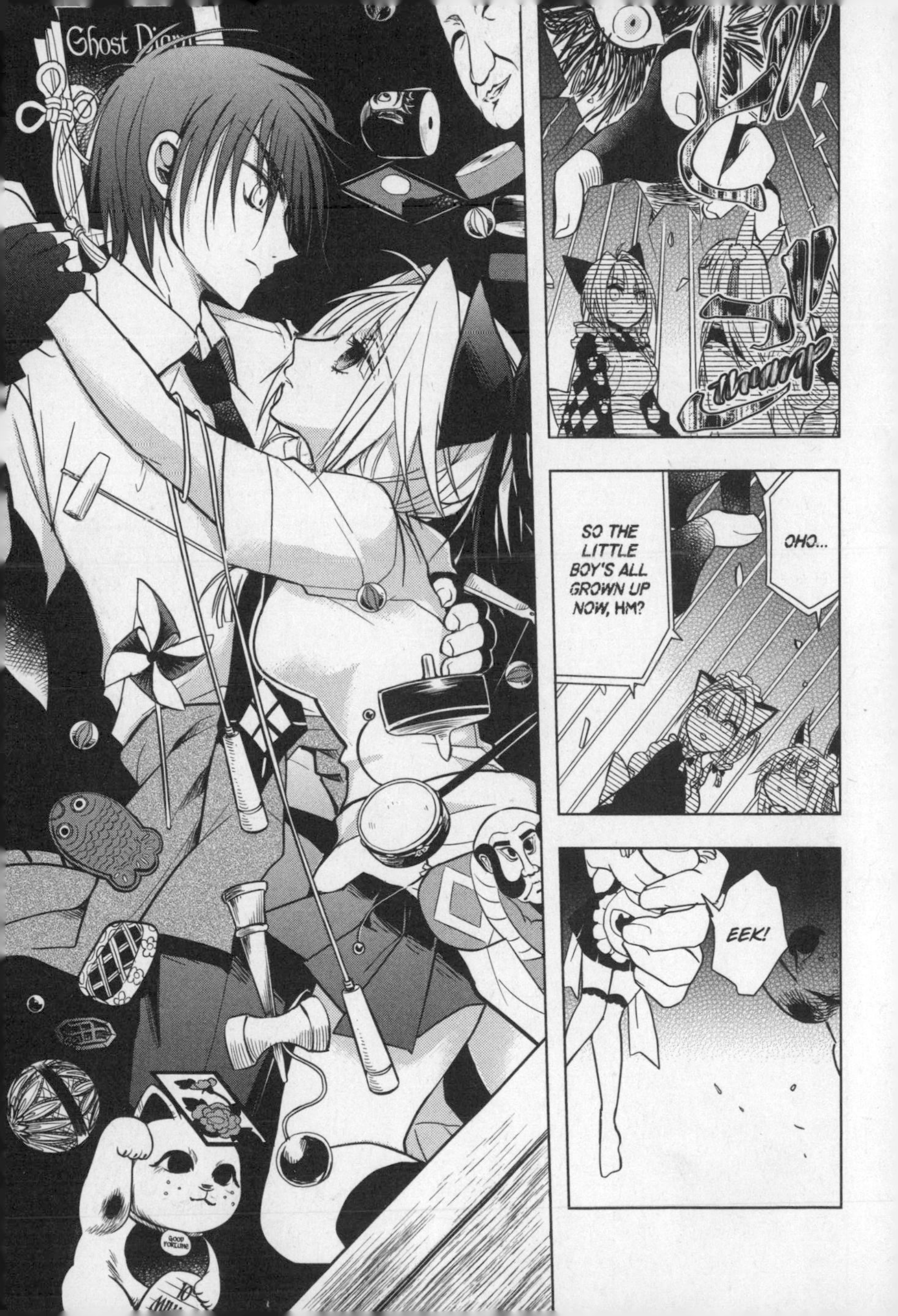

THUMP
OHO...
SO THE LITTLE BOY'S ALL GROWN UP NOW, HM?
EEK!
Ghost Diar
GOOD FORTUNE

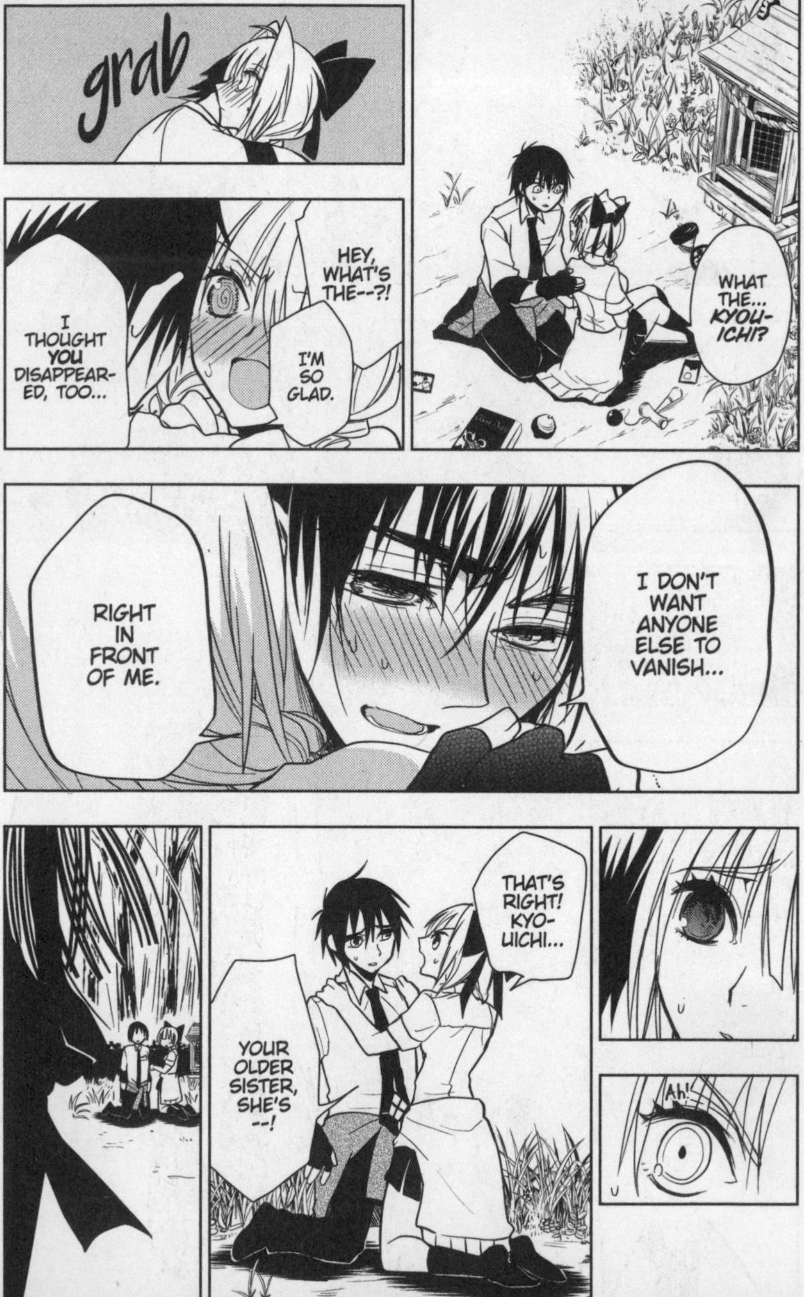
WHAT THE... KYOU-ICHI?
grab
HEY, WHAT'S THE--?!
I'M SO GLAD.
I THOUGHT YOU DISAPPEARED, TOO...
I DON'T WANT ANYONE ELSE TO VANISH...
RIGHT IN FRONT OF ME.
Ah!
THAT'S RIGHT! KYOU-ICHI...
YOUR OLDER SISTER, SHE'S --!

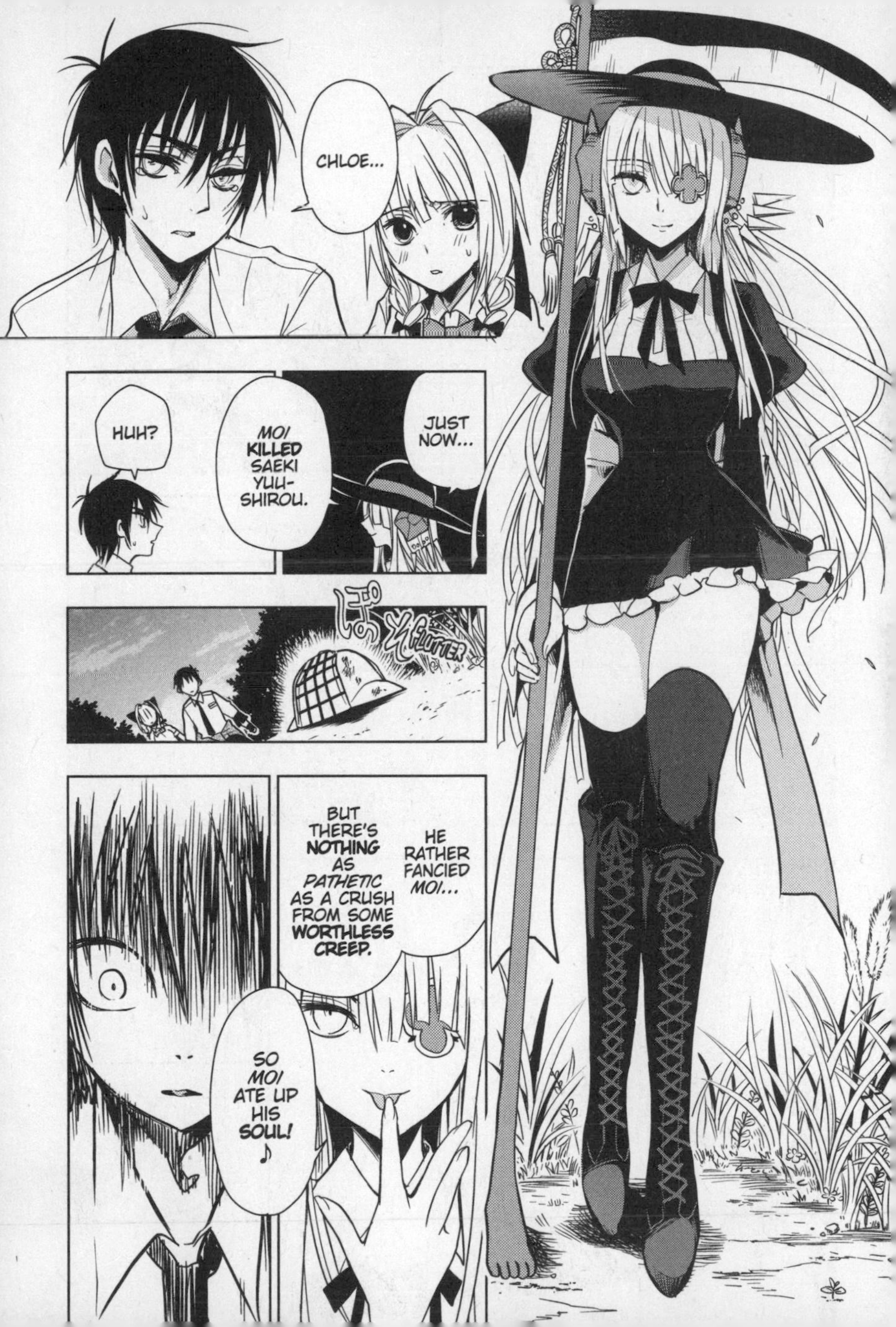
CHLOE...
JUST NOW...
MOI KILLED SAEKI YUU-SHIROU.
HUH?
ぽとっ FLUTTER
HE RATHER FANCIED MOI...
BUT THERE'S NOTHING AS PATHETIC AS A CRUSH FROM SOME WORTHLESS CREEP.
SO MOI ATE UP HIS SOUL! ♪

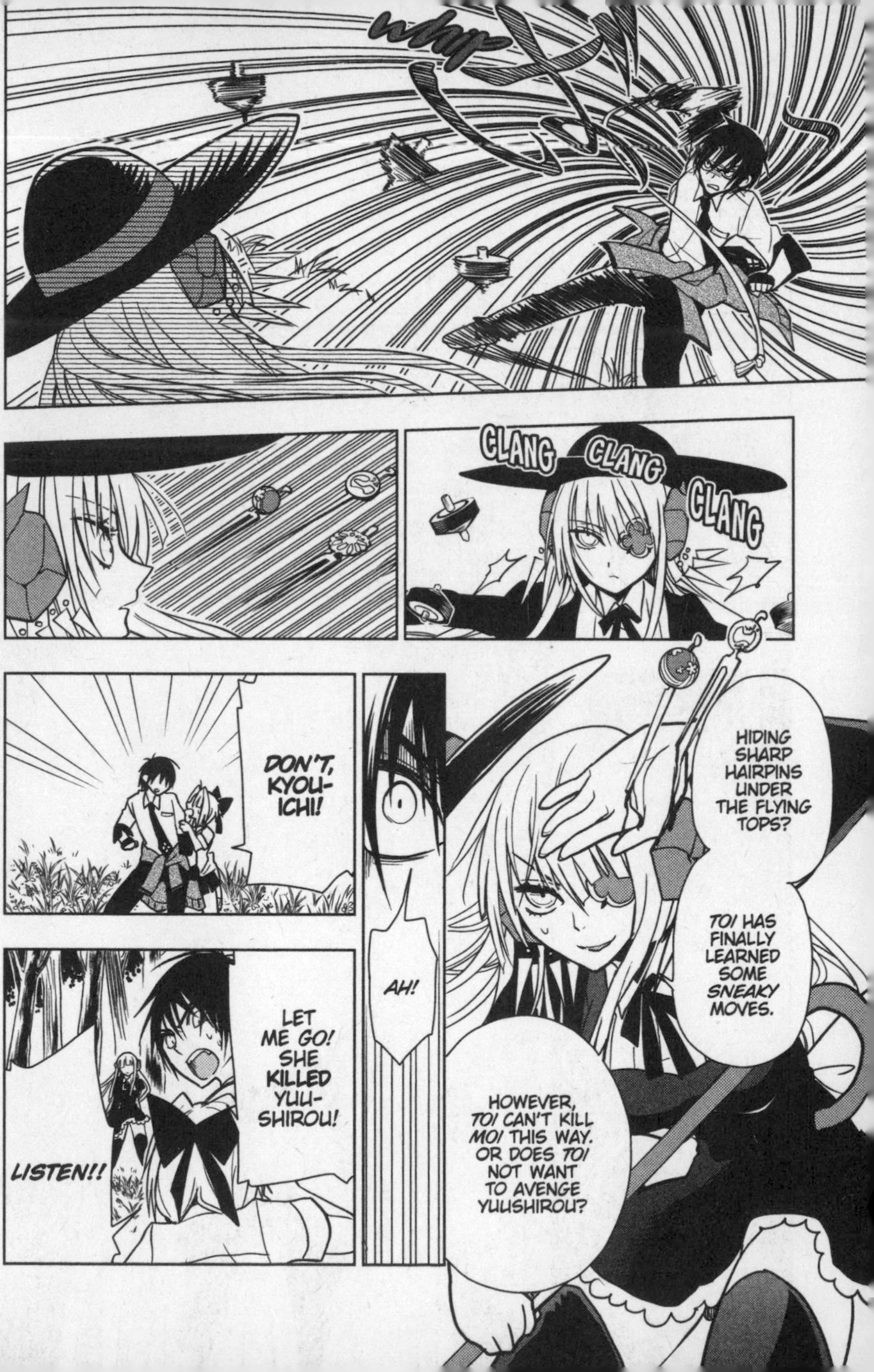

whip
CLANG
CLANG
CLANG
HIDING SHARP HAIRPINS UNDER THE FLYING TOPS?
TOI HAS FINALLY LEARNED SOME SNEAKY MOVES.
HOWEVER, TOI CAN'T KILL MOI THIS WAY. OR DOES TOI NOT WANT TO AVENGE YUUSHIROU?
AH!
DON'T, KYOU-ICHI!
LET ME GO! SHE KILLED YUU-SHIROU!
LISTEN!!

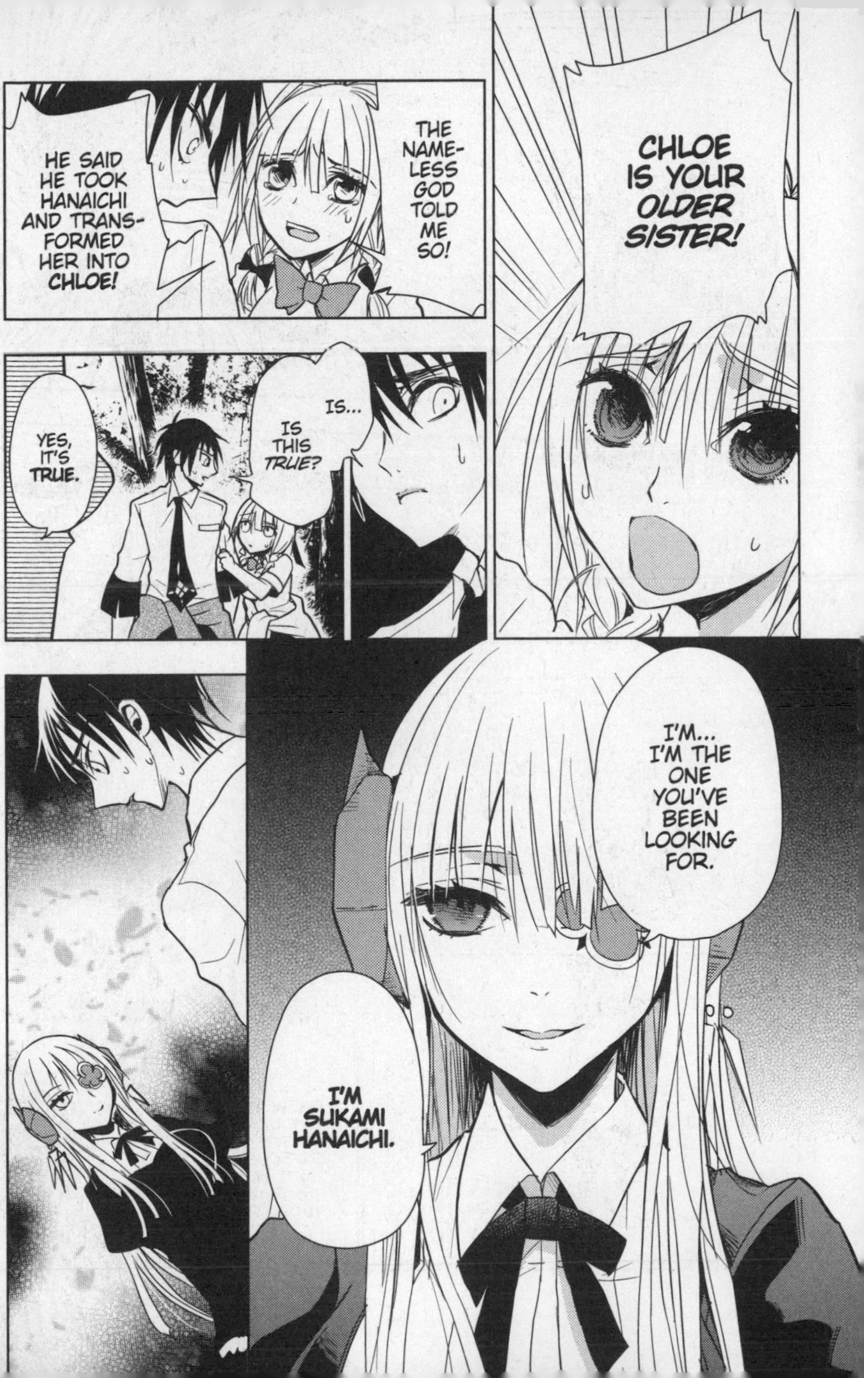
CHLOE IS YOUR OLDER SISTER!
THE NAMELESS GOD TOLD ME SO!
HE SAID HE TOOK HANAICHI AND TRANSFORMED HER INTO CHLOE!
IS... IS THIS TRUE?
YES, IT'S TRUE.
I'M... I'M THE ONE YOU'VE BEEN LOOKING FOR.
I'M SUKAMI HANAICHI.

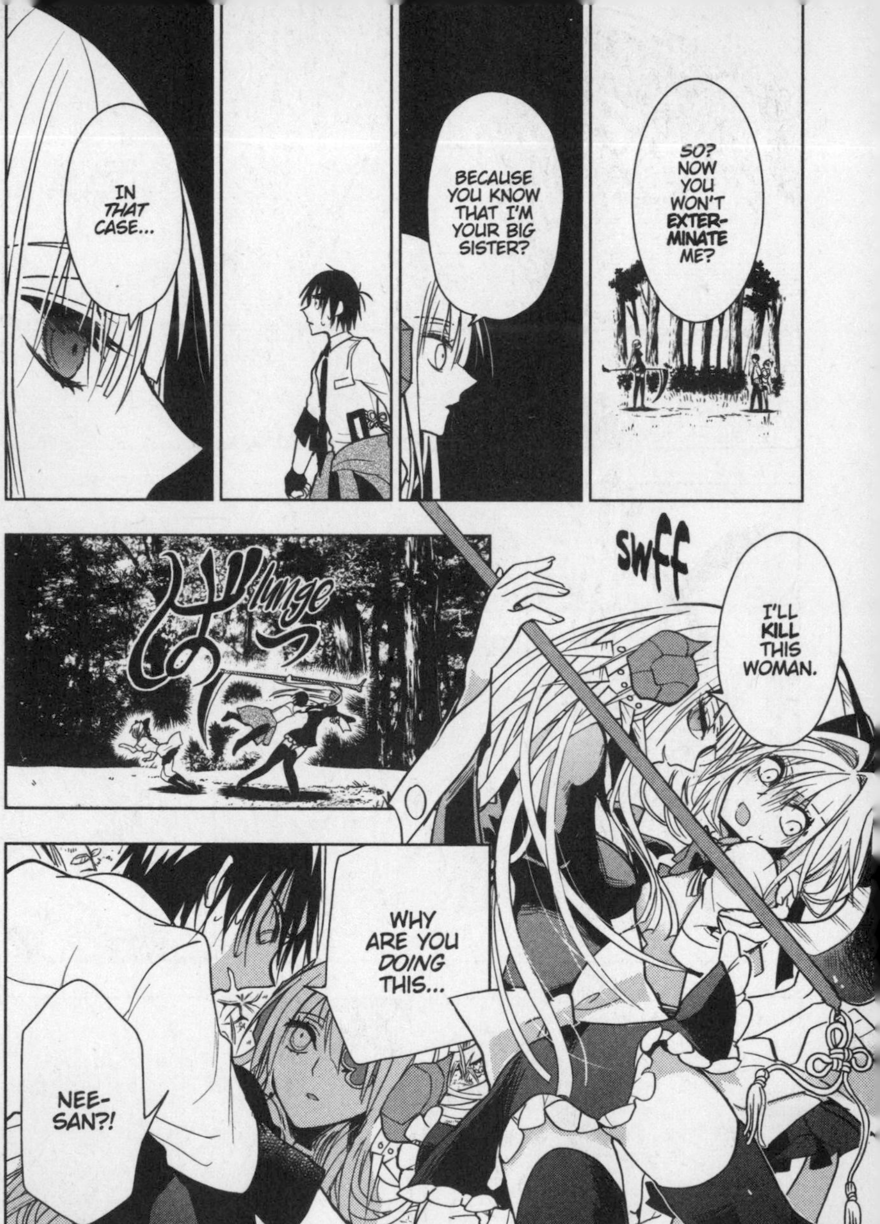
SO? NOW YOU WON'T EXTERMINATE ME?
BECAUSE YOU KNOW THAT I'M YOUR BIG SISTER?
IN THAT CASE...
SWFF
I'LL KILL THIS WOMAN.
Lunge
WHY ARE YOU DOING THIS...
NEE-SAN?!

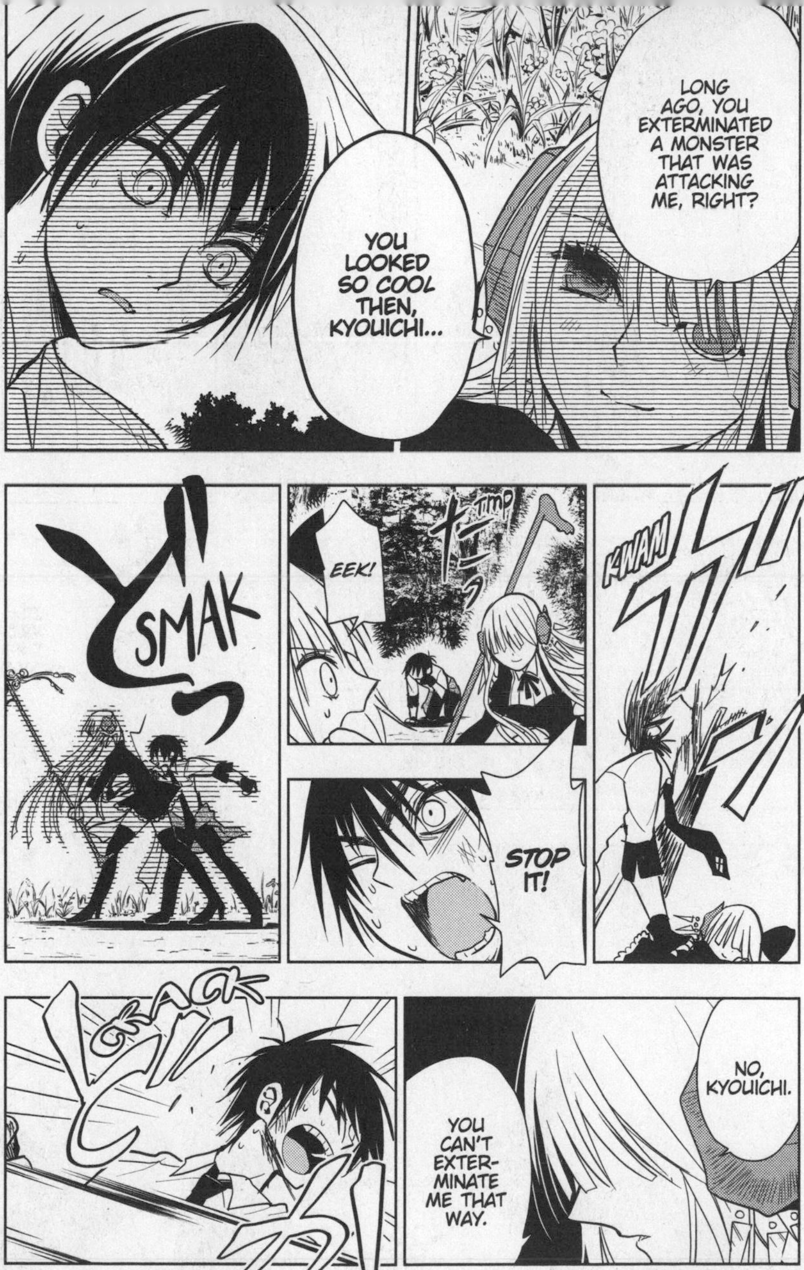
LONG AGO, YOU EXTERMINATED A MONSTER THAT WAS ATTACKING ME, RIGHT?
YOU LOOKED SO COOL THEN, KYOUICHI...
KWAM
TMP
EEK!
STOP IT!
SMAK
NO, KYOUICHI.
YOU CAN'T EXTER-MINATE ME THAT WAY.
CRACK

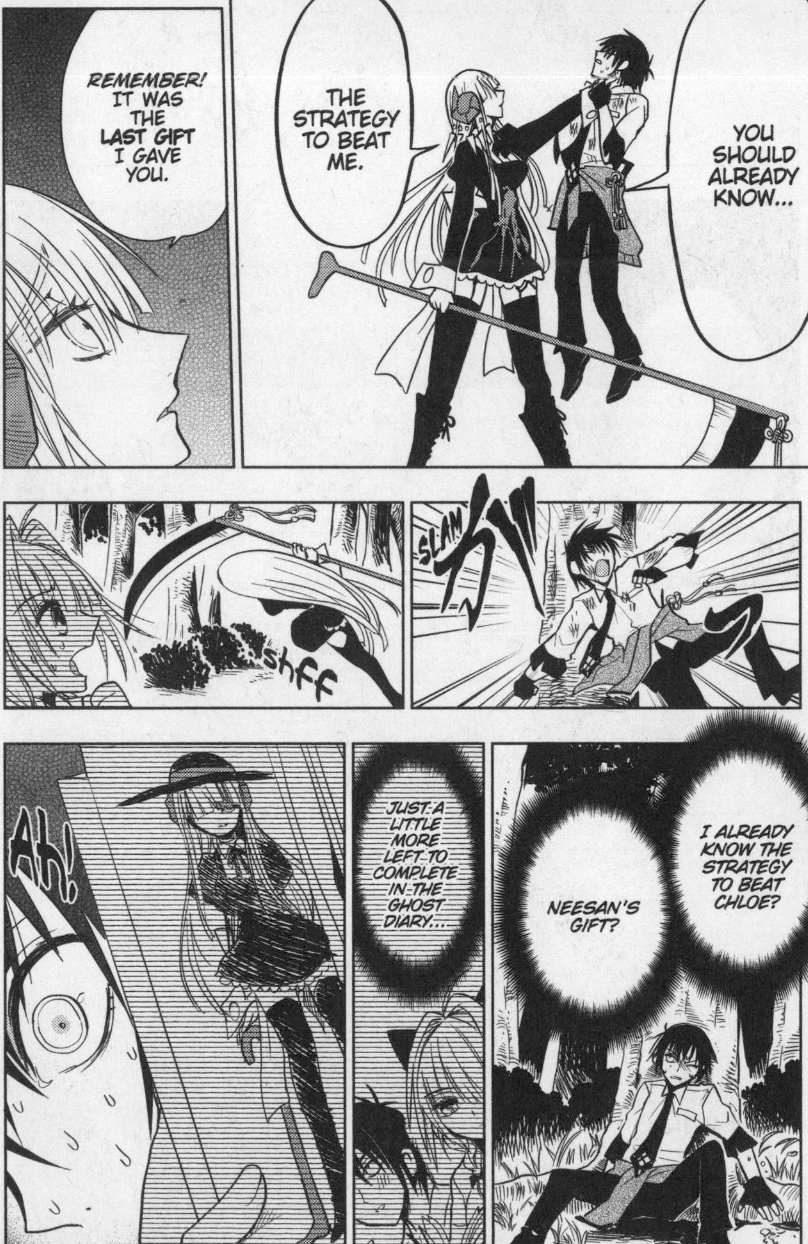
YOU SHOULD ALREADY KNOW...
THE STRATEGY TO BEAT ME.
REMEMBER! IT WAS THE LAST GIFT I GAVE YOU.
SLAM
shff
I ALREADY KNOW THE STRATEGY TO BEAT CHLOE?
NEESAN'S GIFT?
JUST A LITTLE MORE LEFT TO COMPLETE IN THE GHOST DIARY...
Ah!

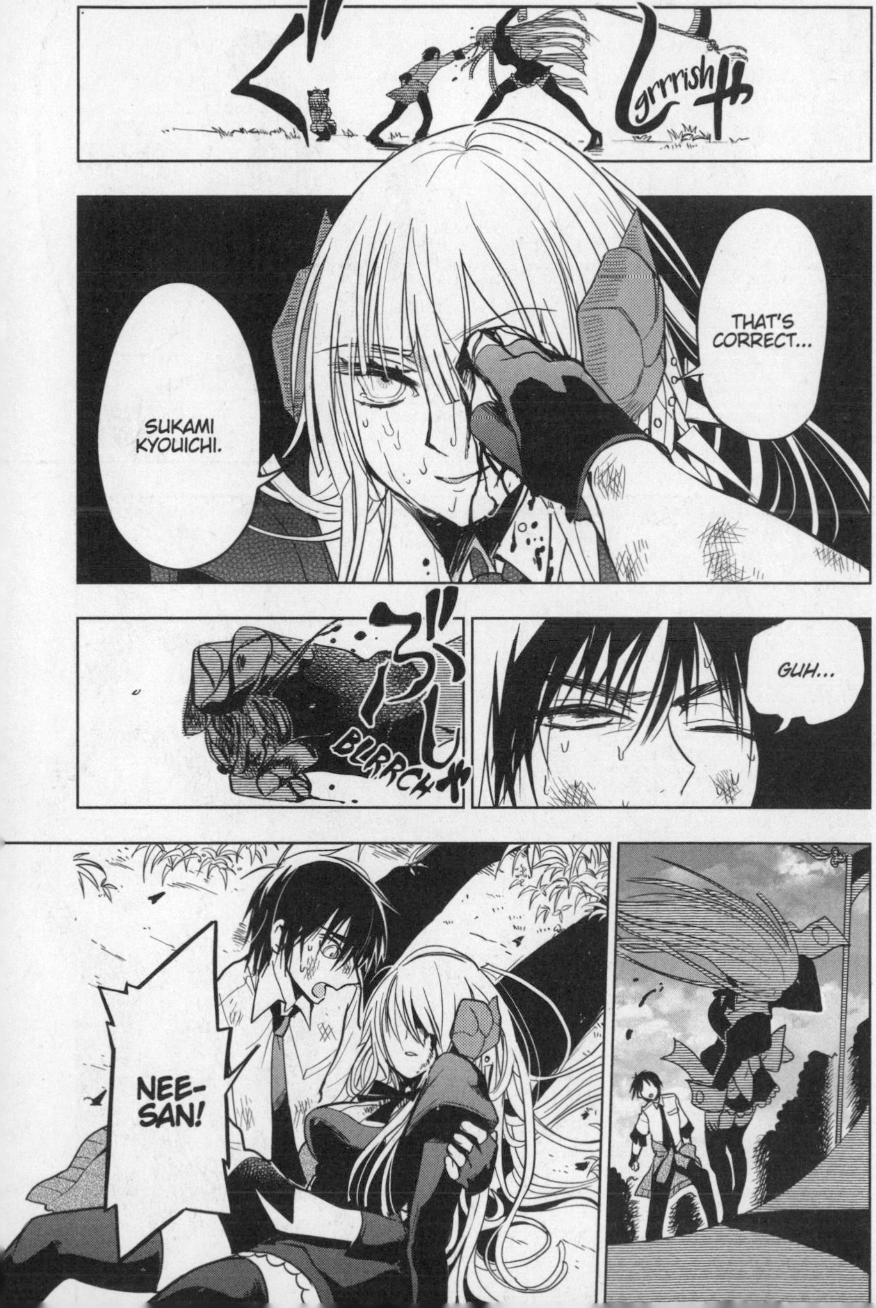
grrrish
THAT'S CORRECT...
SUKAMI KYOUICHI.
GUH...
BLRRCH
NEE-SAN!

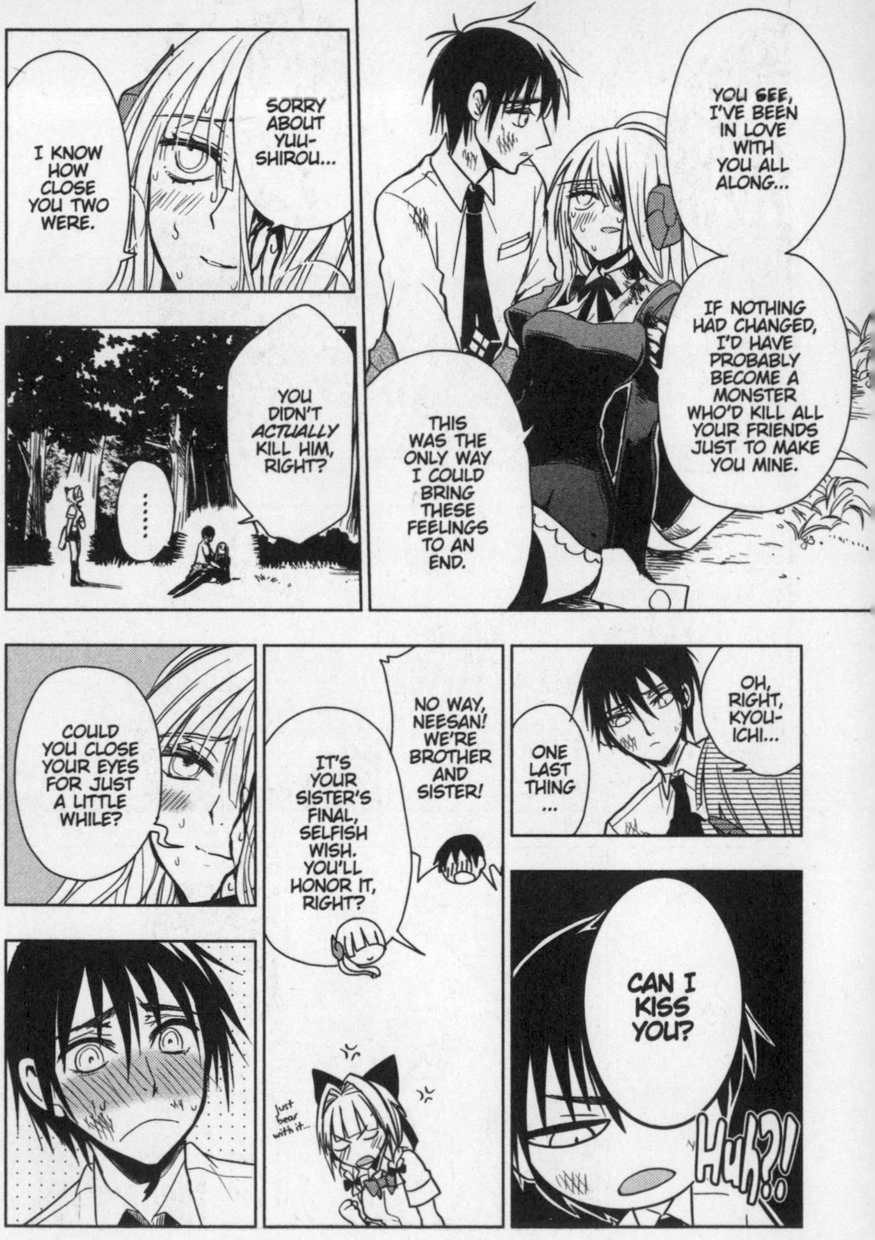

YOU SEE, I'VE BEEN IN LOVE WITH YOU ALL ALONG...
IF NOTHING HAD CHANGED, I'D HAVE PROBABLY BECOME A MONSTER WHO'D KILL ALL YOUR FRIENDS JUST TO MAKE YOU MINE.
THIS WAS THE ONLY WAY I COULD BRING THESE FEELINGS TO AN END.
SORRY ABOUT YUU-SHIROU...
I KNOW HOW CLOSE YOU TWO WERE.
YOU DIDN'T *ACTUALLY* KILL HIM, RIGHT?
......
OH, RIGHT, KYOU-ICHI...
ONE LAST THING ...
CAN I KISS YOU?
HUH?!
NO WAY, NEESAN! WE'RE BROTHER AND SISTER!
IT'S YOUR SISTER'S FINAL, SELFISH WISH. YOU'LL HONOR IT, RIGHT?
just bear with it...
COULD YOU CLOSE YOUR EYES FOR JUST A LITTLE WHILE?

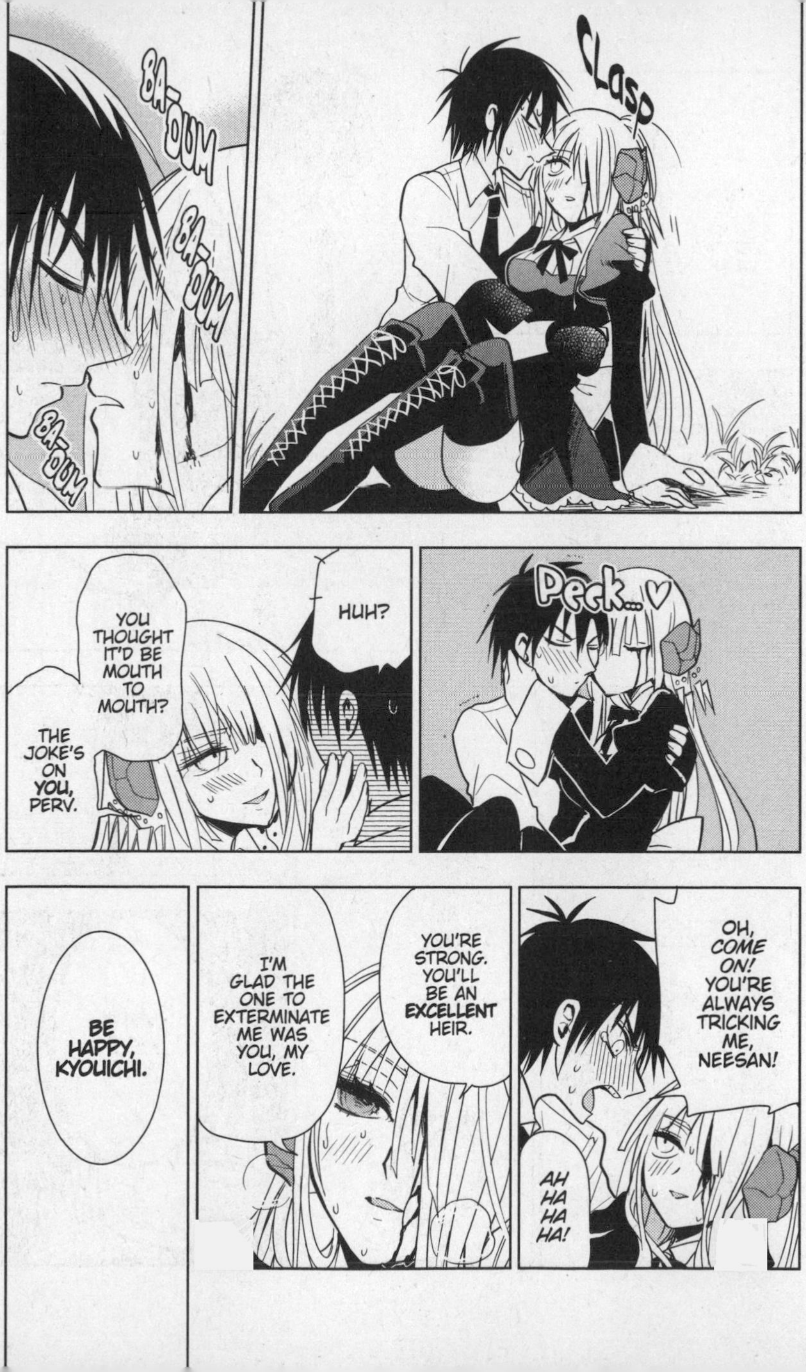
CLASP
BA-DUM
BA-DUM
BA-DUM
Peck...♥
HUH?
YOU THOUGHT IT'D BE MOUTH TO MOUTH?
THE JOKE'S ON YOU, PERV.
OH, COME ON! YOU'RE ALWAYS TRICKING ME, NEESAN!
AH HA HA HA!
YOU'RE STRONG. YOU'LL BE AN EXCELLENT HEIR.
I'M GLAD THE ONE TO EXTERMINATE ME WAS YOU, MY LOVE.
BE HAPPY, KYOUICHI.

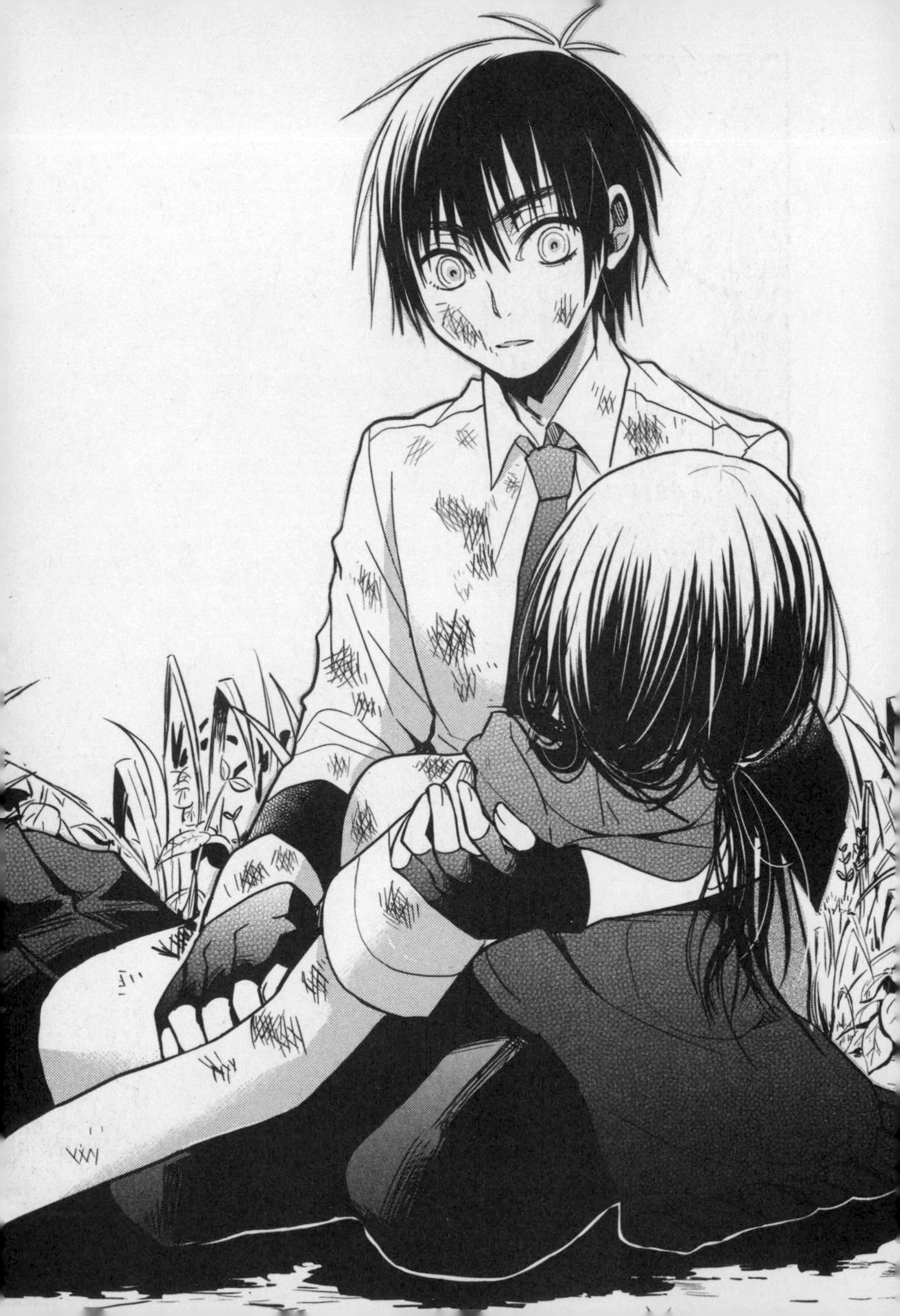

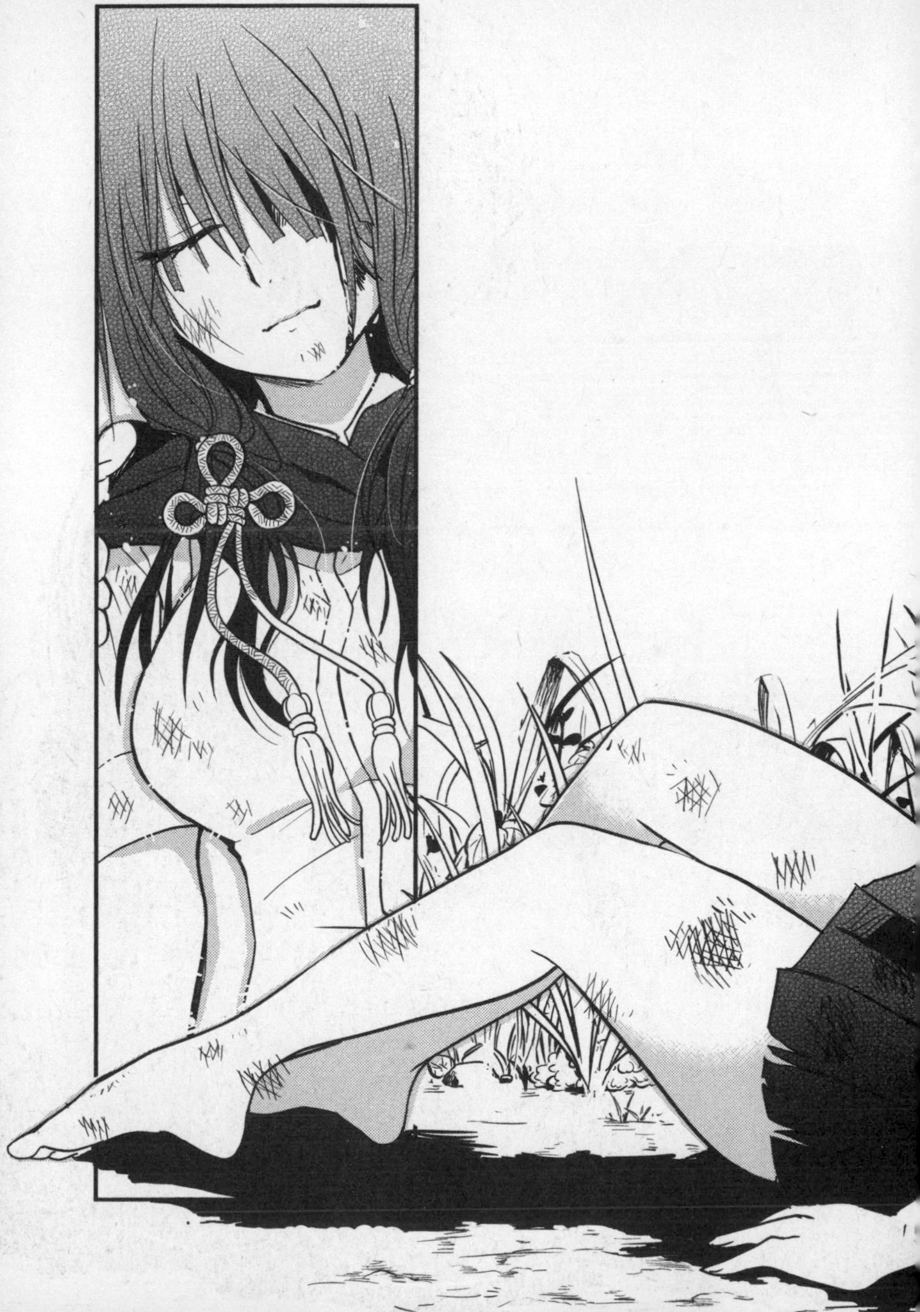

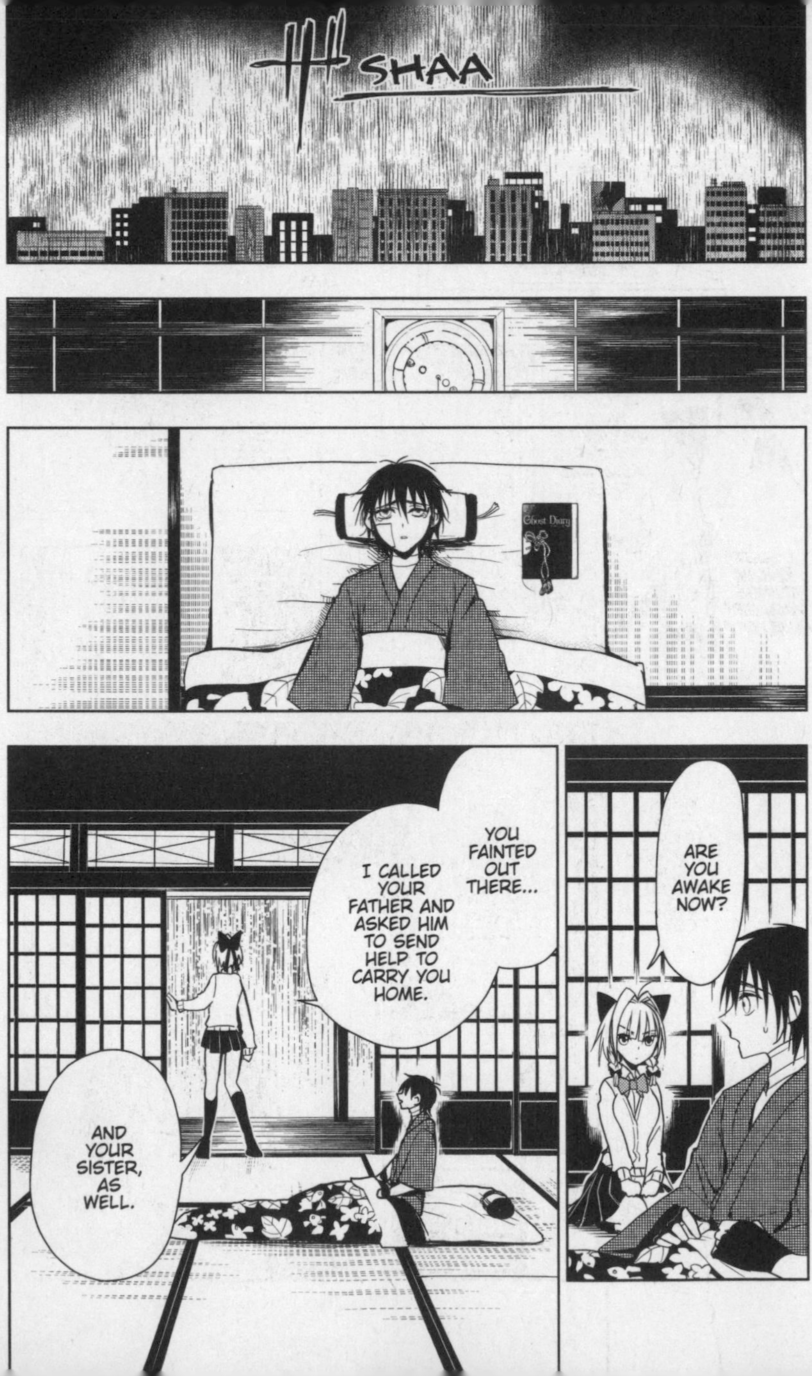
SHAA
Ghost Diary
ARE YOU AWAKE NOW?
YOU FAINTED OUT THERE...
I CALLED YOUR FATHER AND ASKED HIM TO SEND HELP TO CARRY YOU HOME.
AND YOUR SISTER, AS WELL.

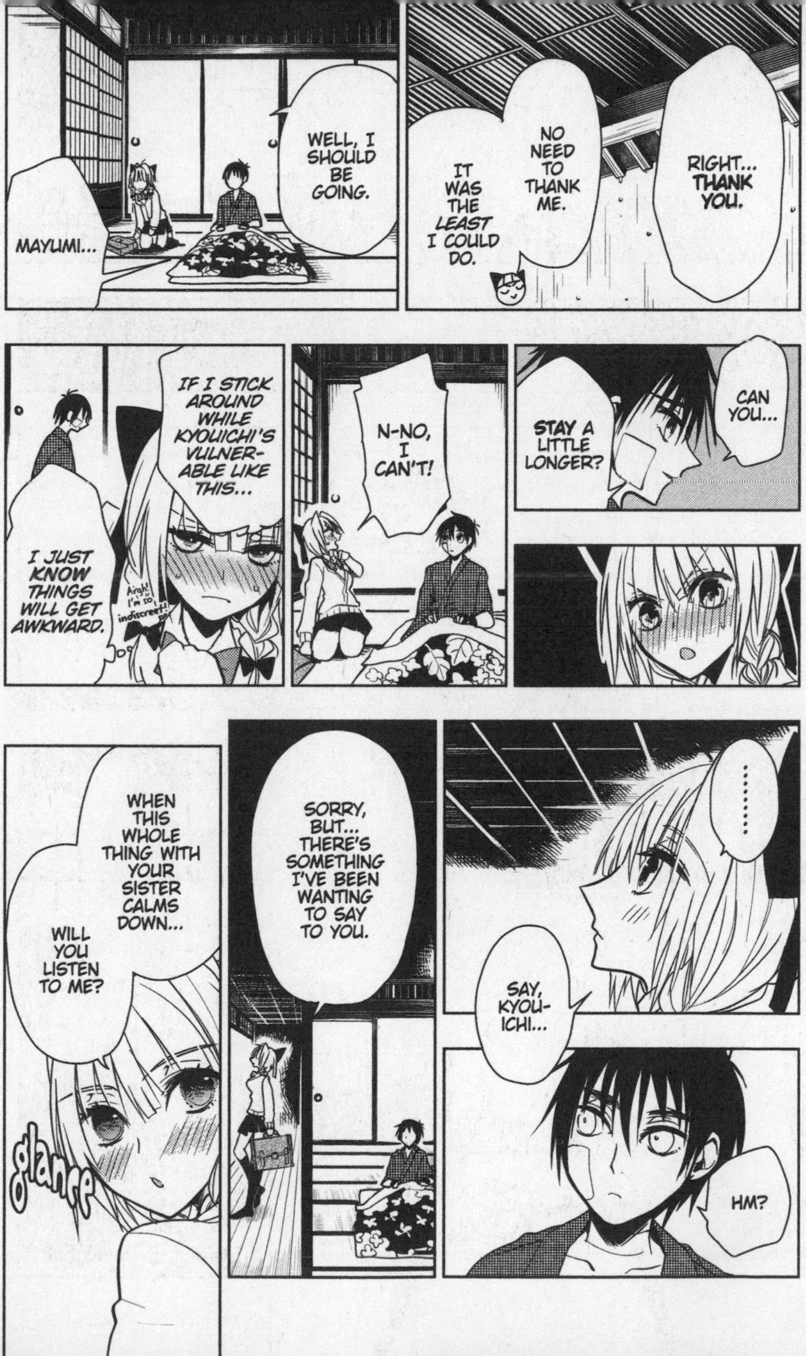
RIGHT... THANK YOU.
NO NEED TO THANK ME.
IT WAS THE LEAST I COULD DO.
WELL, I SHOULD BE GOING.
MAYUMI...
CAN YOU...
STAY A LITTLE LONGER?
N-NO, I CAN'T!
IF I STICK AROUND WHILE KYOUICHI'S VULNER-ABLE LIKE THIS...
I JUST KNOW THINGS WILL GET AWKWARD.
Argh! I'm so indiscreet!
......
SAY, KYOU-ICHI...
HM?
SORRY, BUT... THERE'S SOMETHING I'VE BEEN WANTING TO SAY TO YOU.
WHEN THIS WHOLE THING WITH YOUR SISTER CALMS DOWN...
WILL YOU LISTEN TO ME?
glance

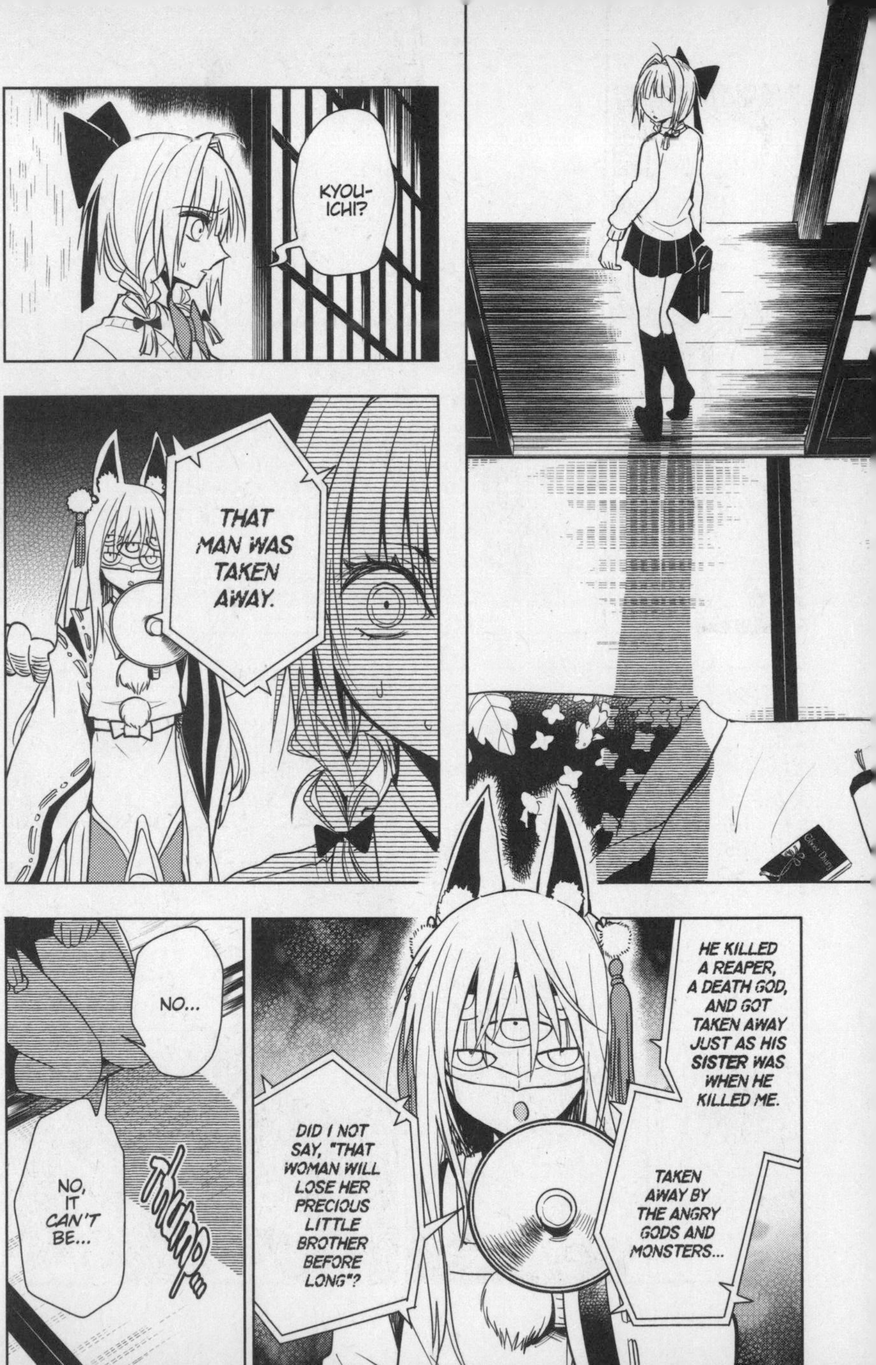
KYOU-ICHI?
THAT MAN WAS TAKEN AWAY.
HE KILLED A REAPER, A DEATH GOD, AND GOT TAKEN AWAY JUST AS HIS SISTER WAS WHEN HE KILLED ME.
TAKEN AWAY BY THE ANGRY GODS AND MONSTERS...
DID I NOT SAY, "THAT WOMAN WILL LOSE HER PRECIOUS LITTLE BROTHER BEFORE LONG"?
NO...
NO, IT CAN'T BE...

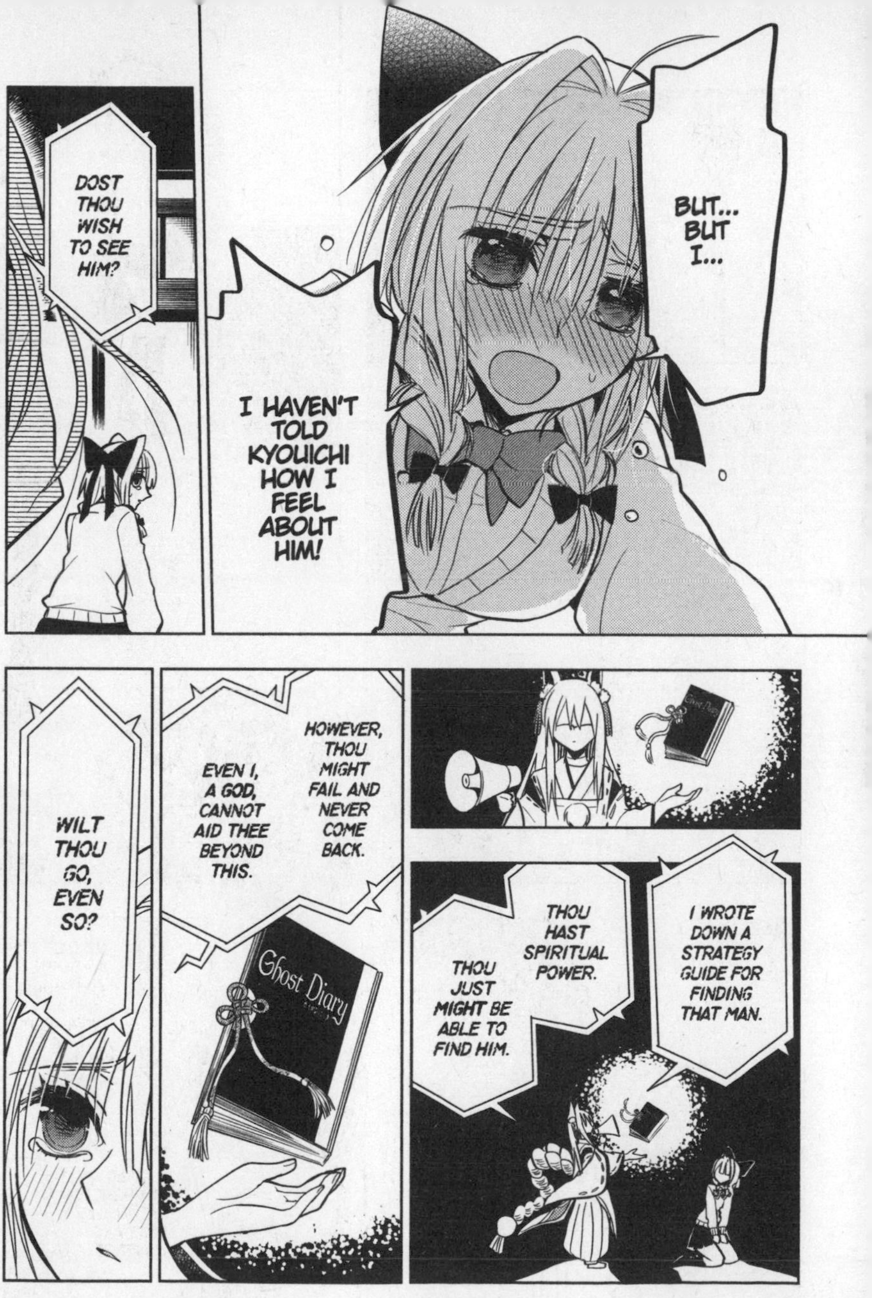
BUT... BUT I...
I HAVEN'T TOLD KYOUICHI HOW I FEEL ABOUT HIM!
DOST THOU WISH TO SEE HIM?
I WROTE DOWN A STRATEGY GUIDE FOR FINDING THAT MAN.
THOU HAST SPIRITUAL POWER.
THOU JUST MIGHT BE ABLE TO FIND HIM.
HOWEVER, THOU MIGHT FAIL AND NEVER COME BACK.
EVEN I, A GOD, CANNOT AID THEE BEYOND THIS.
Ghost Diary
WILT THOU GO, EVEN SO?

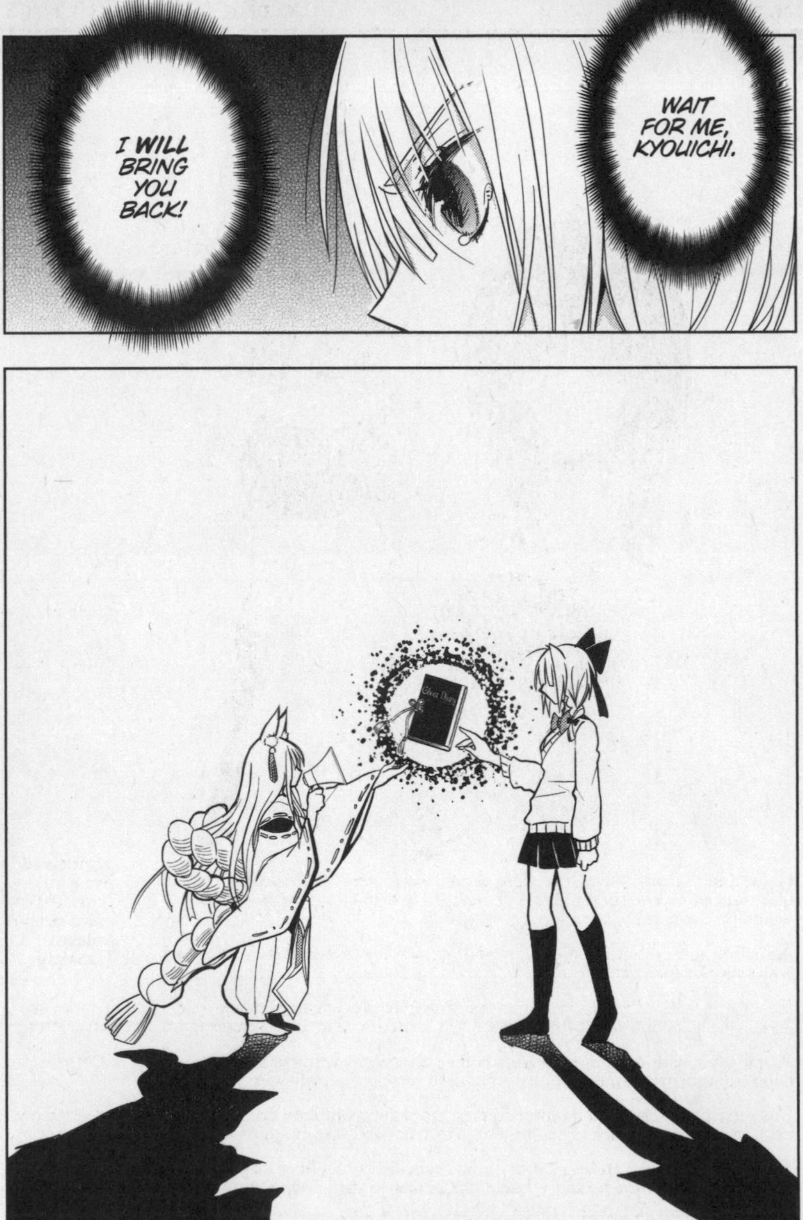

WAIT FOR ME, KYOUICHI.
I WILL BRING YOU BACK!

K a i d a n n i k k i

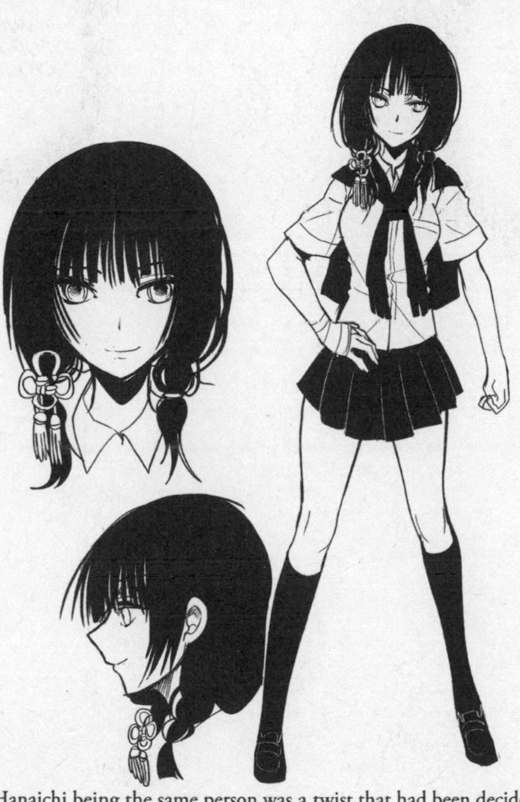

Strong and beautiful, Kyouichi's older sister, Sukami Hanaichi

Chloe and Hanaichi being the same person was a twist that had been decided upon since the series began, but I wonder if I was able to draw it so that it would be a surprise...

Actually, the fact that Kyouichi-kun is short was also a metaphor for how he won't surpass Hanaichi *(ha ha!)*.

Here's a little bit of trivia... So, there are many types of spiritual practitioners: people who call down spirits, people who work magic spells, exorcists who exterminate spirits, etc., etc...

People who work magic spells--such as for possession-casting or curse-poisoning--are often depicted as being women, so I have Hanaichi use more spell-type techniques.

Conversely, exorcists and *onmyou* diviners are stereotypically men, so I have Kyouichi use more exorcist-type techniques...I can be a bit particular about some things *(heh!)*.

Even in Japan, there are apparently several existing family lines of possession-casters and exorcists. As a lover of the occult, I would like to talk to such people someday.

Today's Theme: Sukami Hanaichi

Ghost Diary

カイダンにっき

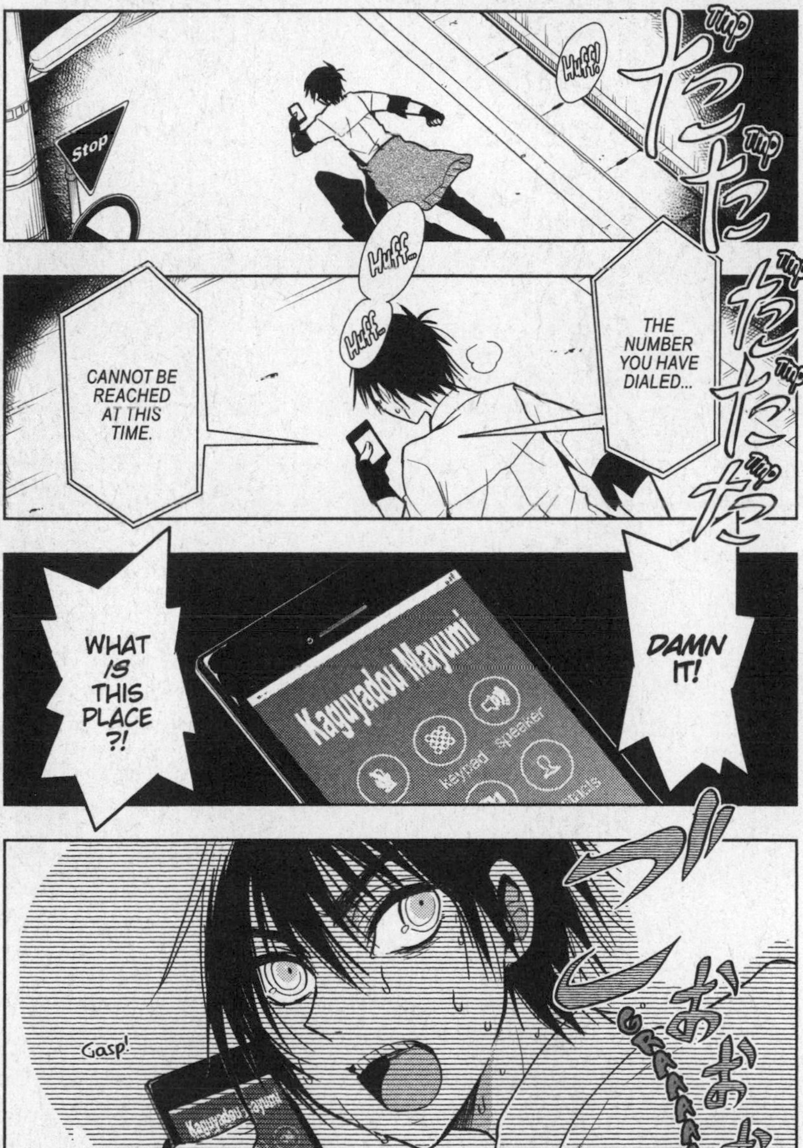

Tmp
Tmp
Huff!
Stop
Tmp
Tmp
Tmp
THE NUMBER YOU HAVE DIALED...
Huff...
Huff...
CANNOT BE REACHED AT THIS TIME.
DAMN IT!
Kaguyadou Mayumi
Speaker
Keypad
WHAT IS THIS PLACE?!
Gasp!
Kaguyadou Mayumi

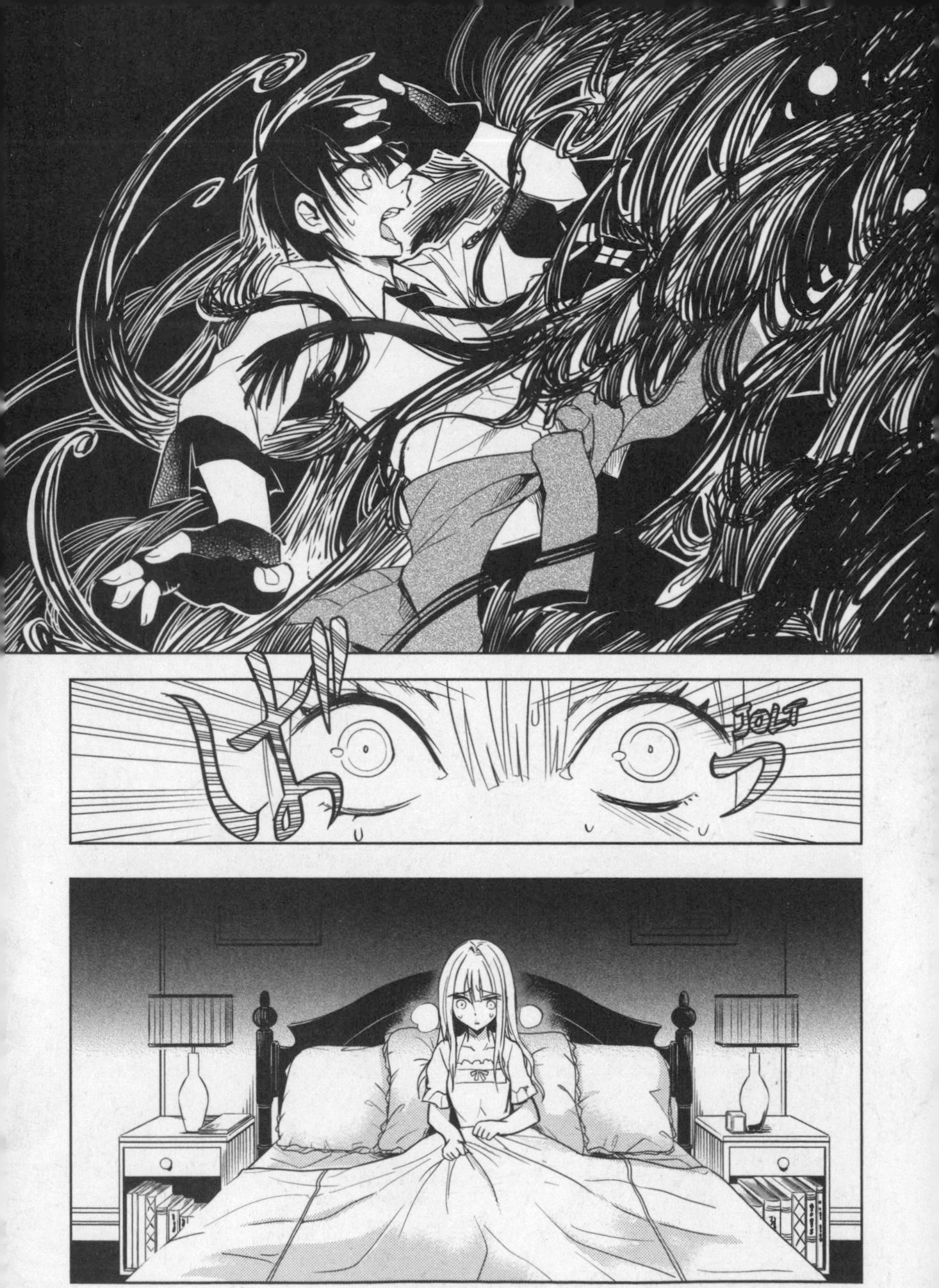
JOLT

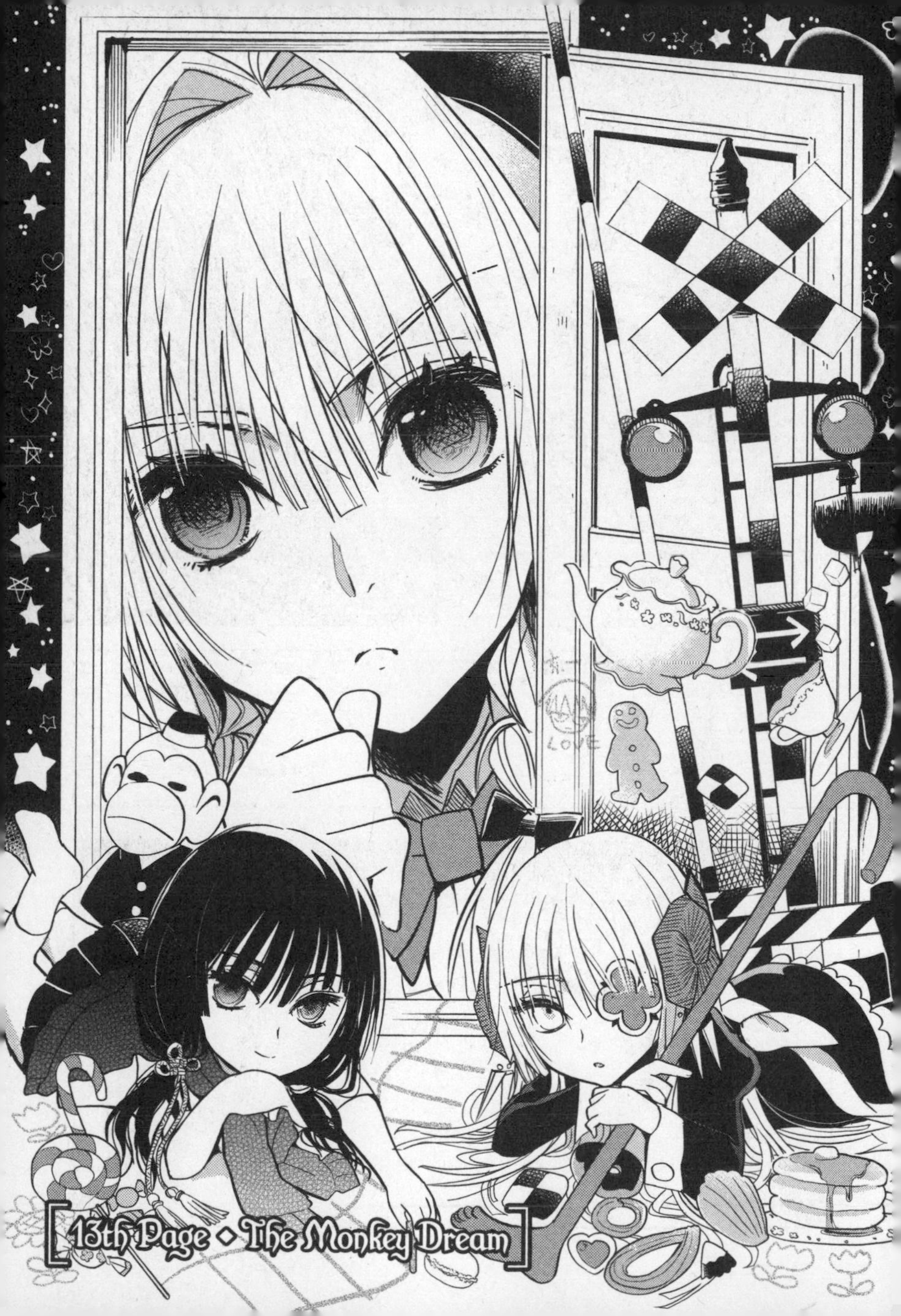
LOVE
13th Page ◆ The Monkey Dream

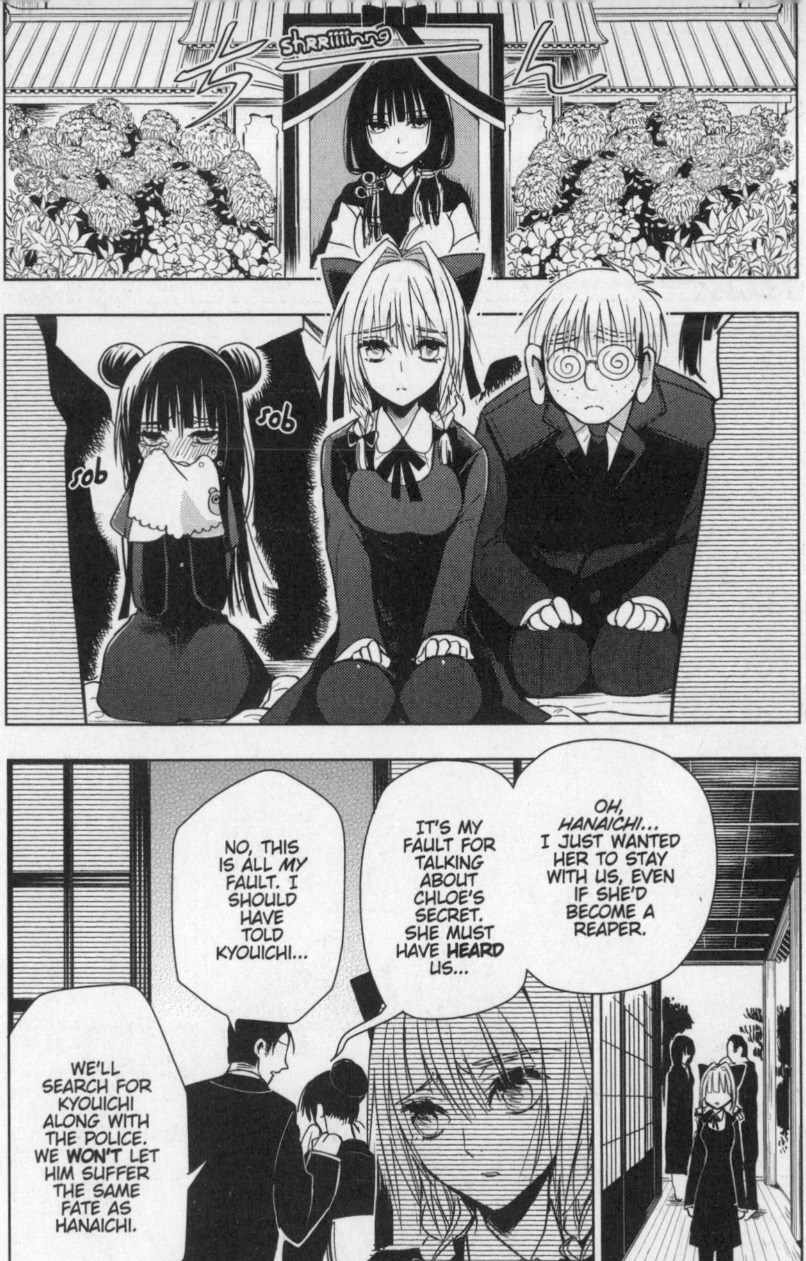
shrriiiinng
sob
sob
OH, HANAICHI... I JUST WANTED HER TO STAY WITH US, EVEN IF SHE'D BECOME A REAPER.
IT'S MY FAULT FOR TALKING ABOUT CHLOE'S SECRET. SHE MUST HAVE HEARD US...
NO, THIS IS ALL MY FAULT. I SHOULD HAVE TOLD KYOUICHI...
WE'LL SEARCH FOR KYOUICHI ALONG WITH THE POLICE. WE WON'T LET HIM SUFFER THE SAME FATE AS HANAICHI.

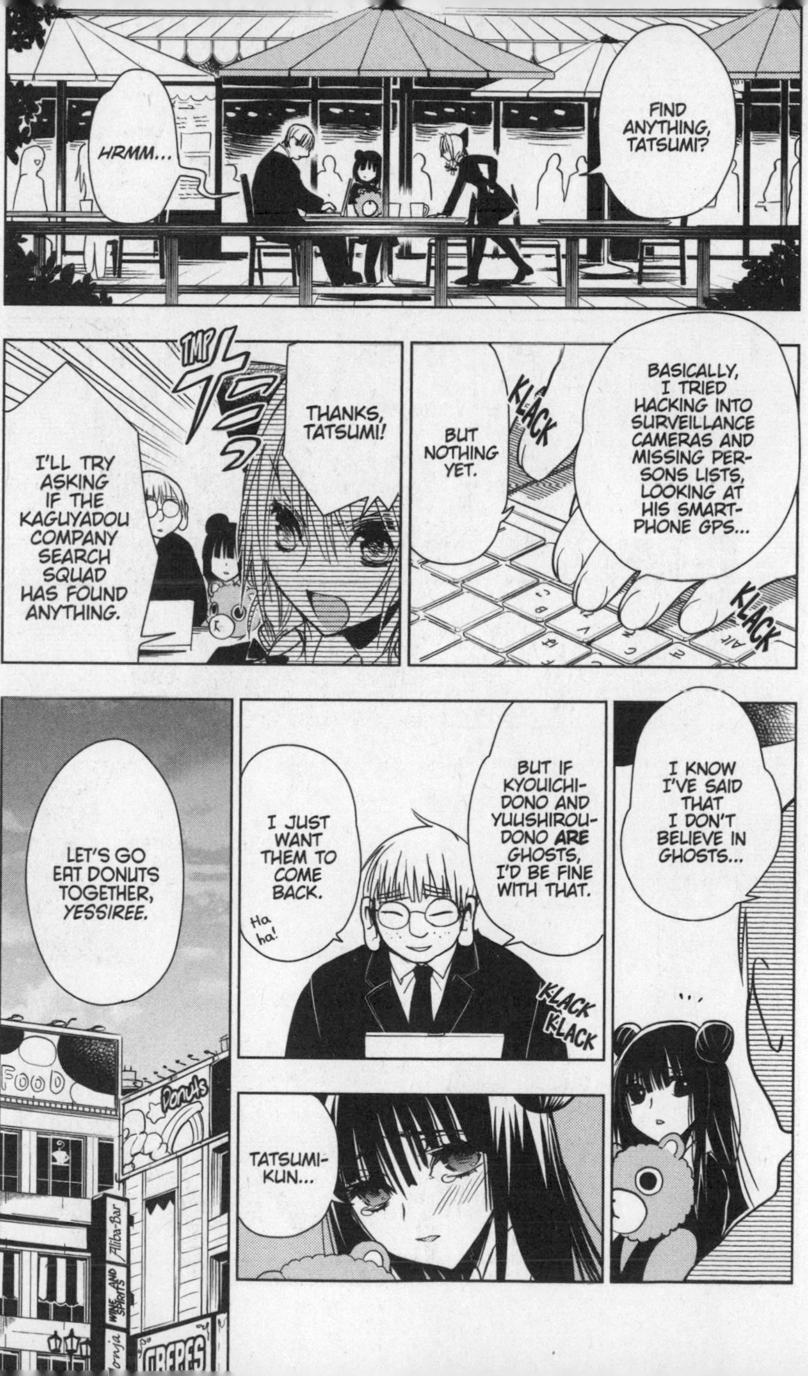
FIND ANYTHING, TATSUMI?
HRMM...
BASICALLY, I TRIED HACKING INTO SURVEILLANCE CAMERAS AND MISSING PERSONS LISTS, LOOKING AT HIS SMARTPHONE GPS...
KLACK
BUT NOTHING YET.
KLACK
TMP
THANKS, TATSUMI!
I'LL TRY ASKING IF THE KAGUYADOU COMPANY SEARCH SQUAD HAS FOUND ANYTHING.
I KNOW I'VE SAID THAT I DON'T BELIEVE IN GHOSTS...
BUT IF KYOUICHI-DONO AND YUUSHIROU-DONO ARE GHOSTS, I'D BE FINE WITH THAT.
I JUST WANT THEM TO COME BACK.
Ha ha!
K-LACK K-LACK
TATSUMI-KUN...
LET'S GO EAT DONUTS TOGETHER, YESSIREE.
FOOD
Donuts
Aliba-Bar
WINE AND SPIRITS
CREPES

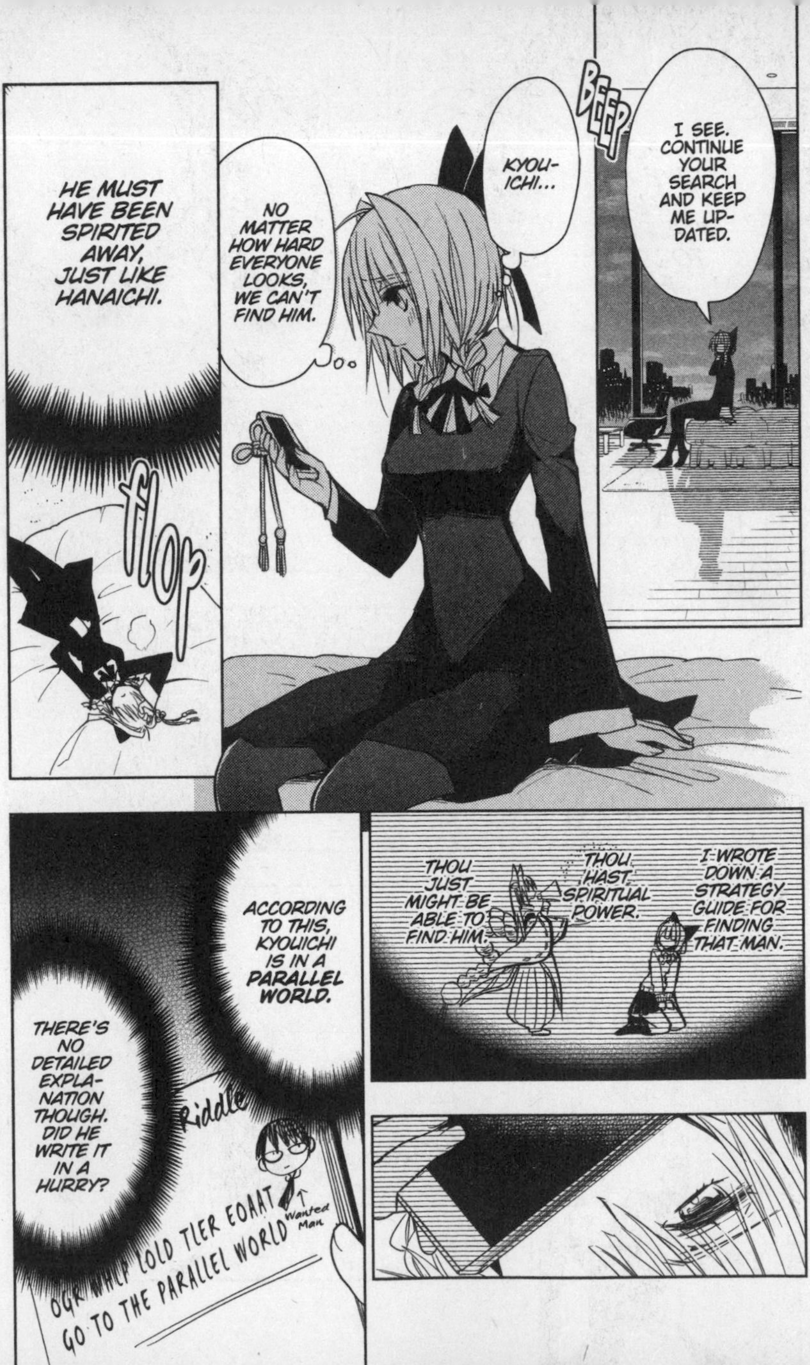
I SEE. CONTINUE YOUR SEARCH AND KEEP ME UP-DATED.
BEEP
KYOU-ICHI...
NO MATTER HOW HARD EVERYONE LOOKS, WE CAN'T FIND HIM.
HE MUST HAVE BEEN SPIRITED AWAY, JUST LIKE HANAICHI.
flop
I WROTE DOWN A STRATEGY GUIDE FOR FINDING THAT MAN.
THOU HAST SPIRITUAL POWER.
THOU JUST MIGHT BE ABLE TO FIND HIM.
ACCORDING TO THIS, KYOUICHI IS IN A PARALLEL WORLD.
THERE'S NO DETAILED EXPLA-NATION THOUGH. DID HE WRITE IT IN A HURRY?
Riddle
Wanted Man
OGK WHLP COLD TLER EOAAT
GO TO THE PARALLEL WORLD

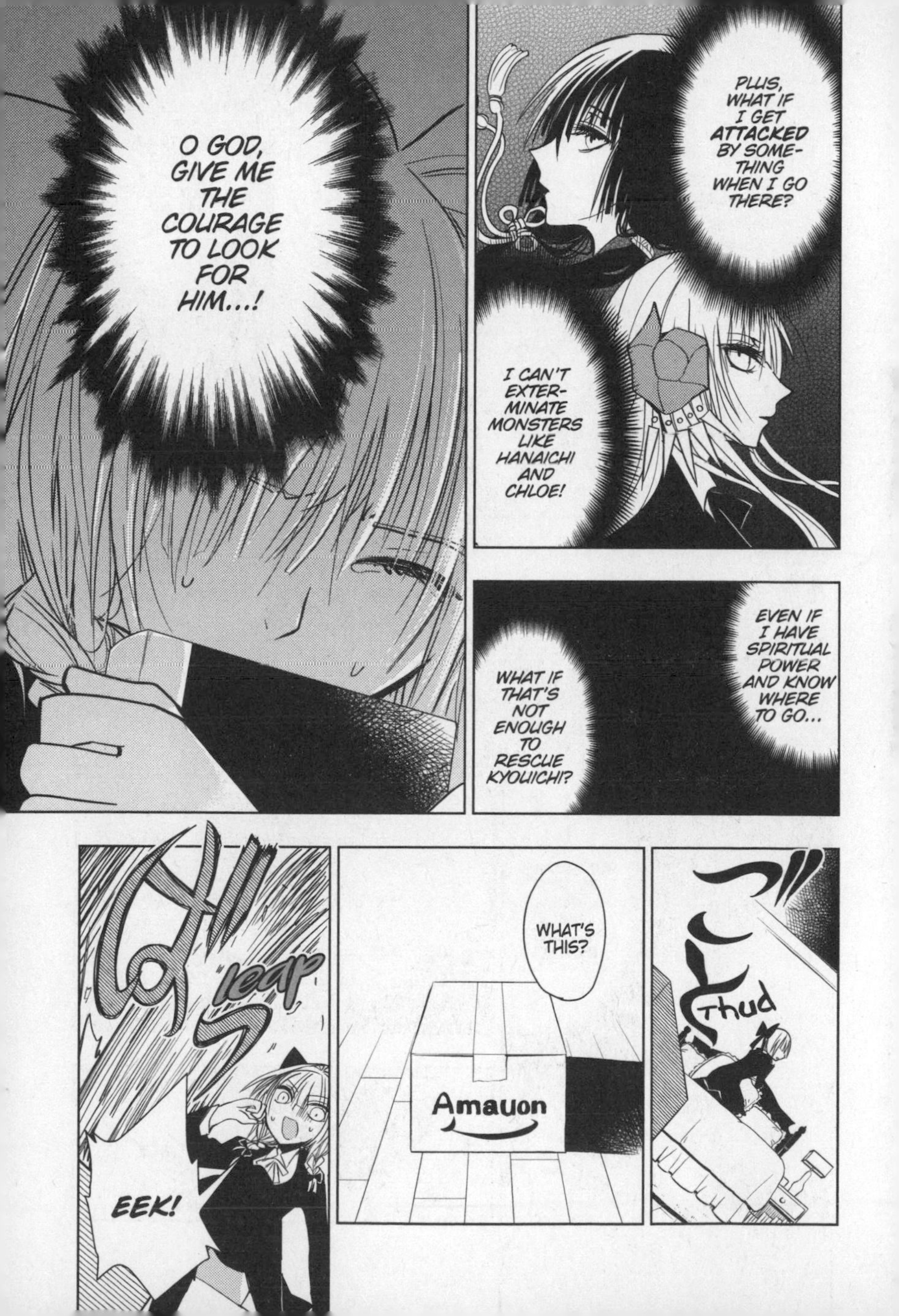
PLUS, WHAT IF I GET ATTACKED BY SOMETHING WHEN I GO THERE?
I CAN'T EXTERMINATE MONSTERS LIKE HANAICHI AND CHLOE!
O GOD, GIVE ME THE COURAGE TO LOOK FOR HIM...!
EVEN IF I HAVE SPIRITUAL POWER AND KNOW WHERE TO GO...
WHAT IF THAT'S NOT ENOUGH TO RESCUE KYOUICHI?
Thud
WHAT'S THIS?
Amauon
leap
EEK!

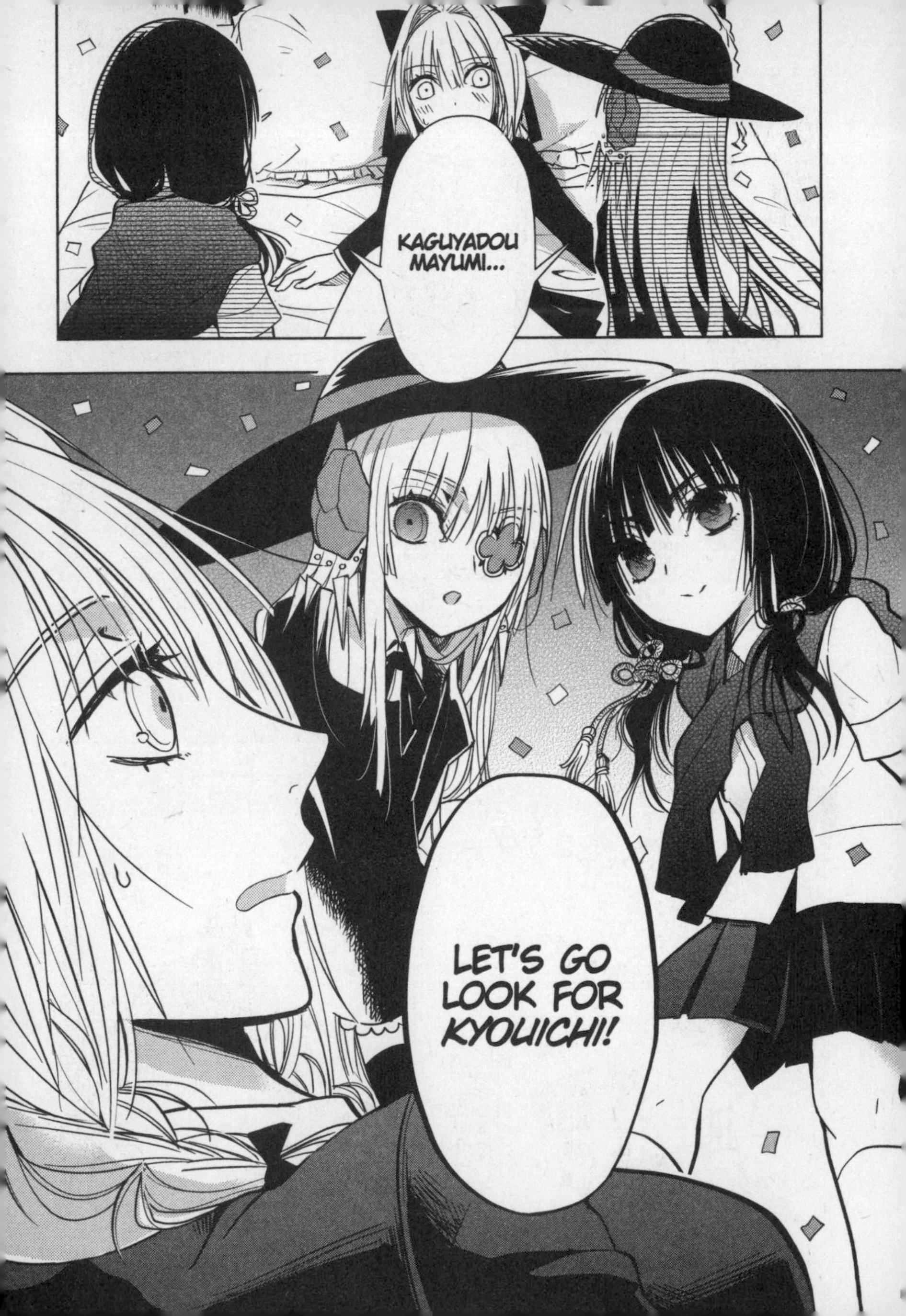
KAGUYADOU MAYUMI...
LET'S GO LOOK FOR KYOUICHI!

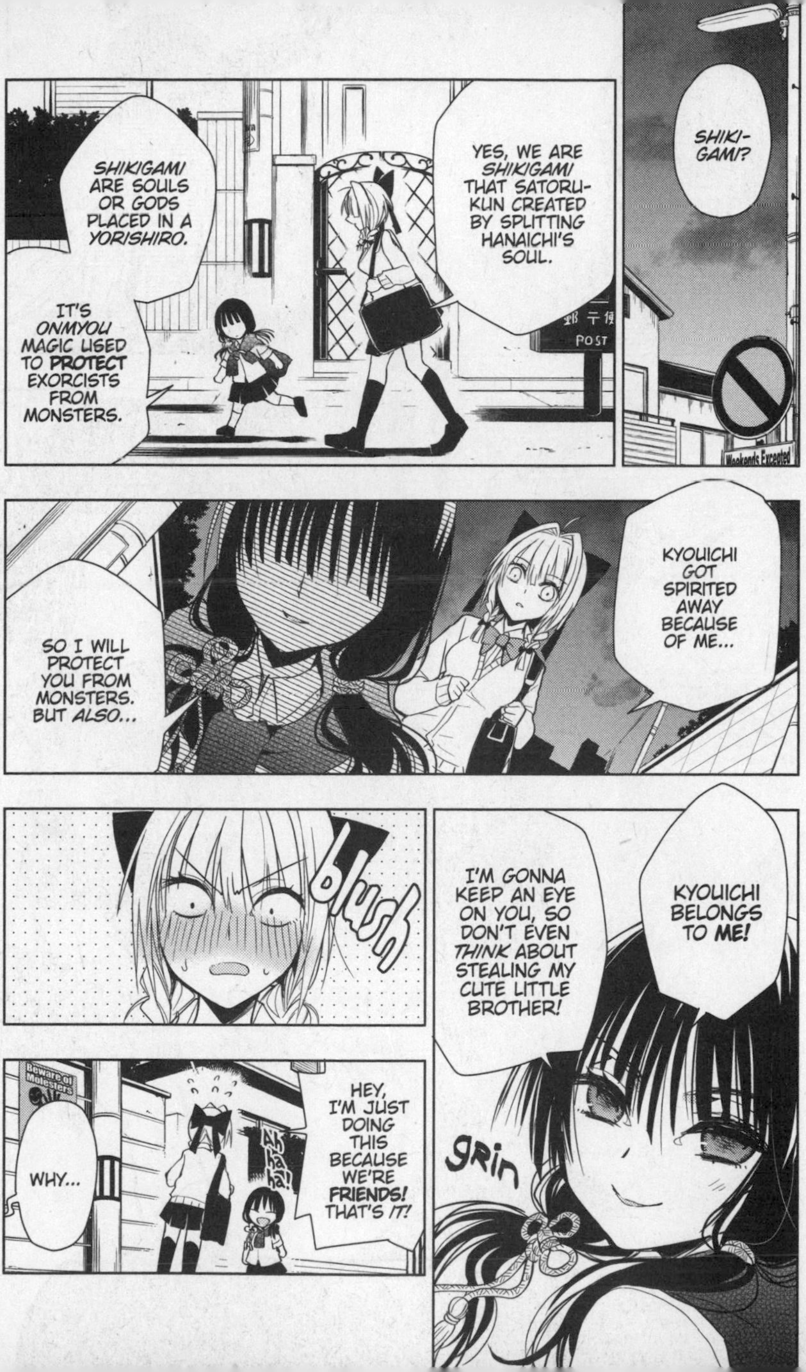
SHIKI-GAMI?
YES, WE ARE SHIKIGAMI THAT SATORU-KUN CREATED BY SPLITTING HANAICHI'S SOUL.
SHIKIGAMI ARE SOULS OR GODS PLACED IN A YORISHIRO.
IT'S ONMYOU MAGIC USED TO PROTECT EXORCISTS FROM MONSTERS.
POST
Weekends Excepted
KYOUICHI GOT SPIRITED AWAY BECAUSE OF ME...
SO I WILL PROTECT YOU FROM MONSTERS. BUT ALSO...
KYOUICHI BELONGS TO ME!
I'M GONNA KEEP AN EYE ON YOU, SO DON'T EVEN THINK ABOUT STEALING MY CUTE LITTLE BROTHER!
grin
blush
HEY, I'M JUST DOING THIS BECAUSE WE'RE FRIENDS! THAT'S IT!
Ah ha ha!
WHY...
Beware of Molesters

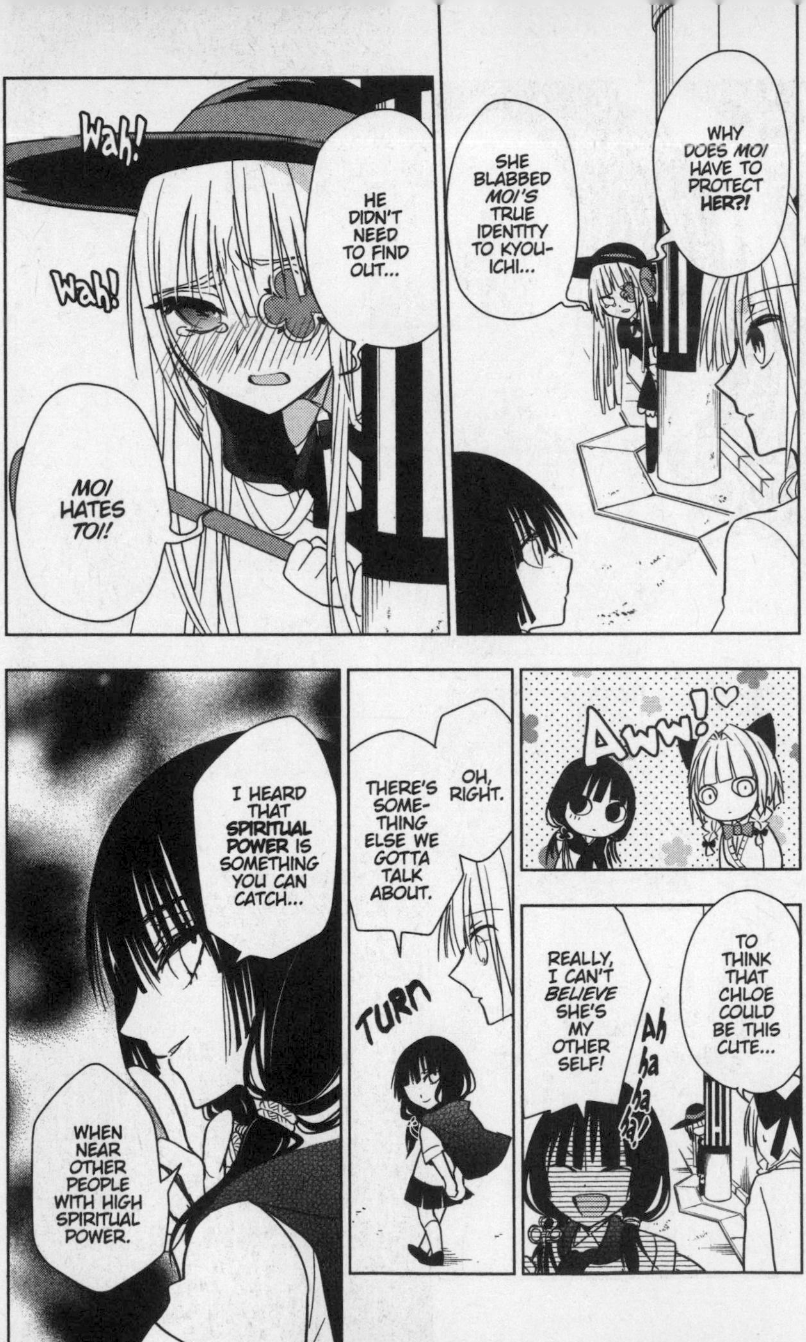
WHY DOES MOI HAVE TO PROTECT HER?!
SHE BLABBED MOI'S TRUE IDENTITY TO KYOU-ICHI...
HE DIDN'T NEED TO FIND OUT...
Wah!
Wah!
MOI HATES TOI!
Aww!
TO THINK THAT CHLOE COULD BE THIS CUTE...
REALLY, I CAN'T BELIEVE SHE'S MY OTHER SELF!
Ahahahaha!
OH, RIGHT.
THERE'S SOMETHING ELSE WE GOTTA TALK ABOUT.
TURN
I HEARD THAT SPIRITUAL POWER IS SOMETHING YOU CAN CATCH...
WHEN NEAR OTHER PEOPLE WITH HIGH SPIRITUAL POWER.

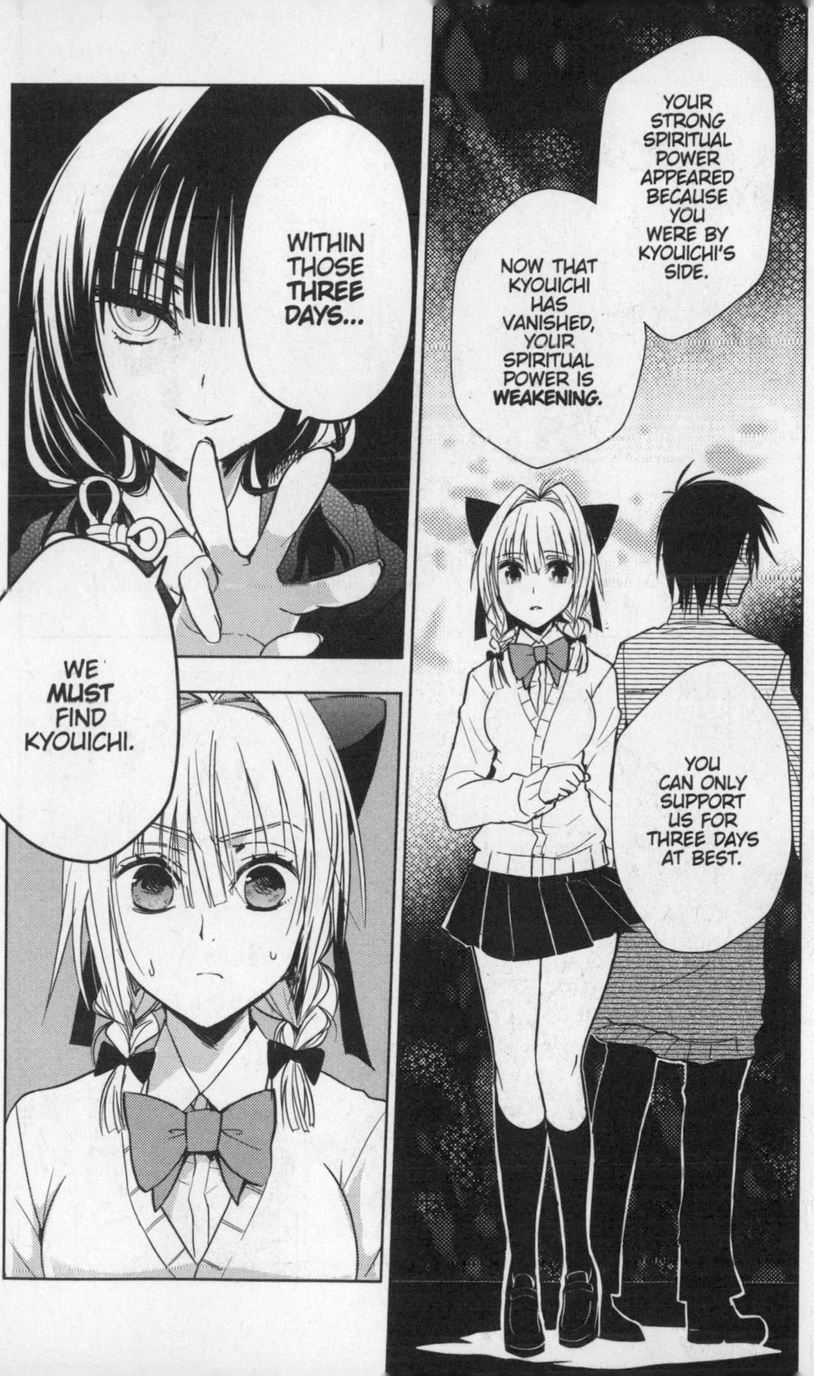

YOUR STRONG SPIRITUAL POWER APPEARED BECAUSE YOU WERE BY KYOUICHI'S SIDE.
NOW THAT KYOUICHI HAS VANISHED, YOUR SPIRITUAL POWER IS WEAKENING.
YOU CAN ONLY SUPPORT US FOR THREE DAYS AT BEST.
WITHIN THOSE THREE DAYS...
WE MUST FIND KYOUICHI.

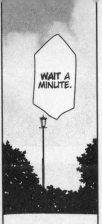

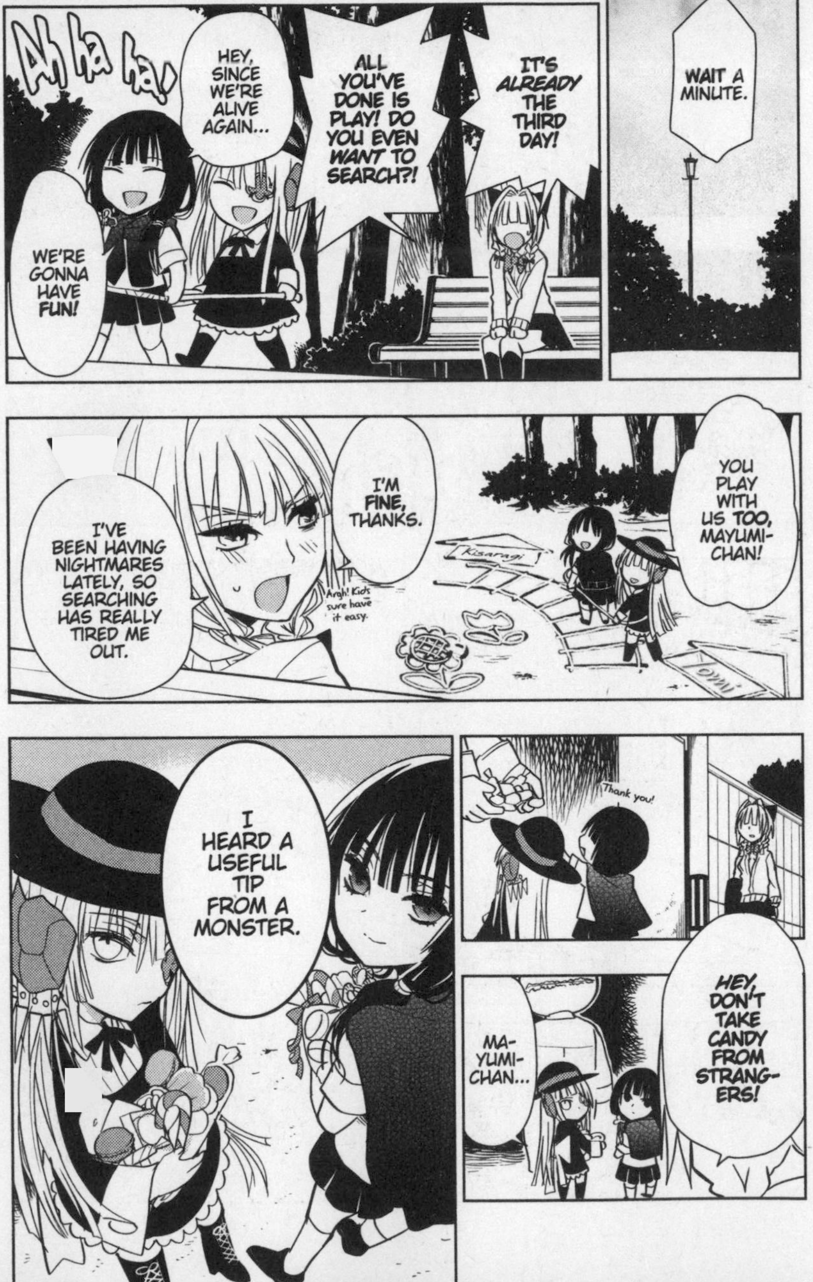
WAIT A MINUTE.
IT'S ALREADY THE THIRD DAY!
ALL YOU'VE DONE IS PLAY! DO YOU EVEN WANT TO SEARCH?!
HEY, SINCE WE'RE ALIVE AGAIN...
Ah ha ha!
WE'RE GONNA HAVE FUN!
YOU PLAY WITH US TOO, MAYUMI-CHAN!
Kisaragi
I'M FINE, THANKS.
Argh! Kids sure have it easy.
I'VE BEEN HAVING NIGHTMARES LATELY, SO SEARCHING HAS REALLY TIRED ME OUT.
Thank you!
HEY, DON'T TAKE CANDY FROM STRANGERS!
MA-YUMI-CHAN...
I HEARD A USEFUL TIP FROM A MONSTER.

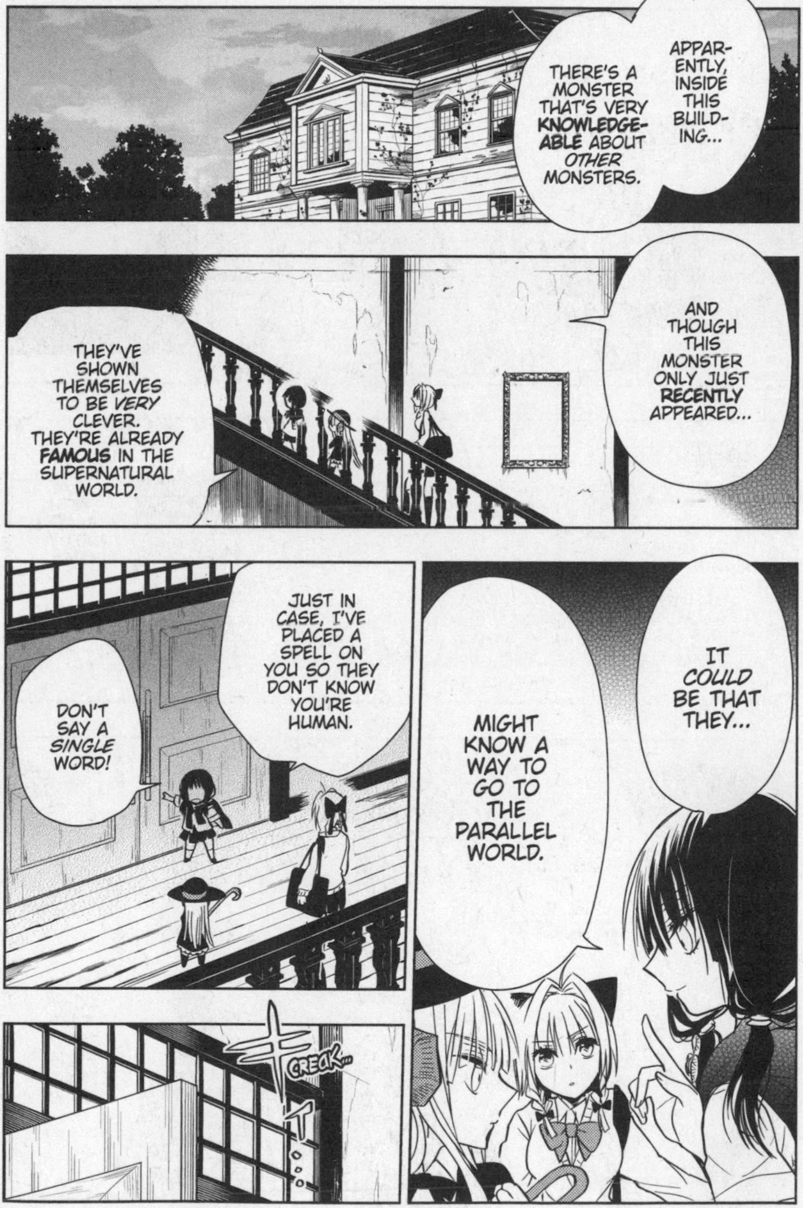
APPARENTLY, INSIDE THIS BUILDING...
THERE'S A MONSTER THAT'S VERY **KNOWLEDGEABLE** ABOUT *OTHER* MONSTERS.
AND THOUGH THIS MONSTER ONLY JUST **RECENTLY** APPEARED...
THEY'VE SHOWN THEMSELVES TO BE *VERY* CLEVER. THEY'RE ALREADY **FAMOUS** IN THE SUPERNATURAL WORLD.
IT *COULD* BE THAT THEY...
MIGHT KNOW A WAY TO GO TO THE PARALLEL WORLD.
JUST IN CASE, I'VE PLACED A SPELL ON YOU SO THEY DON'T KNOW YOU'RE HUMAN.
DON'T SAY A *SINGLE* WORD!
CREAK...

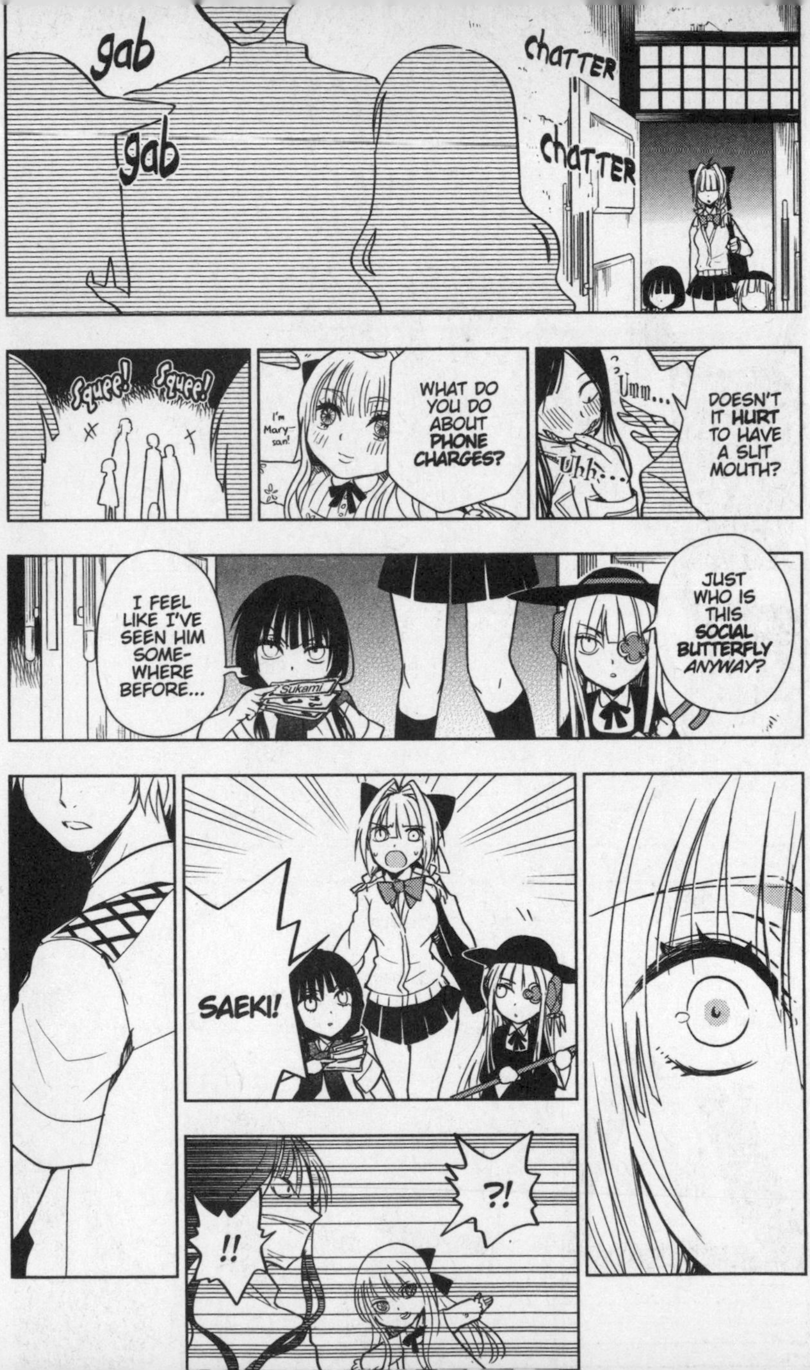
chatter
chatter
gab
gab
DOESN'T IT HURT TO HAVE A SLIT MOUTH?
Umm...
Uhh...
WHAT DO YOU DO ABOUT PHONE CHARGES?
I'm Mary-san!
Squee! Squee!
JUST WHO IS THIS SOCIAL BUTTERFLY ANYWAY?
I FEEL LIKE I'VE SEEN HIM SOME-WHERE BEFORE...
Sukami
SAEKI!
?!
!!

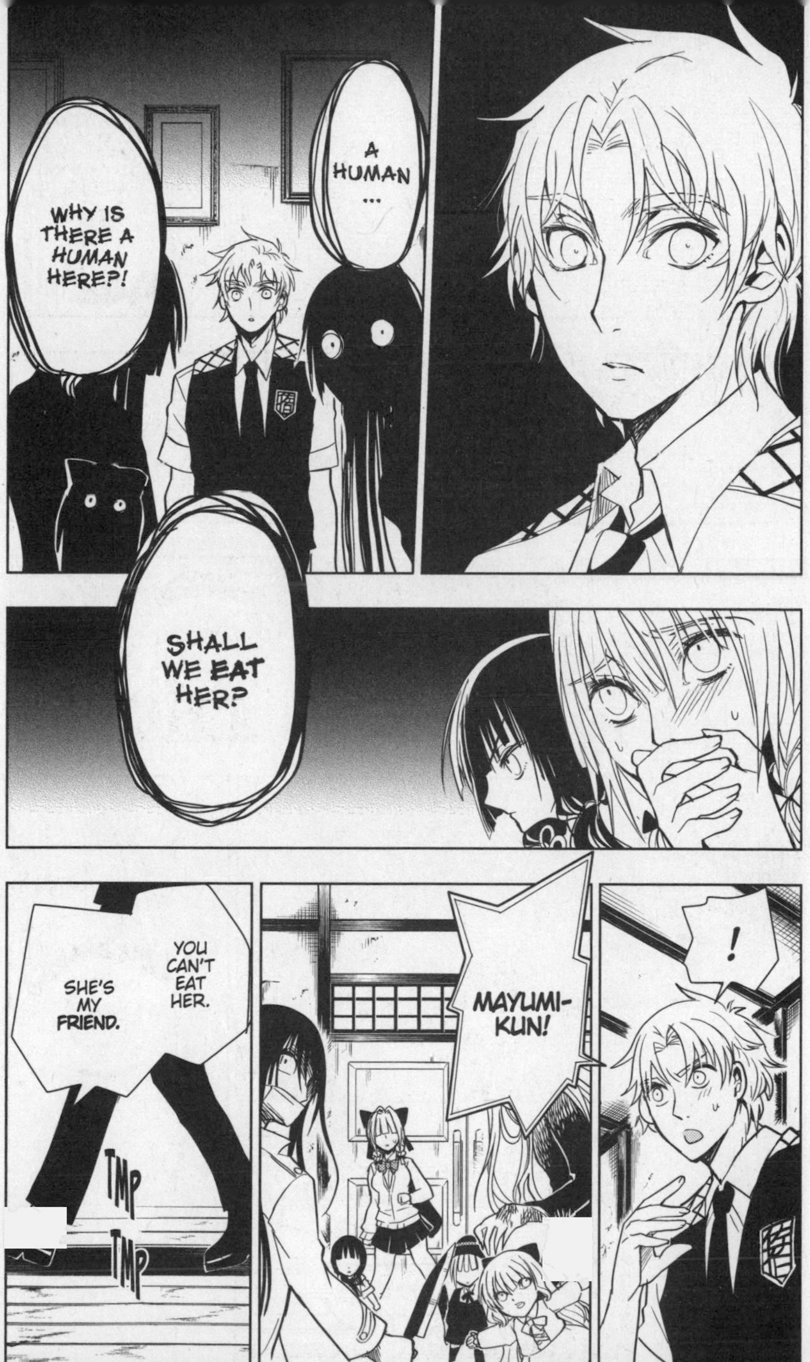
A HUMAN ...
WHY IS THERE A HUMAN HERE?!
SHALL WE EAT HER?
!
MAYUMI-KUN!
YOU CAN'T EAT HER.
SHE'S MY FRIEND.
TMP
TMP

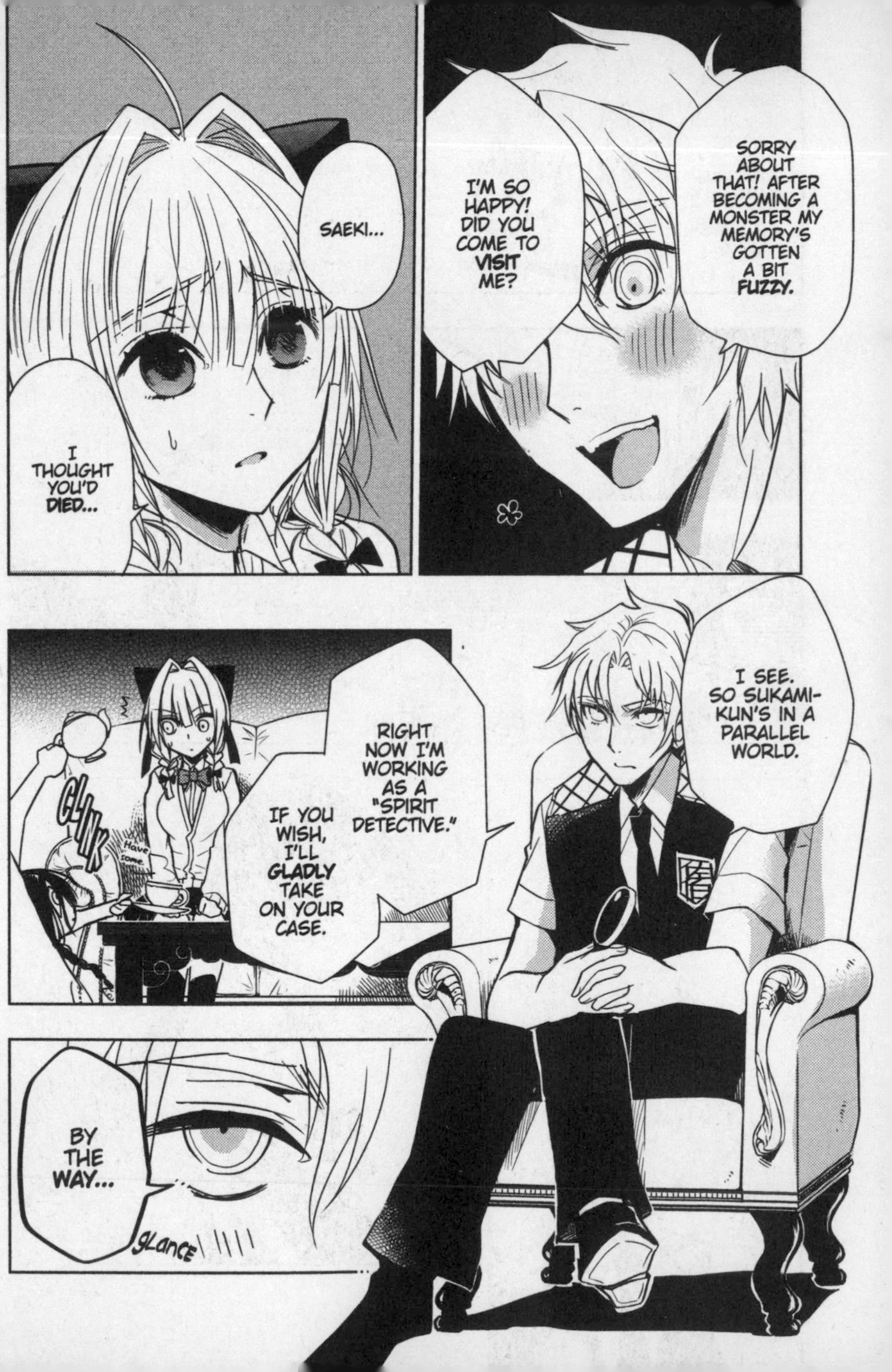
SAEKI...
I THOUGHT YOU'D **DIED...**
I'M SO HAPPY! DID YOU COME TO **VISIT** ME?
SORRY ABOUT THAT! AFTER BECOMING A MONSTER MY MEMORY'S GOTTEN A BIT **FUZZY.**
I SEE. SO SUKAMI-KUN'S IN A PARALLEL WORLD.
RIGHT NOW I'M WORKING AS A "SPIRIT DETECTIVE."
IF YOU WISH, I'LL **GLADLY** TAKE ON YOUR CASE.
CLINK
Have some.
BY THE **WAY...**
glance

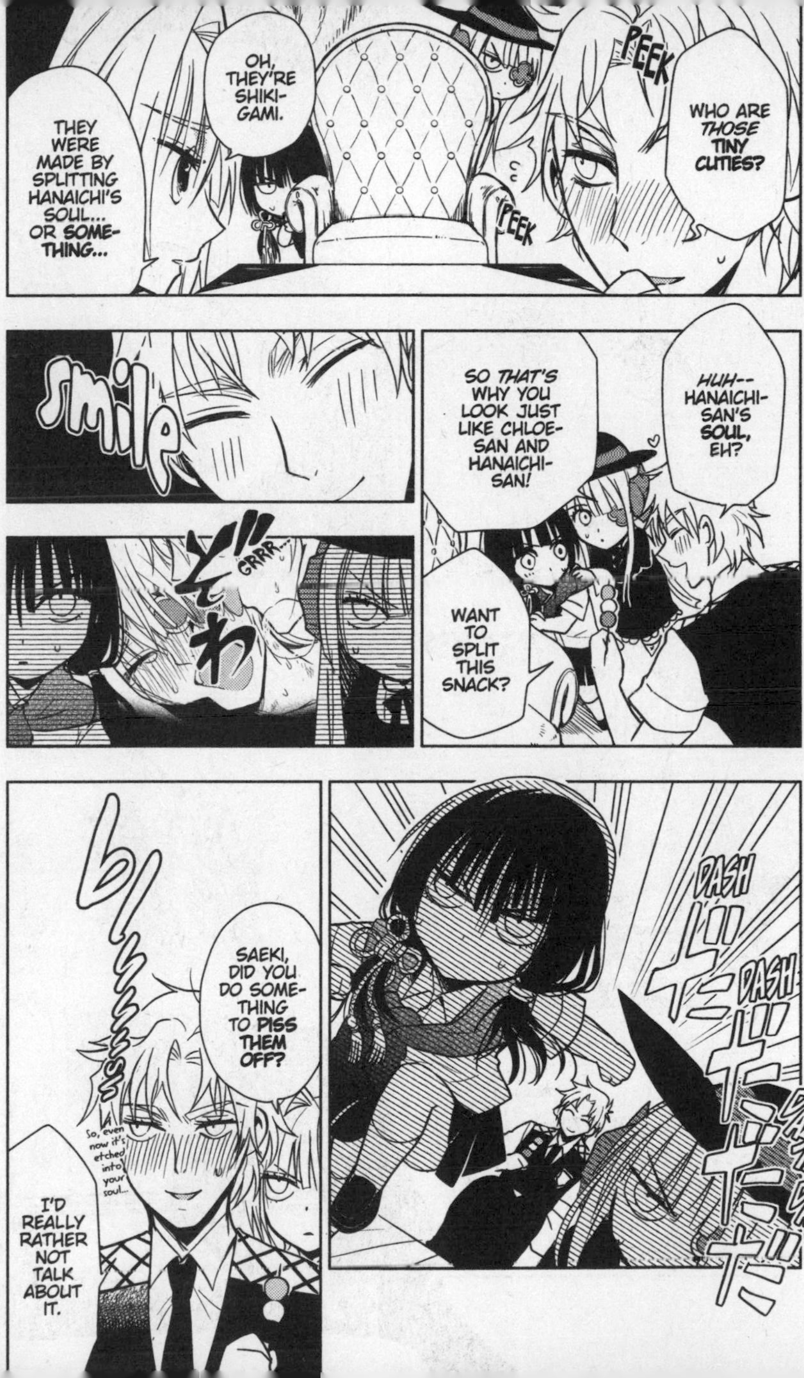
PEEK
WHO ARE THOSE TINY CUTIES?
PEEK
OH, THEY'RE SHIKI-GAMI.
THEY WERE MADE BY SPLITTING HANAICHI'S SOUL... OR SOME-THING...
HUH-- HANAICHI-SAN'S SOUL, EH?
SO THAT'S WHY YOU LOOK JUST LIKE CHLOE-SAN AND HANAICHI-SAN!
WANT TO SPLIT THIS SNACK?
smile
GRRR...
DASH
DASH
DASH
DASH
SAEKI, DID YOU DO SOME-THING TO PISS THEM OFF?
So, even now it's etched into your soul...
I'D REALLY RATHER NOT TALK ABOUT IT.

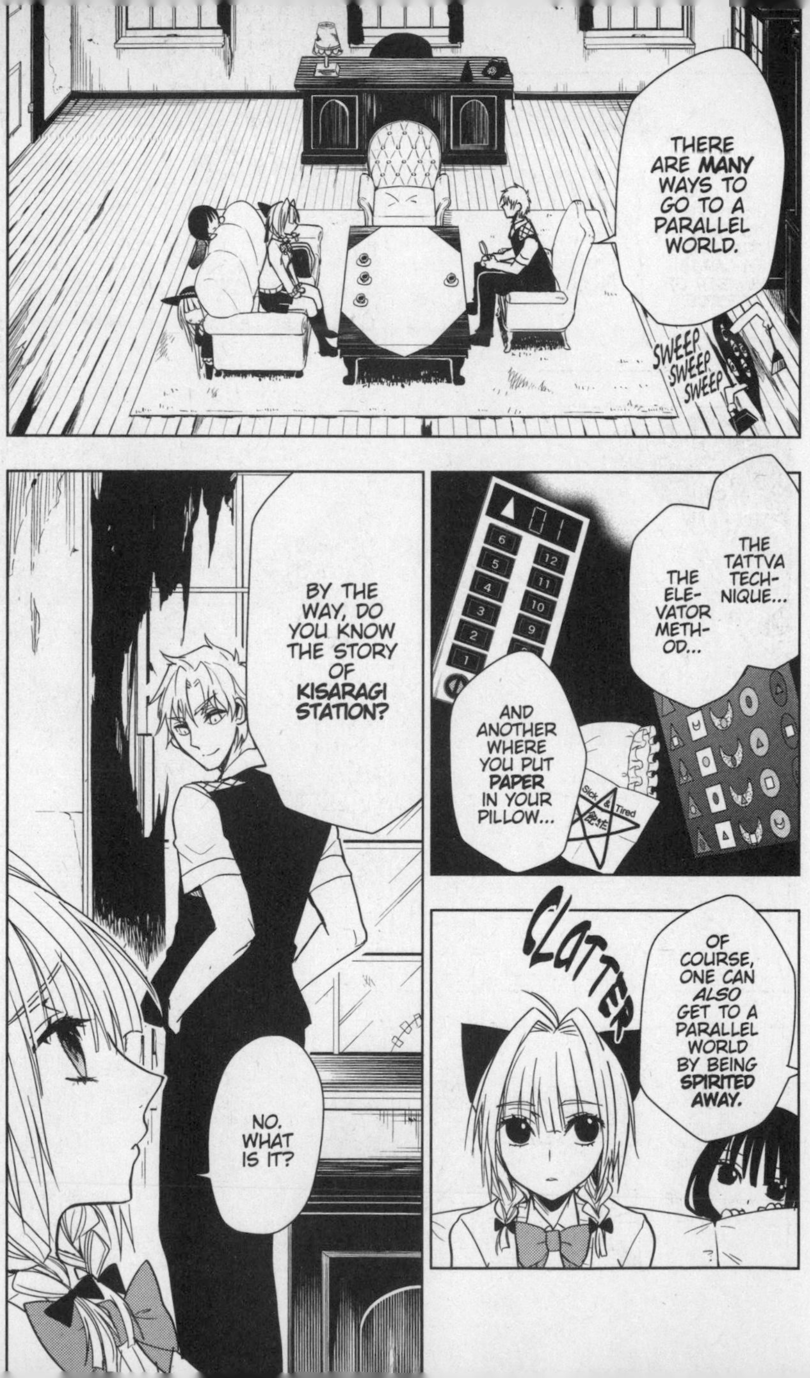
THERE ARE MANY WAYS TO GO TO A PARALLEL WORLD.
SWEEP SWEEP SWEEP
THE TATTVA TECHNIQUE...
THE ELEVATOR METHOD...
AND ANOTHER WHERE YOU PUT PAPER IN YOUR PILLOW...
Sick & Tired
CLATTER
OF COURSE, ONE CAN ALSO GET TO A PARALLEL WORLD BY BEING SPIRITED AWAY.
BY THE WAY, DO YOU KNOW THE STORY OF KISARAGI STATION?
NO. WHAT IS IT?

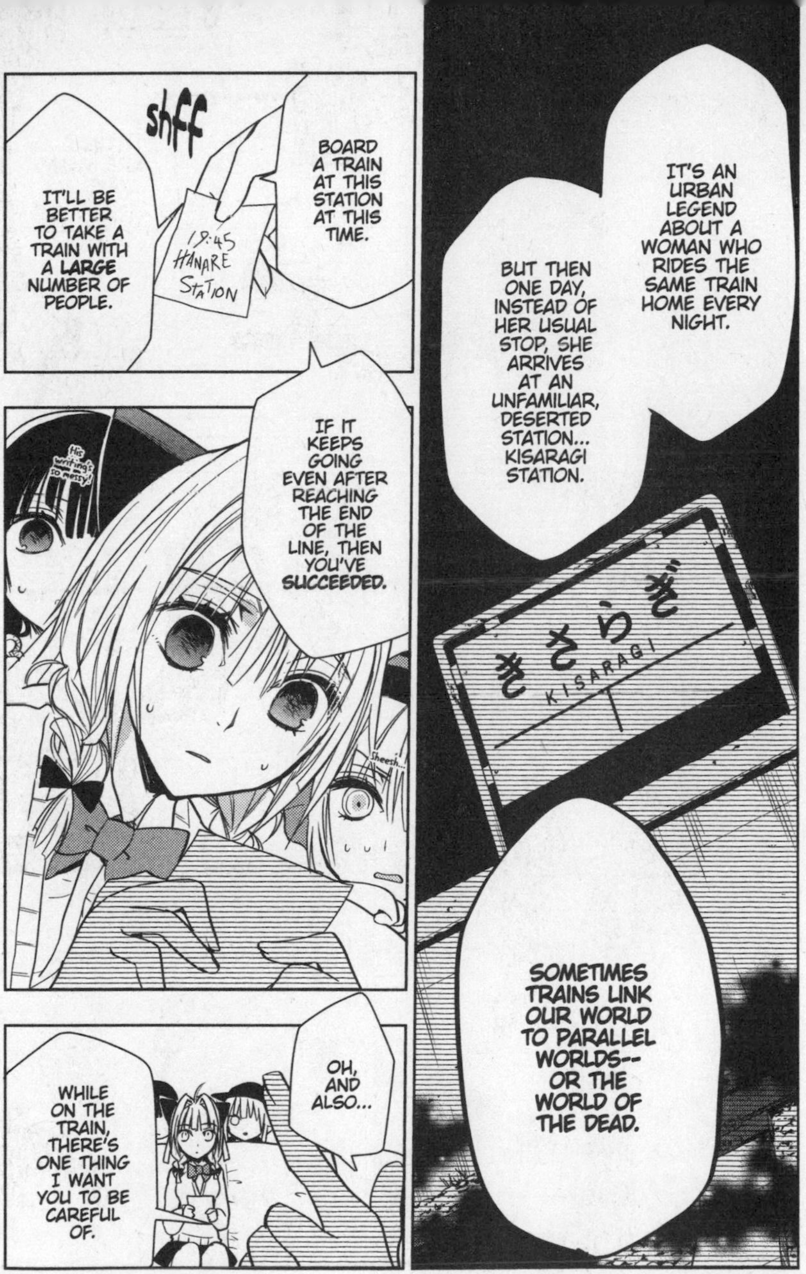
IT'S AN URBAN LEGEND ABOUT A WOMAN WHO RIDES THE SAME TRAIN HOME EVERY NIGHT.
BUT THEN ONE DAY, INSTEAD OF HER USUAL STOP, SHE ARRIVES AT AN UNFAMILIAR, DESERTED STATION... KISARAGI STATION.
きさらぎ
KISARAGI
SOMETIMES TRAINS LINK OUR WORLD TO PARALLEL WORLDS--OR THE WORLD OF THE DEAD.
shff
BOARD A TRAIN AT THIS STATION AT THIS TIME.
19:45 HANARE STATION
IT'LL BE BETTER TO TAKE A TRAIN WITH A LARGE NUMBER OF PEOPLE.
IF IT KEEPS GOING EVEN AFTER REACHING THE END OF THE LINE, THEN YOU'VE SUCCEEDED.
His writing's so messy!
Sheesh...
OH, AND ALSO...
WHILE ON THE TRAIN, THERE'S ONE THING I WANT YOU TO BE CAREFUL OF.

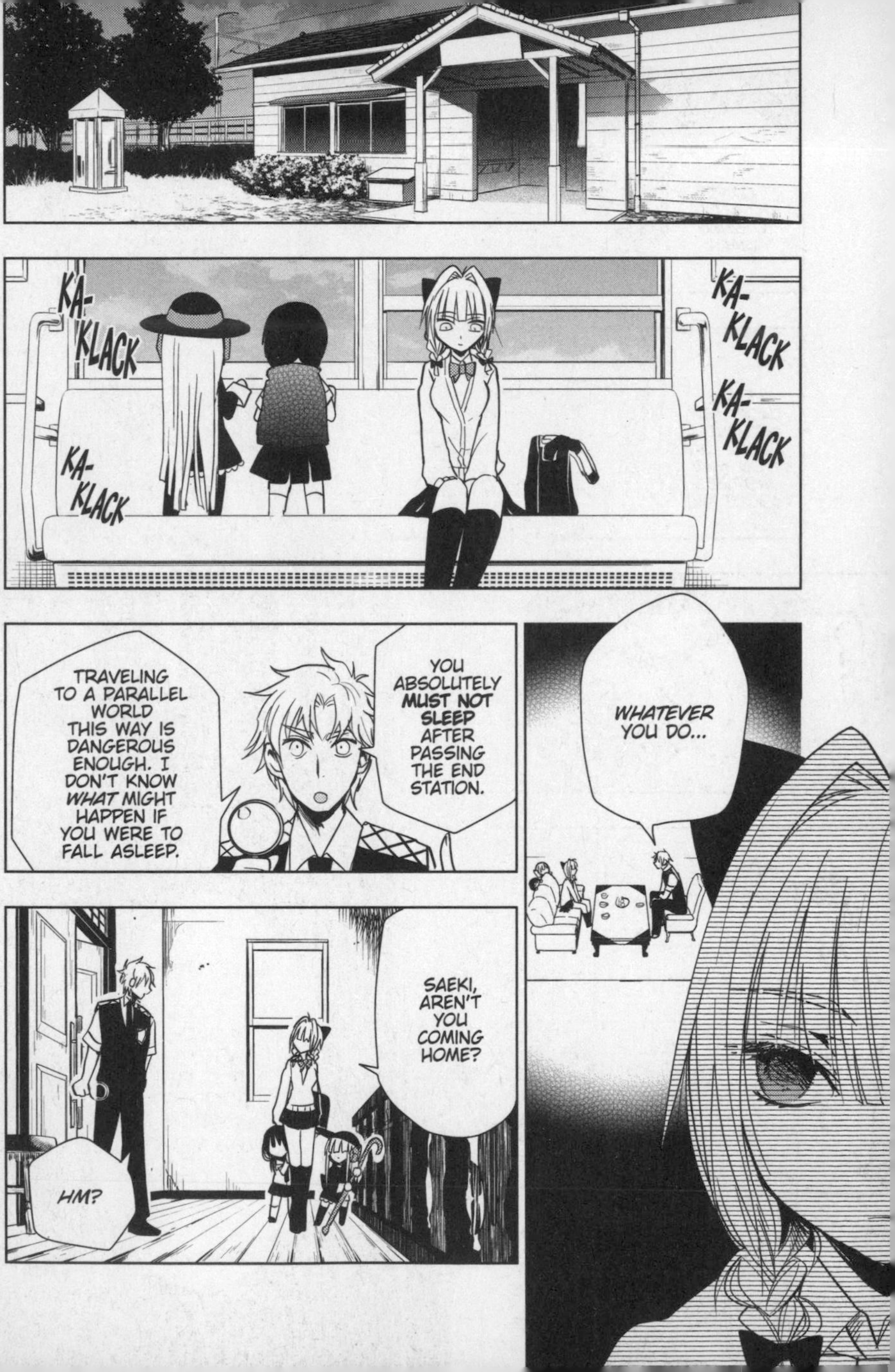
KA-KLACK
KA-KLACK
KA-KLACK
KA-KLACK
WHATEVER YOU DO...
YOU ABSOLUTELY MUST NOT SLEEP AFTER PASSING THE END STATION.
TRAVELING TO A PARALLEL WORLD THIS WAY IS DANGEROUS ENOUGH. I DON'T KNOW *WHAT* MIGHT HAPPEN IF YOU WERE TO FALL ASLEEP.
SAEKI, AREN'T YOU COMING HOME?
HM?

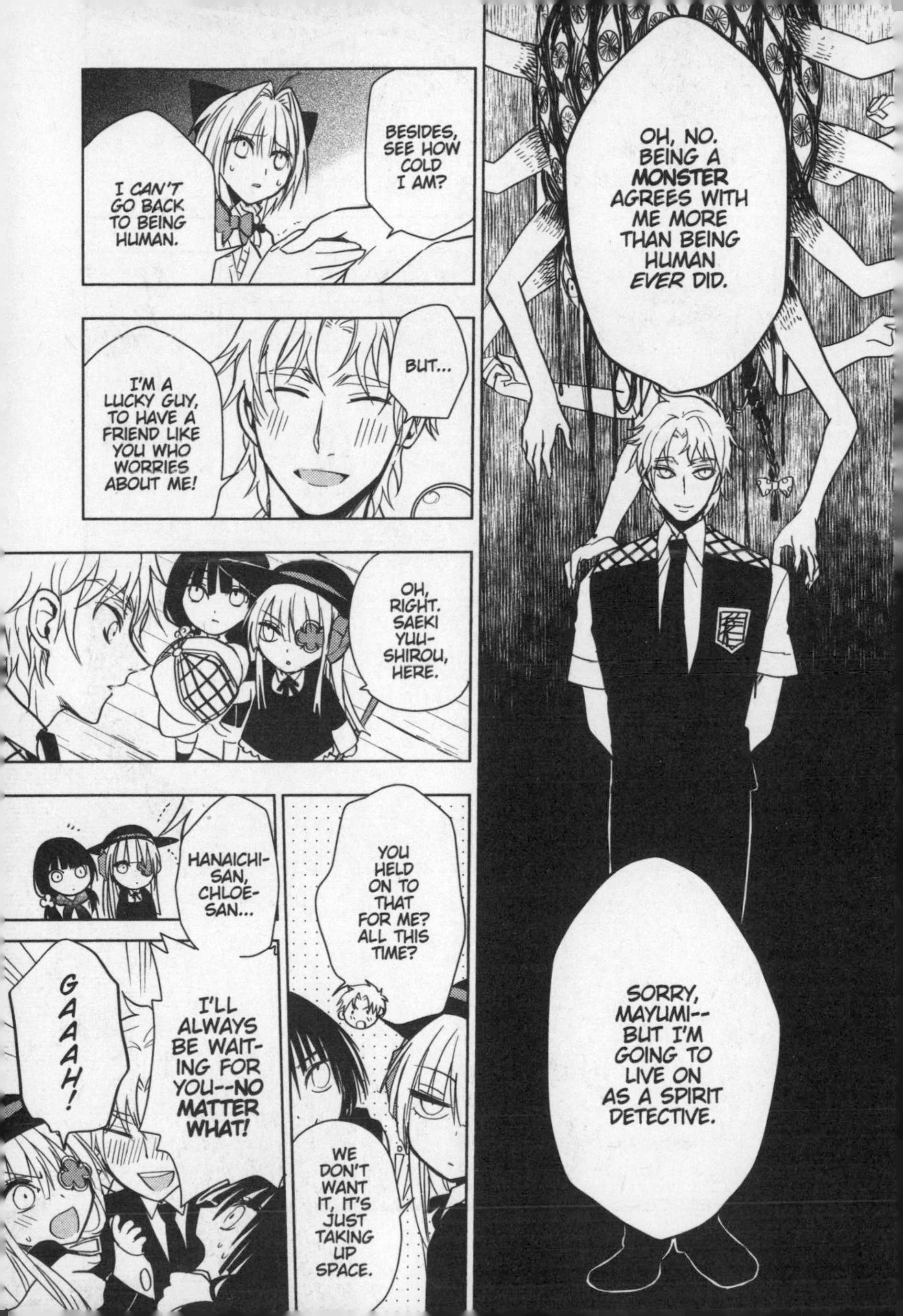
OH, NO. BEING A MONSTER AGREES WITH ME MORE THAN BEING HUMAN EVER DID.
SORRY, MAYUMI--BUT I'M GOING TO LIVE ON AS A SPIRIT DETECTIVE.
BESIDES, SEE HOW COLD I AM?
I CAN'T GO BACK TO BEING HUMAN.
BUT...
I'M A LUCKY GUY, TO HAVE A FRIEND LIKE YOU WHO WORRIES ABOUT ME!
OH, RIGHT. SAEKI YUU-SHIROU, HERE.
YOU HELD ON TO THAT FOR ME? ALL THIS TIME?
HANAICHI-SAN, CHLOE-SAN...
I'LL ALWAYS BE WAITING FOR YOU--NO MATTER WHAT!
GAAAH!
WE DON'T WANT IT, IT'S JUST TAKING UP SPACE.

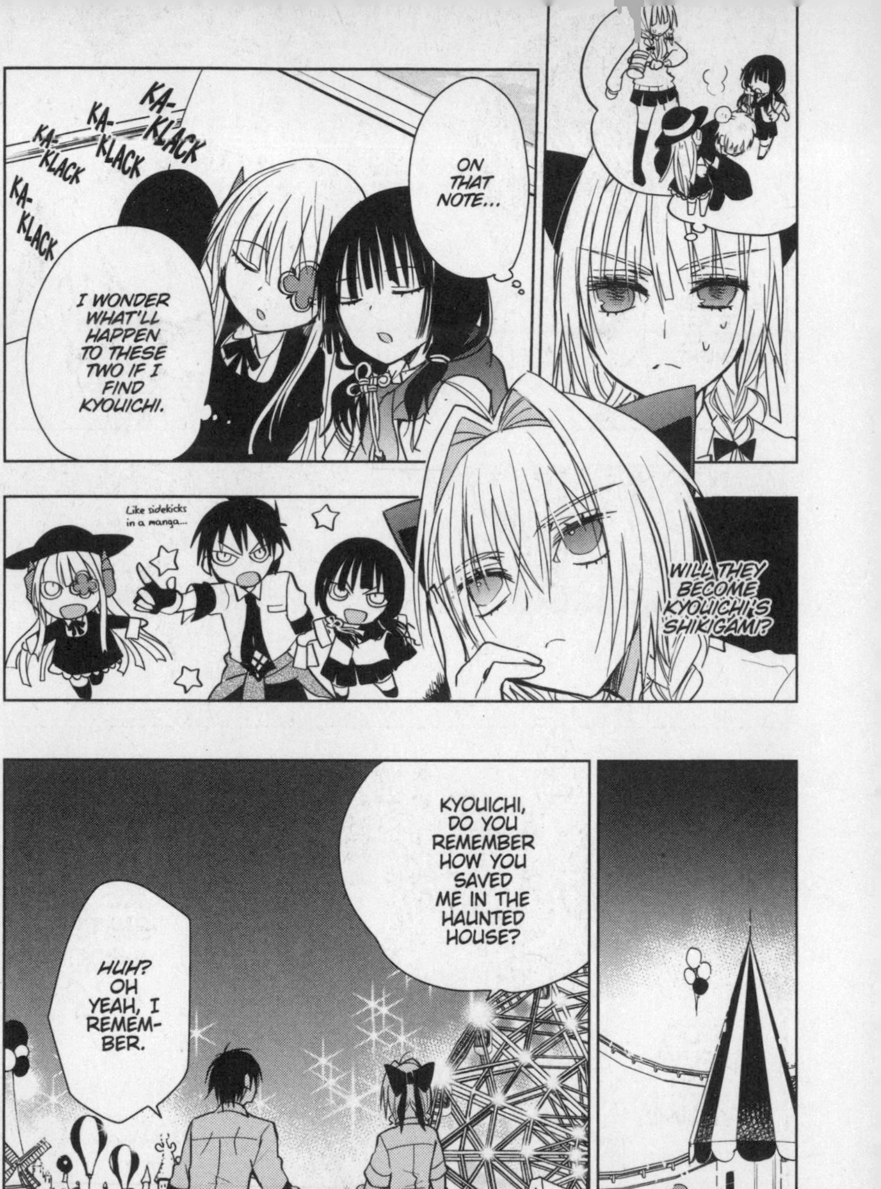
ON THAT NOTE...
KA-KLACK
KA-KLACK
KA-KLACK
KA-KLACK
I WONDER WHAT'LL HAPPEN TO THESE TWO IF I FIND KYOUICHI.
WILL THEY BECOME KYOUICHI'S SHIKIGAMI?
Like sidekicks in a manga...
KYOUICHI, DO YOU REMEMBER HOW YOU SAVED ME IN THE HAUNTED HOUSE?
HUH? OH YEAH, I REMEMBER.

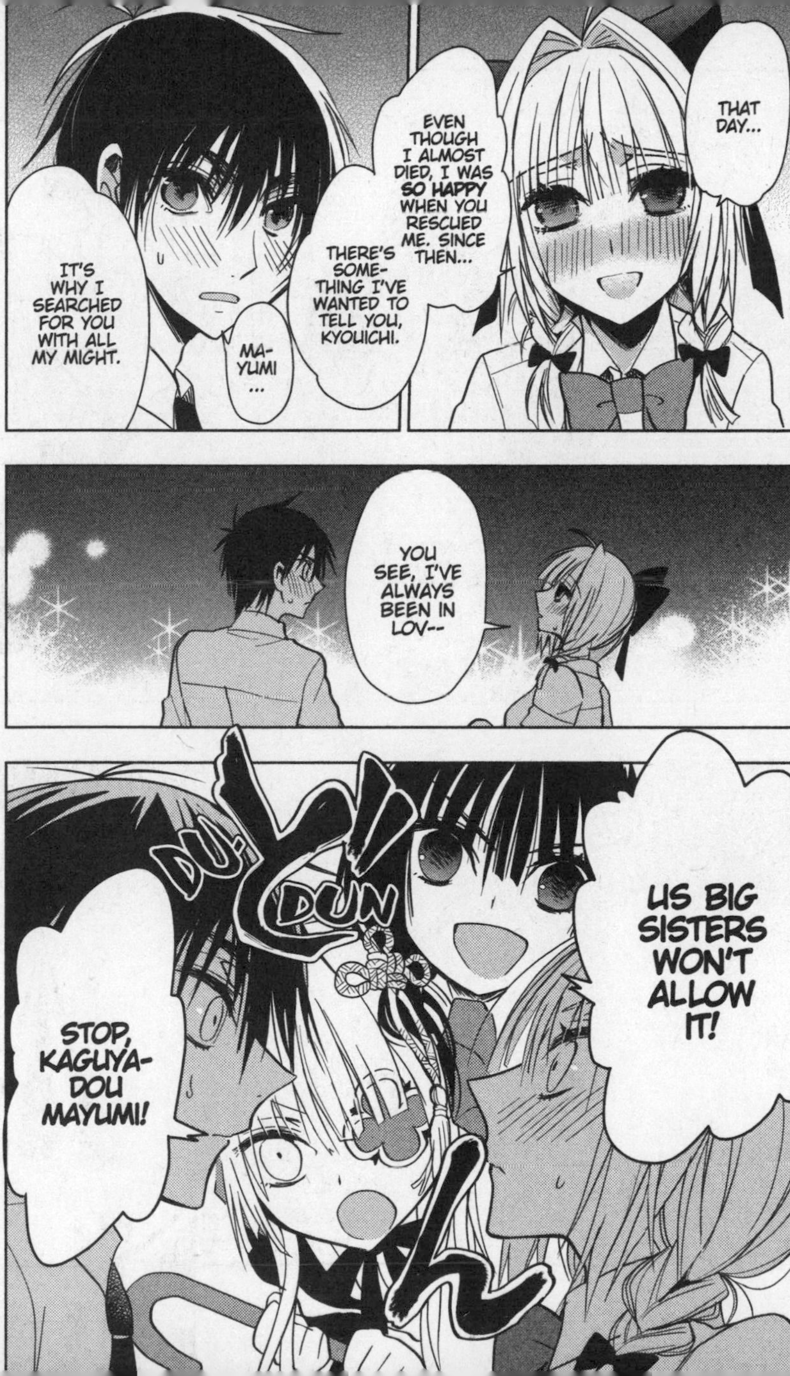
THAT DAY...
EVEN THOUGH I ALMOST DIED, I WAS SO HAPPY WHEN YOU RESCUED ME. SINCE THEN...
THERE'S SOME-THING I'VE WANTED TO TELL YOU, KYOUICHI.
MA-YUMI ...
IT'S WHY I SEARCHED FOR YOU WITH ALL MY MIGHT.
YOU SEE, I'VE ALWAYS BEEN IN LOV--
US BIG SISTERS WON'T ALLOW IT!
DUN
DU!
STOP, KAGUYA-DOU MAYUMI!

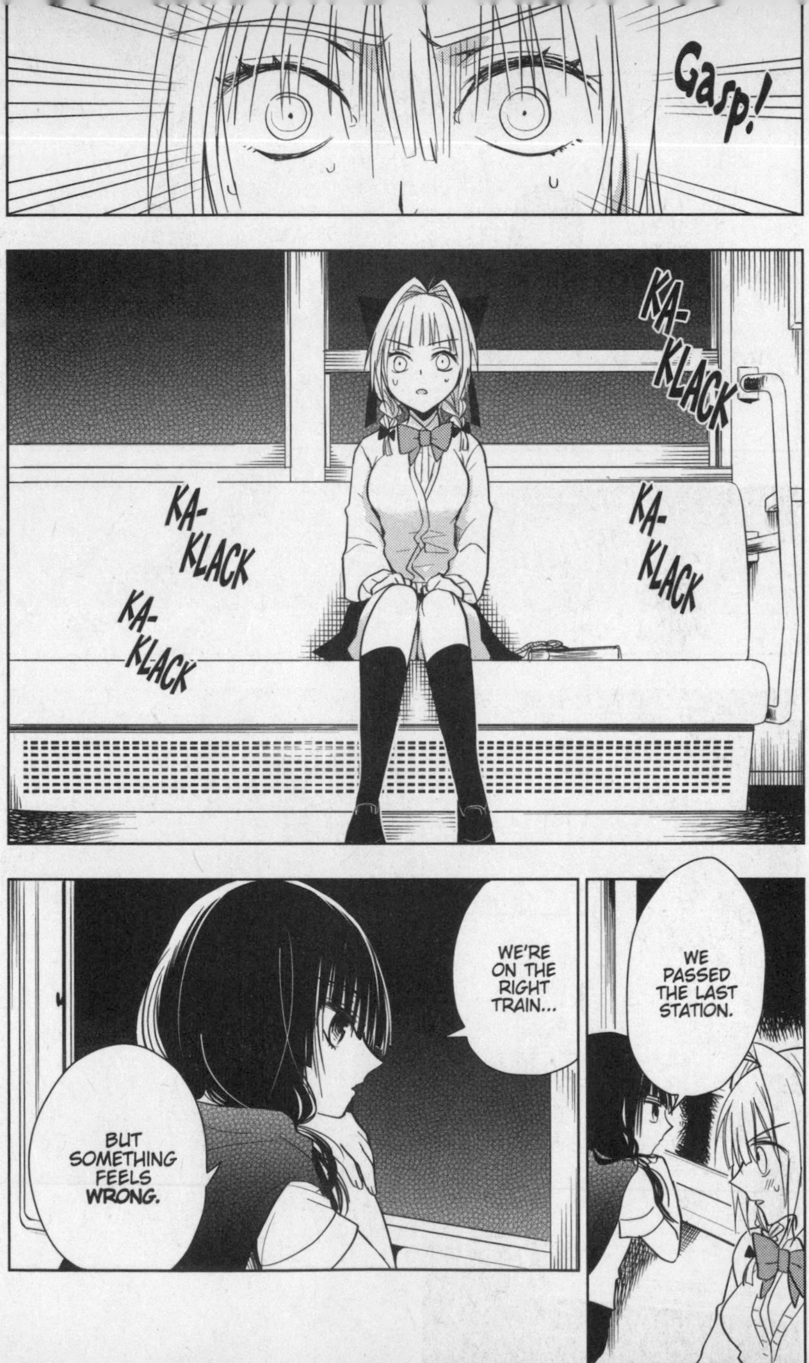
Gasp!
KA-KLACK
KA-KLACK
KA-KLACK
KA-KLACK
WE PASSED THE LAST STATION.
WE'RE ON THE RIGHT TRAIN...
BUT SOMETHING FEELS WRONG.

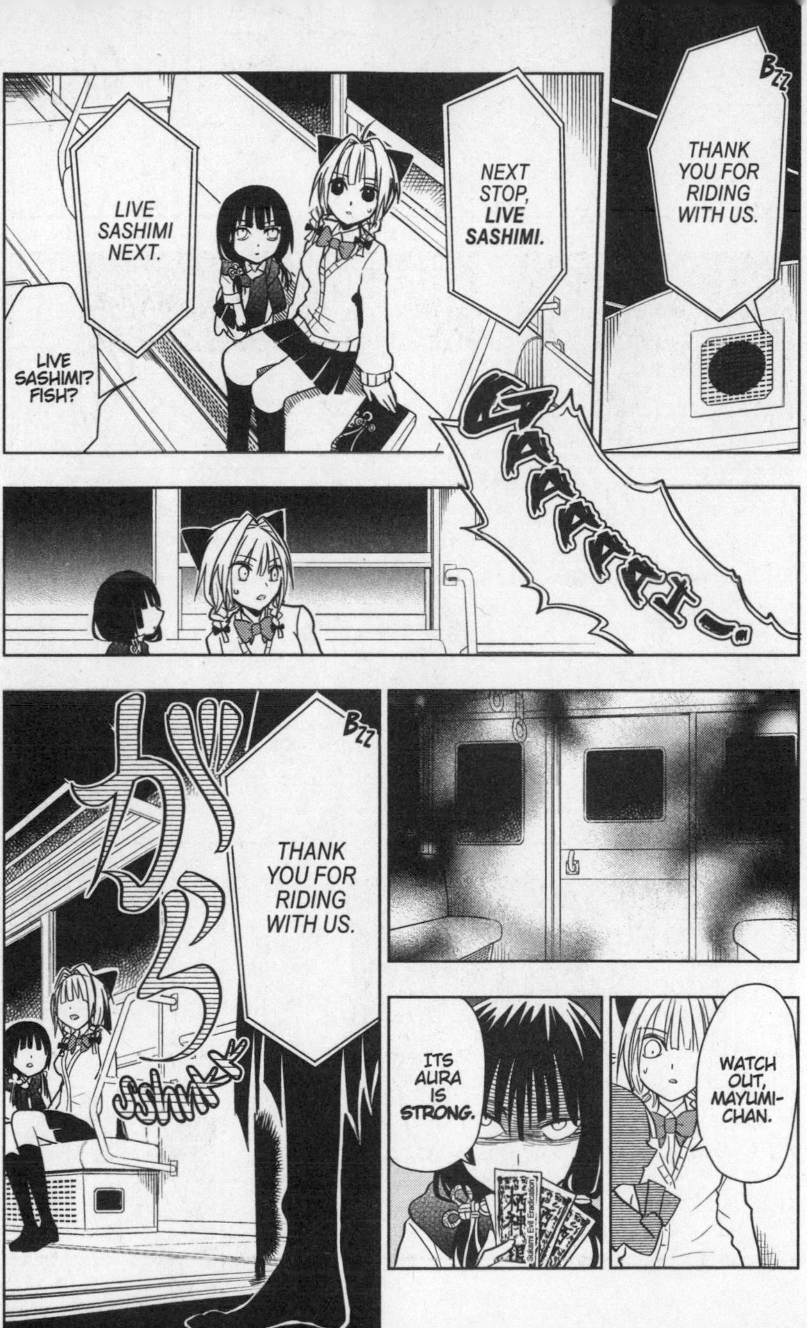
BZZ
THANK YOU FOR RIDING WITH US.
NEXT STOP, LIVE SASHIMI.
LIVE SASHIMI NEXT.
LIVE SASHIMI? FISH?
BZZ
THANK YOU FOR RIDING WITH US.
WATCH OUT, MAYUMI-CHAN.
ITS AURA IS STRONG.

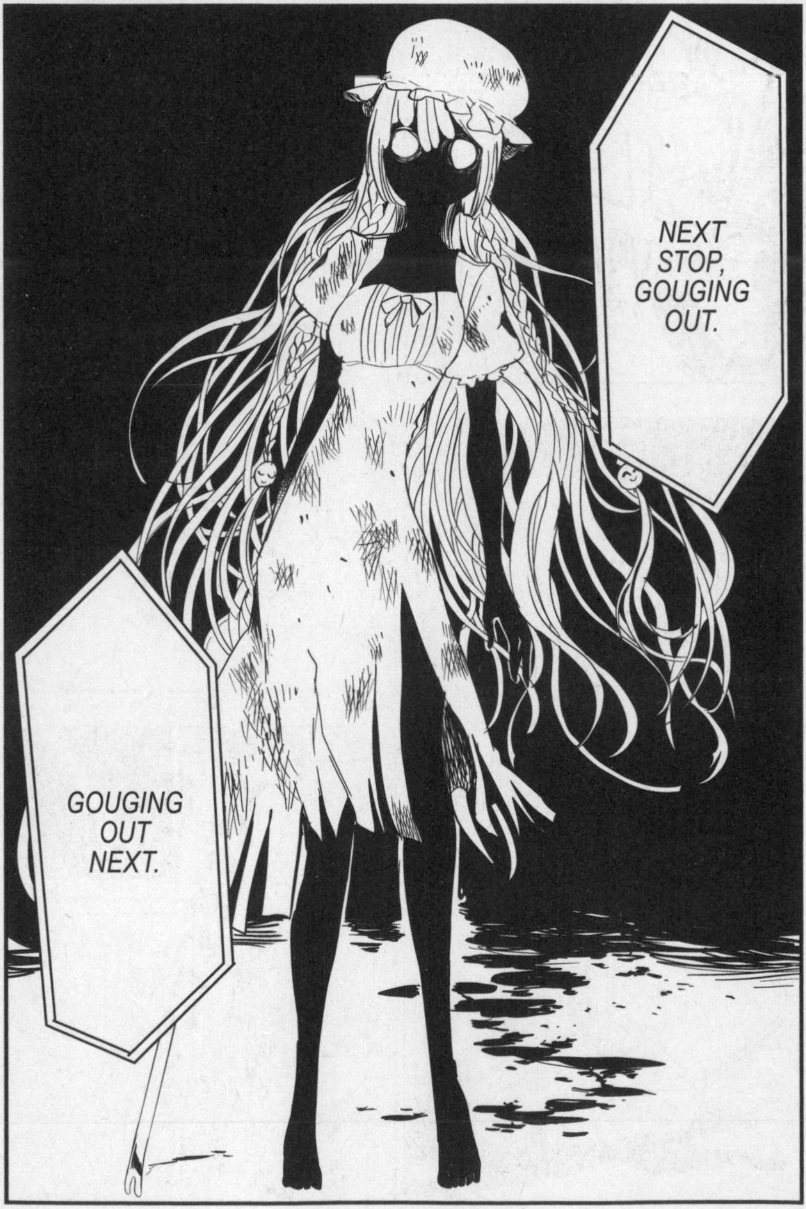
NEXT STOP, GOUGING OUT.
GOUGING OUT NEXT.

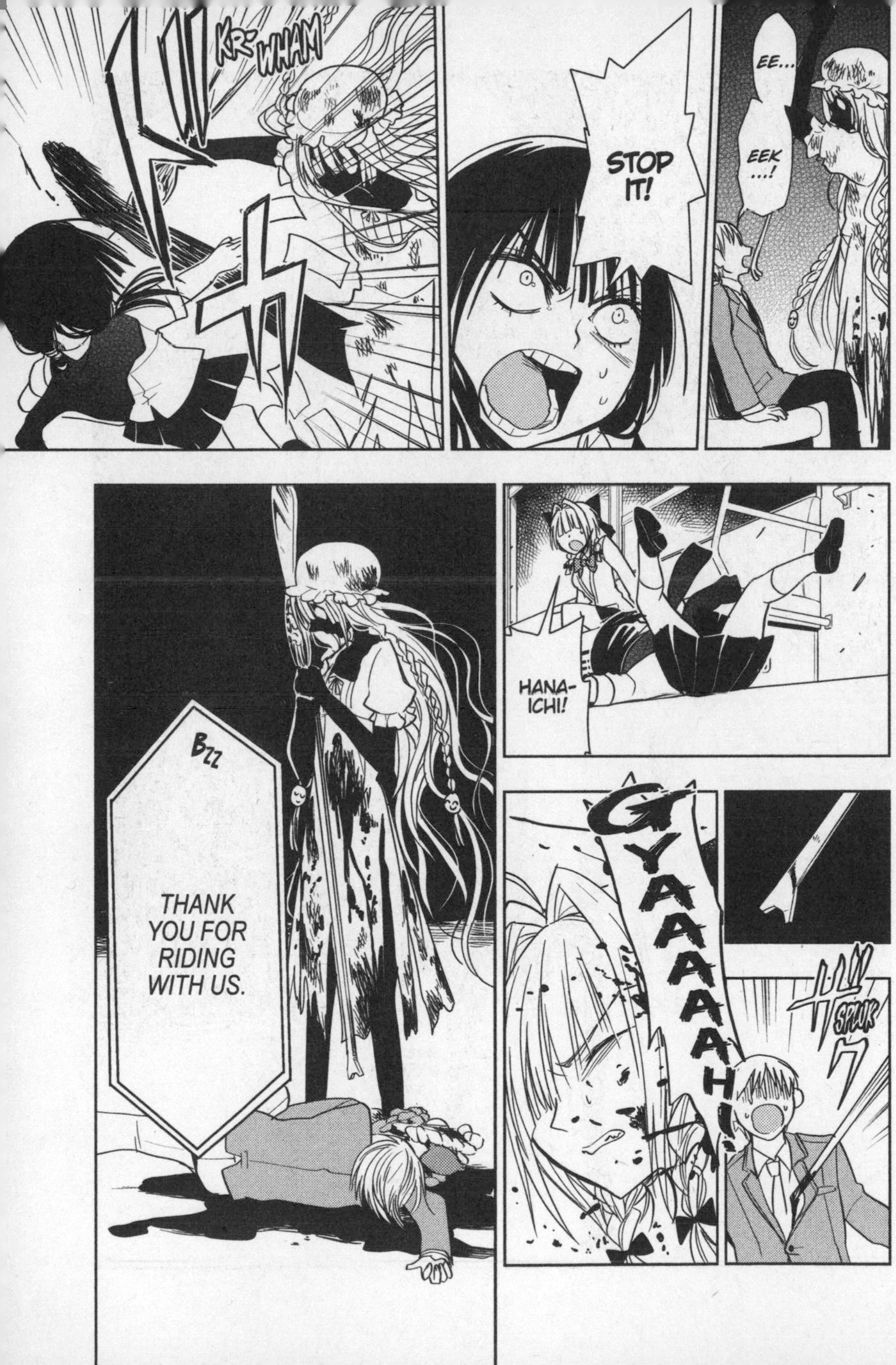
EE...
EEK ...!
STOP IT!
KR-WHAM
HANA-ICHI!
GYAAAAAH!
SPLURK
BZZ
THANK YOU FOR RIDING WITH US.

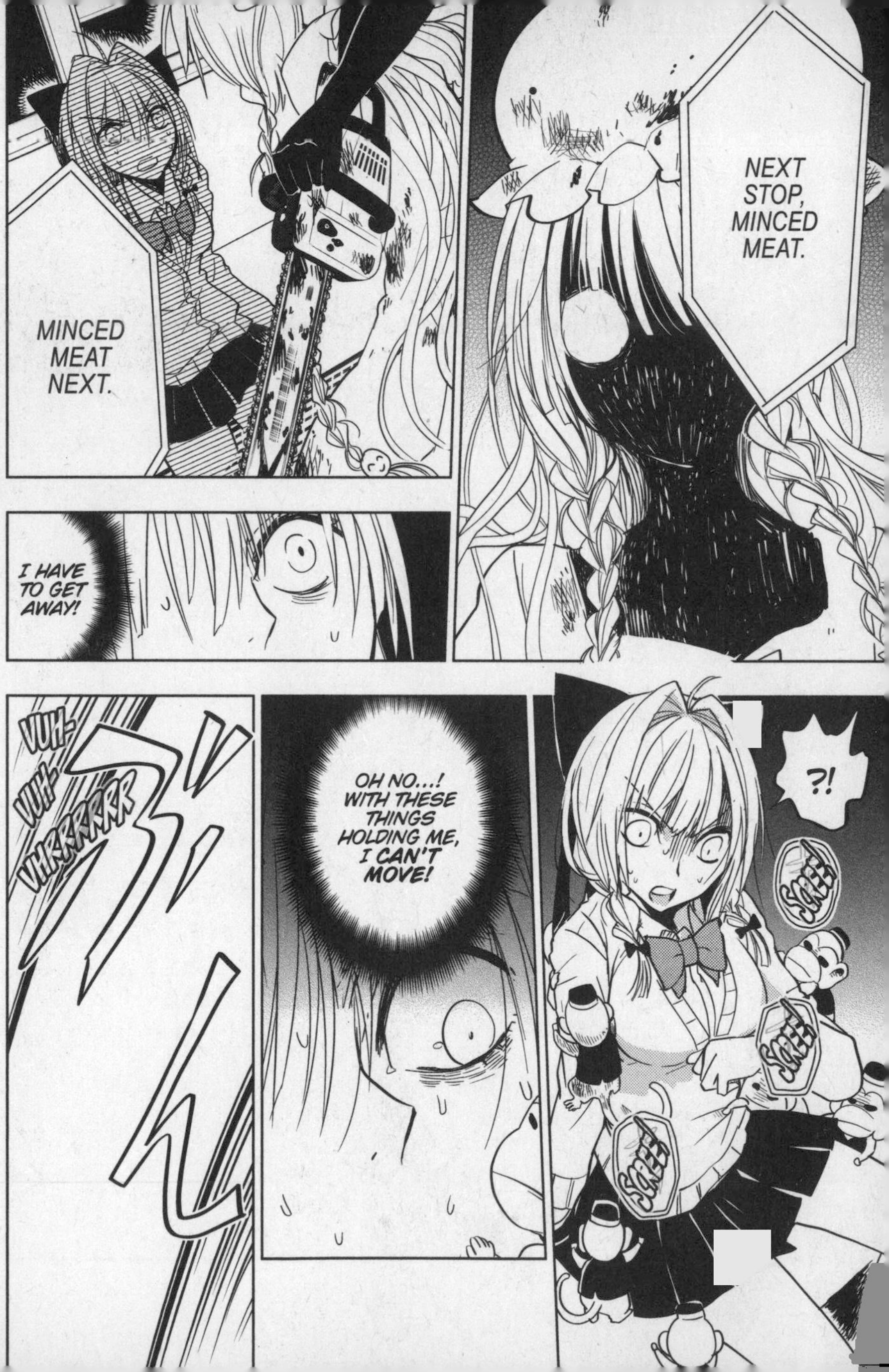
NEXT STOP, MINCED MEAT.
MINCED MEAT NEXT.
I HAVE TO GET AWAY!
?!
SCREE
SCREE
SCREE
OH NO...! WITH THESE THINGS HOLDING ME, I CAN'T MOVE!
VUH-VUH-VHRRRRRRR

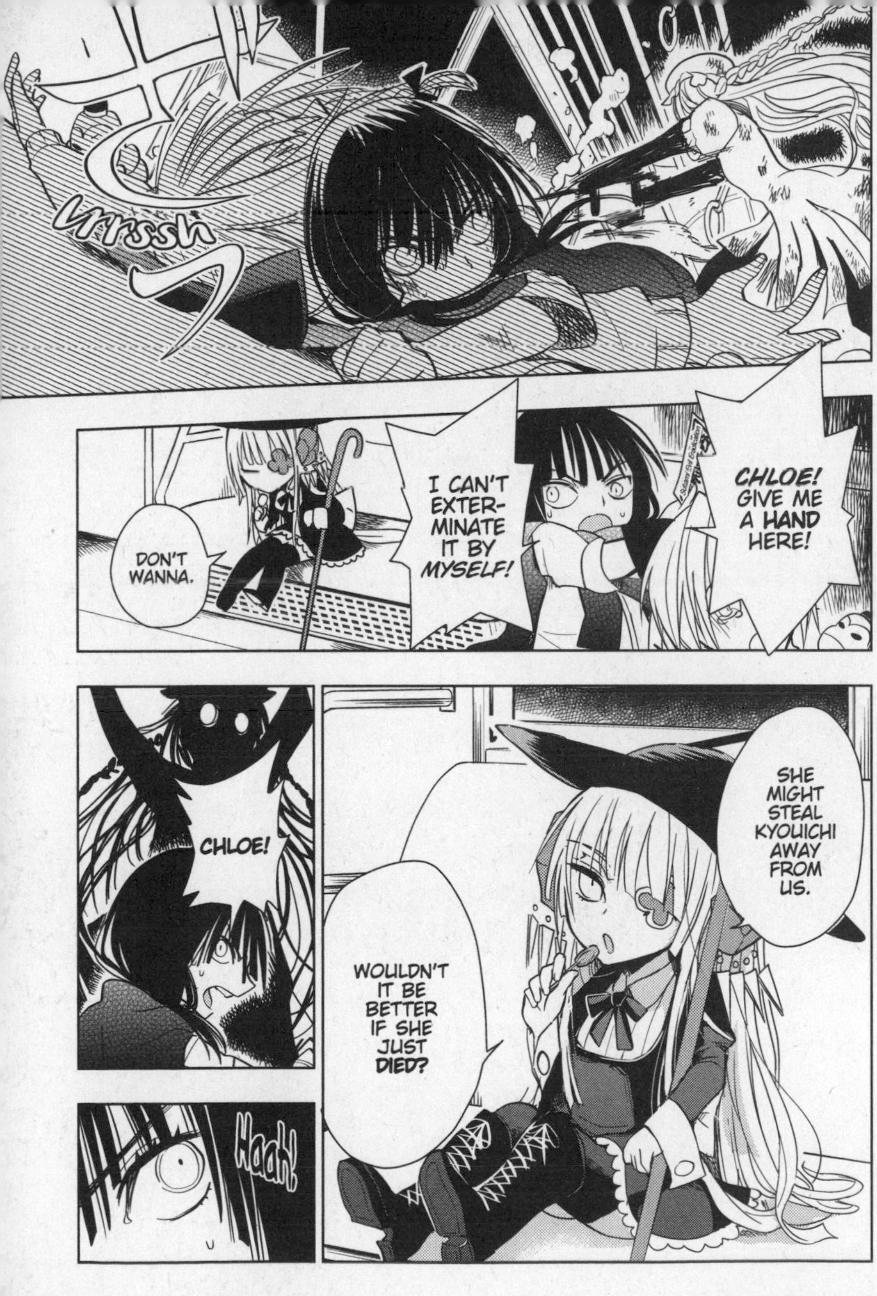
Urrssh
CHLOE! GIVE ME A HAND HERE!
I CAN'T EXTER-MINATE IT BY MYSELF!
DON'T WANNA.
SHE MIGHT STEAL KYOUICHI AWAY FROM US.
WOULDN'T IT BE BETTER IF SHE JUST DIED?
CHLOE!
Haah!

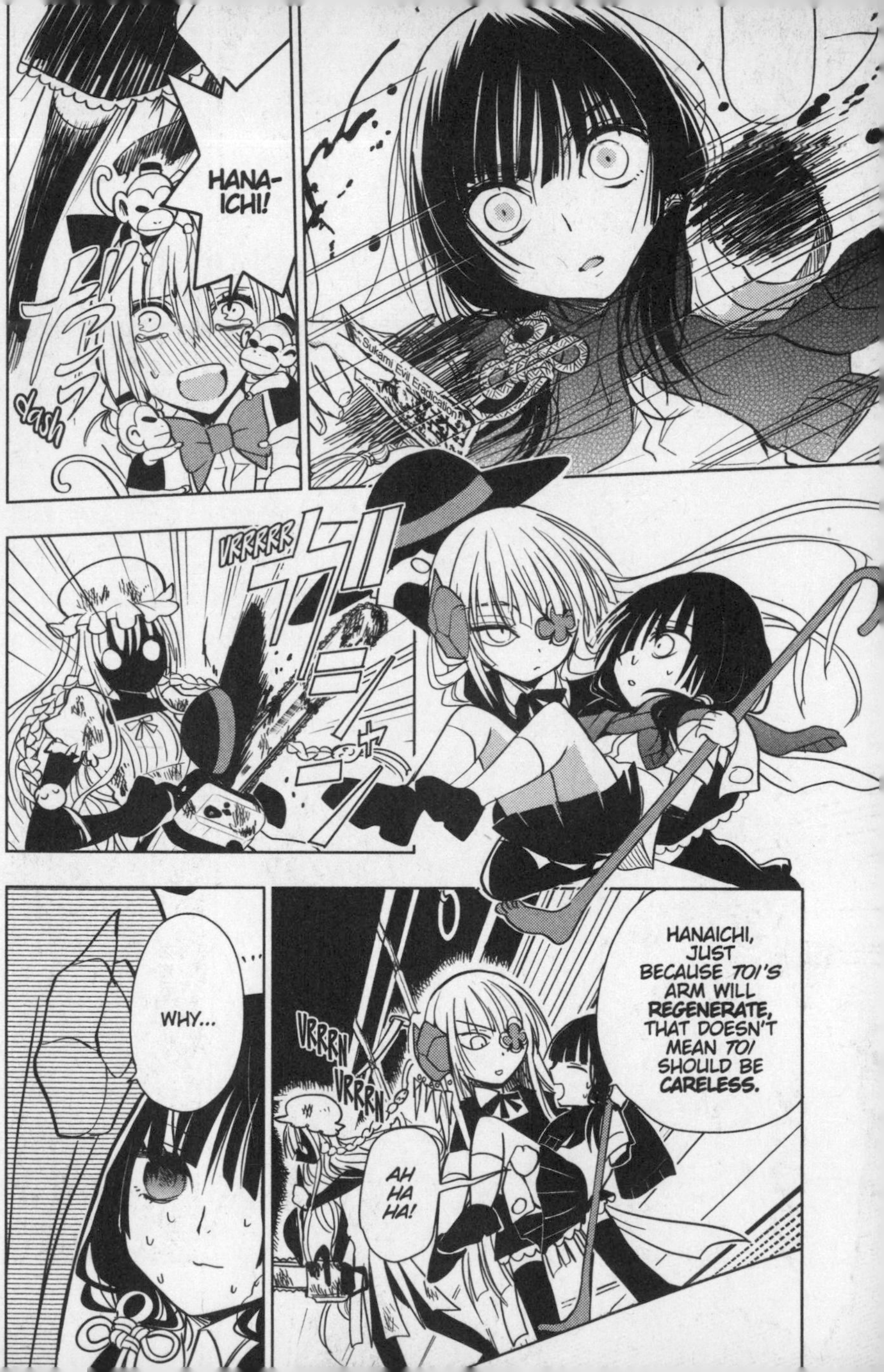
Sukami Evil Eradication
HANA-ICHI!
dash
VRRRRR
HANAICHI, JUST BECAUSE *TOI'S* ARM WILL REGENERATE, THAT DOESN'T MEAN *TOI* SHOULD BE CARELESS.
VRRRN VRRRN
AH HA HA!
...
WHY...

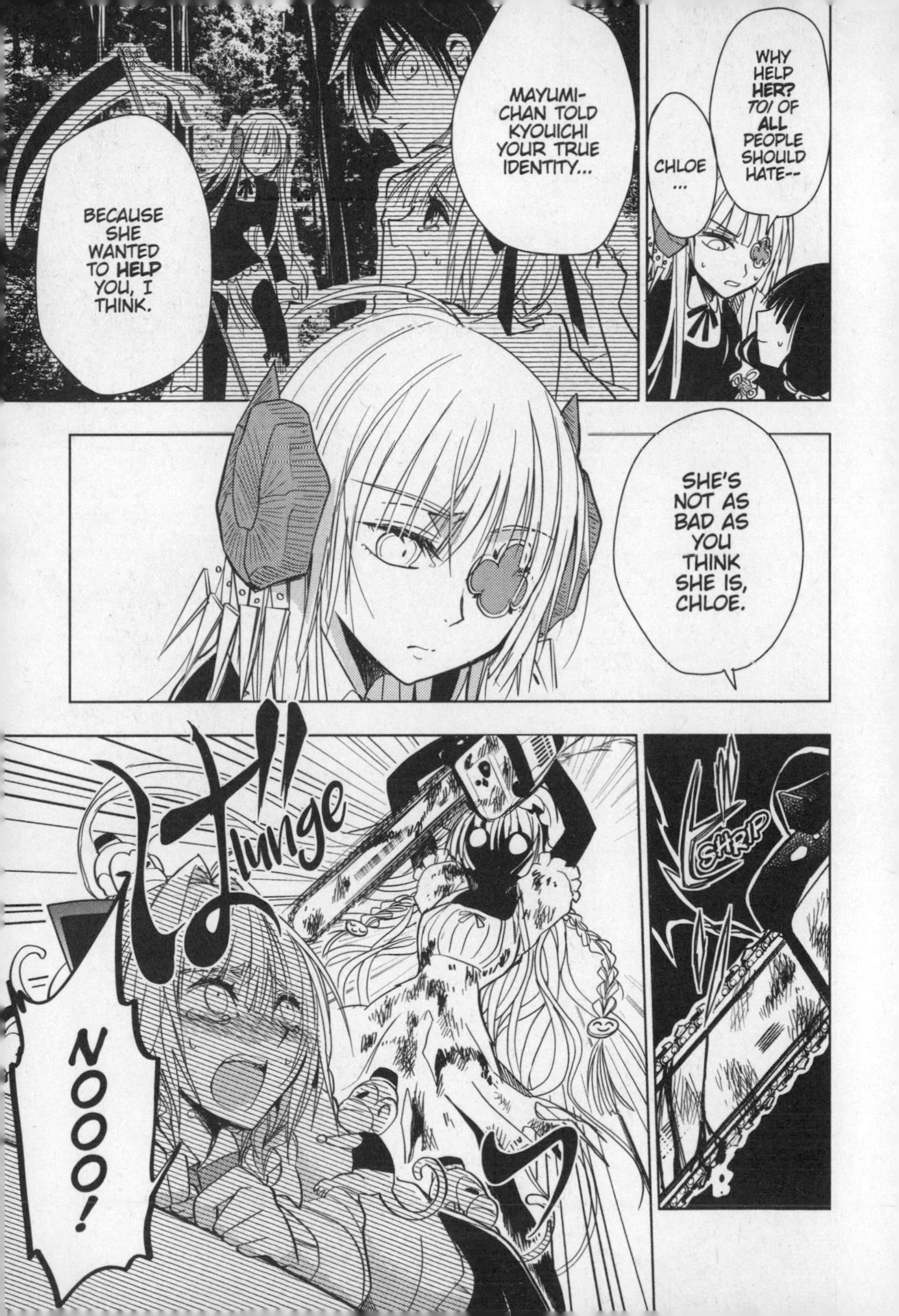
WHY HELP HER? TOI OF ALL PEOPLE SHOULD HATE--
CHLOE ...
MAYUMI-CHAN TOLD KYOUICHI YOUR TRUE IDENTITY...
BECAUSE SHE WANTED TO HELP YOU, I THINK.
SHE'S NOT AS BAD AS YOU THINK SHE IS, CHLOE.
SHRIP
Lunge
NOOO!

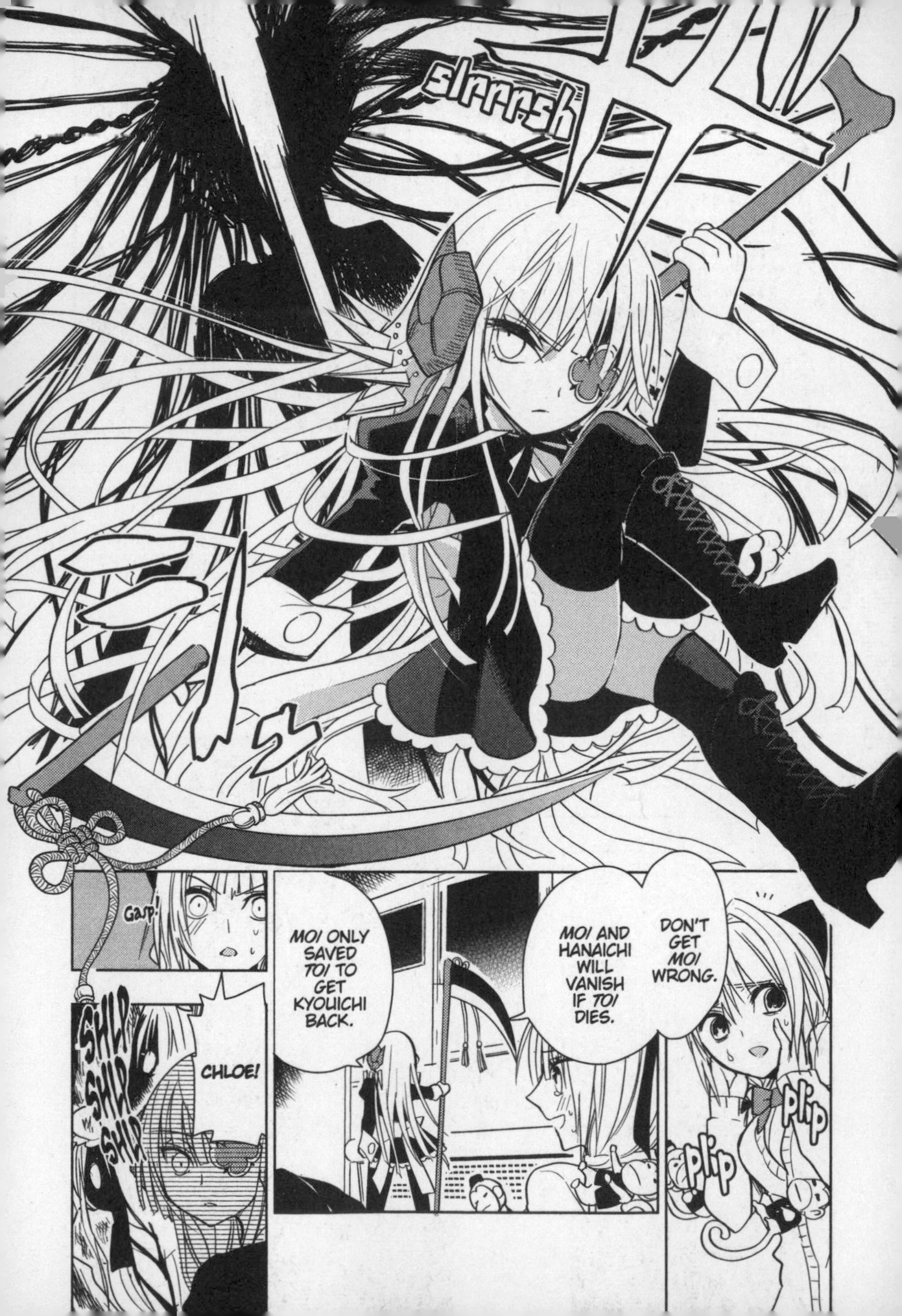
slrrrsh
DON'T GET MOI WRONG.
MOI AND HANAICHI WILL VANISH IF TOI DIES.
MOI ONLY SAVED TOI TO GET KYOUICHI BACK.
plip
plip
Gasp!
CHLOE!
SHLP SHLP SHLP SHLP

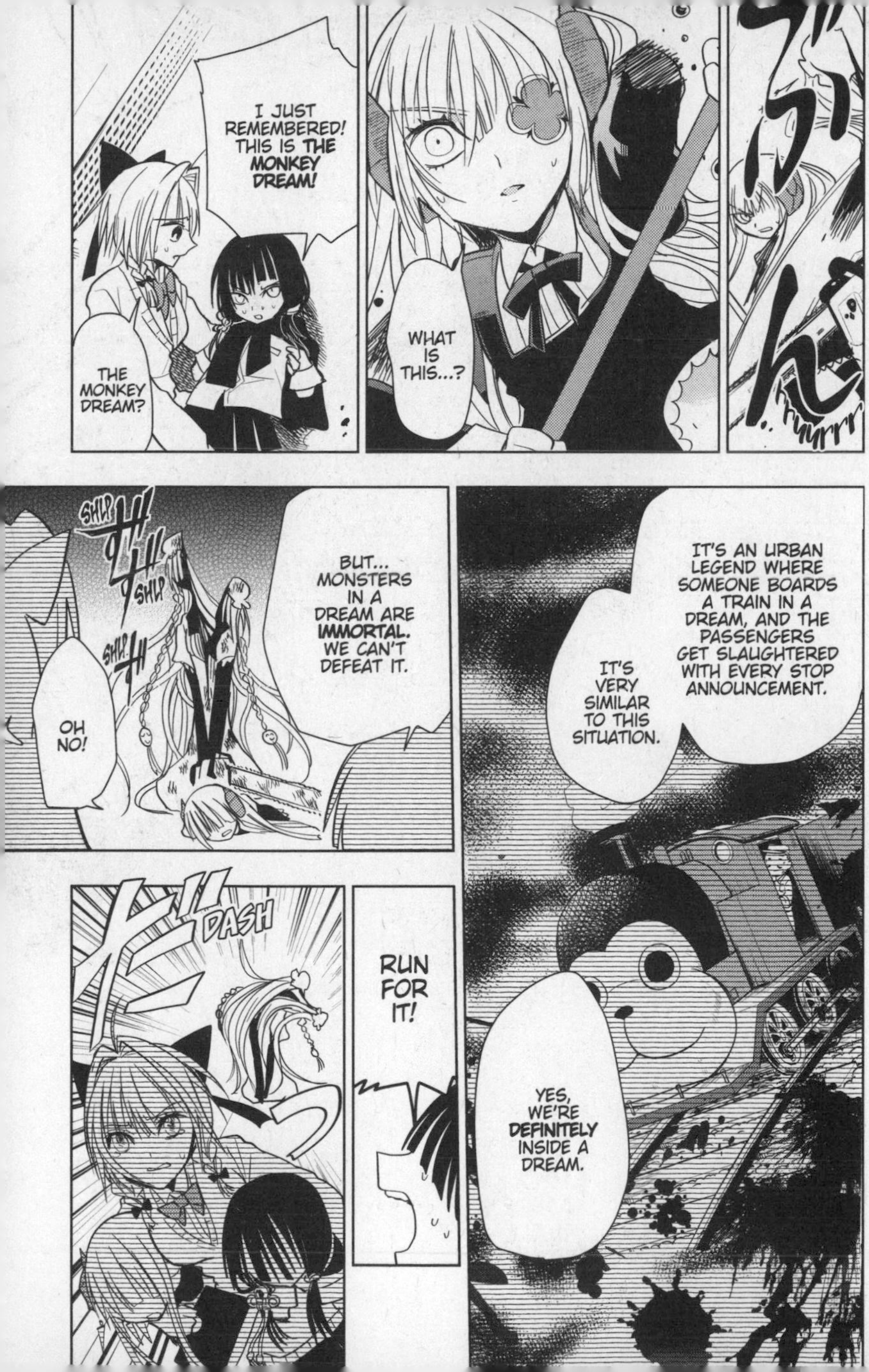
WHAT IS THIS...?
I JUST REMEMBERED! THIS IS THE MONKEY DREAM!
THE MONKEY DREAM?
IT'S AN URBAN LEGEND WHERE SOMEONE BOARDS A TRAIN IN A DREAM, AND THE PASSENGERS GET SLAUGHTERED WITH EVERY STOP ANNOUNCEMENT.
IT'S VERY SIMILAR TO THIS SITUATION.
BUT... MONSTERS IN A DREAM ARE IMMORTAL. WE CAN'T DEFEAT IT.
SHLP
SHLP
SHLP
OH NO!
YES, WE'RE DEFINITELY INSIDE A DREAM.
RUN FOR IT!
DASH

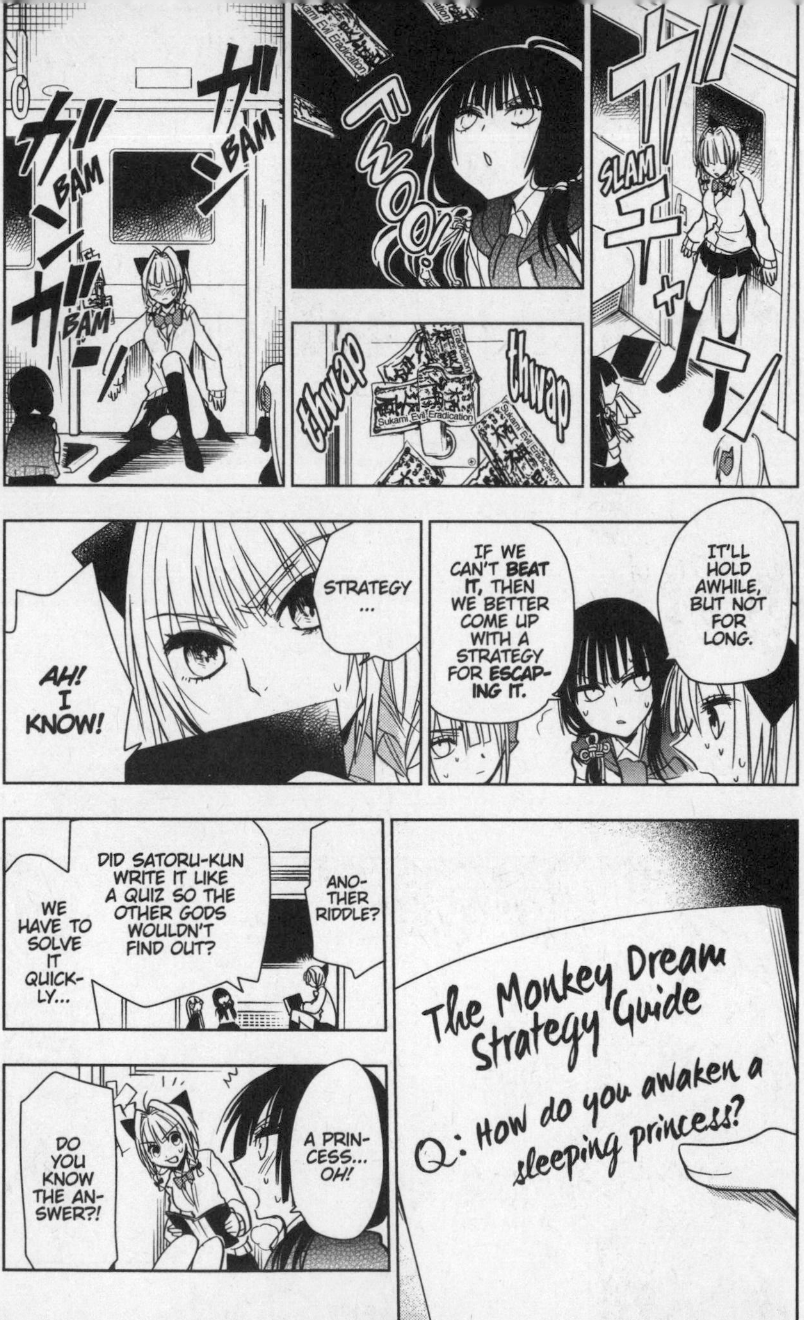
SLAM
FWOO!
Sukami Evil Eradication
BAM
BAM
BAM
thwap
thwap
Sukami Evil Eradication
Sukami Evil Eradication
Sukami Evil Eradication
IT'LL HOLD AWHILE, BUT NOT FOR LONG.
IF WE CAN'T BEAT IT, THEN WE BETTER COME UP WITH A STRATEGY FOR ESCAPING IT.
STRATEGY...
AH! I KNOW!
The Monkey Dream Strategy Guide
Q: How do you awaken a sleeping princess?
ANOTHER RIDDLE?
DID SATORU-KUN WRITE IT LIKE A QUIZ SO THE OTHER GODS WOULDN'T FIND OUT?
WE HAVE TO SOLVE IT QUICKLY...
A PRINCESS... OH!
DO YOU KNOW THE ANSWER?!

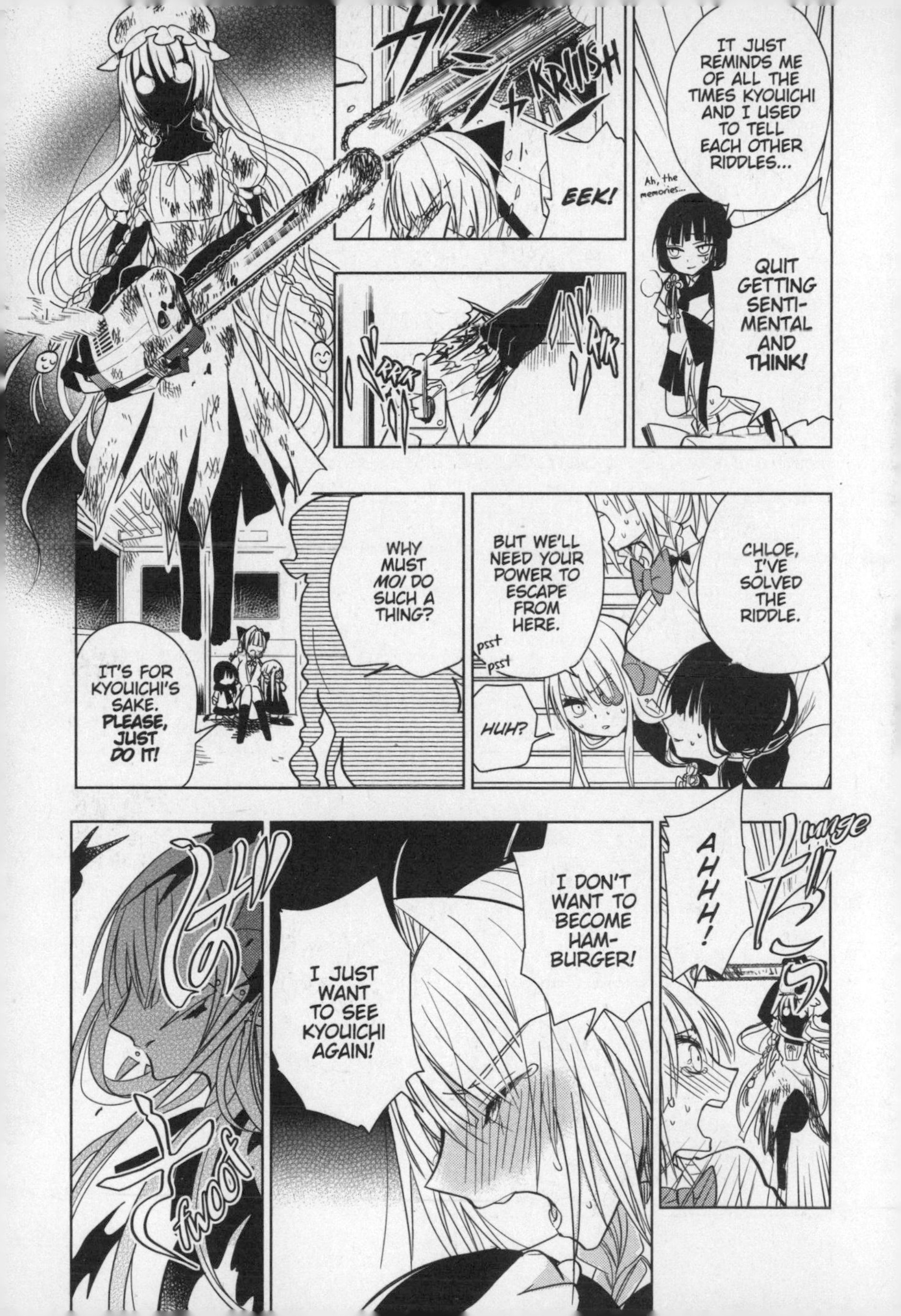
IT JUST REMINDS ME OF ALL THE TIMES KYOUICHI AND I USED TO TELL EACH OTHER RIDDLES...
Ah, the memories...
QUIT GETTING SENTI-MENTAL AND THINK!
KRIIISH
EEK!
RRIK
RRIK
CHLOE, I'VE SOLVED THE RIDDLE.
HUH?
psst psst
BUT WE'LL NEED YOUR POWER TO ESCAPE FROM HERE.
WHY MUST MOI DO SUCH A THING?
IT'S FOR KYOUICHI'S SAKE. PLEASE, JUST DO IT!
lunge
AHHH!
I DON'T WANT TO BECOME HAM-BURGER!
I JUST WANT TO SEE KYOUICHI AGAIN!
fwoof

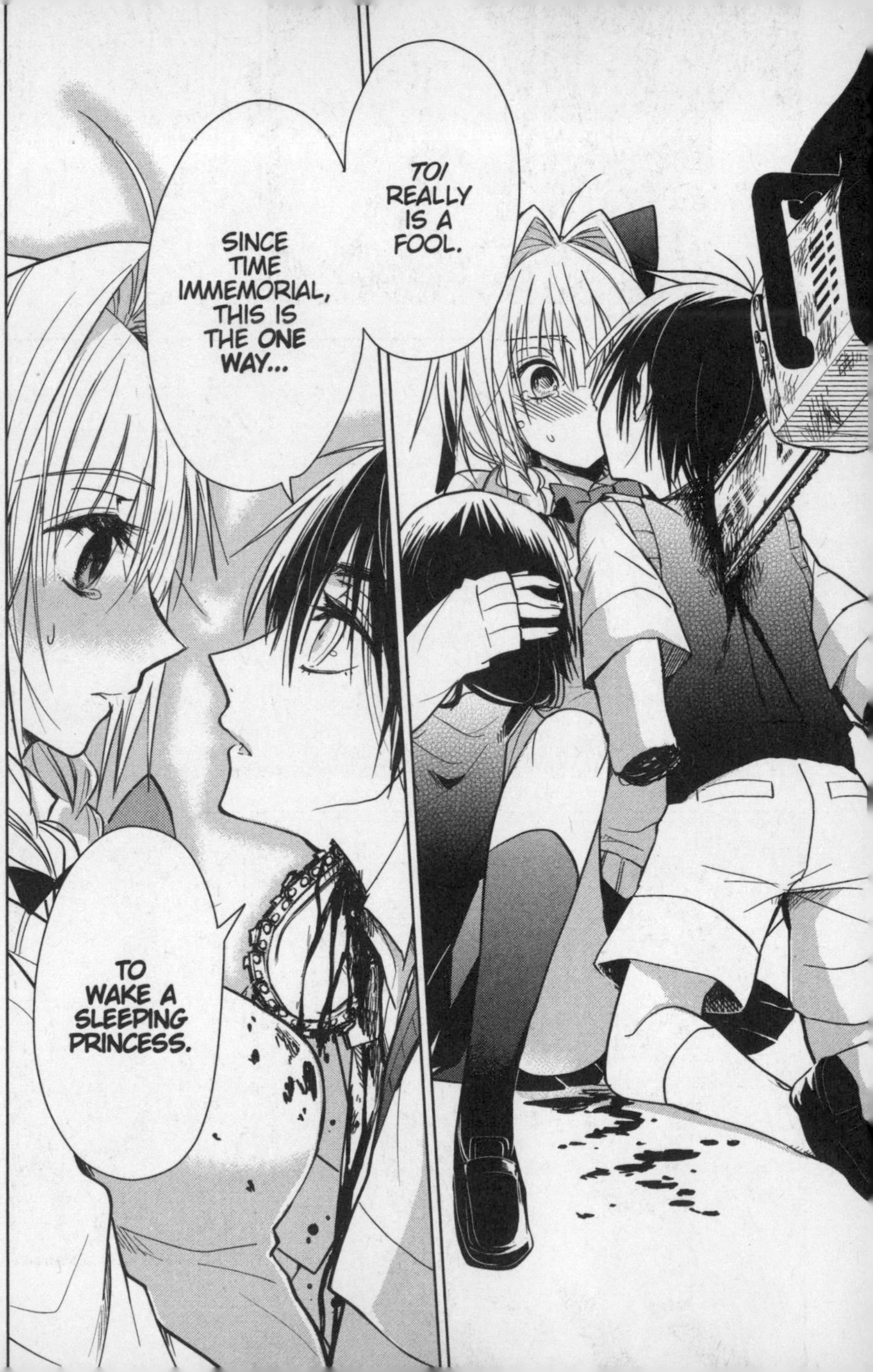
TOI REALLY IS A FOOL.
SINCE TIME IMMEMORIAL, THIS IS THE ONE WAY...
TO WAKE A SLEEPING PRINCESS.

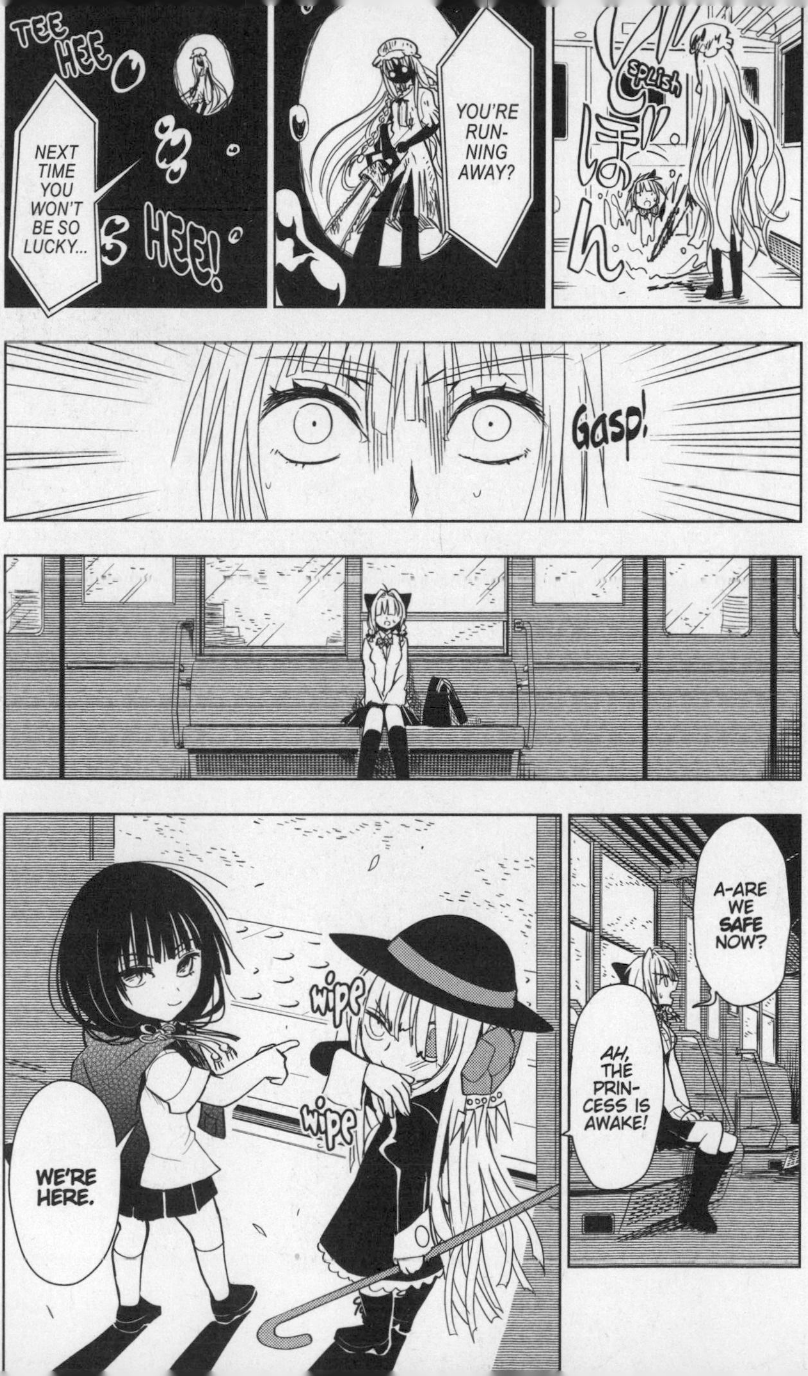
SPLISH
YOU'RE RUN-NING AWAY?
TEE HEE
NEXT TIME YOU WON'T BE SO LUCKY...
HEE!
Gasp!
A-ARE WE SAFE NOW?
AH, THE PRIN-CESS IS AWAKE!
wipe
wipe
WE'RE HERE.

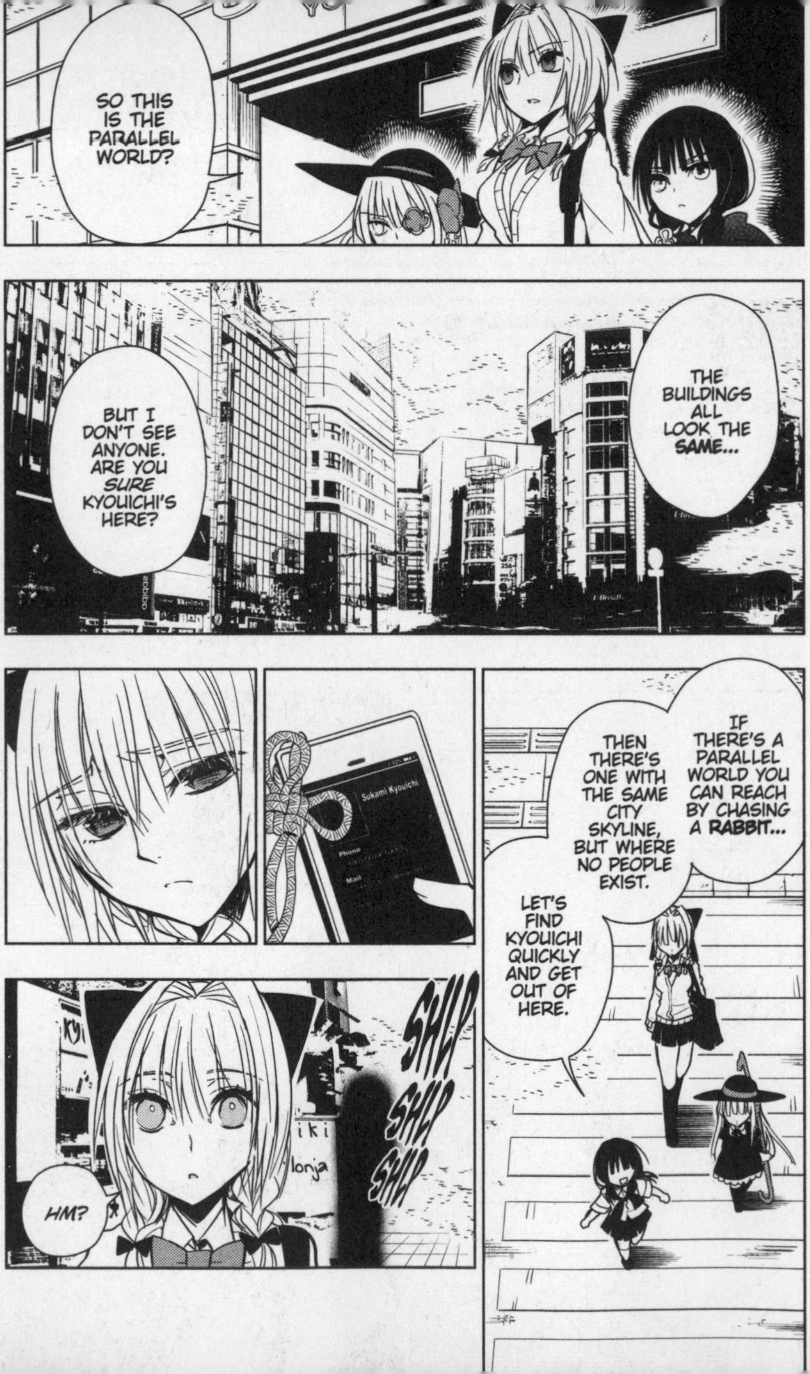

SO THIS IS THE PARALLEL WORLD?
THE BUILDINGS ALL LOOK THE SAME...
BUT I DON'T SEE ANYONE. ARE YOU *SURE* KYOUICHI'S HERE?
Sukami Kyouichi
Phone
Mail
IF THERE'S A PARALLEL WORLD YOU CAN REACH BY CHASING A **RABBIT...**
THEN THERE'S ONE WITH THE SAME CITY SKYLINE, BUT WHERE NO PEOPLE EXIST.
LET'S FIND KYOUICHI QUICKLY AND GET OUT OF HERE.
HM?
SHLP
SHLP
SHLP

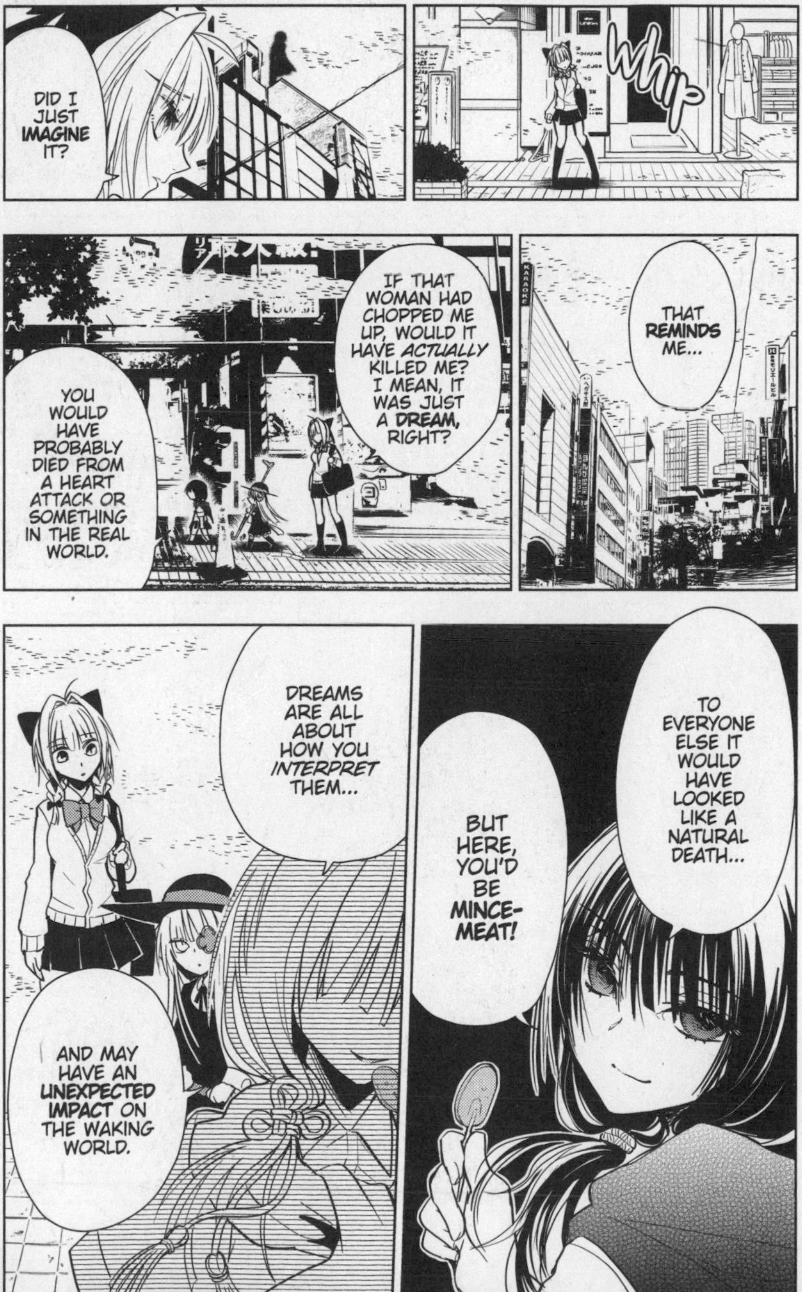

Whip
DID I JUST IMAGINE IT?
THAT REMINDS ME...
IF THAT WOMAN HAD CHOPPED ME UP, WOULD IT HAVE ACTUALLY KILLED ME? I MEAN, IT WAS JUST A DREAM, RIGHT?
YOU WOULD HAVE PROBABLY DIED FROM A HEART ATTACK OR SOMETHING IN THE REAL WORLD.
TO EVERYONE ELSE IT WOULD HAVE LOOKED LIKE A NATURAL DEATH...
BUT HERE, YOU'D BE MINCE-MEAT!
DREAMS ARE ALL ABOUT HOW YOU INTERPRET THEM...
AND MAY HAVE AN UNEXPECTED IMPACT ON THE WAKING WORLD.

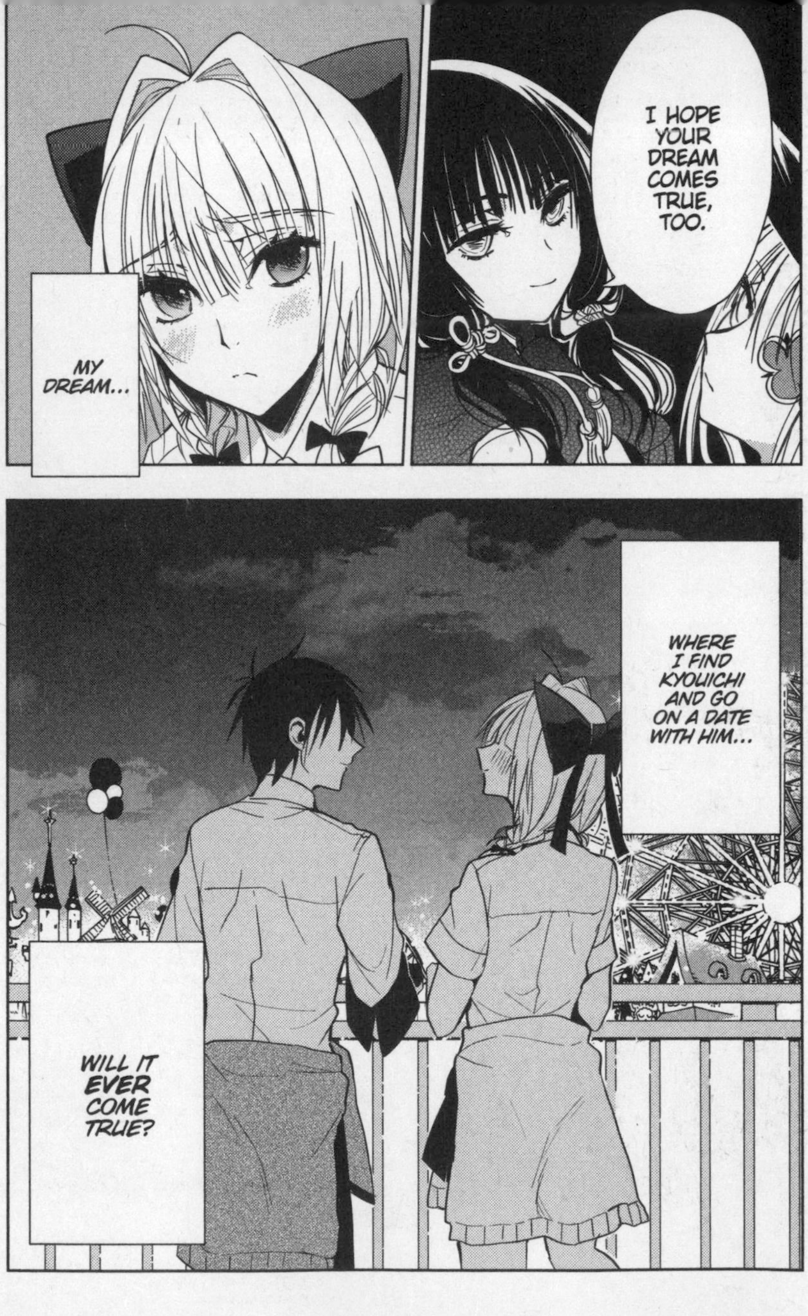
I HOPE YOUR DREAM COMES TRUE, TOO.
MY DREAM...
WHERE I FIND KYOUICHI AND GO ON A DATE WITH HIM...
WILL IT EVER COME TRUE?

Commentary on the Work

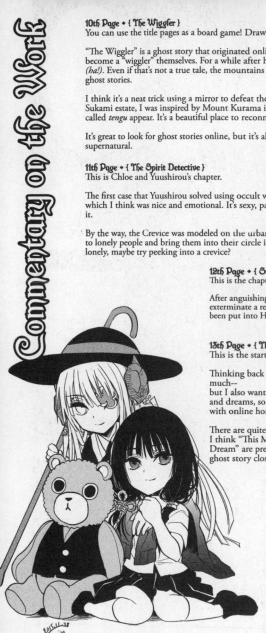

10th Page • { The Wiggler }
You can use the title pages as a board game! Drawing it was tough *(ha ha!)*

"The Wiggler" is a ghost story that originated online. The story is that people who see it go insane and become a "wiggler" themselves. For a while after hearing that story, I had a phobia of the countryside *(ha!)*. Even if that's not a true tale, the mountains and the countryside have many interesting and scary ghost stories.

I think it's a neat trick using a mirror to defeat the wiggler; it really is "fighting fire with fire"! For the Sukami estate, I was inspired by Mount Kurama in Kyoto where it's said that supernatural creatures called *tengu* appear. It's a beautiful place to reconnect with nature.

It's great to look for ghost stories online, but it's also nice to go to visit places connected with the supernatural.

11th Page • { The Spirit Detective }
This is Chloe and Yuushirou's chapter.

The first case that Yuushirou solved using occult wisdom was one that involved the woman he loved, which I think was nice and emotional. It's sexy, painful, and lonely, and I personally had fun drawing it.

By the way, the Crevice was modeled on the urban legend "Crevice People." Apparently they appear to lonely people and bring them into their circle in order to fill the crevices in their hearts. If you get lonely, maybe try peeking into a crevice?

12th Page • { Sukami Hanaichi }
This is the chapter where Kyouichi reunites with Hanaichi.

After anguishing a long time over the question "How should one exterminate a reaper?" I settled on the idea that a *yorishiro* had been put into Hanaichi's body to hold the reaper spirit.

13th Page • { The Monkey Dream }
This is the start of the "Mayumi Arc."

Thinking back on it now, I wondered if it might have been too much--
but I also wanted to include urban legends about parallel worlds and dreams, so I went ahead and drew it. This is also a ghost story with online horror origins.

There are quite a few other ghost stories that involve dreams, and I think "This Man" and "Don't Look in a Mirror During a Lucid Dream" are pretty interesting. "The Monkey Dream" may be a ghost story close to the latter.

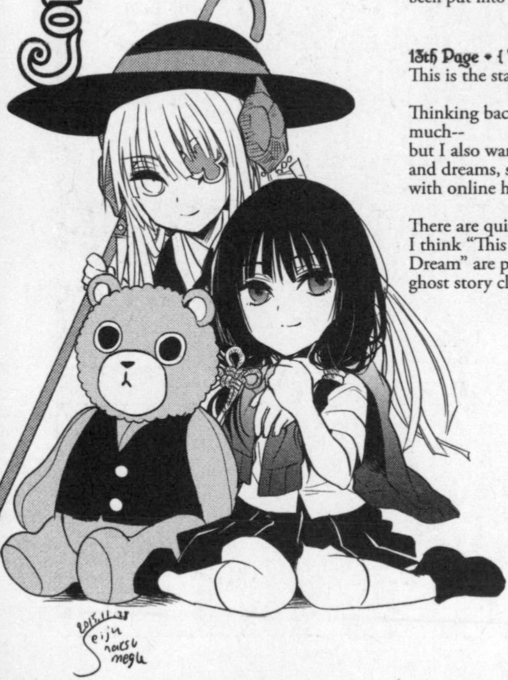

Final Page • { The Phantom Ramen Seller }
When I said, "At the end of *Ghost Diary,* they'll eat ramen," someone said to me, "What is this, *Black Jack?!*"

I thought it would be interesting if a fake Kyouichi appeared as the Phantom Ramen Seller. It was an idea I'd thought of using from the start, and I was finally able to use it in this chapter.

And now, with this chapter, I get the feeling the theme I wanted to draw in *Ghost Diary* has finally come into view.

The series ended in a way that was slightly different from what I'd thought of at the very start, but I think I managed to end it well, with everyone smiling.

—Continued in the Afterword.

Ghost Diary
カイダンにっき

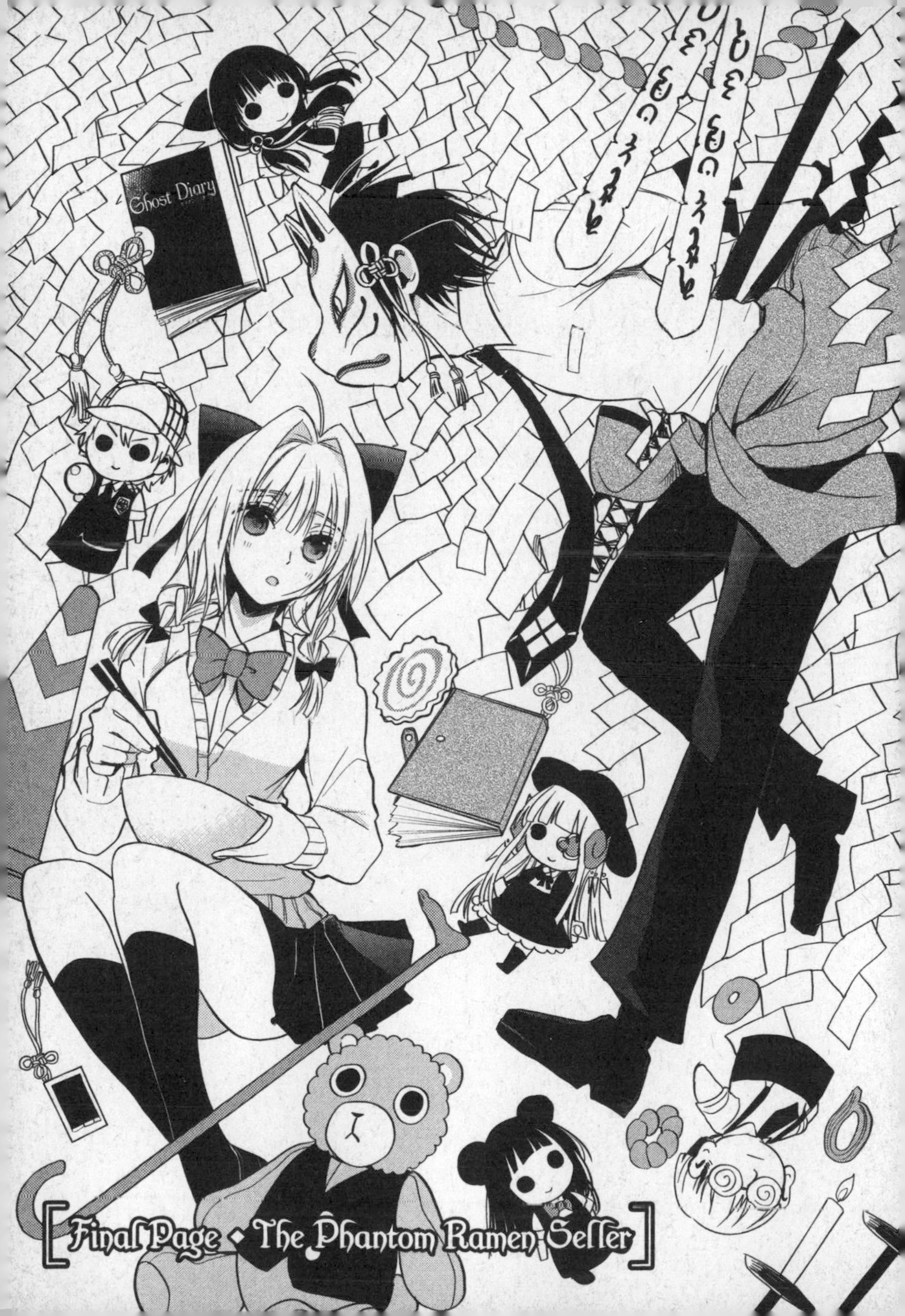
Ghost Diary
Final Page ◆ The Phantom Ramen Seller

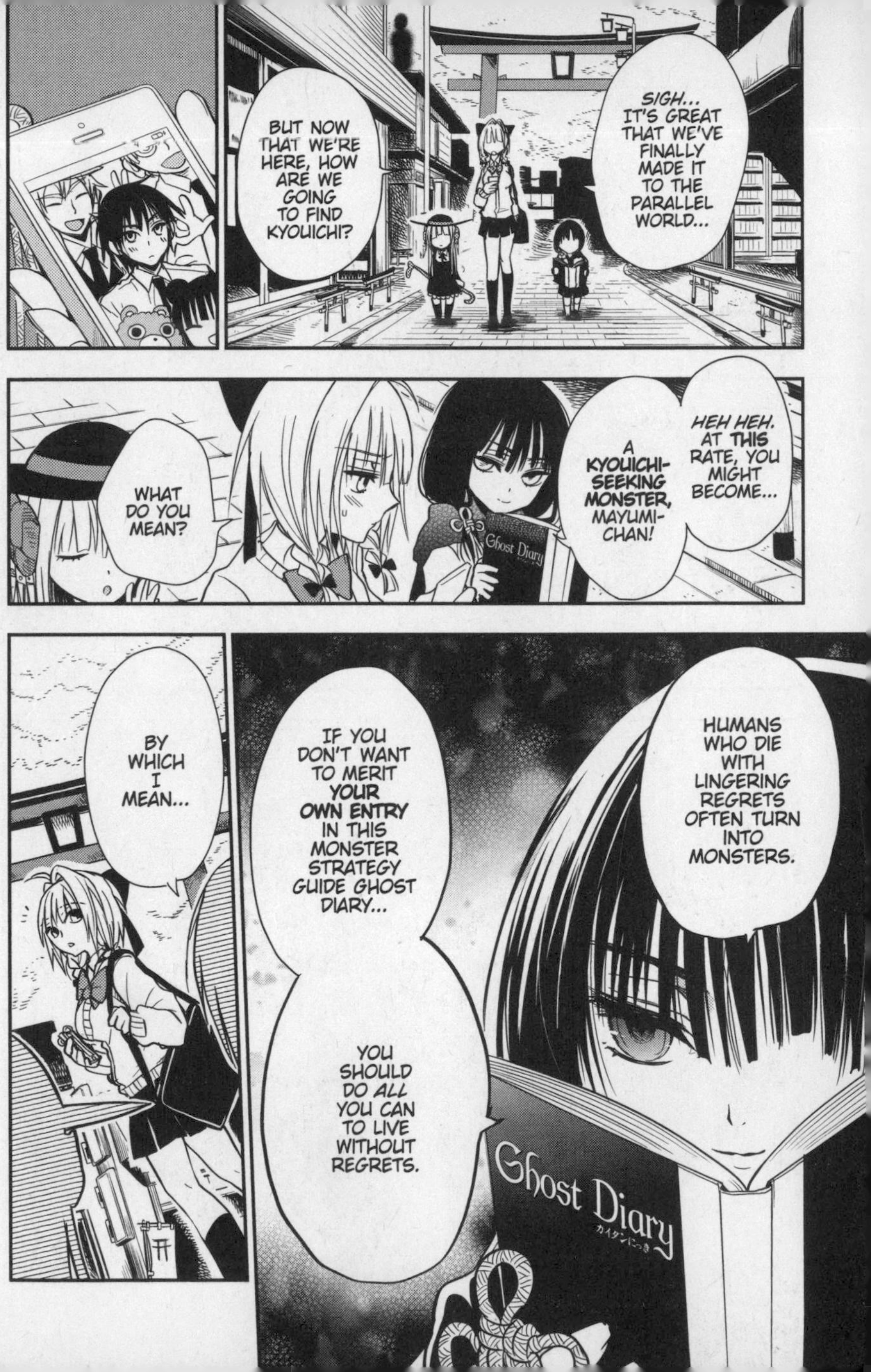
SIGH... IT'S GREAT THAT WE'VE FINALLY MADE IT TO THE PARALLEL WORLD...
BUT NOW THAT WE'RE HERE, HOW ARE WE GOING TO FIND KYOUICHI?
HEH HEH. AT **THIS** RATE, YOU MIGHT BECOME...
A **KYOUICHI-SEEKING MONSTER**, MAYUMI-CHAN!
WHAT DO YOU MEAN?
Ghost Diary
HUMANS WHO DIE WITH LINGERING REGRETS OFTEN TURN INTO MONSTERS.
IF YOU DON'T WANT TO MERIT **YOUR OWN ENTRY** IN THIS MONSTER STRATEGY GUIDE GHOST DIARY...
YOU SHOULD DO *ALL* YOU CAN TO LIVE WITHOUT REGRETS.
Ghost Diary
カイダンにっき
BY WHICH I MEAN...

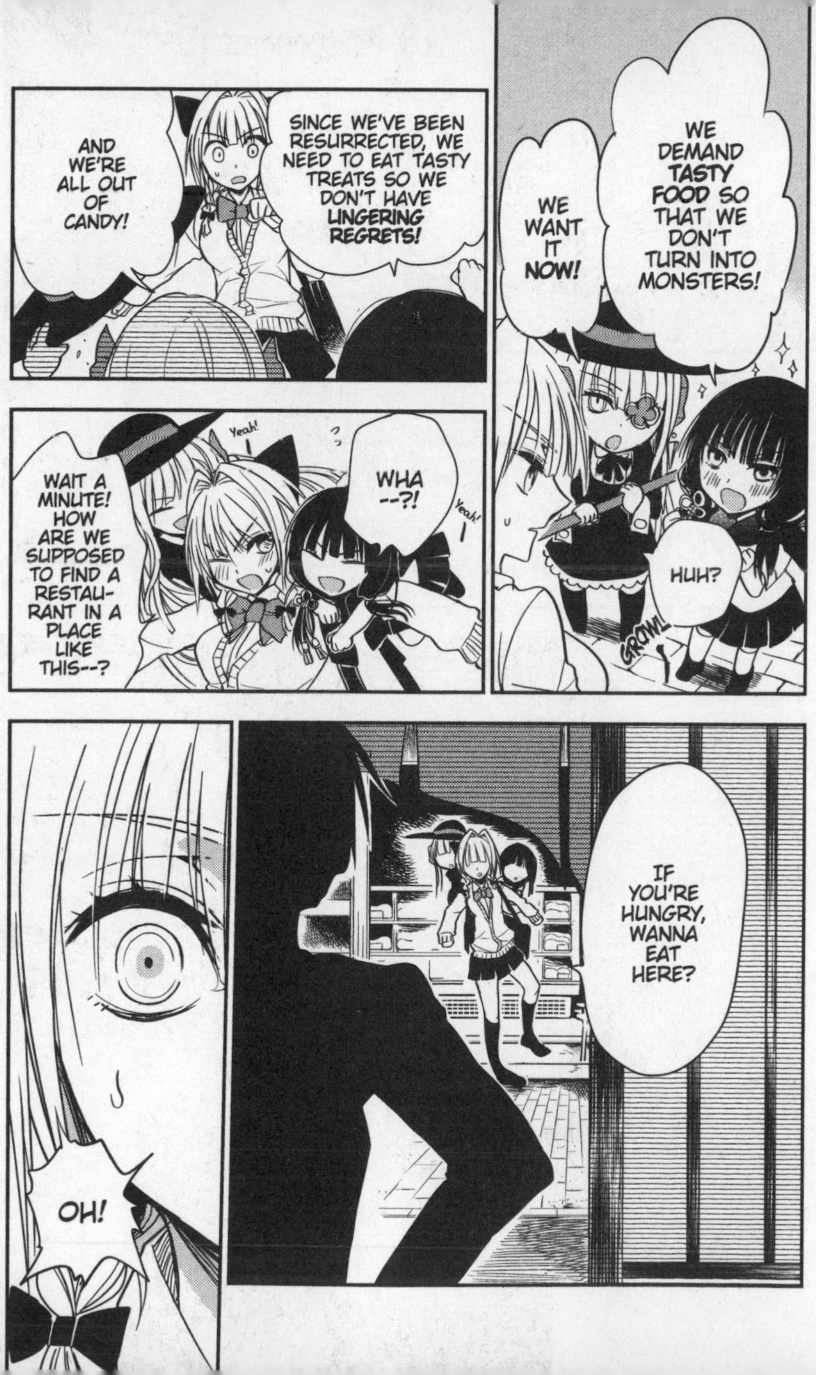
WE DEMAND TASTY FOOD SO THAT WE DON'T TURN INTO MONSTERS!
WE WANT IT NOW!
SINCE WE'VE BEEN RESURRECTED, WE NEED TO EAT TASTY TREATS SO WE DON'T HAVE LINGERING REGRETS!
AND WE'RE ALL OUT OF CANDY!
HUH?
GROWL
WHA--?!
Yeah!
Yeah!
WAIT A MINUTE! HOW ARE WE SUPPOSED TO FIND A RESTAU-RANT IN A PLACE LIKE THIS--?
IF YOU'RE HUNGRY, WANNA EAT HERE?
OH!

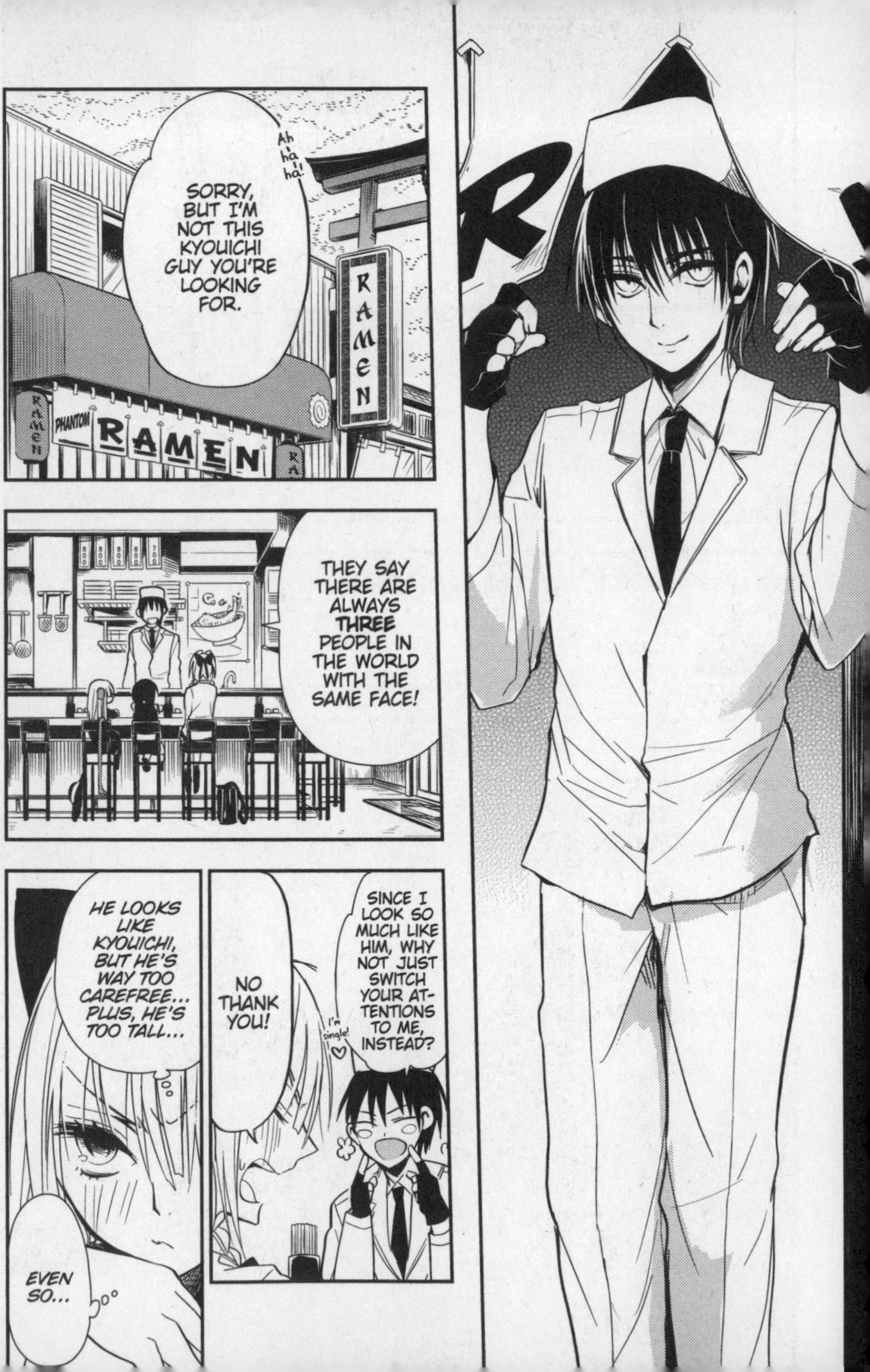

Ah ha ha ha!
SORRY, BUT I'M NOT THIS KYOUICHI GUY YOU'RE LOOKING FOR.
RAMEN
PHANTOM RAMEN
RAMEN
THEY SAY THERE ARE ALWAYS THREE PEOPLE IN THE WORLD WITH THE SAME FACE!
SINCE I LOOK SO MUCH LIKE HIM, WHY NOT JUST SWITCH YOUR AT-TENTIONS TO ME, INSTEAD?
I'm single!
NO THANK YOU!
HE LOOKS LIKE KYOUICHI, BUT HE'S WAY TOO CAREFREE... PLUS, HE'S TOO TALL...
EVEN SO...

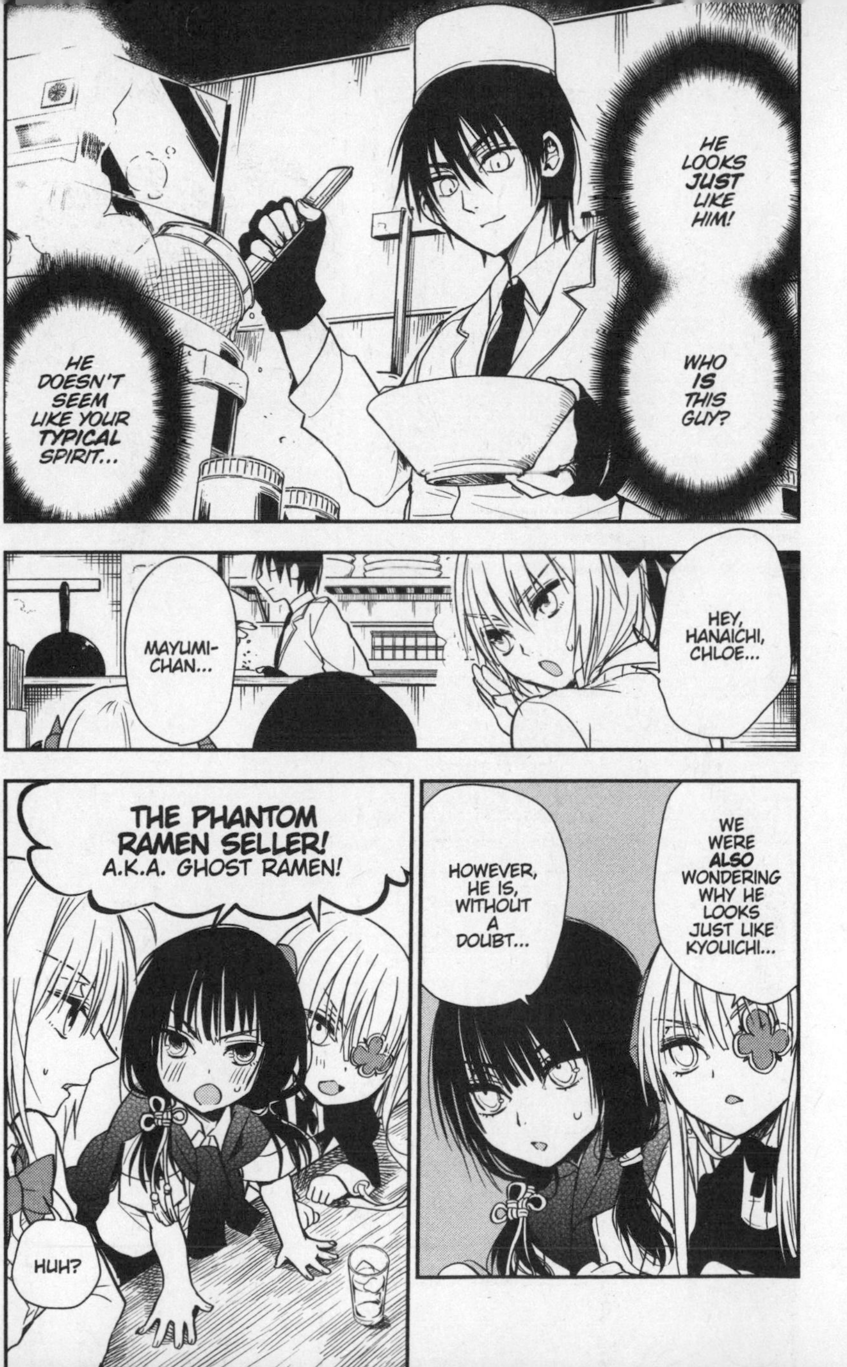
HE LOOKS JUST LIKE HIM!
WHO IS THIS GUY?
HE DOESN'T SEEM LIKE YOUR TYPICAL SPIRIT...
HEY, HANAICHI, CHLOE...
MAYUMI-CHAN...
WE WERE ALSO WONDERING WHY HE LOOKS JUST LIKE KYOUICHI...
HOWEVER, HE IS, WITHOUT A DOUBT...
THE PHANTOM RAMEN SELLER! A.K.A. GHOST RAMEN!
HUH?

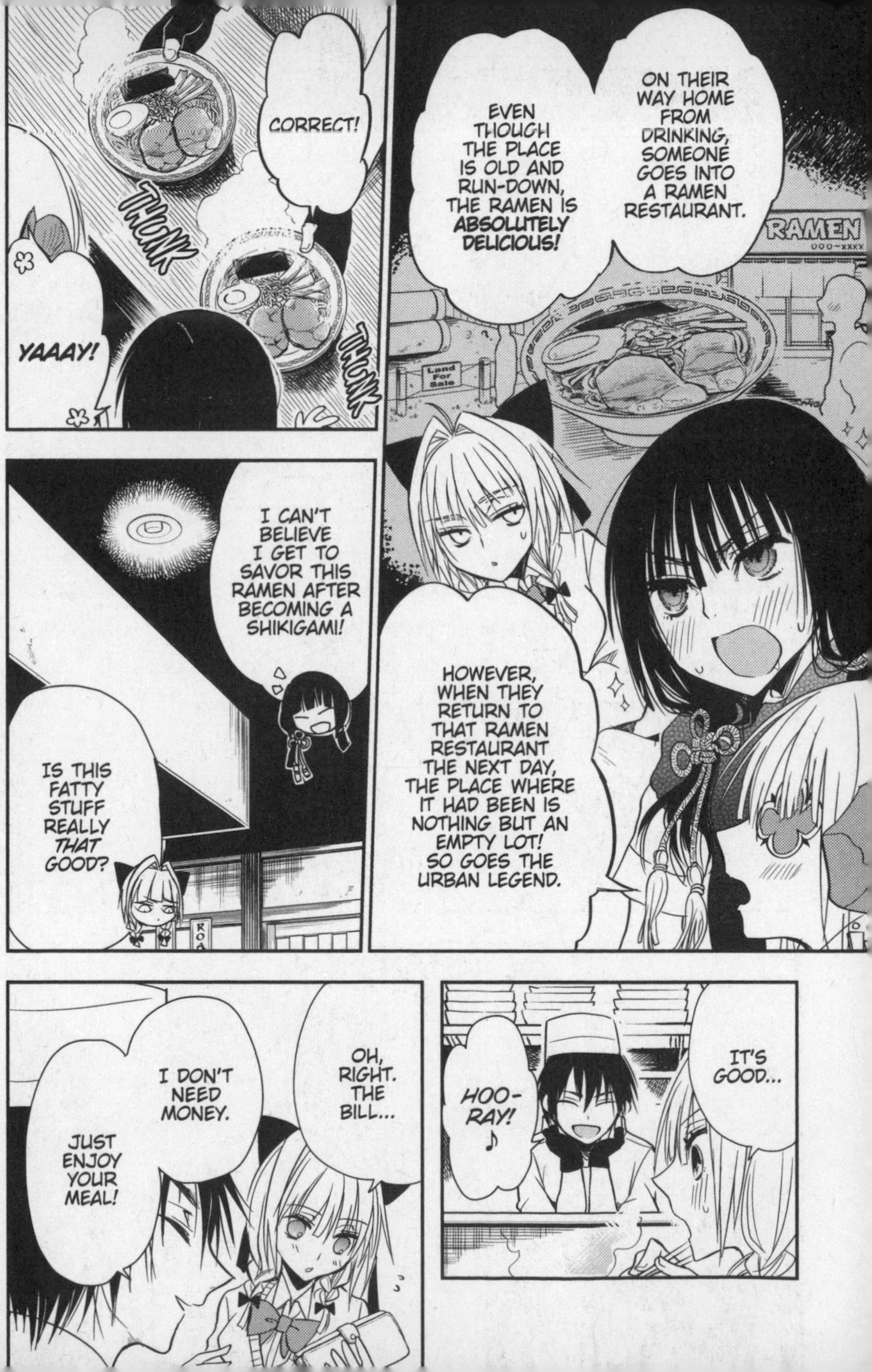

ON THEIR WAY HOME FROM DRINKING, SOMEONE GOES INTO A RAMEN RESTAURANT.
EVEN THOUGH THE PLACE IS OLD AND RUN-DOWN, THE RAMEN IS **ABSOLUTELY DELICIOUS!**
RAMEN
Land For Sale
HOWEVER, WHEN THEY RETURN TO THAT RAMEN RESTAURANT THE NEXT DAY, THE PLACE WHERE IT HAD BEEN IS NOTHING BUT AN EMPTY LOT! SO GOES THE URBAN LEGEND.
CORRECT!
THUNK
THUNK
YAAAY!
I CAN'T BELIEVE I GET TO SAVOR THIS RAMEN AFTER BECOMING A SHIKIGAMI!
IS THIS FATTY STUFF REALLY *THAT* GOOD?
IT'S GOOD...
HOO-RAY! ♪
OH, RIGHT. THE BILL...
I DON'T NEED MONEY.
JUST ENJOY YOUR MEAL!

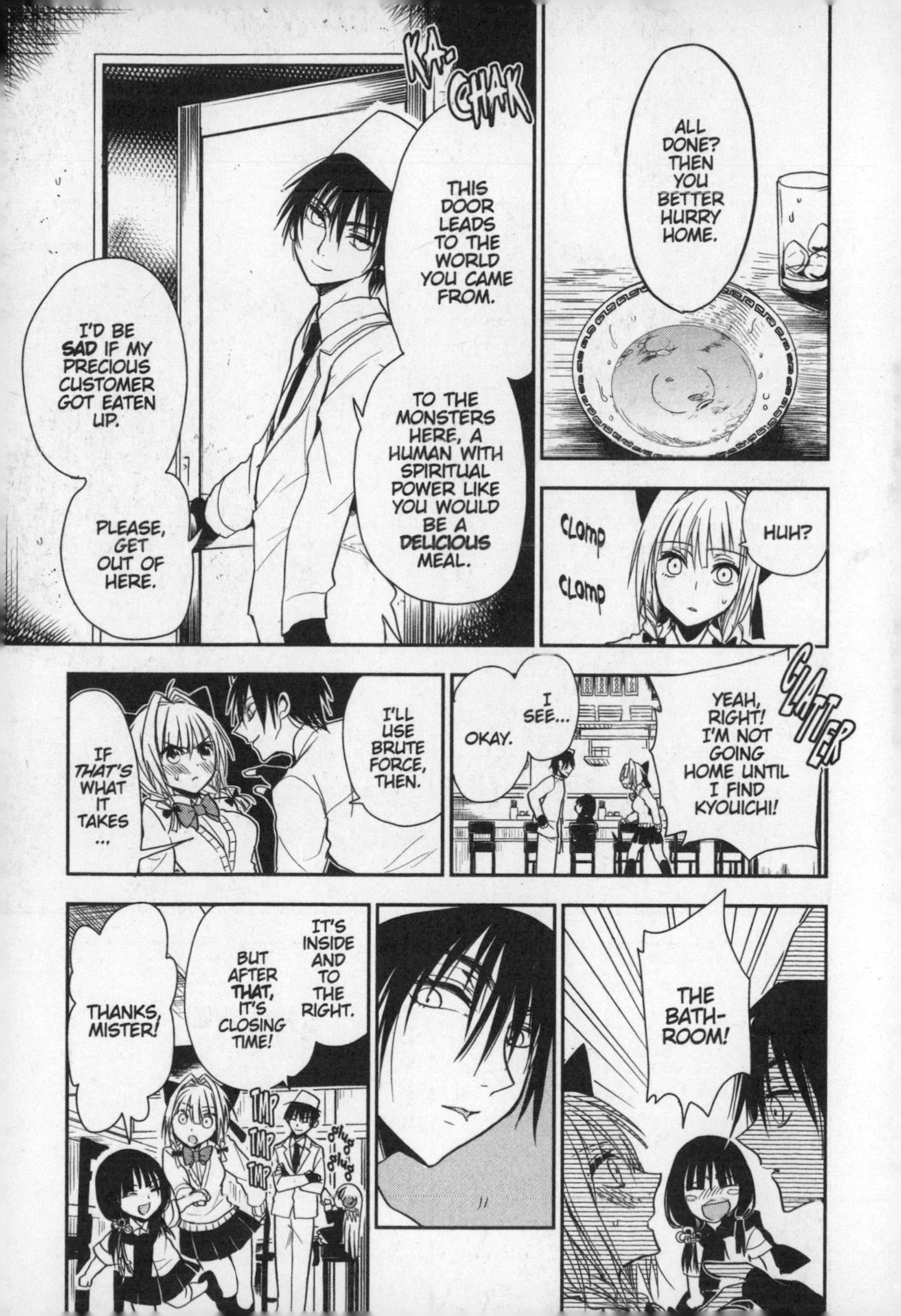
ALL DONE? THEN YOU BETTER HURRY HOME.
CLOMP
CLOMP
HUH?
KA-CHAK
THIS DOOR LEADS TO THE WORLD YOU CAME FROM.
TO THE MONSTERS HERE, A HUMAN WITH SPIRITUAL POWER LIKE YOU WOULD BE A DELICIOUS MEAL.
I'D BE SAD IF MY PRECIOUS CUSTOMER GOT EATEN UP.
PLEASE, GET OUT OF HERE.
CLATTER
YEAH, RIGHT! I'M NOT GOING HOME UNTIL I FIND KYOUICHI!
I SEE...
OKAY.
I'LL USE BRUTE FORCE, THEN.
IF THAT'S WHAT IT TAKES...
THE BATH-ROOM!
IT'S INSIDE AND TO THE RIGHT.
BUT AFTER THAT, IT'S CLOSING TIME!
THANKS, MISTER!
TMP
TMP
TMP
glug
glug

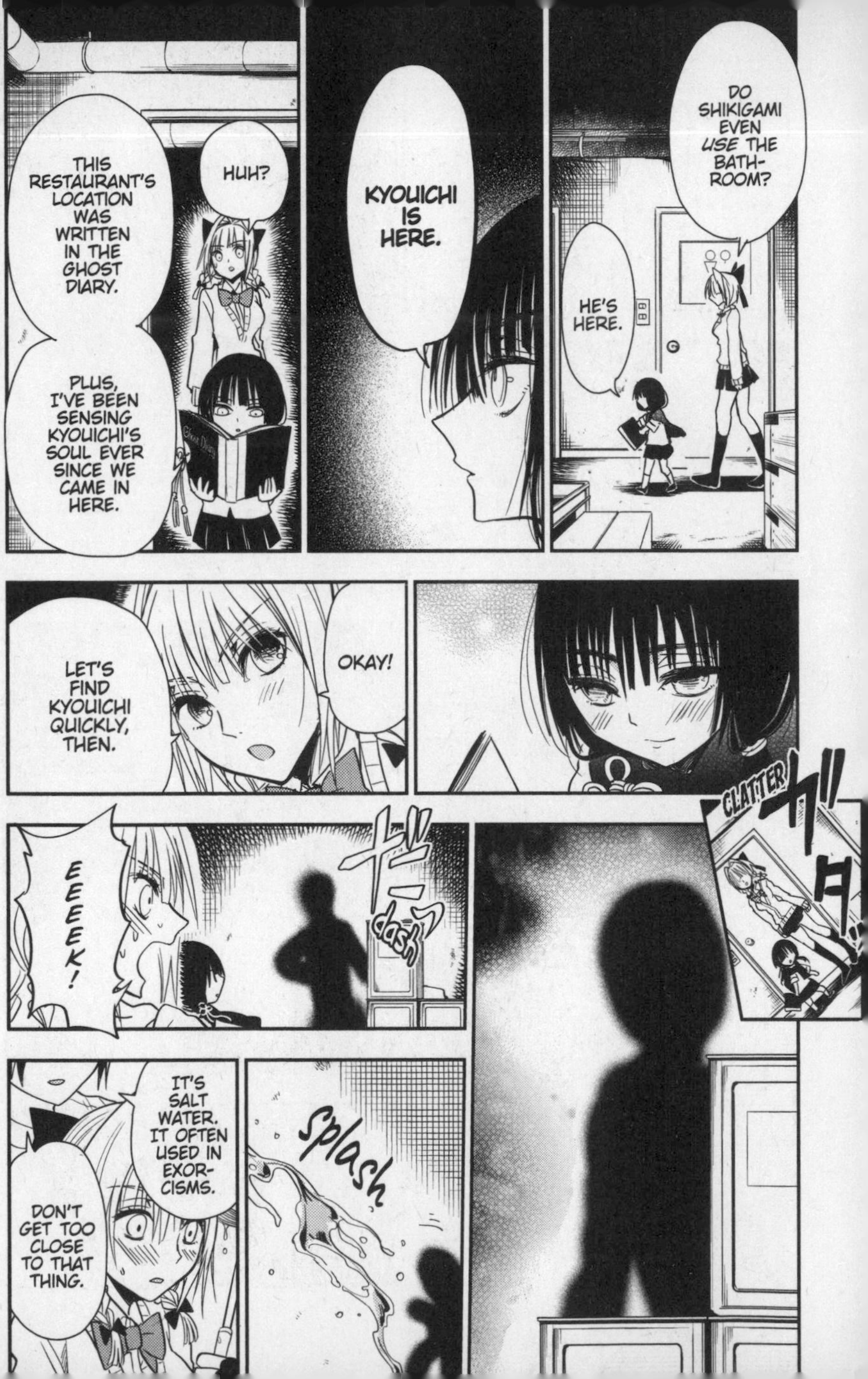
DO SHIKIGAMI EVEN USE THE BATH-ROOM?
HE'S HERE.
KYOUICHI IS HERE.
HUH?
THIS RESTAURANT'S LOCATION WAS WRITTEN IN THE GHOST DIARY.
PLUS, I'VE BEEN SENSING KYOUICHI'S SOUL EVER SINCE WE CAME IN HERE.
LET'S FIND KYOUICHI QUICKLY, THEN.
OKAY!
CLATTER
dash
EEEEEK!
splash
IT'S SALT WATER. IT OFTEN USED IN EXORCISMS.
DON'T GET TOO CLOSE TO THAT THING.

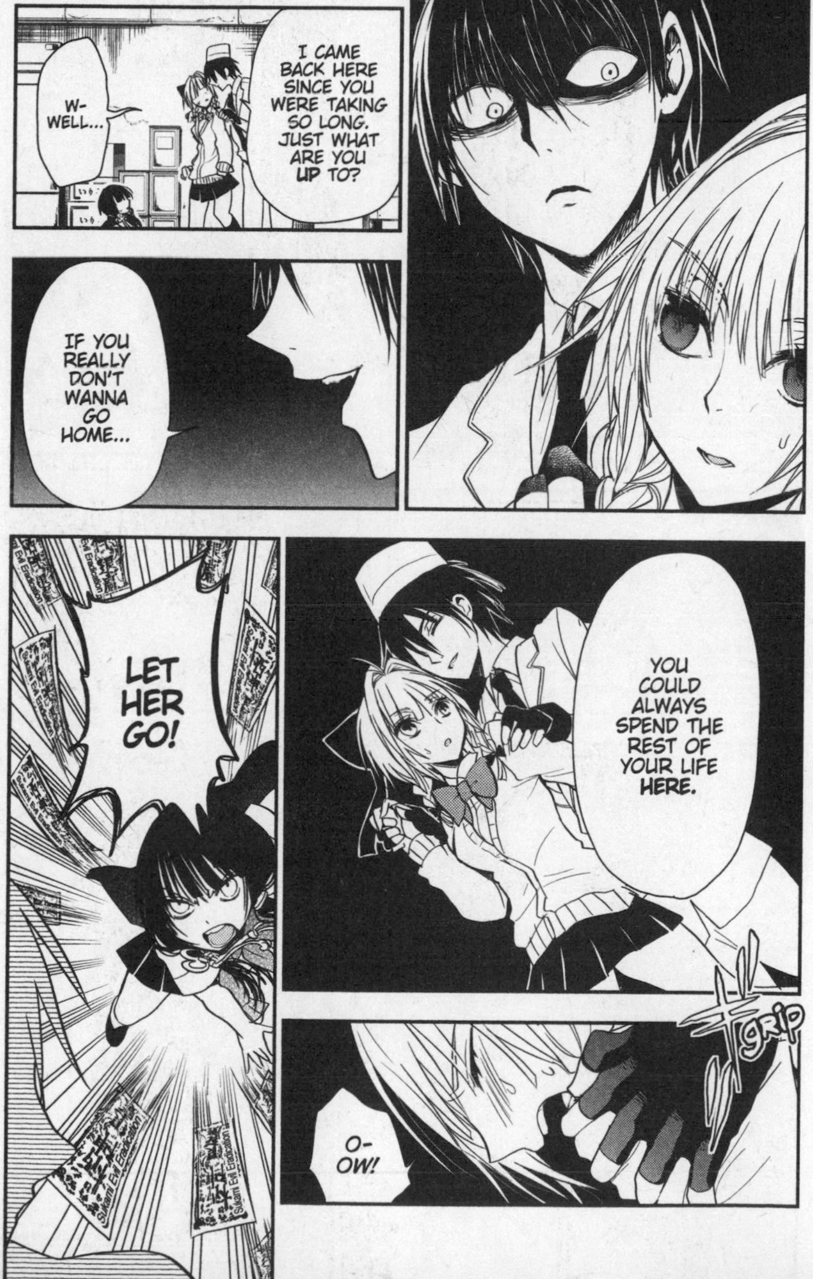
I CAME BACK HERE SINCE YOU WERE TAKING SO LONG. JUST WHAT ARE YOU UP TO?
W-WELL...
IF YOU REALLY DON'T WANNA GO HOME...
YOU COULD ALWAYS SPEND THE REST OF YOUR LIFE HERE.
grip
O-OW!
LET HER GO!
Sukami Evil Eradication

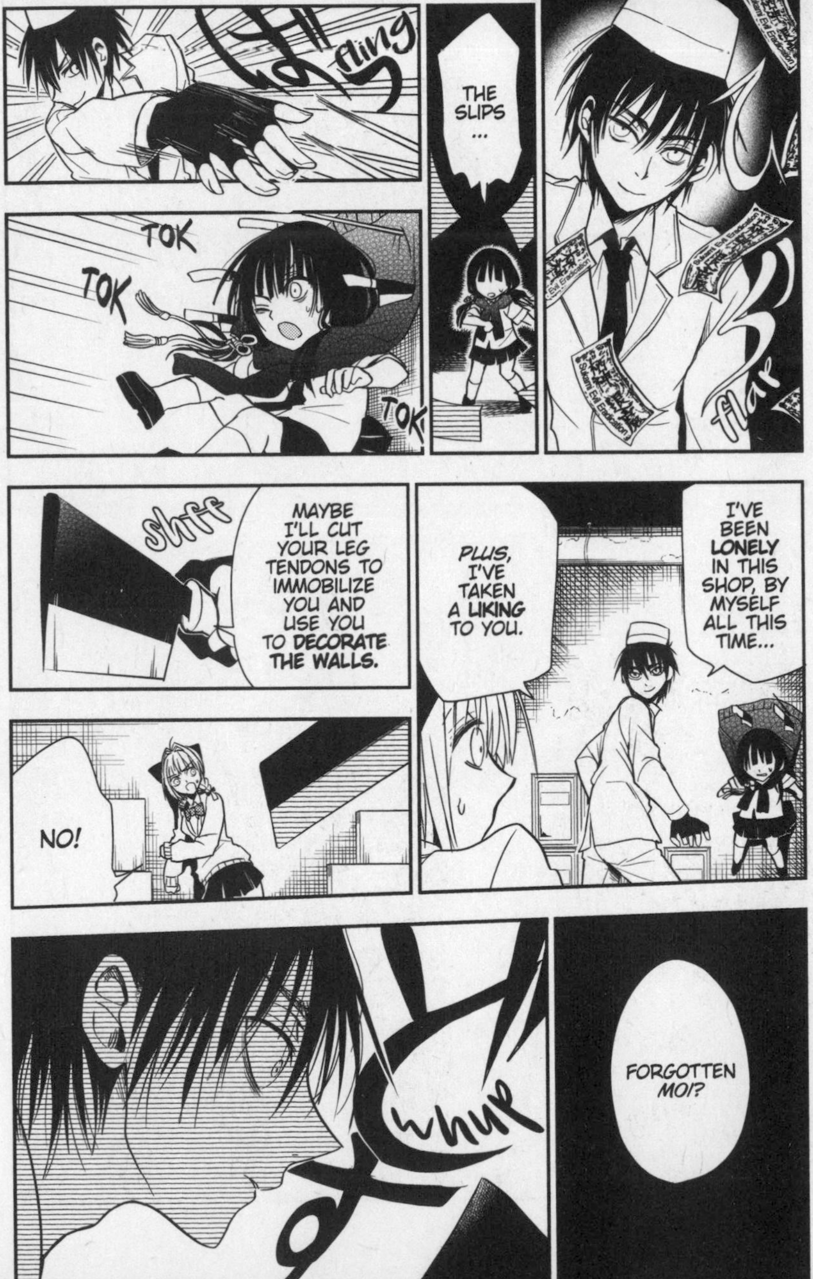
flap
THE SLIPS ...
fling
TOK
TOK
TOK
I'VE BEEN LONELY IN THIS SHOP, BY MYSELF ALL THIS TIME...
PLUS, I'VE TAKEN A LIKING TO YOU.
MAYBE I'LL CUT YOUR LEG TENDONS TO IMMOBILIZE YOU AND USE YOU TO DECORATE THE WALLS.
shfff
NO!
FORGOTTEN MOI?
whup

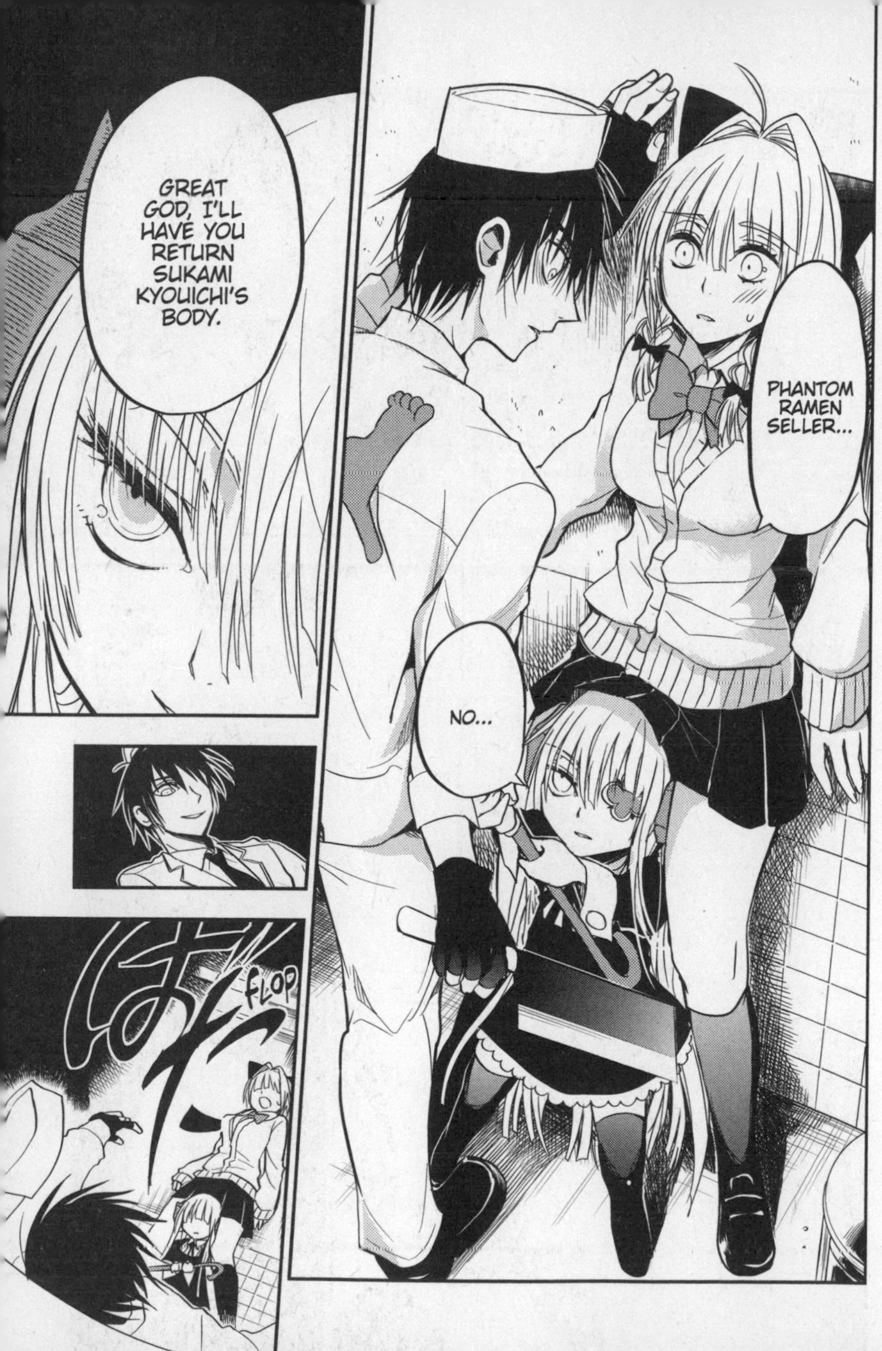
PHANTOM RAMEN SELLER...
NO...
GREAT GOD, I'LL HAVE YOU RETURN SUKAMI KYOUICHI'S BODY.
FLOP

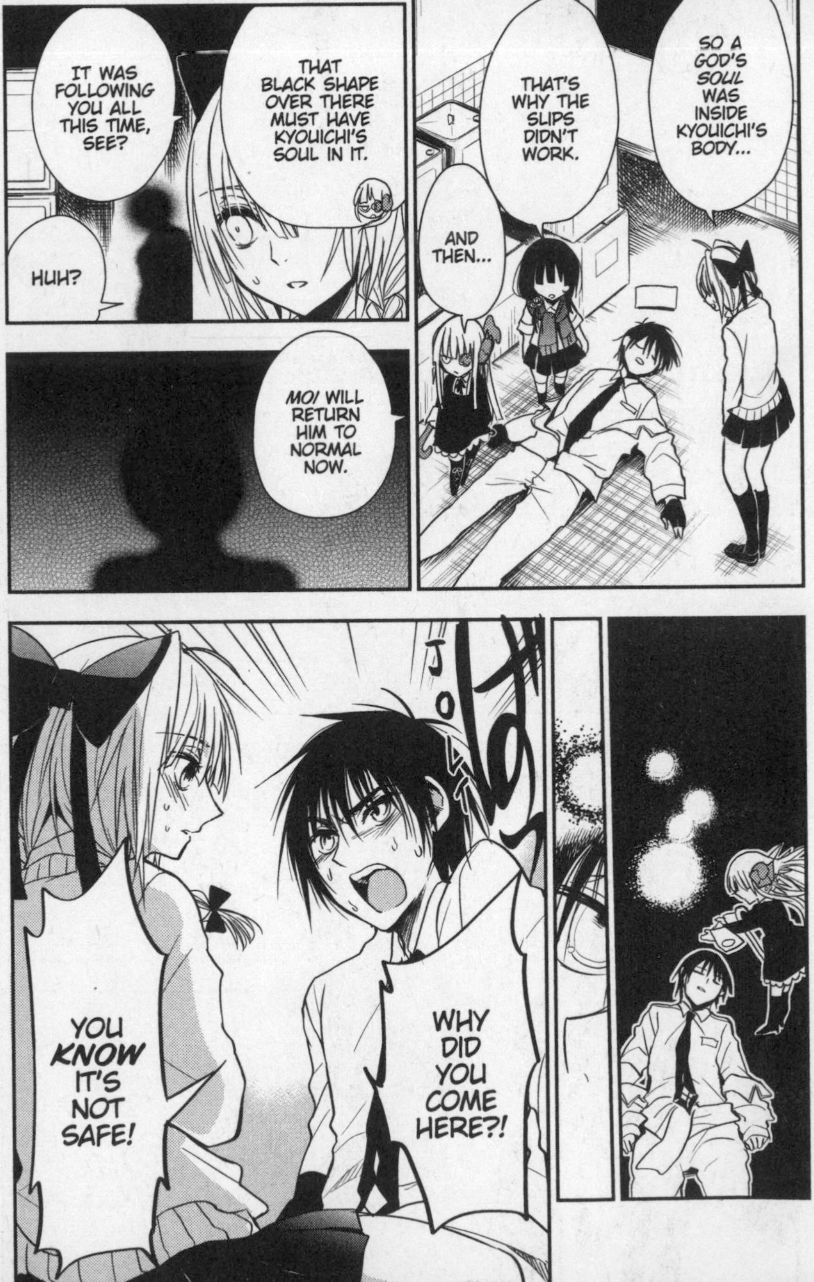
SO A GOD'S *SOUL* WAS INSIDE KYOUICHI'S BODY...
THAT'S WHY THE SLIPS DIDN'T WORK.
AND THEN...
THAT BLACK SHAPE OVER THERE MUST HAVE KYOUICHI'S SOUL IN IT.
IT WAS FOLLOWING YOU ALL THIS TIME, SEE?
HUH?
MOI WILL RETURN HIM TO NORMAL NOW.
JOLT
WHY DID YOU COME HERE?!
YOU ***KNOW*** IT'S NOT SAFE!

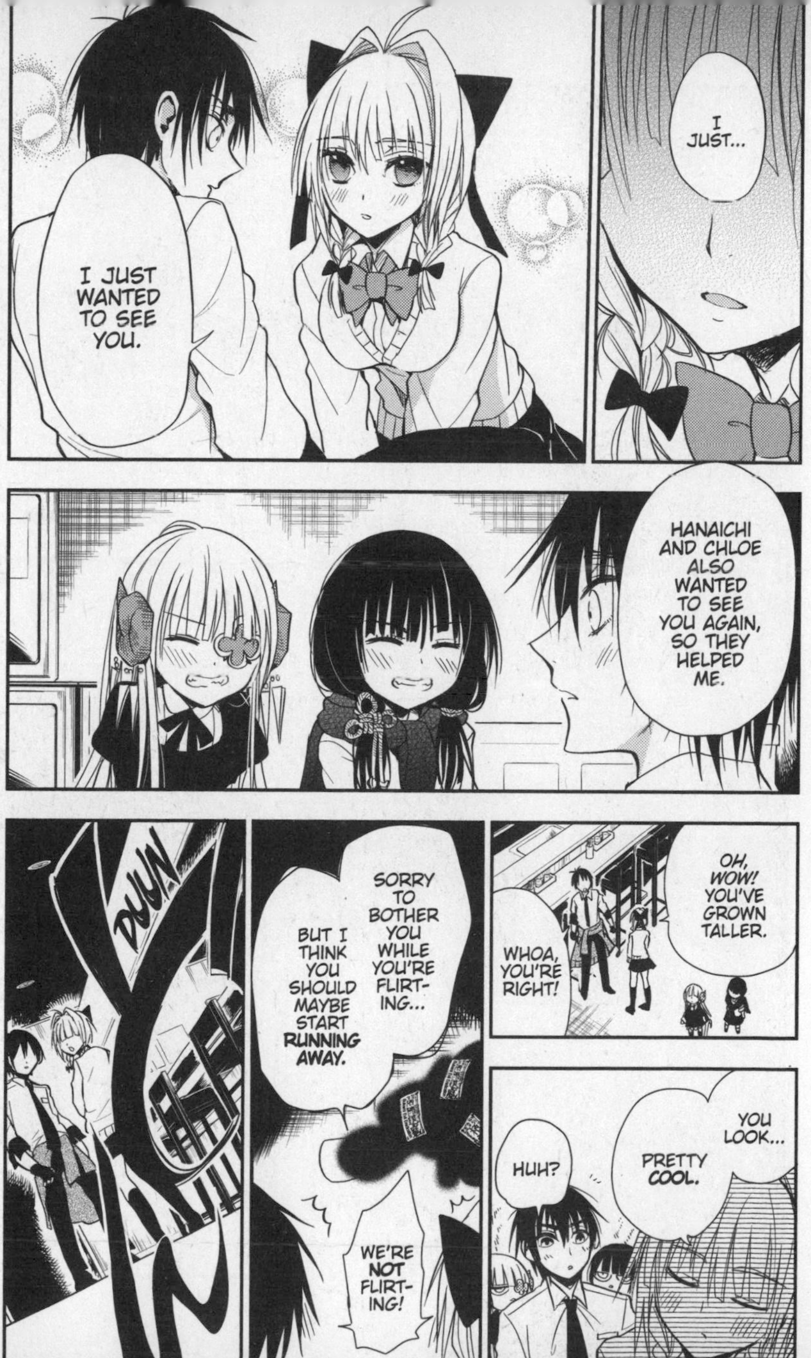

I JUST...
I JUST WANTED TO SEE YOU.
HANAICHI AND CHLOE ALSO WANTED TO SEE YOU AGAIN, SO THEY HELPED ME.
OH, WOW! YOU'VE GROWN TALLER.
WHOA, YOU'RE RIGHT!
YOU LOOK...
PRETTY **COOL**.
HUH?
SORRY TO BOTHER YOU WHILE YOU'RE FLIRT-ING...
BUT I THINK YOU SHOULD MAYBE START **RUNNING AWAY**.
WE'RE **NOT** FLIRT-ING!
DUUN

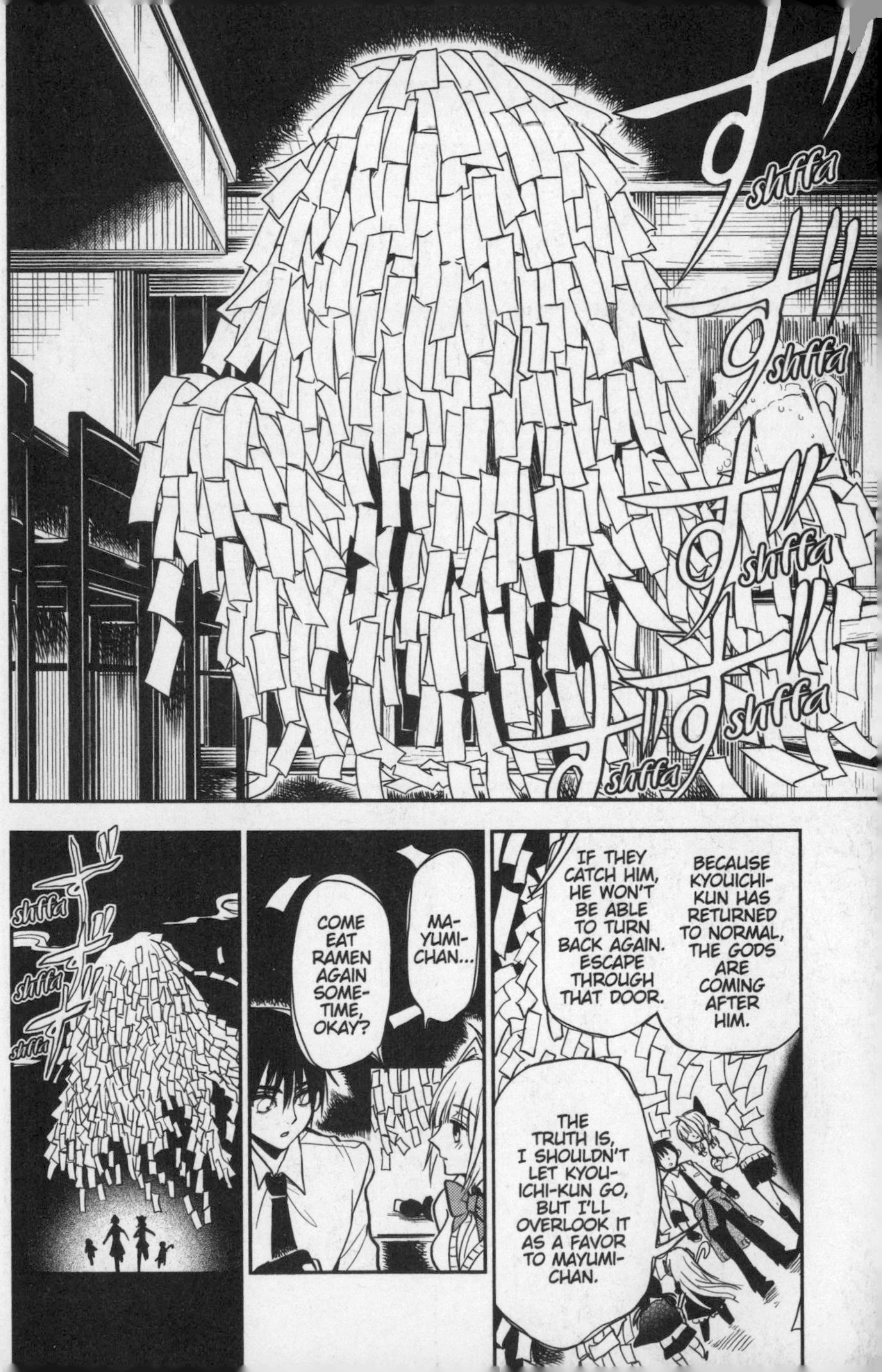
shffa
shffa
shffa
shffa
shffa
BECAUSE KYOUICHI-KUN HAS RETURNED TO NORMAL, THE GODS ARE COMING AFTER HIM.
IF THEY CATCH HIM, HE WON'T BE ABLE TO TURN BACK AGAIN. ESCAPE THROUGH THAT DOOR.
THE TRUTH IS, I SHOULDN'T LET KYOUICHI-KUN GO, BUT I'LL OVERLOOK IT AS A FAVOR TO MAYUMI-CHAN.
MAYUMI-CHAN...
COME EAT RAMEN AGAIN SOMETIME, OKAY?
shffa
shffa
shffa

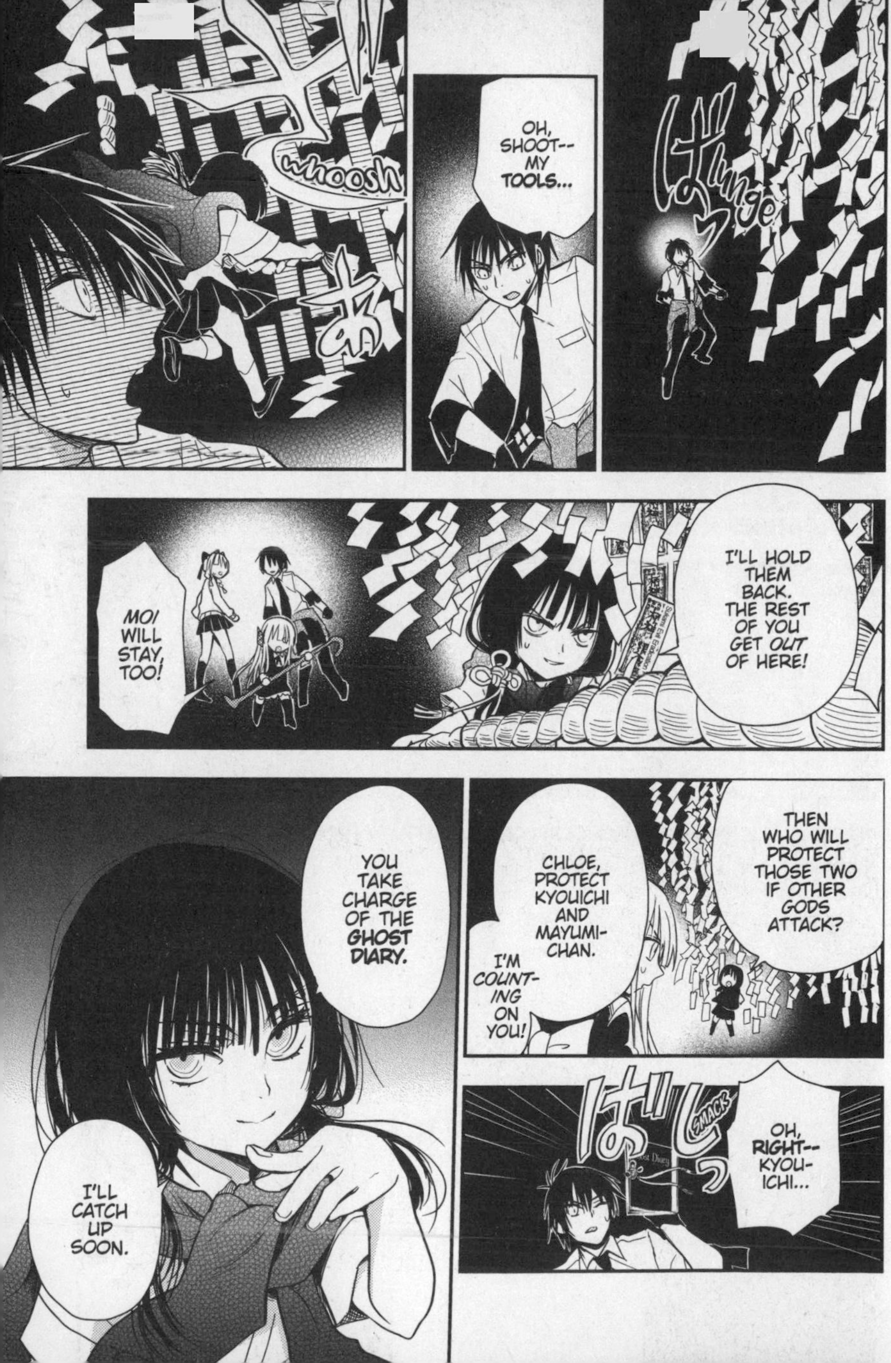
lunge
OH, SHOOT-- MY TOOLS...
whoosh
I'LL HOLD THEM BACK. THE REST OF YOU GET *OUT* OF HERE!
MOI WILL STAY, TOO!
THEN WHO WILL PROTECT THOSE TWO IF OTHER GODS ATTACK?
CHLOE, PROTECT KYOUICHI AND MAYUMI-CHAN.
I'M COUNTING ON YOU!
YOU TAKE CHARGE OF THE **GHOST DIARY.**
SMACK
OH, **RIGHT**-- KYOUICHI...
I'LL CATCH UP SOON.

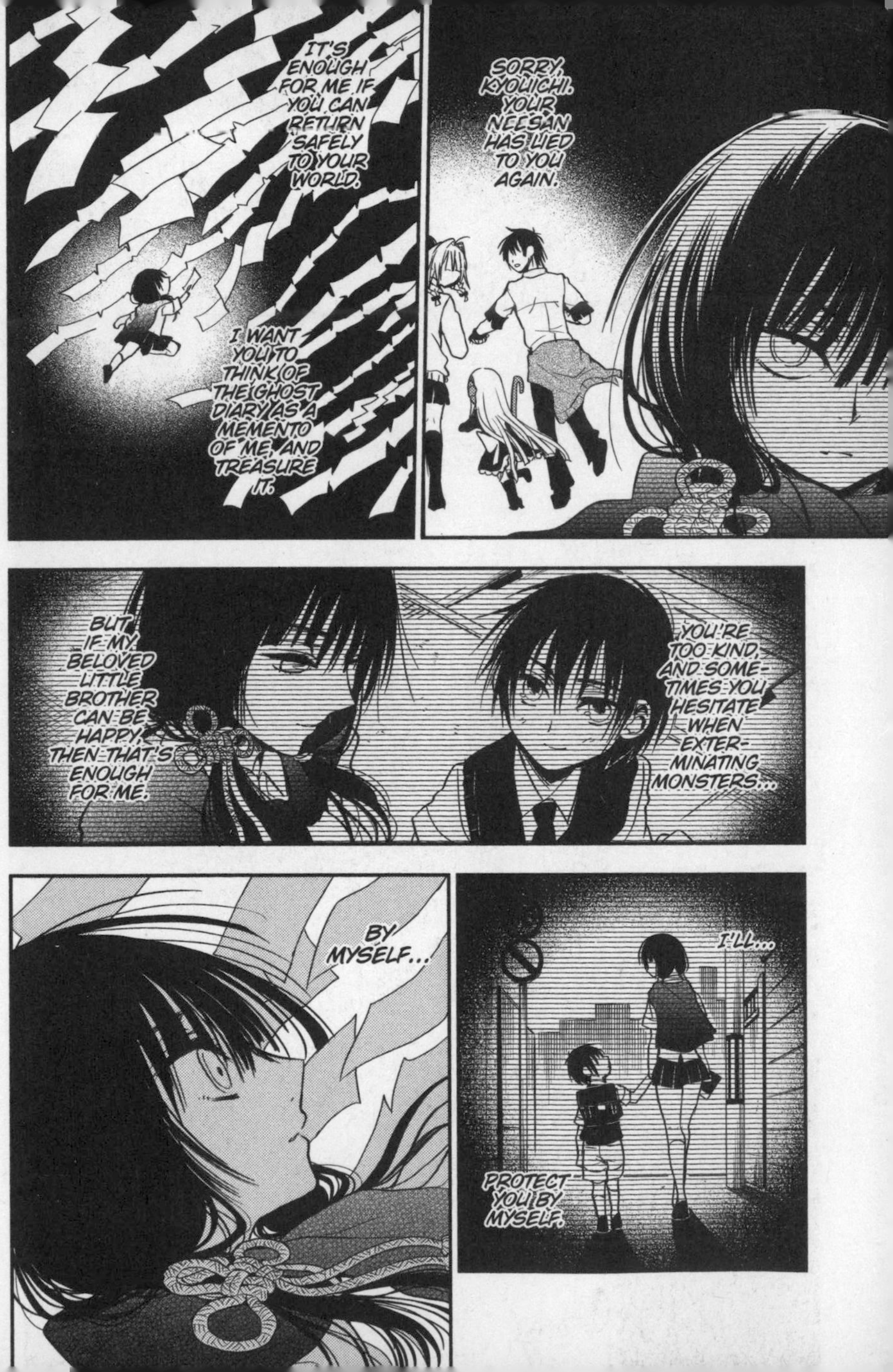
SORRY, KYOUICHI. YOUR NEESAN HAS LIED TO YOU AGAIN.
IT'S ENOUGH FOR ME IF YOU CAN RETURN SAFELY TO YOUR WORLD.
I WANT YOU TO THINK OF THE GHOST DIARY AS A MEMENTO OF ME, AND TREASURE IT.
YOU'RE TOO KIND, AND SOME-TIMES YOU HESITATE WHEN EXTER-MINATING MONSTERS...
BUT IF MY BELOVED LITTLE BROTHER CAN BE HAPPY, THEN THAT'S ENOUGH FOR ME.
I'LL...
PROTECT YOU BY MYSELF.
BY MYSELF...

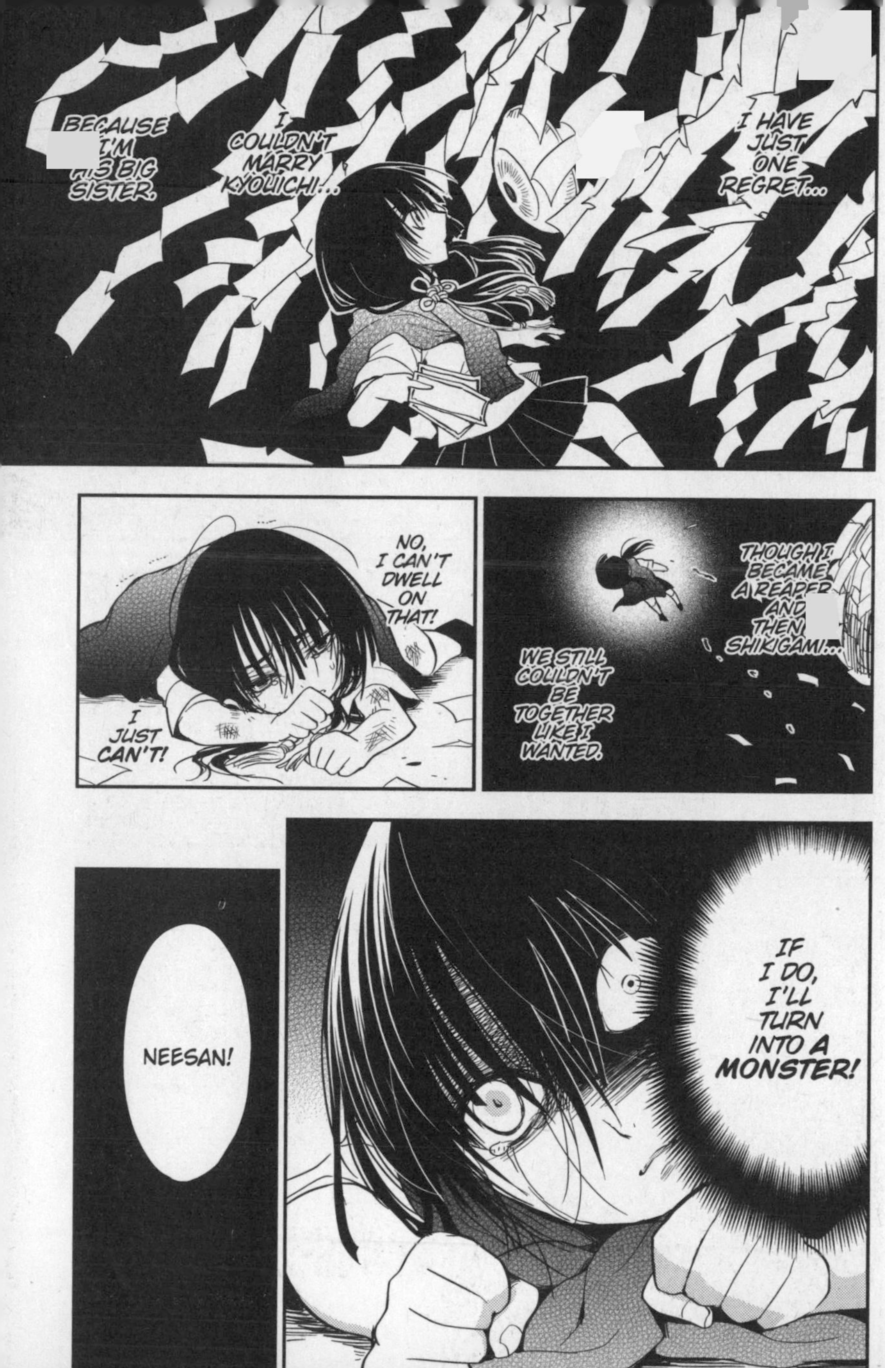
I HAVE JUST ONE REGRET...
I COULDN'T MARRY KYOUICHI...
BECAUSE I'M HIS BIG SISTER.
THOUGH I BECAME A REAPER AND THEN SHIKIGAMI...
WE STILL COULDN'T BE TOGETHER LIKE I WANTED.
NO, I CAN'T DWELL ON THAT!
I JUST CAN'T!
IF I DO, I'LL TURN INTO A MONSTER!
NEESAN!

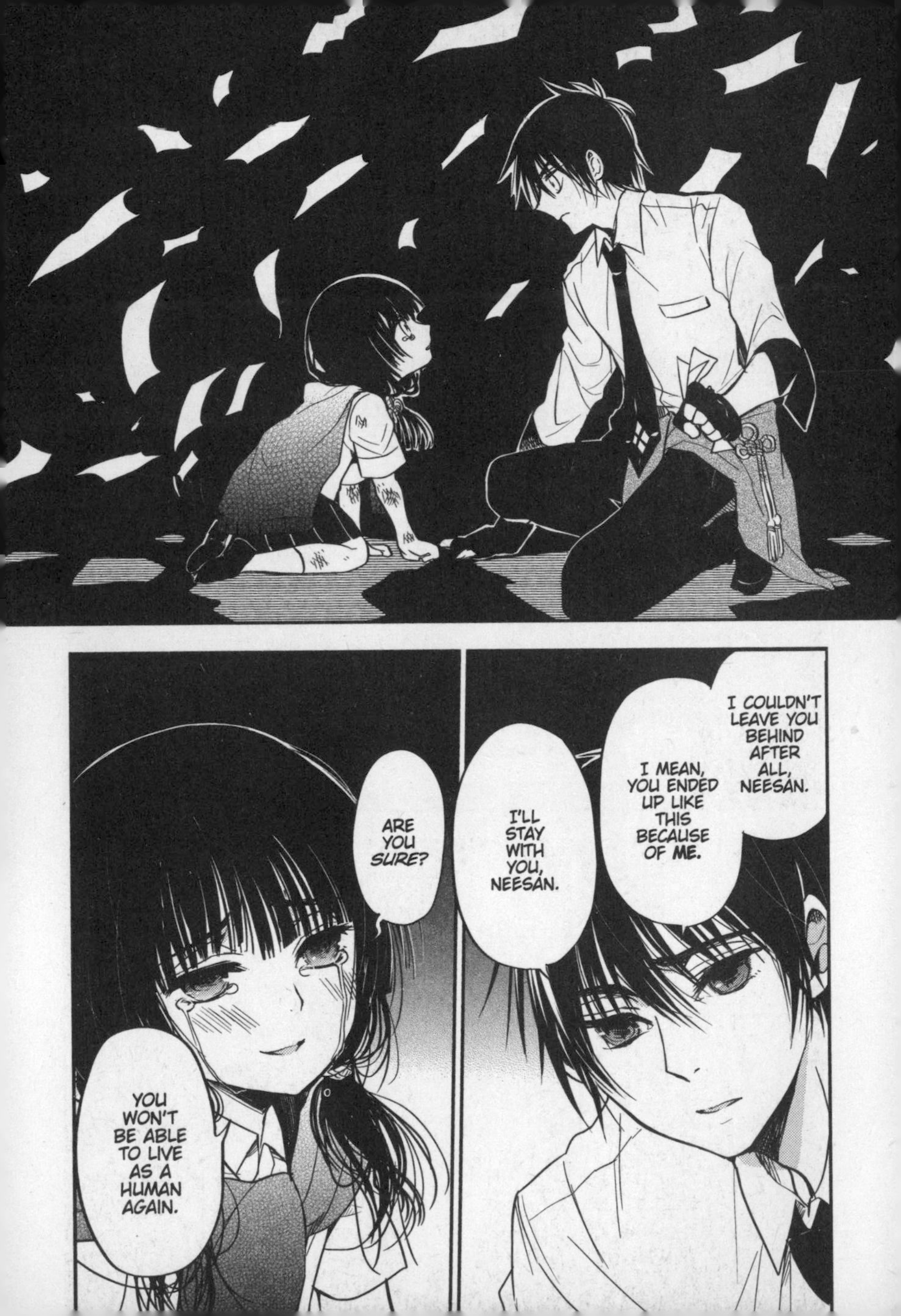

I COULDN'T LEAVE YOU BEHIND AFTER ALL, NEESAN.
I MEAN, YOU ENDED UP LIKE THIS BECAUSE OF ME.
I'LL STAY WITH YOU, NEESAN.
ARE YOU SURE?
YOU WON'T BE ABLE TO LIVE AS A HUMAN AGAIN.

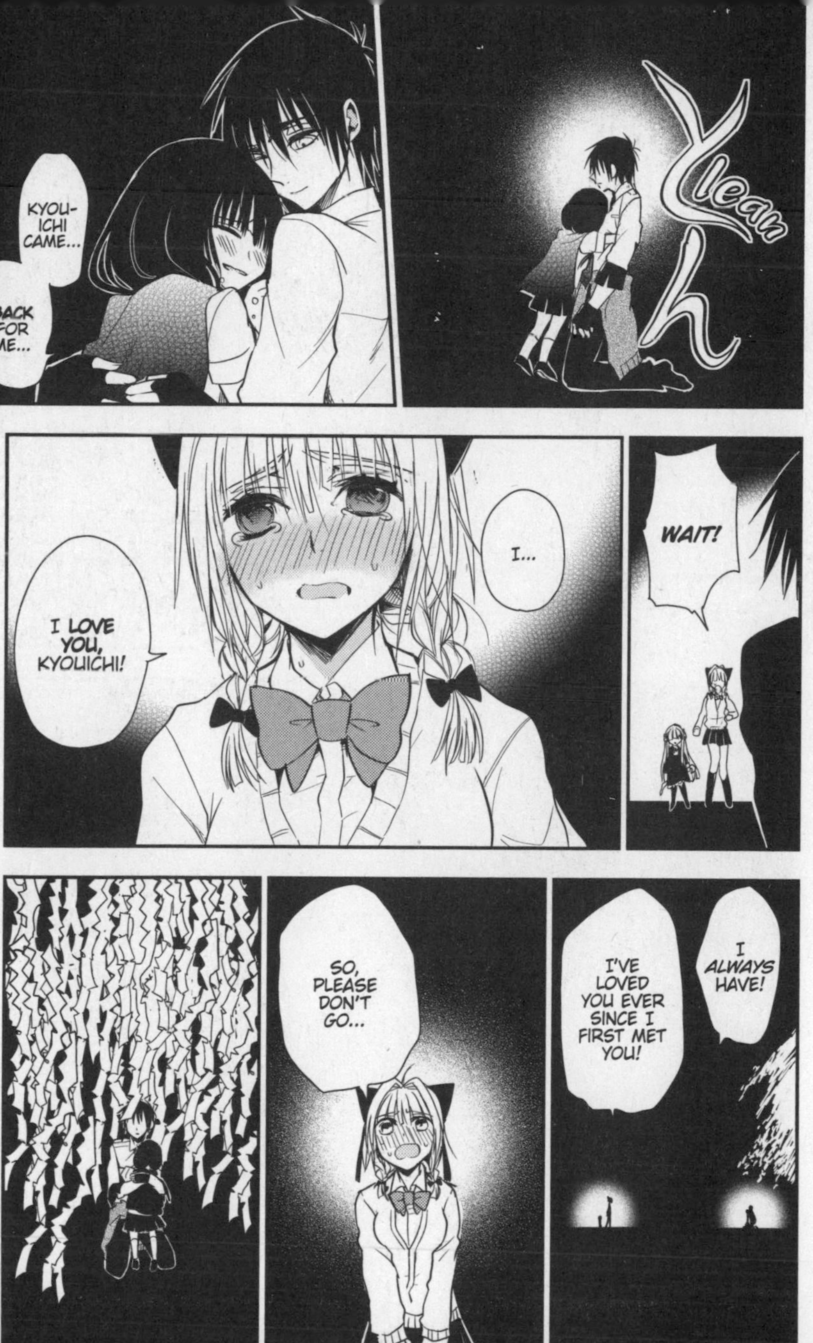
KYOU-ICHI CAME...
BACK FOR ME...
WAIT!
I...
I LOVE YOU, KYOUICHI!
I ALWAYS HAVE!
I'VE LOVED YOU EVER SINCE I FIRST MET YOU!
SO, PLEASE DON'T GO...

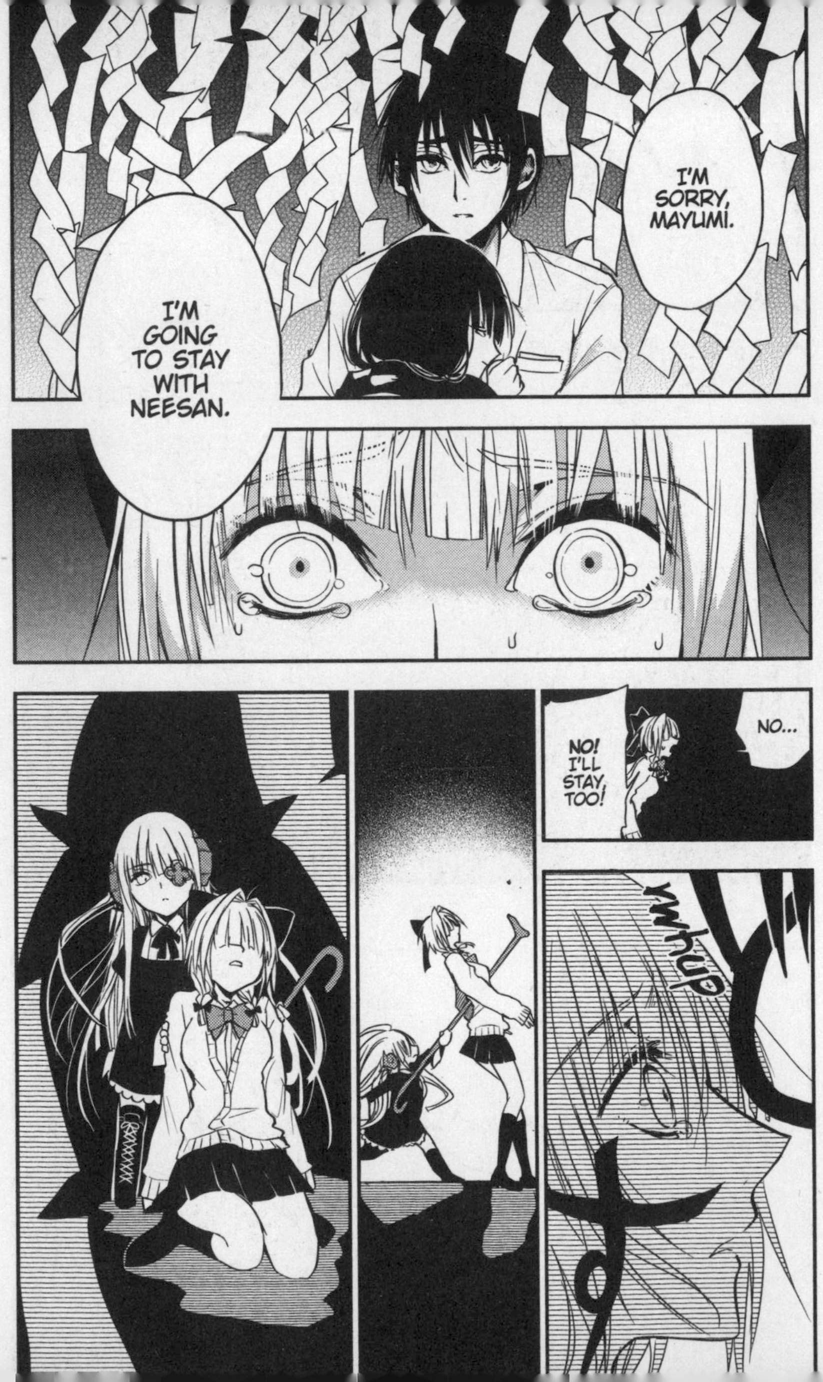
I'M SORRY, MAYUMI.
I'M GOING TO STAY WITH NEESAN.
NO...
NO! I'LL STAY, TOO!
hup

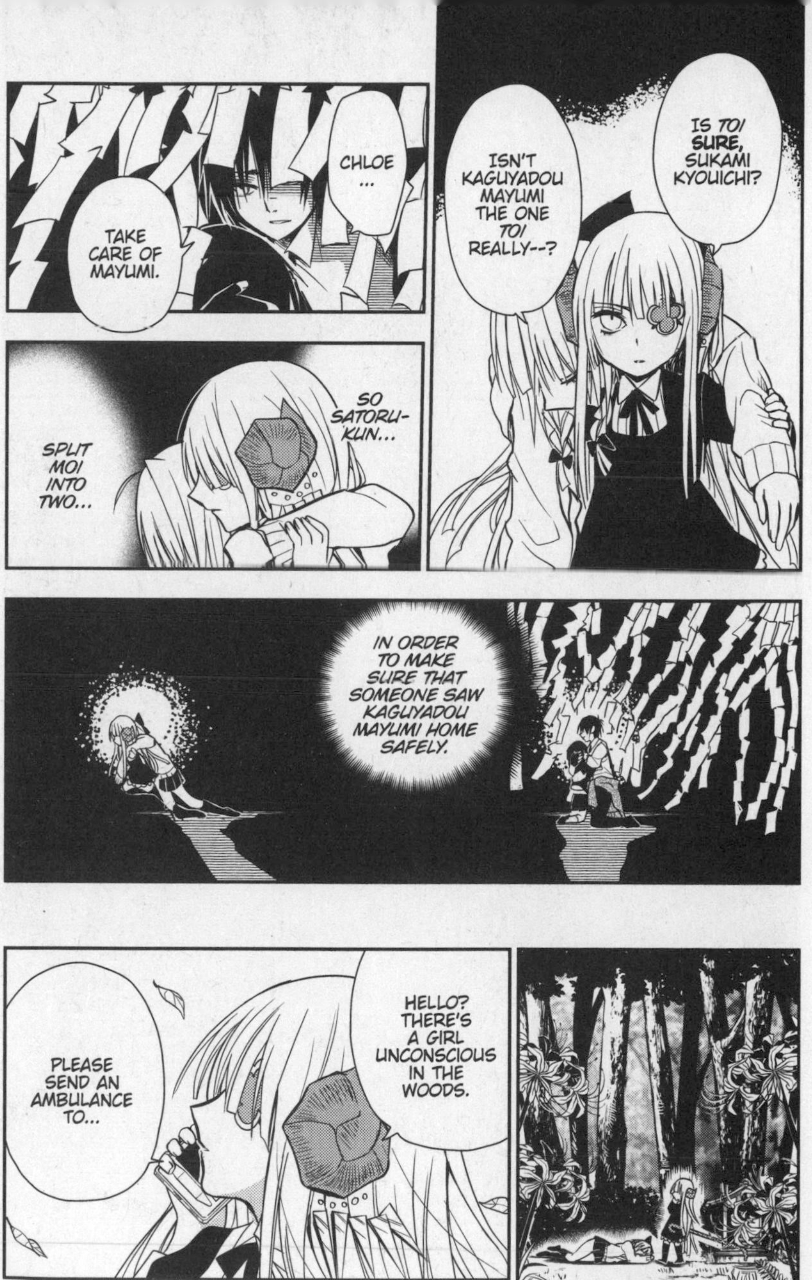
IS TOI SURE, SUKAMI KYOUICHI?
ISN'T KAGUYADOU MAYUMI THE ONE TOI REALLY--?
CHLOE ...
TAKE CARE OF MAYUMI.
SO SATORU-KUN...
SPLIT MOI INTO TWO...
IN ORDER TO MAKE SURE THAT SOMEONE SAW KAGUYADOU MAYUMI HOME SAFELY.
HELLO? THERE'S A GIRL UNCONSCIOUS IN THE WOODS.
PLEASE SEND AN AMBULANCE TO...

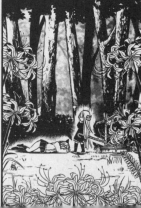

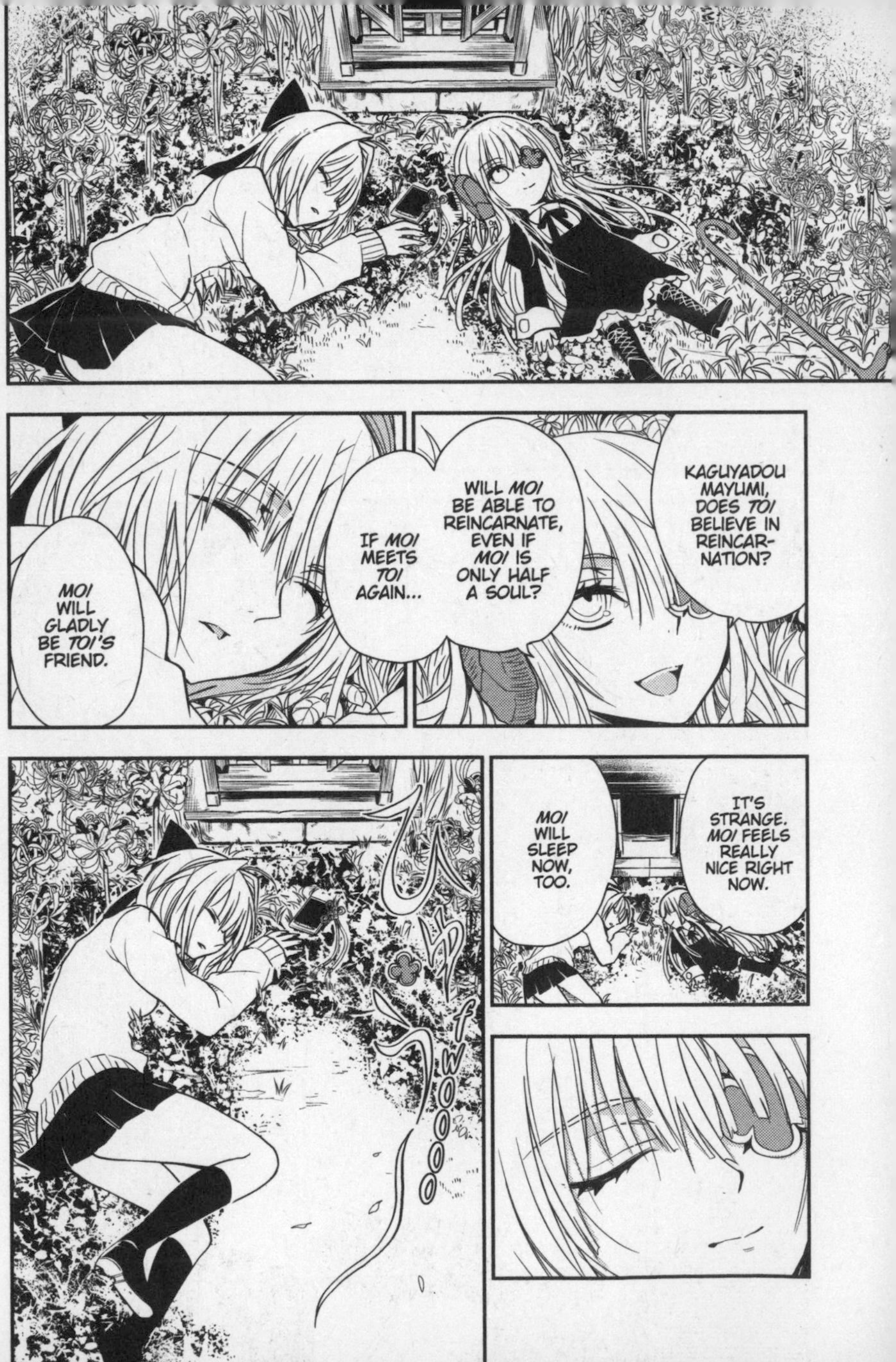
KAGUYADOU MAYUMI, DOES *TOI* BELIEVE IN REINCAR-NATION?
WILL *MOI* BE ABLE TO REINCARNATE, EVEN IF *MOI* IS ONLY HALF A SOUL?
IF *MOI* MEETS *TOI* AGAIN...
MOI WILL GLADLY BE *TOI*'S FRIEND.
IT'S STRANGE. *MOI* FEELS REALLY NICE RIGHT NOW.
MOI WILL SLEEP NOW, TOO.
fwoooooo

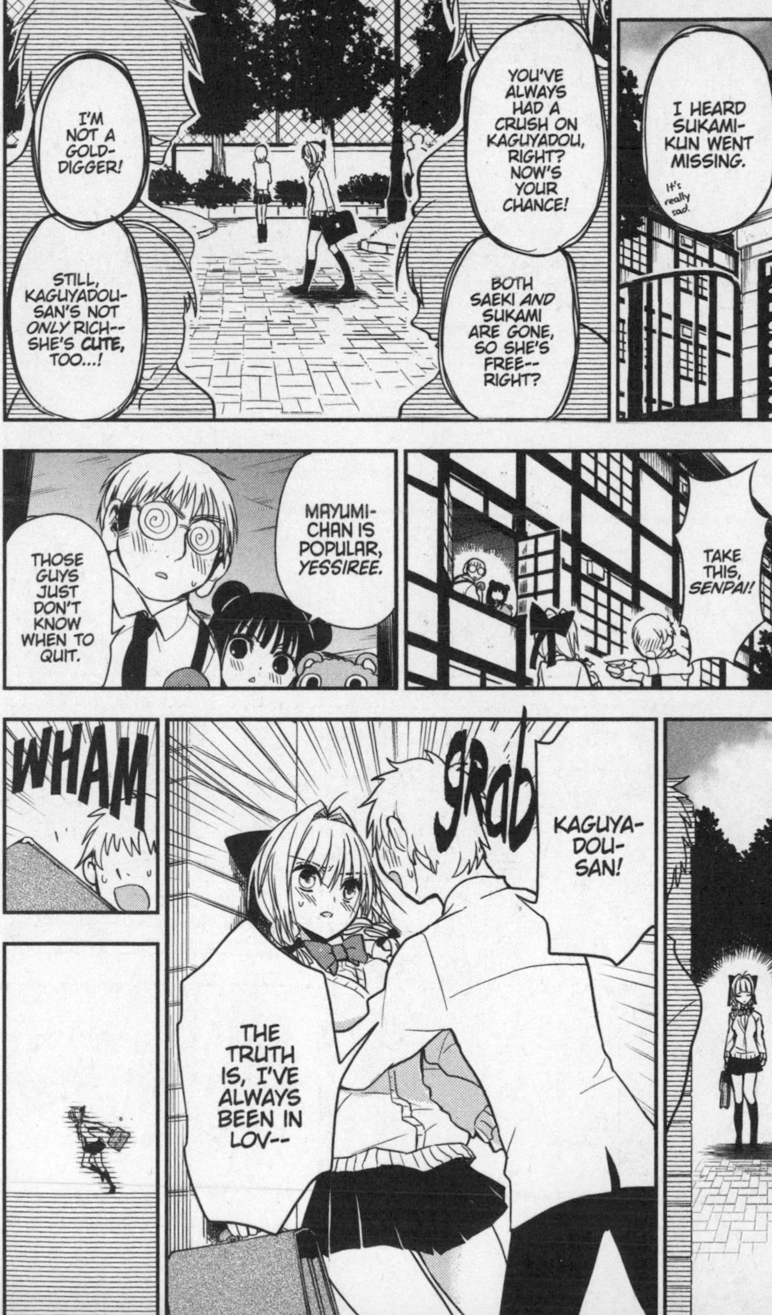

I HEARD SUKAMI-KUN WENT MISSING.
It's really sad.
Mangekyo
YOU'VE ALWAYS HAD A CRUSH ON KAGUYADOU, RIGHT? NOW'S YOUR CHANCE!
BOTH SAEKI AND SUKAMI ARE GONE, SO SHE'S FREE--RIGHT?
I'M NOT A GOLD-DIGGER!
STILL, KAGUYADOU-SAN'S NOT ONLY RICH--SHE'S CUTE, TOO...!
TAKE THIS, SENPAI!
MAYUMI-CHAN IS POPULAR, YESSIREE.
THOSE GUYS JUST DON'T KNOW WHEN TO QUIT.
KAGUYA-DOU-SAN!
GRAB
THE TRUTH IS, I'VE ALWAYS BEEN IN LOV--
WHAM

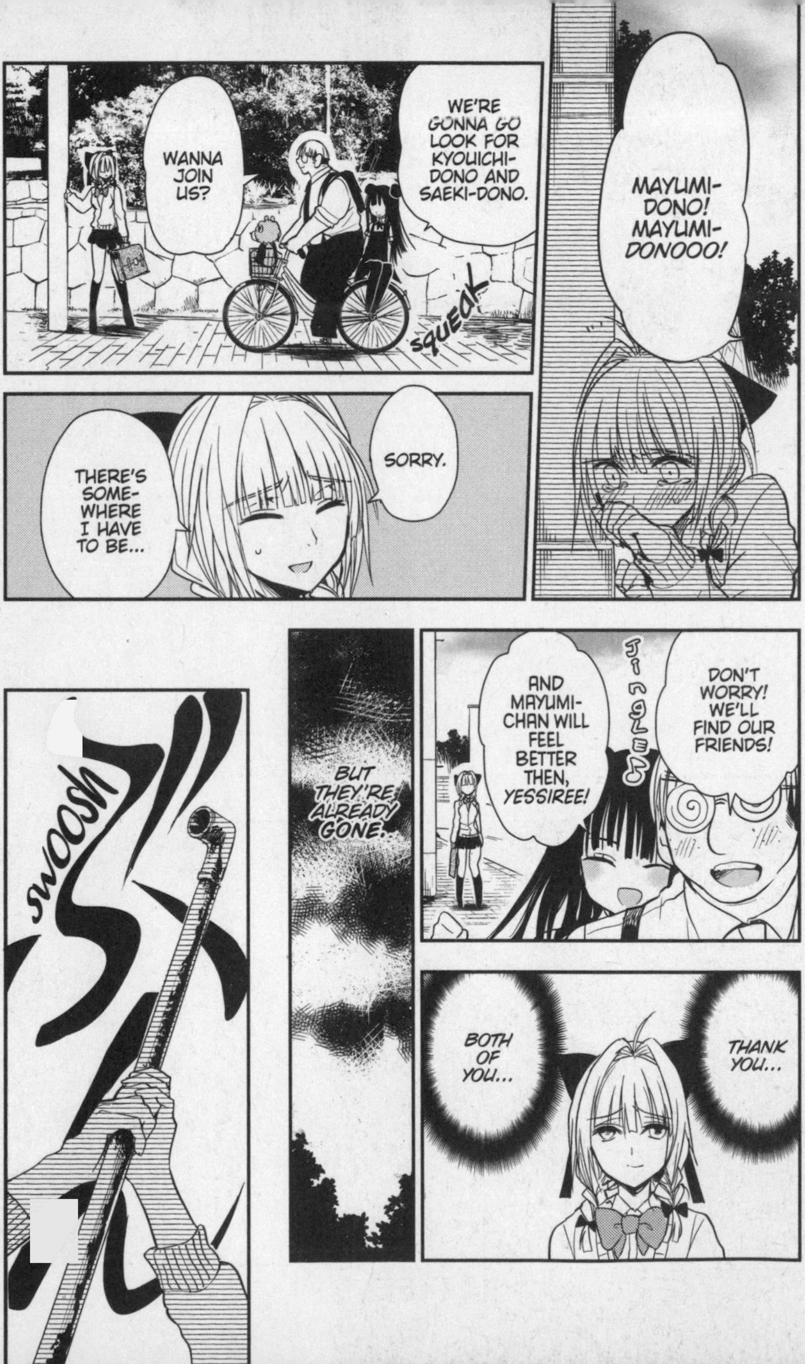

MAYUMI-DONO! MAYUMI-DONOOO!
WE'RE GONNA GO LOOK FOR KYOUICHI-DONO AND SAEKI-DONO.
WANNA JOIN US?
squeak
SORRY.
THERE'S SOME-WHERE I HAVE TO BE...
DON'T WORRY! WE'LL FIND OUR FRIENDS!
Jingle
AND MAYUMI-CHAN WILL FEEL BETTER THEN, YESSIREE!
THANK YOU...
BOTH OF YOU...
BUT THEY'RE ALREADY GONE.
swoosh

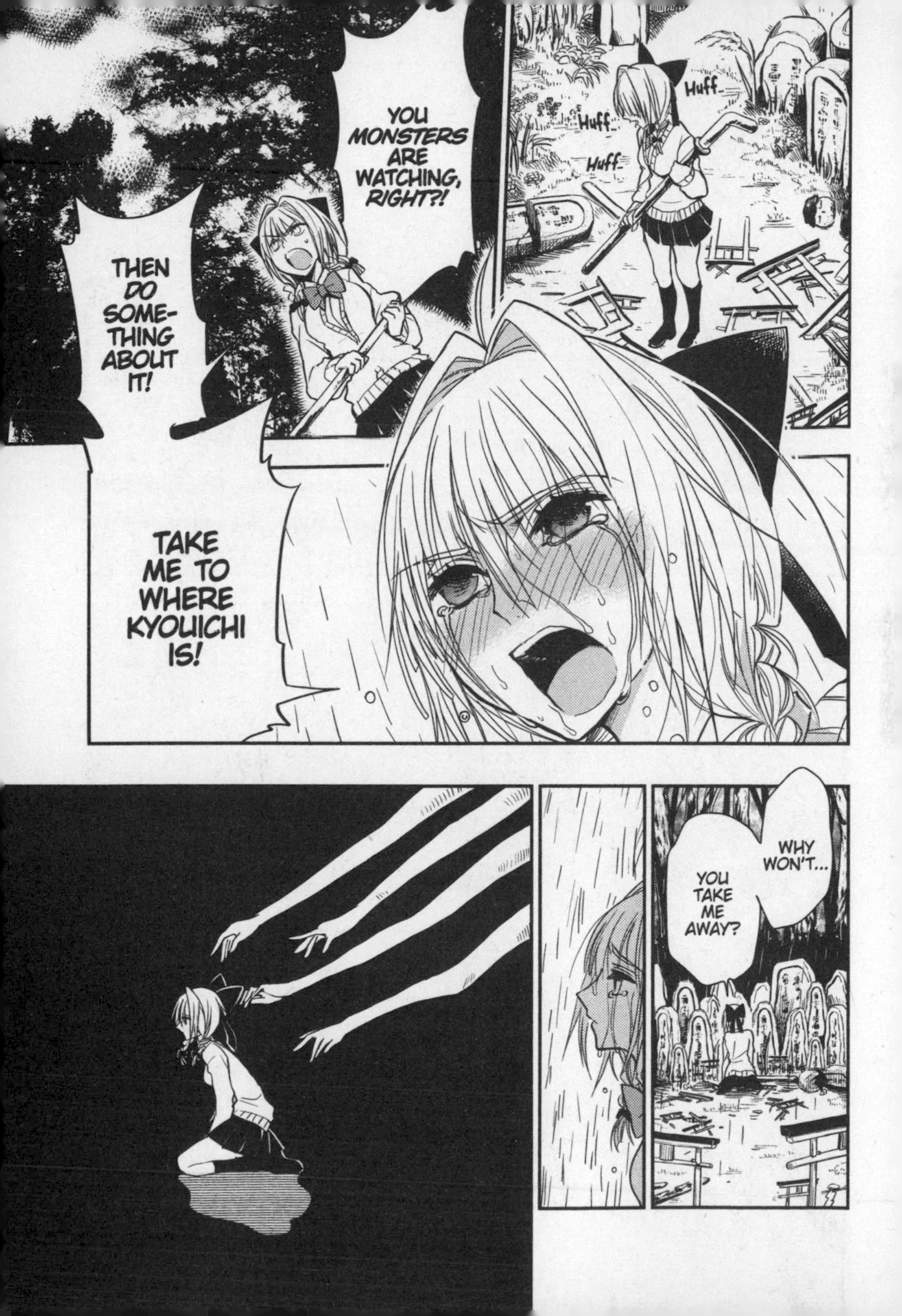
Huff
Huff
Huff
YOU MONSTERS ARE WATCHING, RIGHT?!
THEN DO SOME-THING ABOUT IT!
TAKE ME TO WHERE KYOUICHI IS!
WHY WON'T...
YOU TAKE ME AWAY?

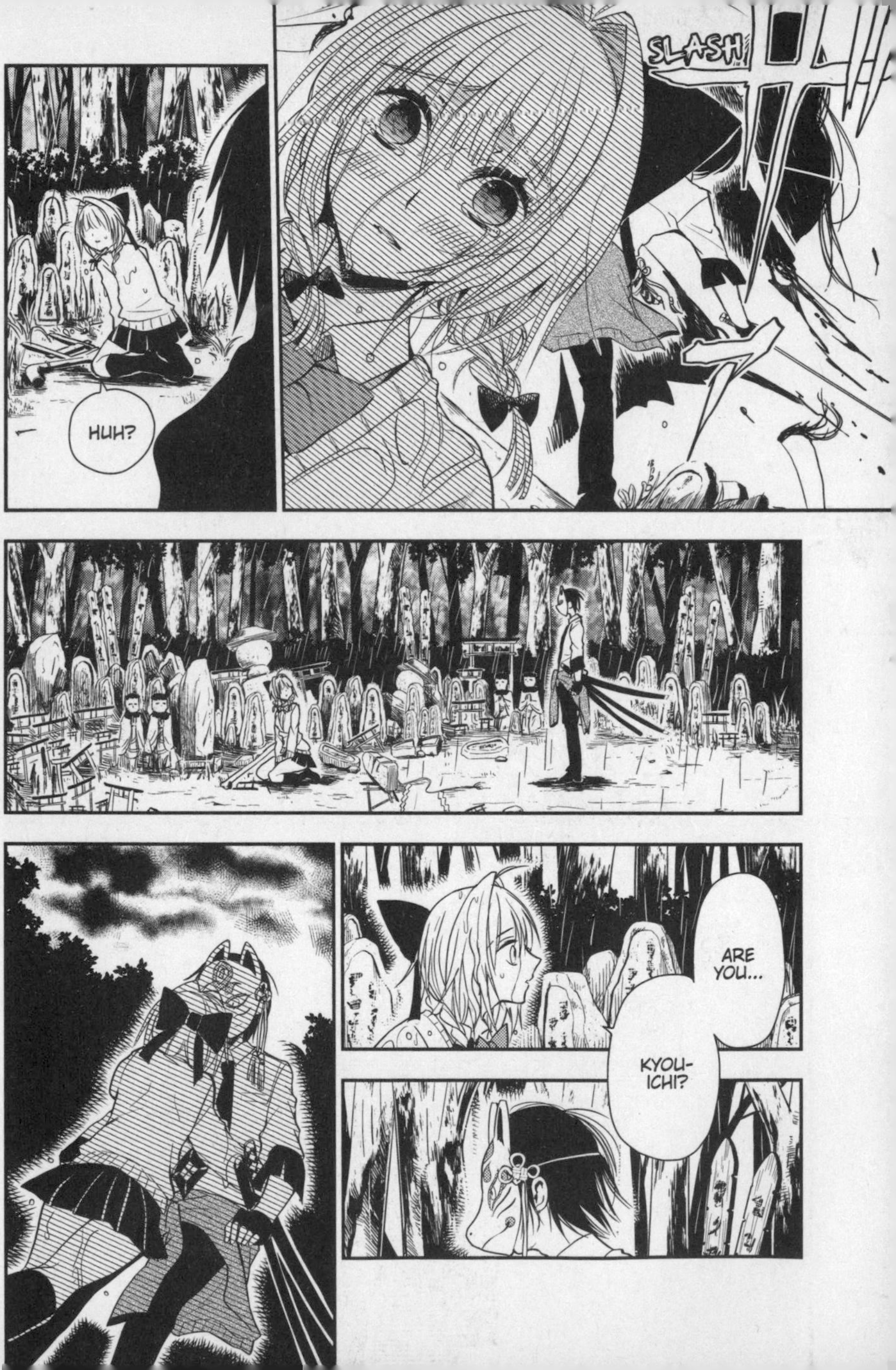
SLASH
HUH?
ARE YOU...
KYOU-ICHI?

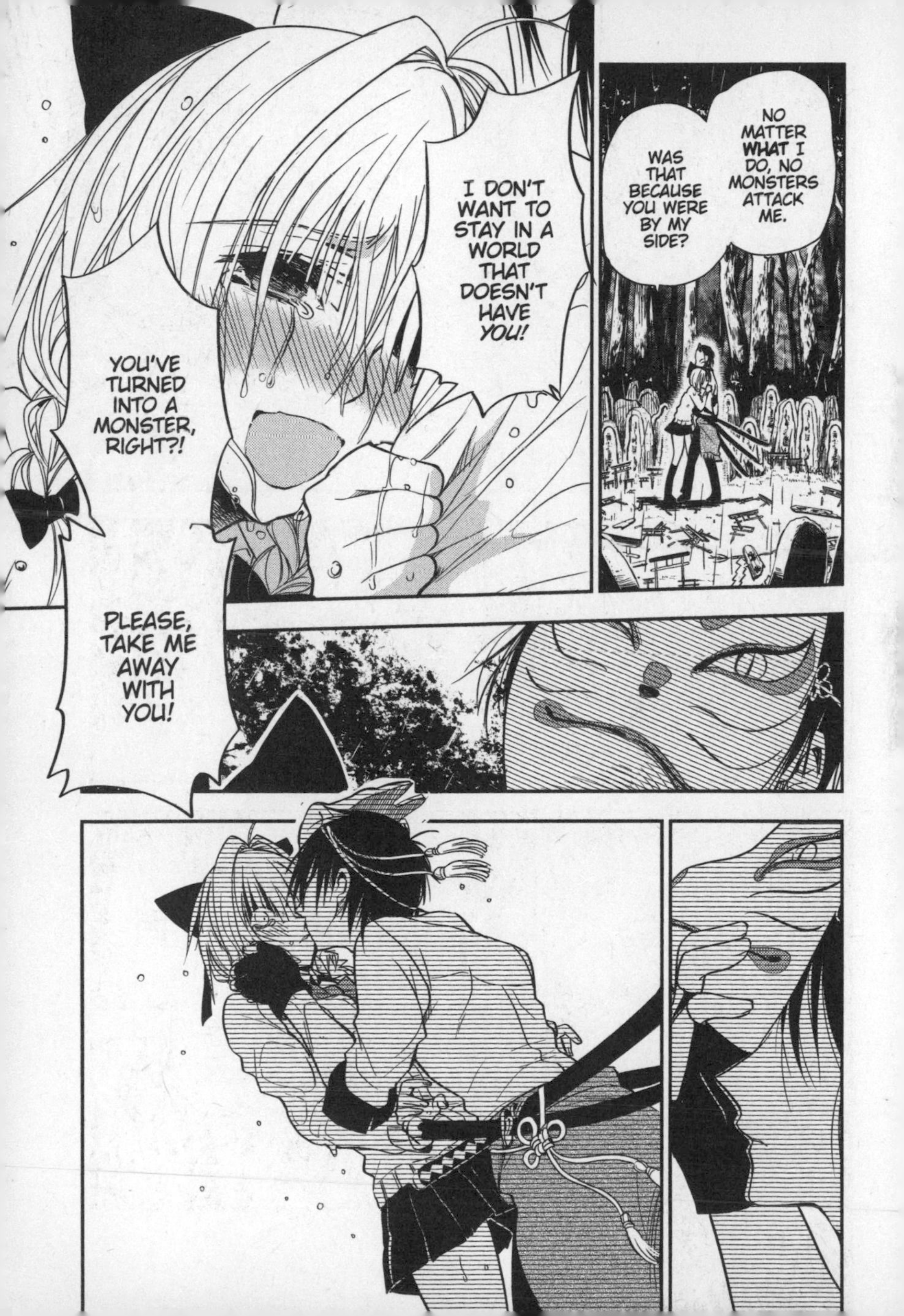
NO MATTER WHAT I DO, NO MONSTERS ATTACK ME.
WAS THAT BECAUSE YOU WERE BY MY SIDE?
I DON'T WANT TO STAY IN A WORLD THAT DOESN'T HAVE YOU!
YOU'VE TURNED INTO A MONSTER, RIGHT?!
PLEASE, TAKE ME AWAY WITH YOU!

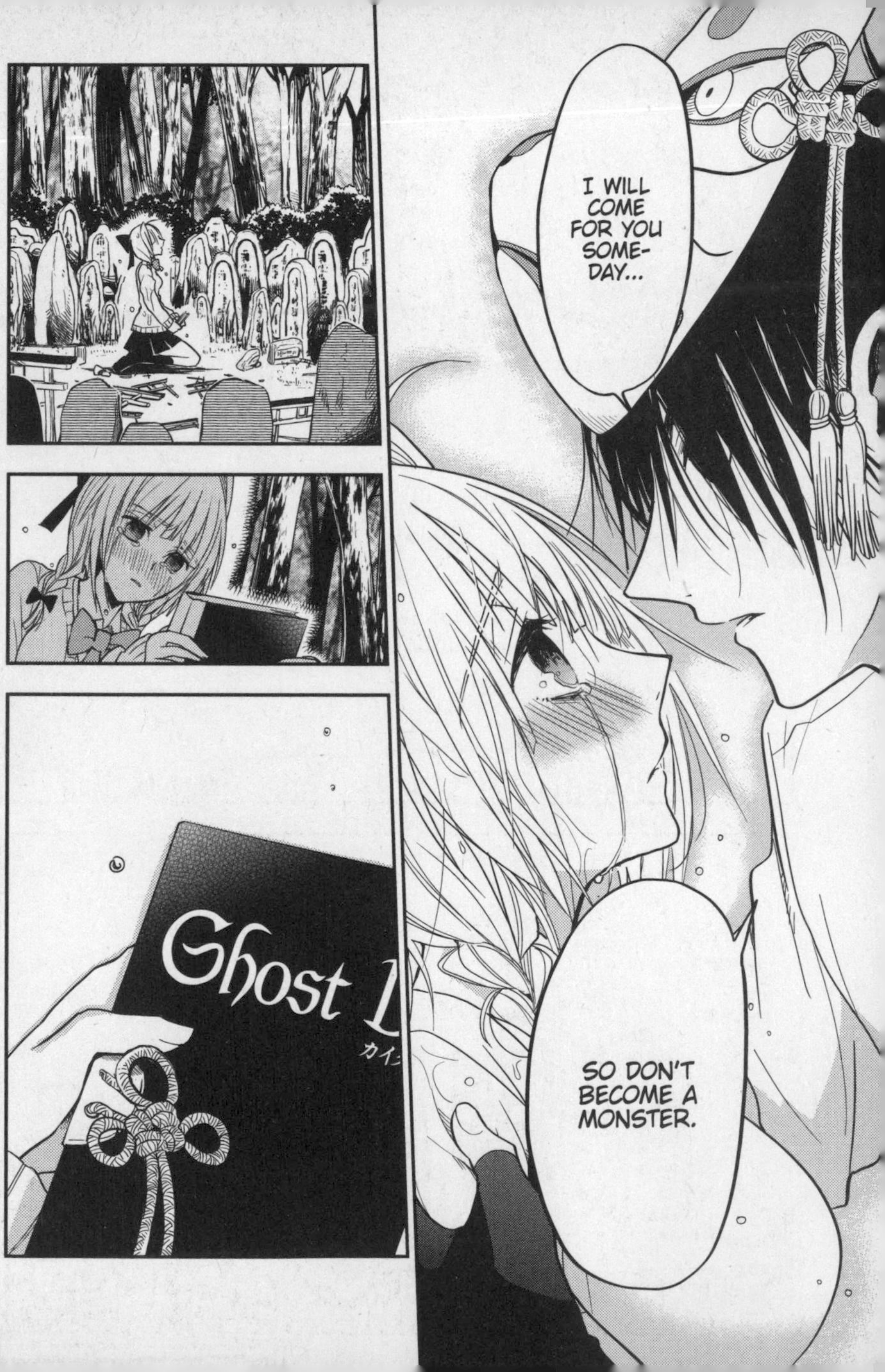
I WILL COME FOR YOU SOME-DAY...
SO DON'T BECOME A MONSTER.
Ghost

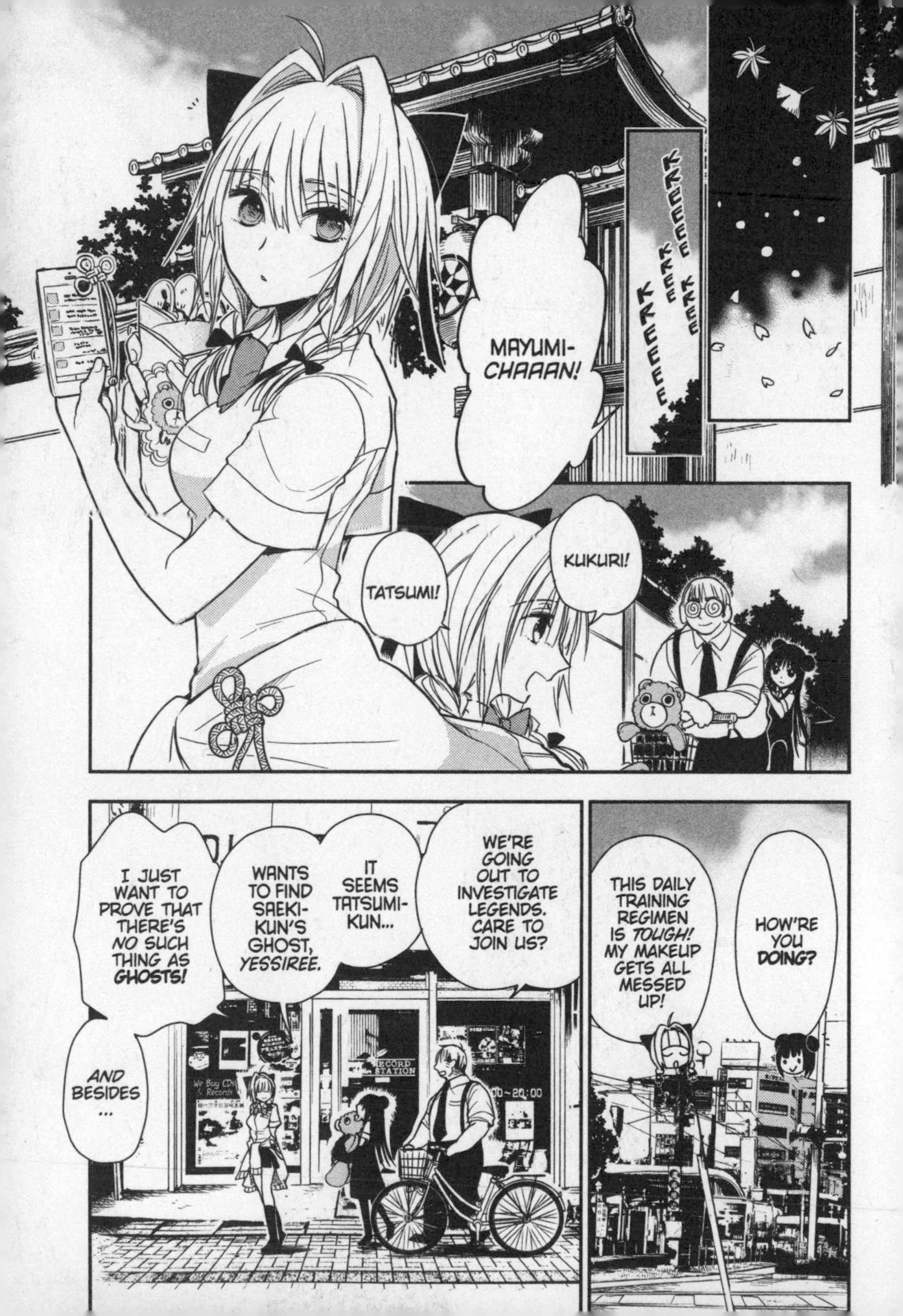
KREEEE KREE KREE KREEEE
MAYUMI-CHAAAN!
KUKURI!
TATSUMI!
HOW'RE YOU DOING?
THIS DAILY TRAINING REGIMEN IS TOUGH! MY MAKEUP GETS ALL MESSED UP!
WE'RE GOING OUT TO INVESTIGATE LEGENDS. CARE TO JOIN US?
IT SEEMS TATSUMI-KUN...
WANTS TO FIND SAEKI-KUN'S GHOST, YESSIREE.
I JUST WANT TO PROVE THAT THERE'S NO SUCH THING AS GHOSTS!
AND BESIDES ...
RECORD STATION
We Buy CDs & Records
00~20:00

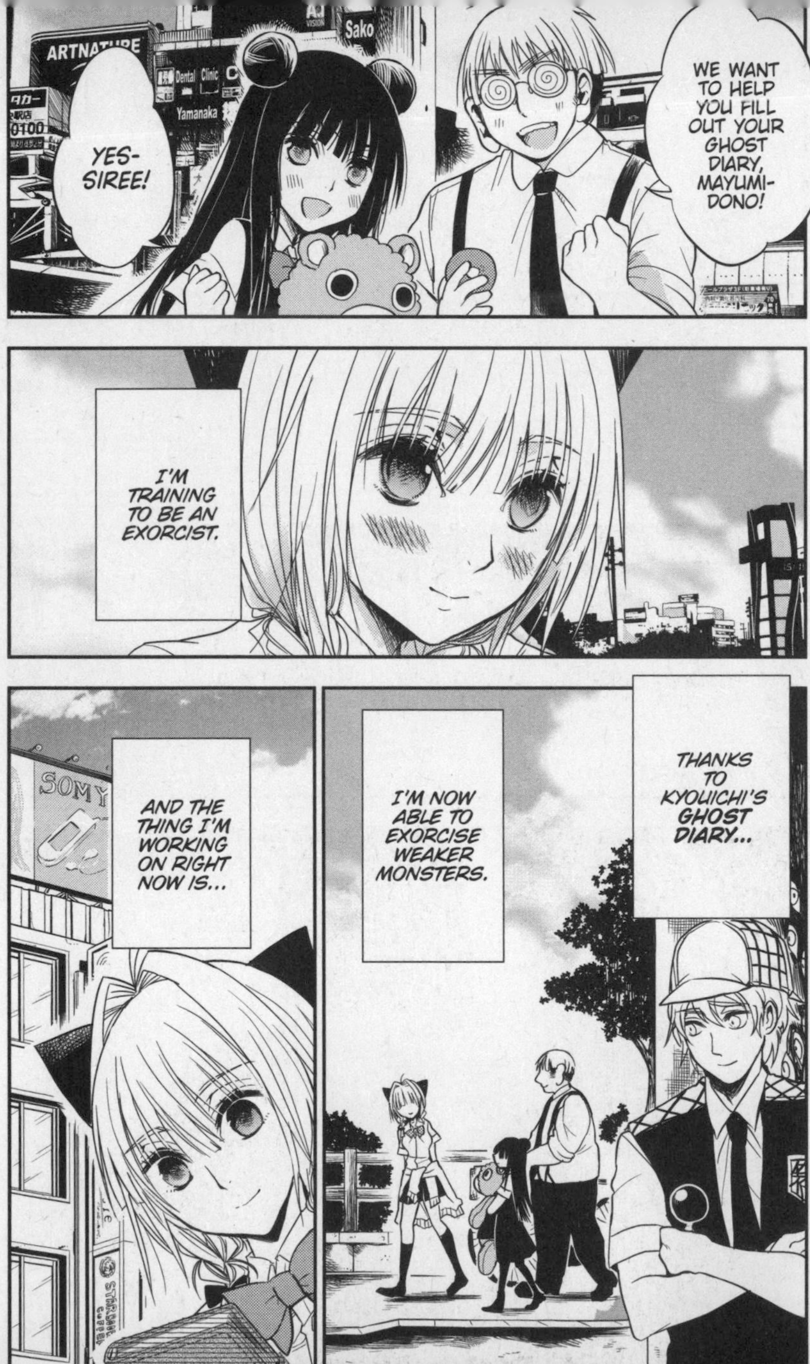
WE WANT TO HELP YOU FILL OUT YOUR GHOST DIARY, MAYUMI-DONO!
YES-SIREE!
I'M TRAINING TO BE AN EXORCIST.
THANKS TO KYOUICHI'S GHOST DIARY...
I'M NOW ABLE TO EXORCISE WEAKER MONSTERS.
AND THE THING I'M WORKING ON RIGHT NOW IS...

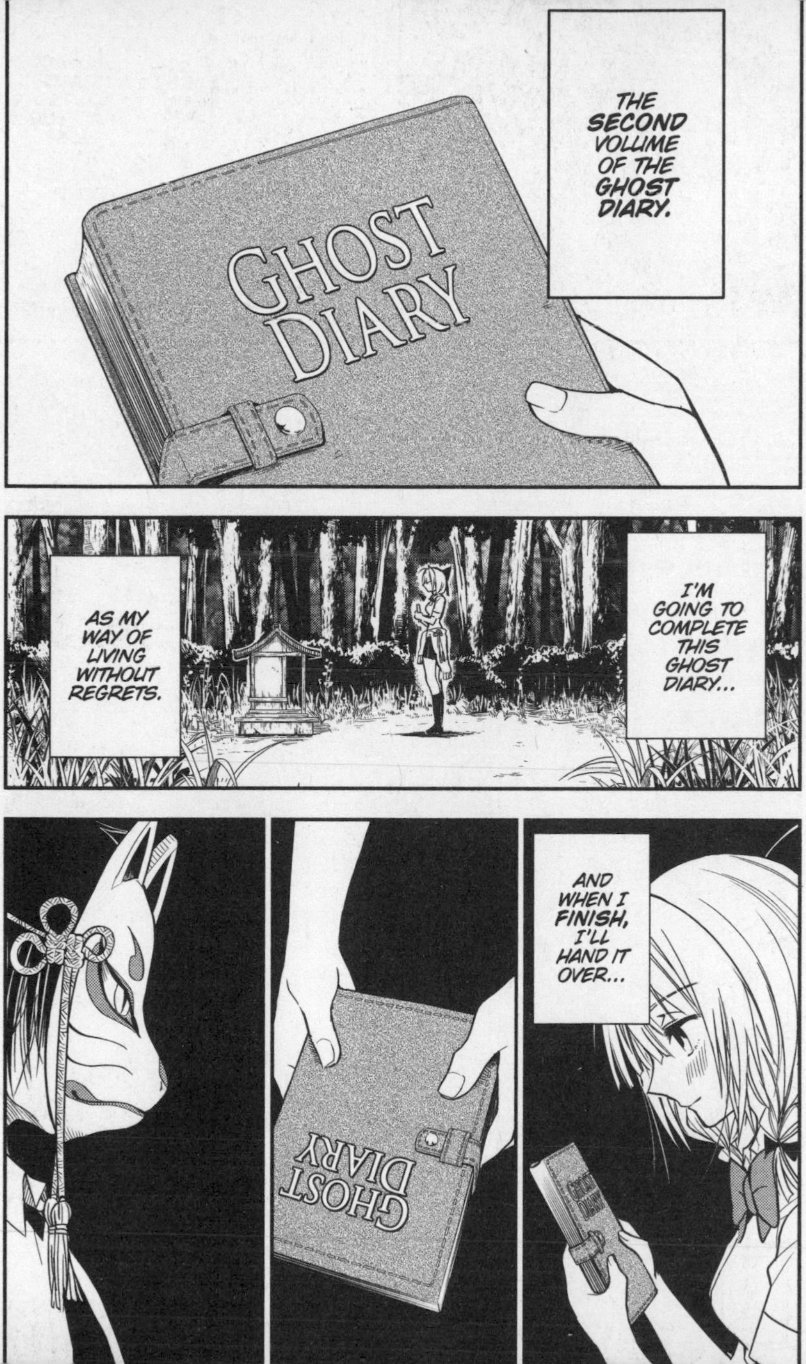
THE SECOND VOLUME OF THE GHOST DIARY.
GHOST DIARY
I'M GOING TO COMPLETE THIS GHOST DIARY...
AS MY WAY OF LIVING WITHOUT REGRETS.
AND WHEN I FINISH, I'LL HAND IT OVER...

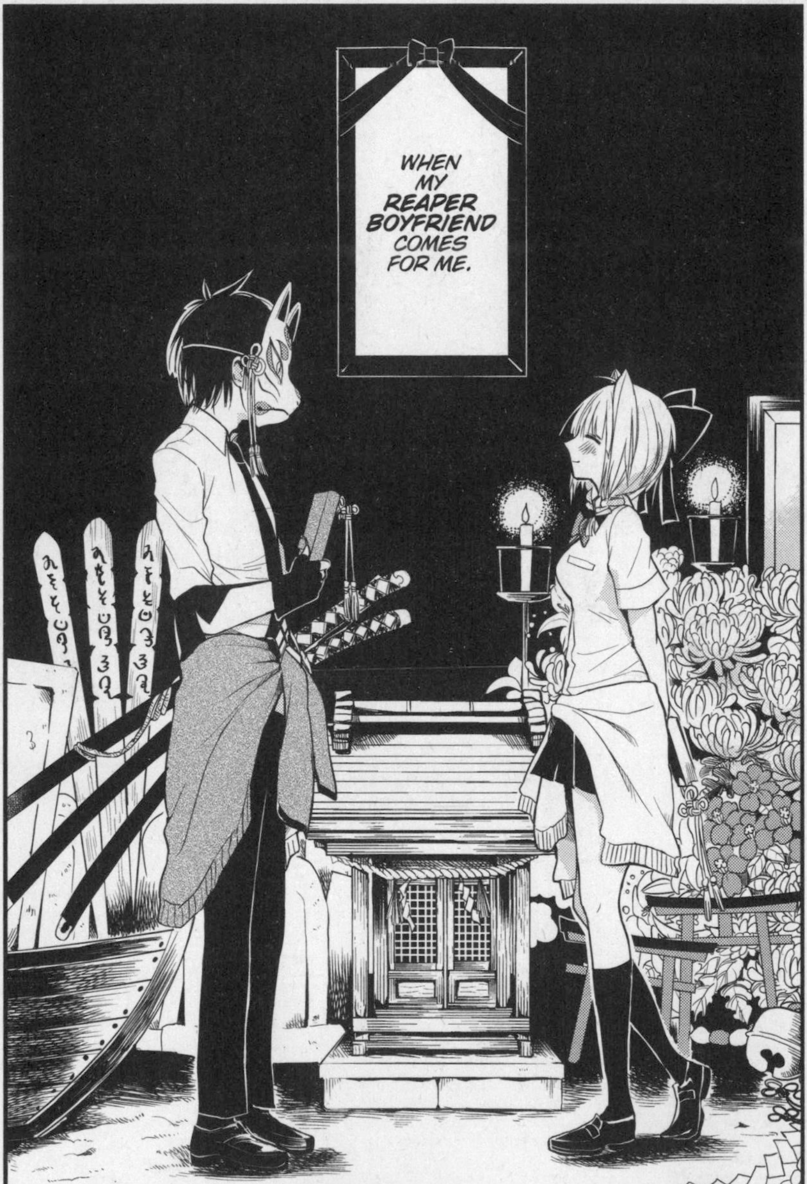
WHEN MY REAPER BOYFRIEND COMES FOR ME.

[FIN]